D0311586

24,30

Mathematics, Pedagogy, and Secondary Teacher Education

San Diego Christian College
2100 Greenfield Drive
El Cajon, CA 92019

510.712
M426p

Mathematics, Pedagogy, and Secondary Teacher Education

Thomas J. Cooney
Stephen I. Brown
John A. Dossey
Georg Schrage
Erich Ch. Wittmann

Heinemann
A division of Reed Elsevier Inc.
361 Hanover Street
Portsmouth, NH 03801-3912
Offices and agents throughout the world

©1996 by Thomas J. Cooney, Erich Ch. Wittman, George Schrage, John Dossey, and Stephen I. Brawn.

All rights reserved. No part of this book may be reproduced in any form or by electronic or mechanical means, including information storage and retrieval systems, without permission in writing from the publisher, except by a reviewer, who may quote brief passages in a review.

Printed paperback edition 1999.

Acquisitions Editor: Leigh Peake
Cover Designer: Tom Allen/Pear Graphic Design
Manufacturing Coordinator: Deanna Richardson

Library of Congress Cataloging-in-Publication Data
The Library of Congress has cataloged the single hardcover volume as follows:

Mathematics, pedagogy, and secondary teacher education / Thomas J. Cooney . . .
    [et al.]
        p.   cm.
    Includes bibliographical references (p. –).
    ISBN 0-325-00115-4 (acid-free paper)
    1. Mathematics—Study and teaching (Secondary) 2. Mathematics
teachers—Training of. I. Cooney, Thomas J.
QA11.M3758   1996
510.' 71'2—dc20   96-19145
                                        CIP

Printed in the United States of America on acid-free paper
10 09 08 07 06   VP   7 8 9 10 11

To Our Friend and Colleague, Georg:

whose brilliance and spirit of adventure provide all of us visions for facing obstacles in mathematics education and in life.

Contents

Preface   ix

Prologue   xi

One

**THINKING ABOUT BEING
A MATHEMATICS TEACHER**

Thomas J. Cooney

1

Two

**DEVELOPING A TOPIC ACROSS
THE CURRICULUM: FUNCTIONS**

Thomas J. Cooney

27

Three

**DESIGNING TEACHING:
THE PYTHAGOREAN THEOREM**

Erich Ch. Wittman

97

Four

ANALYZING SUBJECT MATTER: FUNDAMENTAL IDEAS OF COMBINATORICS

Georg Schrage

167

Five

MODELING WITH FUNCTIONS

John Dossey

221

Six

POSING MATHEMATICALLY: A NOVELETTE

Stephen I. Brown

281

Preface

Mathematics, Pedagogy, and Secondary Teacher Education is intended for both preservice and inservice teachers who wish to experience some of the fundamental ideas expressed in the documents published by the National Council of Teachers of Mathematics that are commonly referred to as the Standards. The text encourages the reader to seek connections between pedagogy and content in a number of ways. Pedagogical ideas are part of the substance of each piece. Often these ideas are exemplified in various classroom vignettes or in a variety of interview settings. Readers are also encouraged to imagine the implications for teaching of their own experiences as learners. Consequently, both the content and the format of the text differ significantly from most texts that deal with the teaching of mathematics at the secondary level.

We want to begin with a note about the structure of this work. *Mathematics, Pedagogy, and Secondary Teacher Education* is being published in two different forms—as a single text and as a series of smaller books. Each of these smaller books is identical to the corresponding chapter in the larger text. Because each chapter is rich in material for exploration, we felt that inservice and preservice instructors should have the flexibility to choose and assign the topics that best match their teaching goals. It is important to note that "Thinking About Being a Mathematics Teacher" addresses ideas central to the other pieces. We therefore recommend that you always use this piece whenever you are assigning one of the other smaller books.

The specific documents that our work draws upon as well as the focus of each of the individual pieces is described and illustrated in both the Prologue and in the piece by Thomas Cooney titled, "Thinking About Being a Mathematics Teacher." That piece also explicitly addresses some of the underlying principles of the Standards.

For a quick overview of the content of each of the chapters as well as a brief statement of the general pedagogical direction of the entire text, the reader may wish to look at the letter from the authors to Dr. Riskit that begins on page ix of the Prologue.

Both the writing of the text and related research were supported by a grant received from the National Science Foundation (#TPE-9050016) in 1990 in which the authors were principal investigators. (The views expressed in this text are not necessarily those of the National Science Foundation.) The authors all received help from their coauthors and from insightful reviews by many colleagues. In particular we would like to thank Glenda Lappan, John Siskar, Frederick Reiner, Phares O'Daffer, Jerry Becker, Marilyn Nickson (Great Britain), Mike Shaughnessy, Douglas Grouws, and Nicholas Rouche (Belgium) for their most helpful reviews. We are also grateful to Thomas Giambrone, Robin Woodbury (a doctoral student at the University at Buffalo), and Hunter Ballew for sending us helpful comments based on their use of drafts of some of the chapters. The following people (all University of Georgia doctoral students at the time of their contributions) helped in the design and writing of "Developing a Topic Across the Curriculum" and some provided extensive feedback to authors of the other pieces. Melvin Wilson, Barry Shealy, Tingyao Zheng, Bridget Arvold, and Nichola Oppong. Joao Ponte from the University of Lisbon and Antoine Stam, a professor in the Business School at the University of Georgia, also contributed ideas for "Developing a Topic Across the Curriculum."

There is obviously more material in this text than can be included in a single course. Reading the Prologue and "Thinking About Being a Mathematics Teacher" should enable the instructor to make some decisions about what to include, exclude, or modify. We hope our attempt to integrate content and pedagogy is helpful to other instructors as they seek ways of promoting reform in the teaching of mathematics.

Prologue
Stephen I. Brown

I- A FIRST CLASS MEETING

It is May 25, 1995 and this is the first session of a course entitled Integrating Mathematics and Pedagogy. It is being offered to a class of about fifteen students who are at various stages of their professional development as teachers. Nine are in their junior year in an undergraduate course in teacher education. Six are experienced teachers, who have taught for a number of years, ranging from two to seventeen. The professor, Dr. Riskit, has taught for about twenty years, but she has not used this text before, nor taught a course with this title. Dr. Riskit holds a joint appointment in the school of education and in the mathematics department.

Dr. Riskit: Welcome to the first session of this course. Some of you may be relieved to find out that in some ways I am in the same boat as you. I know that you have not taken this course before. But, guess what? I have not taught it before. The course represents a novel point of view with regard to teacher education. The title of the material we'll be working with, *Mathematics, Pedagogy and Secondary Teacher Education,* suggests that novelty. The material was inspired by a number of documents written in the late 1980s and early to mid 1990s that attempted to reform the way we think about teaching and learning. Are any of you familiar with those documents? They were published by organizations such as the National Council of Teachers of Mathematics and the Mathematics Association of America. Some of you are well aware of these organizations, but others probably have not yet heard of them.

Elster: Yes, I think I know what you mean. They were the rage at the time and though I took in-service course work that focused on those books, I must confess that I have not done as much as I would have liked in my teaching. I always felt I needed additional support. I hope this course will help.

Dr. Riskit: I hope so. Elster, can you tell us all what some of the books are that you are referring to?

Elster: One of them has a cute title. It is *Everybody Counts.* There's another with the word *Standards* in the title. Oh yes. There was another with even a cuter title, *On the Shoulders of Giants.* I think it was taken from a quote by Isaac Newton, referring to his indebtedness to his predecessors.

Tova: Elster is right about the word *Standards* in the title. But actually, I think there were several books with that title—one dealing with new curriculum in mathematics, another with assessment of learning, and something else I can't remember.

Dr. Riskit: Terrific, Tova. We'll come to the third topic, which deals with the professional education of teachers later on, but as you can tell, we have several experienced teachers in the course. We will have to find ways of making use of your expertise. Maybe we can begin right now. Do either of you want to give us an overview of some of the key ideas about teaching and learning that appear in the collections you just mentioned?

Elster: A biggie has to do with problem solving. It is *the* central idea.

Yung: Hasn't math always been about solving problems? What is new about that concept?

Dr. Riskit: Good question, Yung. Even when I was a student in the 1950s we were expected to solve problems in math classes. Anyone want to answer Yung's question?

Tova: The most important one is that students are not only given problems to solve but they are taught specific strategies for dealing with what they do not yet know how to solve. The idea of problem solving as coping with the unknown is relatively new. Also, students are not only expected to *produce* solutions but to *reflect* on the processes they use and to think through what they learn from failed efforts as well as successful ones.

Dr. Riskit: Good point, Tova. You have actually said a number of different interesting things about problem solving. We will be looking at these matters a lot in this course. Speaking about problem solving, let's not try to solve all our problems about the content of this course at once. Does anyone else want to mention one or two other ideas that appear in those earlier documents?

John: There are a lot of suggestions for relating math to other fields. I think the word "connections" is used to describe the relationship.

Dr. Riskit: Yes, and what are some tools that are used to make that connection?

Yung: What do you mean by a tool?

Dr. Riskit: Another good question. Well . . . think of some examples in which you applied math to the real world. What did you need to do to make the connection?

Nova: Frequently we made use of functions . . . looking at dependent and independent variables.

Yung: We also heard about modeling, but how do functions compare with modeling?

Dr. Riskit: That is something we will find out more about in these materials *[Silence, as Dr. Riskit waits three seconds for someone in the class to ask a question or make a statement]*

Tova: Didn't you mention when I spoke with you in your office last semester that you had communicated with the authors of the materials? Can you tell us something about them?

Dr. Riskit: Actually, I was so intrigued by the contents when I saw them listed in a catalogue that I wrote to them and asked them to tell me a little bit about how the materials came about. If you wait one minute, I will go into my office and get that letter for you.

[Dr. Riskit returns in a few minutes and reads the letter to the class.]

Dear Dr. Riskit:

Many thanks for your interest in *Mathematics, Pedagogy and Secondary Teacher Education.* As you can tell from even a quick glance at any of the individual pieces, we take an unusual approach in enabling teachers to connect their experience in learning mathematics with issues in pedagogy. We feel that such reflection is critical if teachers are to weave together important issues of pedagogy.

The materials were created as part of a project on the integration of pedagogy and mathematics sponsored by the National Science Foundation in the early to mid 1990s. Each of the individual pieces provides a different kind of focus on the relationship of educational issues to mathematics.

"Thinking About Being a Mathematics Teacher" (by Thomas Cooney) invites students to consider a variety of general but important questions— including why it is that they decided to become mathematics teachers and what their image is of teaching mathematics.

"Designing Teaching: The Pythagorean Theorem" (by Erich Wittmann) selects a topic that has, in one form or other, received the equivalent of several days of attention in the secondary school curriculum. Introducing the topic in a myriad of ways, the author raises implications for rethinking a number of issues of a more general nature. Included among them are the relationship of geometric and algebraic ways of thinking and the relationship between formal and informal proofs.

"Developing a Topic Across the Curriculum: Functions" (by Thomas Cooney) presents functions as both a mathematical entity in its own right and as a unifying mathematical tool that enables us to relate mathematics to the real world. The students are invited to explore a number of different views of the concept of function with the expectation that they will deepen their appreciation of its mathematical complexity and at the same time develop a point of view regarding its teaching.

Like both the Pythagorean theorem and functions, the topic of combinatorics has a robust history. It is rooted in the concept of counting and though it was included in the college curriculum in the past, it has appeared in only a perfunctory way (mostly as part of course work in probability) at the secondary school level. It represents a body of subject matter that could be incorporated in a number of different ways into existing curriculum. "Analyzing Subject Matter: Fundamental Ideas of Combinatorics" (by Georg Schrage) demonstrates how much depth exists in problems that are easily stated and understood, but difficult to analyze.

Modeling is a relatively new topic to the secondary school scene, though the topic is one that has captured the fancy of practicing mathematicians for a long time. "Modeling with Functions" (by John Dossey) is offered in an effort to suggest how mathematics can be applied and related to the real world, to other fields, and to itself as well. This piece clarifies what a model is and shows us how we make use of models in mathematical thinking even when we are not explicitly aware that we are doing so.

"Posing Mathematically" (by Stephen Brown) is "novel" in both format and content. It is written in the style of a novel and it focuses on a way of thinking about mathematics and about pedagogy that is just beginning to receive attention. As is the case of modeling or functions, it represents a mind-set that invites us to rethink virtually any subject matter in the curriculum. The author integrates strategies for problem posing with those of problem solving and draws heavily upon the often overlooked insight that no problem is solved without first being posed. A related insight is that a problem well posed is half solved, something that also has not always been well appreciated in the history of mathematics.

Taken together, these pieces exemplify the principles of teaching and learning mathematics that are advocated in a number of recent documents created by teams of mathematicians and educators. In particular we refer you to *Curriculum and Evaluation Standards for School Mathematics* (NCTM, 1989); *Everybody Counts* (National Research Council, 1989); *Reshaping School Mathematics: A Philosophy and Framework for Curriculum* (National Research Council, 1990); *The Professional Teaching Standards* (NCTM, 1991); *Assessment Standards for School Mathematics* (NCTM, 1995), *On the Shoulders of Giants* (Steen, 1990).

Each of the above authors, as well as those who have written for this collection, assumes that learning is an act of *experiencing* and *acting* upon the world rather than merely *receiving* it. Activities are provided throughout to encourage teachers to reflect upon their own beliefs and practices about teaching and learning. So you see that the teachers are encouraged to connect their own learning of mathematical topics with issues related to teaching and learning.

Again, many thanks for your interest. We hope you find this letter useful in deciding upon what text to use for the course.

Sincerely,

The Authors

Tova: Wow, this collection will give us a lot to think about..

Dr. Riskit: Well that's true. So far we have heard about the content of the material in a general way. Now I would like you to get a feeling for it in a more detailed way even before we start using it.

Dr. Riskit thinks for a while. She had originally planned to offer a brief introductory lecture on course requirements and on the nature of the material for the course. Based upon the realization that there was such diverse talent and experience in the course, she decides to modify her original plan. She decides it would be better for them to talk to each other and to try to come to an understanding of the nature of the material on their own.

She decides to pass out a questionnaire for students to provide some information about themselves that would be of interest both to her and to each other. While they are filling out information about their backgrounds and indicating their names and phone numbers, she mulls over how to proceed.

Since the publisher offers the material either as a single text or as smaller books based on the chapters, she hasn't yet decided on what material she should ask the students to purchase for class. This means that none of them have the material in front of them. However, she does have her copy of the full text as well as two copies from the library. She realizes that there are many different kinds of overviews that the students might explore and finally hits upon the following scheme that encourages them to think about the organization of the course as well.

She decides to organize the class into three groups: two teams of undergraduates and another group of experienced teachers. Here is the assignment that she decides to have them begin in class:

For the undergraduate groups: Look for common features that appear in the different chapters. That is, look for similarity of format despite major differences.

For the group of experienced teachers: There is no way we can cover all six chapters in one semester and I would like to take your insights into consideration in guiding my selection of the extensive content in this book. In order to give me a better idea of your interests and your experiences, skim the five content chapters and recommend how you would sequence the material for the course.

Each group is engaged in a lively discussion that continues until nearly the end of the first class meeting. Dr. Riskit realizes that there will not be enough time to have each of the groups report back to the entire class. She also realizes that it would be worthwhile for each of the members of each group to think further about these matters before returning to discuss these matters further. Dr. Riskit therefore decides to give a written assignment to each person. Below is the assignment due for the next session about three days later:

> Write a paper of approximately two typewritten pages that (1) summarizes what your small group has discussed and then (2) reacts to some of the issues that have been discussed or locates new ones that had not been raised in the group discussion.

Dr. Riskit has not yet decided how she will make use of these individual essays when the students return to their small groups for the next class meeting, but she has given assignments of this sort before and she will think about how to proceed over the weekend.

II - THE FIRST ASSIGNMENT
YUNG'S APPROACH:

Yung is a member of the first group. She found it a little unsettling to meet with other members of the small group to skim through the text before having the opportunity of doing so on her own. She was mostly interested in the subject matter that she would have to learn. Nevertheless, she found this book to be arranged in an interesting way and was more excited than she thought she would be in coming up with her paper. Below is her first draft:

> The first thing that struck us as a group was the diversity we found among the chapters. We were concerned that we would not be able to locate common elements in these chapters. We weren't sure where to begin. At first, we started to look only for an organization that was common in all of the chapters. We looked for an identical format. It was hard to find one. We eventually decided to be a little less literal. We did that in two ways. First we chose to look for common elements that most of the chapters had, even if they did not appear in all of them. Then we decided to search for *common points of view* even if these points of view were expressed differently in each of the chapters.

We noticed that most of the chapters began with a dialogue. The dialogues seemed to take place in a classroom and they involved reaction of students to activities or questions that teachers had. All of these dialogues were lively. The students did not always answer correctly; nor did they always understand what the teacher was trying to convey. In that sense there was a "real world" quality to the dialogues like what we might find in our own classes.

When I got home I began to think some more about these dialogues. Why were they there? In most cases the dialogue appeared at the beginning of the chapter and occasionally later on. In one or two of the chapters, they reappeared throughout. I liked reading dialogues rather than being lectured at about what is important and what is right. When I thought more about these dialogues, I was really enticed by them. They seem to set the stage for thinking about teaching and learning as social activities. The teacher frequently encourages students to react to what other students are saying. I am going to enjoy thinking more about the classroom as a social environment.

I realize now that there is a second common feature. That is, there are many invitations for students to work cooperatively in small groups. Students were asked to have conversations about controversial matters and they were encouraged to write both individual and group essays in conjunction with these conversations. I had always thought that people decided to study math rather than English or history because they did not have to write essays and because there was nothing really controversial. I am a little concerned about viewing math as like these other subjects. But I am enjoying writing this essay more than I thought I would.

A third feature that seems to pervade the chapters is a focus on something we discussed in our first class. That is there is a problem solving orientation in each of the chapters. Sometimes they are referred to as "Reflective Problems." Sometimes they are just activities or questions to think about.

A fourth feature of the chapters is one that I thought about only after beginning this assignment. It relates to the title of the course: *Integrating Mathematics Content and Pedagogy*. What is being integrated here? Each of the chapters has mathematical sections and each of them has sections in which there are teaching ideas. In some of the chapters these sections intertwine; in others they appear to be parallel. I decided to speak to my uncle who is a math teacher and asked him about his own education. Apparently, he was taught mathematics in his math courses and he was taught how to teach math in his education courses. In this book something else seems to be happening. Not only are the two different concerns integrated in the same course, but we are encouraged to use ourselves as a laboratory. In the process of learning mathematics, we think of ourselves as teachers.

There is an intriguing and challenging feature that integrates math and pedagogy—as the letter to Dr. Riskit by the authors suggested. We are encouraged to think about how we react to a new idea as a student; and no sooner do we seem to have begun to understand it than we are asked what the implications might be for us as teachers. I love the prospect of thinking of myself as a laboratory of sorts.

ELSTER'S APPROACH:

Elster has been assigned to the group of experienced teachers. He finds the assignment virtually impossible to carry out. He realizes that it would be possible to design the course in such a way that the class covers selected excerpts from each of the chapters. In that case, he thinks that the first few sections of each chapter could be chosen. On the other hand, he realizes that it would be possible to select only one or two chapters in their entirety. But he finds it hard to figure out which ones ought to be chosen without knowing more about Dr. Riskit's interests and intentions and without knowing a lot about the content of each of the chapters—something he cannot grasp in the short period of time needed to do the assignment. Part of his problem is that some of the chapters deal with specific content. The Pythagorean theorem and combinatorics are examples of that. Some of the chapters deal more with process that can be applied to any content. Posing mathematically and the chapter on modeling are such examples. He sees the functions chapter as having dual functions. (He smiles when he appreciates this turn of phrase.)

Elster is in a quandary. He feels that it is not the job of students to define what a course ought to be about or how it ought to be organized. He looks at the sheet that Dr. Riskit passed out in class with the names and phone numbers of all of the students in the course. He remembers that she did encourage them to contact each other at home should they feel the need for reaction from colleagues. Elster decides to call up a couple of other people in his small group to help him think through what he might write. He called up two of the students in the class. Tova agreed with him completely and even suggested that they not do the assignment until getting more information and justification from Dr. Riskit. Tova was more distressed than Elster, however. She was thinking of dropping the course and taking it next year when it would be offered by someone who Tova believed would know what she was doing. Even if Dr. Riskit was the teacher again, at least she would have had enough experience after teaching it once to know what she wanted to do in the course. Another student, Nova, loved the assignment. She said that she liked the prospect of participating with the instructor not only on how things should be taught, but also what should be taught. She said she liked to think of teaching as a form of collaboration between students and teacher. Elster had stomach cramps and decided to sleep on the matter. He was willing to think about it further but was looking for some approach that would be helpful to the teacher but that would not actually require advice of the sort she was requesting.

Reflective Problems

1. Given what you know so far, what are some issues that you feel should be addressed in thinking about how the course should be organized? Are there issues that you think might be troublesome for undergraduates but not for experienced teachers? Vice versa? Why?

2. What is your opinion about Elster's reaction? Do you think it is appropriate for Dr. Riskit to pose the second assignment to the group of experienced teachers?

3. Dr. Riskit has asked all of the students to bring copies of their papers to class. She will ask the students to get together in small groups with their individual papers. What kinds of activities would you recommend that they do in these groups? Why? Assume a brainstorming mode in answering this question.

4. Dr. Riskit formed groups consisting of either undergraduates or experienced teachers. Do you think she might have gained some advantages by mixing members of both groups?

5. Write a brief essay in which you react to this prologue. Then try to find someone who reacts to it differently from you. Discuss what you think accounts for the difference. Save your papers for future reflection.

Thinking About Being
a Mathematics Teacher

Here, we begin by inviting you to explore what mathematics means to you and your views of the teaching and learning of mathematics. We also invite you to consider the way mathematics and the teaching of learning of mathematics are characterized in the NCTM *Standards* and how these perspectives might relate to your professional development. Let us begin by exploring a question that affects all of us—regardless of our career stage.

WHY DID YOU CHOOSE TO BECOME
A MATHEMATICS TEACHER?

Reflective Problem 1

Before reading this section, answer the following questions. You may want to write your responses down.

1. Why did/do you want to become a mathematics teacher?

2. If you were to start your education or career over again and you couldn't be a mathematics teacher, what career would you choose? Why?

What influenced you to become a teacher of mathematics? A love of mathematics? A love of working with young people? Financial reasons? Job security? Family circumstances? Do you think your decision was based more on people who influenced you or on circumstantial events in your life? Each of us is attracted to mathematics education for a variety of reasons that depend on our personal biography and circumstances. There is probably not one single reason but rather a collection of reasons and circumstances that influenced our decision.

Think about what people may have influenced you to become a teacher of mathematics. What were their characteristics? What was there about those people that influenced you? Most of us were influenced as young people by parents, community leaders, teachers, coaches, friends, or others whom we admired and with whom we had sustained contact. We admired them for some reason—most likely a certain strength of character, perhaps manifested by warmth and caring, or a certain intellectual curiosity.

We can also ask the mirror-image question about ourselves: Which of *our* characteristics will likely influence the students we teach? How is it that we can create a context within which our students will develop a love of mathematics, curiosity, and a desire to learn? We should never lose sight of the fact that as teachers we will likely influence students in many ways. An important question is, "How can we influence them in a way that honors their growth as thinking and caring individuals?"

To what extent do you think you chose to become a mathematics teacher because of circumstances in your life? Some people chose teaching because of perceived job security or because they feel that teaching fits their particular life-style. To what extent do you think events in your life determined that teaching was the most viable career option for you? Which of the following two factors likely influenced you the most: the subject of mathematics or a desire to work with young people? As you reflect upon your own background, do you remember always being interested in mathematics? Always wanting to help others? To what extent were these factors important (or not) in your decision to become a mathematics teacher?

WHAT COMES TO YOUR MIND WHEN YOU THINK OF MATHEMATICS?

Reflective Problem 2

Consider the following questions. Write down your responses.

1. If someone were to ask me what mathematics is, I would say

   _____.

2. To me, the essence of mathematics is

   _____.

3. The thing that I enjoy most about doing mathematics is

   _____.

Mathematics means many things to many people. For some, mathematics is the study of patterns. Some patterns are simple number patterns that young children can explore. Other patterns are exceedingly complex and are understood by only a few of the world's most renowned mathematicians. While the topics and levels of sophistication may vary greatly, there is nothing about a pattern-seeking conception of mathematics that prevents students of all ages from engaging in a search for relationships, forming conjectures about those relationships, and studying the conditions under which those relationships hold true.

Many see mathematics as a search for abstract relationships that hold "eternal truths." Others see mathematics as an outgrowth of human invention rather than the discovery of what has been there forever. Still others are less interested in the philosophical debate about how mathematics was created and are more interested in the practical side of mathematics. For these latter people, mathematics is seen as a tool for solving practical problems, for example, determining the cost of purchasing a car. Others see mathematics as a kind of puzzle—determining which pieces fit together to make a coherent whole. These people often think of mathematics as a matter of solving unique kinds of problems, perhaps couched in a puzzle format as in the well-known problem of identifying digits associated with each letter in the following arrangement.

$$
\begin{array}{c}
\text{S E N D} \\
+ \underline{\text{M O R E}} \\
\text{M O N E Y}
\end{array}
$$

In *Mathematics, Pedagogy, and Secondary Teacher Education* we try to capture a variety of perspectives about what constitutes mathematics. The following five problems are examples of those presented by the various authors. Do not solve them now but rank-order them in terms of your interest level in solving them.

1. The first two numbers that have three divisors are 4 and 9. These numbers are the first two squares (beyond 1). A reasonable conjecture would be that all squares greater than 1 have three divisors. Is that true? Investigate.

2. ABCD is a unit square. E, F, G, and H are midpoints (Figure 1). What percent of ABCD is shaded?

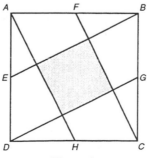

Figure 1

3. Suppose a 20 cm by 20 cm sheet of construction paper had its corners cut out so that it could be folded to make a box (Figure 2). What size corners should be cut out in order to maximize the volume of the box?

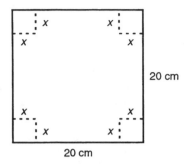

Figure 2

4. A single domino shows a pair of numbers both between 0 and 6. A complete set of dominoes consists of a certain number of dominoes such that every pair of this kind occurs exactly once. How many dominoes are in a set?

5. Prices for pizzas at Gumpy's Pizza and at Pizza Shack are shown below. What advice would you give your friends about purchasing pizza from the two pizza restaurants?

| *Gumpy's Pizza* | | *Pizza Shack Pizza* | |
Diameter	*Cost*	*Diameter*	*Cost*
20 cm	$6.50	25 cm	$7.00
30 cm	$9.00	35 cm	$10.75
40 cm	$12.50	45 cm	$15.50

Compare your ranking with those of other classmates. Are your rankings similar to theirs or not? Do you think your classmates hold a view of mathematics similar to or different from yours?

One of the authors had the following interview with a teacher several years ago.

I: If you were to think of something that is as different from mathematics as you could imagine, what would it be?

T: That's an interesting question. (*Pause*) I guess I would say hard rock music.

I: And why do you say that?

T: Well that kind of music seems so bizarre. It doesn't seem to have any structure—at least none that I can detect or appreciate. On the other hand, mathematics is very structured. Everything fits together. There are no pieces just laying out there not connected to anything else.

Although we might disagree (or not) with the teacher's analysis of hard rock music and the certainty of mathematics, we nevertheless gain a glimpse of what she thinks mathematics is. Notice that thinking of mathematics as a structure is an important part of her view of mathematics.

Exploration 1

Find a willing friend and ask him or her the following question: If you could think of something that is as different from mathematics as possible, what would it be? Explore why he or she picked whatever was picked. Write a one-page report on what you think your friend's view of mathematics is.

Let us now return to Reflective Problem 2. Consider your response and complete the following activity.

Reflective Problem 3

Write a one- to two-page statement of what mathematics means to you. Include your responses to the various questions posed in this section.

WHAT INFLUENCES OUR VIEWS OF MATHEMATICS?

While we enjoy doing mathematics at some level and generally have a positive attitude toward mathematics, there are many people who hold quite a different view of the subject. For some people, studying mathematics creates considerable anxiety and tension. They think mathematics is a subject that is accessible only to the selected few. Indeed, our society often promotes the view that mathematics is something to be avoided. Consider the cartoon in Figure 3.

Figure 3

What view of mathematics do you think is communicated in this cartoon?

Furinghetti (1993) has observed that various scenes in movies often depict a certain negativism toward mathematics. For example, she notes that in the film *A Streetcar Named Desire,* Blanche tells her suitor, falsely, that she is a teacher. When asked if she teaches mathematics, Blanche flatly denies that she has anything to do with mathematics, as if such an association would be an affront to her femininity. Furinghetti (1993) also observed that Woody Allen, in *Radio Days*, asks a classmate to recite mathematical formulae to illustrate what a disagreeable character the classmate really is. A number of years ago, a toy company produced a Barbie doll that said, "Math is tough." While the doll was taken off the market, it is easy to see why so many people were offended by a company suggesting that mathematics is a subject inherently difficult for women.

··

Exploration 2

Identify instances in newspapers, television, or the movies where a particular view about mathematics is conveyed. Describe the situation. Write a brief analysis about what you think the impact might be on others regarding their view of mathematics.

··

We are often surrounded by circumstances that communicate a certain elitism toward mathematics that is generally counterproductive to helping students see the beauty and joy in doing mathematics. We have all encountered individuals who communicate in a bragging sort of way that they don't know much about mathematics. We are a product of this society. Yet, for the most part, we don't share that view. For us, mathematics is an enjoyable subject, not discounting the fact that we may have had many difficult and trying experiences when learning mathematics. We cannot deny the fact that many of our students' views of mathematics, and perhaps our own as well, are influenced by the culture in which we live. To the extent to which this culture communicates a negative view of mathematics, we are faced with the challenge of communicating to our students that mathematics is a subject accessible to all.

WHAT DO THE NCTM *STANDARDS* SAY ABOUT MATHEMATICS?

The view of mathematics communicated in the NCTM *Standards* places considerable emphasis on various processes in doing mathematics, particularly communication, reasoning, and problem solving. We will consider the nature of each of these processes as addressed in the *Standards*.

MATHEMATICS AS COMMUNICATION

We can think of communication in at least two different ways. First, there is the need to communicate to others what we mean by the mathematics we are using. Second, we can use mathematics to communicate information about the real world. The following activity emphasizes mathematical communication in the sense of using mathematical terms to help another student draw a figure.

Exploration 3

Work in groups of three. One person should be shown Figure 4 or a similarly drawn figure. This person should give directions to a second person who is to draw the figure but who cannot see the figure. The first person cannot see what the second person is drawing and hence is unaware of the result of the directions given. The third person should note what mathematical terms are used by the first person.

Figure 4

When the first person completes his/her directions, the three participants should discuss the process and observe whether the second person drew the figure correctly or not. The third person should note ways that the mathematical language was used effectively and how it might have been used better, if possible.

Mathematics also provides a means by which we can describe and analyze real-world phenomena.

Exploration 4

Identify several instances in newspapers, television, or the movies where mathematics is used to communicate information. Write a short essay on the role mathematics can play in communicating this information to the general public.

MATHEMATICS AS REASONING

Mathematics by its very nature involves different kinds of reasoning processes. The NCTM *Standards* emphasize four different kinds of reasoning: inductive, deductive, proportional, and spatial. *Inductive reasoning* involves a process by which we recognize what is common to a set of examples and then generalize the observed property to a more inclusive set. For example, if we square an odd number and subtract one from the square, we obtain the following examples.

$$3^2 - 1 = 8 \qquad 5^2 - 1 = 24 \qquad 7^2 - 1 = 48 \qquad 9^2 - 1 = 80 \qquad 11^2 - 1 = 120$$

We can make several observations. First, the resulting numbers are all even. Second, the resulting numbers are all multiples of 8. Third, the numbers all end in 0, 4, or 8. We could, therefore, form the following generalizations.

- The square of an odd number less one is an even number.
- The square of an odd number less one is a multiple of 8.
- The square of an odd number less one results in a number that ends in 0, 4, or 8.

Deductive reasoning can help us establish whether conjectures are true by using logic that proceeds from the general to the specific. Often deductive reasoning fits one of the two following patterns.

Modus Ponens	*Modus Tollens*
If p, then q	If p, then q
p	not q
Therefore q	Therefore not p
---	---
If a figure is a square, then the figure is a parallelogram	If a figure is a square, then the figure is a parallelogram
ABCD is a square	ABCD is not a parallelogram
Therefore ABCD is a parallelogram	Therefore ABCD is not a square

Deductive reasoning also occurs in the form of a series of deductions called the *chain rule* as indicated below.

$$p \rightarrow q \ (\text{read ``}p \text{ implies } q\text{''})$$
$$q \rightarrow r$$
$$\text{Therefore } p \rightarrow r$$

The following example illustrates this kind of reasoning.

If ABCD is a square, then ABCD is a rectangle.
If ABCD is a rectangle, then ABCD is a parallelogram.
Therefore if ABCD is a square, then ABCD is a parallelogram.

Let us return to the second of the three conjectures stated above. We can establish it by using deductive reasoning.

If n is an odd number, then it can be expressed as $n = 2k + 1$, where k is some integer.

Therefore $n^2 = (2k + 1)^2 = 4k^2 + 4k + 1$. If we subtract one, we have $4k^2 + 4k$, which can be factored $4k(k + 1)$. Since either k or $k + 1$ must be even, we can see that the expression $4k^2 + 4k$ must be a multiple of eight since it has a factor of four and a factor of two.

You may want to consider how the first and third conjectures can be established using deductive reasoning.

It does not follow that all conclusions based on inductive reasoning are true. We saw that the first two square numbers (beyond 1), 4 and 9, have three factors. Twenty-five also has exactly 3 factors: 1, 5, and 25. We might conjecture that all square numbers (beyond 1) have 3 factors. But 16 has 5 factors! Neither is it the case that when a generalization is reached using inductive reasoning, the truth of the generalization can be established. For example, Goldbach (1690–1764) observed that any even number greater than 2 can be represented as the sum of two prime numbers. Observe that $4 = 2 + 2$, $20 = 17 + 3$, and $52 = 47 + 5$. This conjecture is called *Goldbach's conjecture*. While computers have yet to find a counterexample, neither has anyone created a proof for Goldbach's conjecture. Similarly, the seventeenth-century mathematician Pierre de Fermat (1608–1665) stated what became known as "Fermat's Last Theorem," which can be stated as follows:

The equation $a^n + b^n = c^n$ is not solvable in integers for any $n > 2$.

While this theorem seemed to be true (no counterexamples could be found), a proof for the theorem did not appear until 1994. This proof is still being studied by mathematicians.

Another kind of reasoning discussed in the NCTM *Standards* is that of *proportional reasoning*. Two quantities vary proportionally when, as their corresponding values increase or decrease, the ratios of the two quantities are always equivalent. If, for example, x and y vary proportionally with x as the independent variable, then there is a multiplicative relationship between x and y such that for each value of x, $y = kx$, k being a constant. Does it follow that if $y = x + 1$, then x and y vary proportionally? Would $(y - 1)$ and x vary proportionally? A second characteristic of two quantities that vary proportionally, is that for every unit change in x, there is a constant change in y. Proportional reasoning can be used to solve rather trivial problems like, "If 3 tickets to a movie cost $12, how much do 12 tickets cost?" A more complex problem might be, "If a 4" by 6" photograph is enlarged to fit an 8" by 10" frame, does the photo need to be cropped? If so, what part of the picture would have to be cropped?" Without question, proportional reasoning is a central part of mathematical thinking.

A fourth kind of reasoning highlighted in the NCTM *Standards* is *spatial reasoning*, which involves reasoning with two- or three-dimensional objects. Consider, for example, what kind of cross section of a cube (Figure 5) would result in the following planar figures.

1.   a square
2.   a rectangle
3.   an isosceles triangle
4.   an equilateral triangle
5.   an isosceles trapezoid

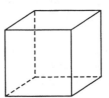

Figure 5

Given these different cross sections, we could ask how their areas could be determined. These tasks require spatial reasoning.

Exploration 5

Suppose the cube above was a unit cube. What would be the area of the largest possible rectangular cross section? The largest possible square cross section? The largest possible triangular cross section?

MATHEMATICS AS PROBLEM SOLVING

Problem solving has always been recognized as an important part of doing mathematics. As mentioned in the NCTM *Standards* there is more to problem solving than just getting answers, e.g., learning and using strategies for solving problems, verifying and interpreting results, reflecting on the solution process, posing new problems, and generalizing results where appropriate. George Polya's classic book *How to Solve It* emphasizes strategies for solving problems and the value gained from looking back on the solution process. The asking of questions like "What happens if?" or "What if not?" provides means of generating problems to be considered that are "cousins" to the initial problem.

Consider the following problem that was shared with one of the authors by a Japanese colleague.

Jack is in a race with 15 other boys. At the beginning of the race Jack is fifth from the last. At the end of the race he is third. How many boys did he pass?

When people solve this problem, they inevitably draw some sort of representation of the runners and then locate Jack in that representation. But some assumptions need to be made. How many boys are in the race? What do we mean by fifth from the last? What does it mean to finish third? If Jack passes one boy, and then that boy passes Jack, and then finally Jack passes that boy again, is that one pass or two passes for Jack? Does it matter whether Jack passes the two boys who are initially first and second and consequently other boys finish first and second in the race or whether he never passes the two boys who initially lead the race? We might say that while the problem seems simple enough, it is hopelessly vague. Yet, there is much here to be valued. When mathematics is applied to real-world problems, certain assumptions must be made about the context or conditions of the problem being addressed. For example, mathematical models for weather predictions make certain assumptions about climatic conditions. To the extent that those assumptions are correct, the mathematical models can predict weather rather accurately. But when some event occurs that was not accounted for in the model, the prediction goes awry—the model failed to account for all of the relevant factors. The racing problem invites students to consider assumptions necessary to solve the problem.

Another facet of problem solving is developing general solutions from specifically solved problems. Suppose we made the following representation for the race with Jack and assume that he can pass a person only once and that he does not pass the initial two leaders in the race. Jack's assumed position is marked.

Beginning of race: B_1 B_2 B_3 B_4 B_5 B_6 B_7 B_8 B_9 B_{10} B_{11} $\underline{\mathbf{B_{12}}}$ B_{13} B_{14} B_{15} B_{16}

End of race: B_1 B_2 $\underline{\mathbf{B_{12}}}$ B_3 B_4 B_5 B_6 B_7 B_8 B_9 B_{10} B_{11} B_{13} B_{14} B_{15} B_{16}

Under these assumptions, we can see that Jack passes 9 other boys (B_3 through B_{11} inclusive). The question then becomes, how can we determine that he passes 9 boys without drawing the representations, that is, using only the numbers in the problem? What symbolic representations would we need? This might be important if we were trying to solve the following problem where drawing a representation for the number of girls in the race would not be a reasonable approach.

Exploration 6

Jackie was in a race with 200 other girls. At the beginning of the race she was 50th from last. At the end of the race she was 10th. How many other girls did she pass?

1. Identify other assumptions that could be made in Jack's race and determine what the solutions would be under these assumptions.

2. How would these assumptions affect the solutions to the problem with Jackie?

3. What conditions in the problems could be changed to create other types of problems?

MATHEMATICS AS CONNECTIONS

An important emphasis in the NCTM *Standards* is that of *connections*. In general connections are of two types. First, there are the connections between mathematics and real-world situations. The chapter on mathematical modeling emphasizes this type of connection. In a more pervasive way, this type of mathematical connection can help us think quantitatively as we make decisions that affect our lives. The second type of connection exists within mathematics itself and is rooted in the structure of mathematics.

With respect to the first type of connection, suppose we were operating a flower shop and we wanted to determine what price for flowers and plants would give us a reasonable return on our investment. What factors should we consider and what mathematics would be involved? Clearly we must sell them for a price greater than what we paid for them and yet not so high that everyone is discouraged from buying them. But how do we find a reasonable price between these two extremes? What are the factors to be considered? The cost of the plants and flowers for the store owners? The cost of renting or buying the shop? The volume of the business—how many plants or flowers can be handled in a given year? What the competition sells the plants or flowers for? The salaries for the shop owners and for other employees? Does it make a difference whether special days, e.g., Valentine's Day, come on a weekend or during the week? While experience and trial and error may be helpful in determining prices, there are a number of factors that need to be considered and modeled in order to determine prices that return a reasonable profit.

Exploration 7

Contact owners of a small business who sell a particular product. Ask them what factors contribute to their determination of the prices and what factors seem to influence sales. Write a brief report on what you found and what role you see mathematics plays (or could play) in determining a fair price.

Mathematical connections also include connections within mathematics—the second type of connection. These kinds of connections, for example, can be between algebraic and geometric relationships or between various theorems in the same mathematical domain. Consider the relationships between the following situations.

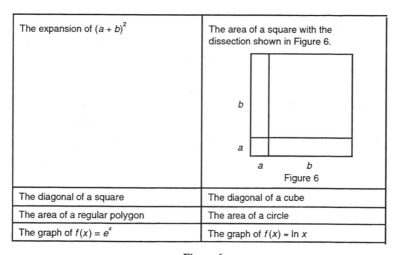

The expansion of $(a + b)^2$	The area of a square with the dissection shown in Figure 6.
The diagonal of a square	The diagonal of a cube
The area of a regular polygon	The area of a circle
The graph of $f(x) = e^x$	The graph of $f(x) = \ln x$

Figure 6

WHAT VIEW DO YOU HAVE ABOUT THE TEACHING AND LEARNING OF MATHEMATICS?

In a previous section you were asked to consider your view of mathematics. The following activity invites you to consider your view of teaching mathematics.

Reflective Problem 4

Consider analogies with the following possibilities and decide which one(s) best fit your notion of what it means to be a mathematics teacher. Provide a rationale as to why you made the selection that you did.

newscaster	orchestra conductor	physician
missionary	gardener	engineer
social worker	entertainer	coach

How does your selection and rationale compare with those of your classmates?

As the above activity suggests, there are many facets to the teaching of mathematics. Indeed, perhaps each of us can identify with some aspect of all of the possible selections.

Reasons for teaching mathematics vary from teacher to teacher. Some enjoy seeing the sparkle in students' eyes when they comprehend something they had not previously understood or the thrill of helping students master a subject that they had previously considered "unlearnable." Others like to present problems and engage themselves and their students in solving problems to which neither teacher nor student knows the answer. Still others may teach mathematics because they feel that learning mathematics teaches students to master details and to become disciplined in their approach to learning.

There are many facets to becoming an effective teacher of mathematics. The NCTM *Professional Standards for Teaching Mathematics* (1991) emphasizes the importance of posing tasks that are based on sound and significant mathematics, posing questions and tasks that elicit, engage, and challenge each student's thinking, listening to students' ideas, enabling students to investigate mathematical ideas and to validate their own mathematical reasoning. In this section we will consider these emphases as they relate to 1. the teaching of mathematics for *all* students, 2. infusing technology into classroom teaching, and 3. assessing students' understanding of mathematics.

THE NOTION OF CULTURAL DIVERSITY

The notion of cultural diversity includes issues of gender, race and ethnicity, and cultural backgrounds of students. The NCTM *Standards* emphasize that tasks and means of teaching mathematics should provide contexts in which all students are encouraged to learn. In many ways, often implicitly and unknowingly, we communicate a certain orientation toward mathematics through the use of our language and methods of teaching mathematics. Damarin (1990), for example, notes that terms such as *mastery*, mathematical *power*, *attack* problems, apply *strategies*, and *torpedo* generalizations convey a certain aggressiveness that is sometimes offensive to women. Damarin poses the following questions for our consideration as we reflect on our teaching of mathematics.

> How deeply rooted in competition is mathematics instruction?
>
> How can students be encouraged to use "sharing time" to share their own mathematical problems of the economics of allowances, the allotment of time to activities, or quantitative goal setting?
>
> What are some good problems involving quadratic equations that do not involve trajectories (which Damarin tends to associate with bullets and bombs)? (146)

Damarin's purpose is to raise our consciousness in how we talk about and teach mathematics so that we communicate that mathematics is for all students. A key point made by Damarin (1990) is that the means by which we teach mathematics may be biased in favor of students who thrive on competition and verbal learning—characteristics that may work against women and minorities.

The culture of the classroom can be an important determiner of how and whether students learn mathematics. With respect to the teaching of African Americans, Stiff (1990) writes, "The emphasis on making connections, mathematical communication, and cooperative learning, for example, should permit teachers to give a greater sense of security to all students but will make it equally important that teachers understand and value the elements of the culture that make African-Americans unique from others" (156). Urie Treisman, for example, was able to affect dramatically the performance of African-American students in their calculus course at the University of California at Berkeley by explicitly teaching them strategies of cooperation. These strategies were part of the student culture of his Asian pupils but were assumed to be a form of cheating by African Americans in the course. A key component of Treisman's success was the creation of a culture that expected success. The popular film *Stand and Deliver*, which features the teaching of Jaime Escalante, also emphasizes how the creation of a success-oriented classroom produces (Hispanic) students who make significant progress in learning mathematics.

Cuevas (1990) offers specific suggestions for teachers who are dealing with immigrant students or students whose first language is not English. Included are avoiding idioms or language that is particularly couched in the predominant language, being aware of the students' cultural backgrounds when developing mathematical ideas, and providing contexts in which students can share ideas with one another before making presentations to the entire class.

Each of these authors, in different ways, is raising the issue about the role of language in the teaching and learning of mathematics. Students whose backgrounds are not from the dominant culture will likely experience difficulties in learning mathematics if the medium by which they learn is primarily verbal based on the language of the dominant culture. While language will always be an important part of teaching mathematics, it need not be the only means by which mathematics is taught. What is sometimes missed, however, is that the medium by which mathematics is learned may have a lot to do with what and how well it gets learned. The current popularity of using cooperative learning groups stems in part from an emphasis on mathematical communication, but also reflects a desire to better accommodate the needs of diverse student populations.

Another aspect of attending to cultural diversity is the use of problems and situations that have meaning to the students. Even puzzlelike problems that are seemingly "culture free" are more likely to be of interest to students who come from backgrounds where there is a sense of gratification associated with solving puzzles. Damarin's (1990) contention that problems involving quadratics often involve ballistics highlights the fact that some mathematics problems are couched in contexts that may, at the very least, be uninteresting to students, and, at worst, be offensive to them. Given the advancement of women in athletics and in the business world, and of men in such professions as nursing, it is no longer the case that problems necessarily have to be selected to fit stereotyped roles in society. Yet, culture is important to the selection of problems. For example, students from a rural background may not be interested in problems that seemingly address issues common to urban life, and vice versa. While good textbooks often provide an array of problems from different social contexts, teachers should create and use problems that encourage the best possible performance from their students.

Wilson and Padron (1994) provide the following analysis regarding the challenges we face in addressing issues of cultural diversity.

> Schools are trying to provide mathematics for all students through essentially the same practices that have reduced the subject to preparation for the next mathematics class with little relevance to daily living. Students are still placed in tracks, textbooks have essentially the same format and content, curriculum guides are lists of mathematical topics, and teachers' lesson plans consist of exercises to be assigned and textbook pages to be completed. The problem is extensive and can be approached from several perspectives, but we would like to focus on the power of teachers and teacher education programs to make a difference. (47)

The authors show how different cultures approach the same computational problem. For example, they write that students from different countries use the division algorithm in different ways as indicated below (Wilson & Padron, 52).

Venezuela	United States

$$
\begin{array}{c|c}
540 & \\
90 & 45 \\
\hline
0 & 12
\end{array}
$$

$$
\begin{array}{r}
12 \\
45\overline{)540} \\
\underline{45} \\
90 \\
\underline{90} \\
0
\end{array}
$$

While 24 ÷ 5 yields the same numerical answer regardless of what algorithm is used, we can envision quite different and culture-dependent answers to the following question.

Create a story in which the answer to the problem 24 ÷ 5 is

1. 4
2. 5
3. 4.8
4. $4\dfrac{4}{5}$

The stories that people create will reflect their experiences—which, by definition, will be unique to that person. While we might think that 24 ÷ 5 is culture free, certainly the real-world context in which that computation has meaning is anything but culture free.

Exploration 8

Identify a partner and debate the following issue:

Mathematics is culture free. We should not be concerned about the nature of problems students solve so long as they are doing significant mathematics.

Flip a coin. If it comes up heads, you argue in support of the above position while your partner argues to the contrary. If it comes up tails, you argue to the contrary while your partner argues in support of the position.

Carry on the debate for about 10 minutes. At the end of that time, stop the debate and list the arguments made by each person. Compare your and your partner's list with those from other pairs of debaters.

In the following activity, consider the different types of problems that are often found in textbooks. The purpose of the activity is to consider the possibility that the problems students solve may carry with them certain biases in terms of students' interests. The argument can be made that students should encounter a wide range of problems to enable them to appreciate cultures that are different from their own. Would you agree or disagree with such an argument?

Exploration 9

Work in a group of four students and consider the following problems. Analyze the problems in terms of their potential interest level for students in terms of gender, socioeconomic status, and cultural background. Compare your group's analysis with critiques from other groups in the class. (You need not solve the problems.)

1. Kathy has to cut the lawn, which approximates a square 80 feet by 80 feet. She wants to determine whether she should cut the lawn back and forth in vertical strips, whether she should cut the lawn in strips parallel to the diagonal of the square, or cut it in a spiral path. Which path would you recommend to Kathy and why?

2. Andy needs to fertilize a plot of land that measures 150 feet by 200 feet. How much will it cost him if 10 pounds of fertilizer covers 1,000 square feet and each 10-pound bag costs $10?

3. A city transit system is going to increase fares 10 cents per trip. If someone makes two trips a day, how much more will it cost the person over a year if he uses the city transportation 5 times a week, 50 weeks a year?

4. Teresa's free throw shooting average is 70%. If she plays in two games over the weekend and makes 15 out of 21 free throws, has she done better or worse than her average? Justify your answer.

5. Indiana Jones is traveling down a river filled with piranhas in a Brazilian rain forest. When he is going downstream he can cover 1 mile in three minutes. When his boat goes upstream, it takes 15 minutes to cover the mile. What is the speed of the current?

6. The weight of a body is inversely proportional to the square of its distance from the center of the earth. If a man weighs 180 pounds on the earth's surface, what will he weigh 200 miles above the earth? Assume the radius of the earth is 4,000 miles.

7. If a number is increased by 4 times its reciprocal, the sum is $4\frac{1}{6}$. Find the number.

8. If there are 70 tennis players who enter a tournament and play single elimination, how many matches will be played in the tournament?

THE ROLE OF TECHNOLOGY IN TEACHING

There can be little question that technology is playing an increasingly important role in the teaching of mathematics. This raises serious questions about
what mathematics should be taught given our capacity to solve much more
computationally difficult problems. Still, it seems likely that in the foresee-
able future some skills will remain important to the learning of secondary
school mathematics. Technology can facilitate the solving of certain problems
that might be difficult to solve using standard, algebraic means. For example,
graphing calculators can enable us to solve equations that might not be solvable by means usually available to secondary students. Too, technology can
give us a different perspective on traditional topics. Consider, for example,
the solving of equations such as $x^3 - x = 20$ or $2(x - 5) = 11 - x$. The cubic
equation can be solved using graphing calculators in which two functions are
graphed ($f(x) = 20$ and $f(x) = x^3 - x$), the solution designated by their point(s)
of intersection. The linear equation can be easily solved by traditional algebraic means. But it can also be solved by considering the intersection of the
graphs of two functions, $f(x) = 2(x - 5)$ and $f(x) = 11 - x$. Such a solution process provides students with not only a geometric interpretation of solving linear equations (or equations more generally), but also a context for students to
develop a broader understanding of what it means to solve equations. Similarly, we could use spreadsheets to solve equations by generating values for
each member of the original equation. By using successive approximations,
if necessary, we can determine the values for which the expressions $2(x - 5)$
and $11 - x$ assume the same value.

Exploration 10

Solve the following equations in three ways (if possible): using standard
algebraic techniques, using a graphing calculator, and using a spreadsheet. (You may need to approximate some solutions.)

1. $-3x + 5 = 4(2 - x)$
2. $3^x = 135$
3. six $x = .5\ x$
4. $x^2 - 5 = |x|$

THE IMPORTANCE OF ASSESSMENT

The NCTM *Standards* emphasize reform not only in teaching but also in the
means by which we assess students' learning. The issue of assessment in the
reform process is of major importance in mathematics education today. The

fact that the National Council of Teachers of Mathematics developed an entire set of standards on assessment is in itself indicative of the importance being given to assessment. In some sense our instruction and what we assess is dependent on what we think mathematics is and what we consider our role as teachers of mathematics to be. If we think mathematics is essentially a matter of acquiring skills and computing, then our tests will likely engage students in doing a large number of skills or computations. On the other hand, if we think our role as teachers is to help students understand the structure of mathematics, then our tests will likely consist of problems that require students to use various forms of deductive reasoning—as, for example, when we ask students to write proofs in geometry. Still other teachers may think that their role as teachers is to help students see how mathematics is a tool for solving real-world problems. Such a view of mathematics and of the teaching of mathematics will lead to test questions couched in real-world contexts.

The evidence is mounting that our beliefs and attitudes toward mathematics influence how we teach mathematics and how we assess students' learning of mathematics. (See, for example, Thompson, 1992.) While it is unclear whether our instruction drives what we test or whether, conversely, what we test drives what we teach, in the practical world of the classroom instruction and assessment are integrally related. There is no shortage of references on assessment in mathematics education that provide suggestions on how to create interesting items for students, how to use portfolios as a means of assessing student growth, and how we can provide contexts that encourage students to demonstrate their full understanding of the mathematics in question. (See, for example, NCTM (1991b), MSEB (1993), and the 1990 and 1993 NCTM yearbooks.) These various assessment techniques are too comprehensive to address here. One issue, however, is essential to the notion of integrating content and pedagogy, namely, the use of open-ended questions.

Open-ended questions are designed to encourage students to demonstrate their reasoning processes, to give evidence of their depth of understanding of mathematics, and to provide a context for assessing their ability to communicate mathematically. We should be clear that having a depth of understanding is quite a different matter from doing a difficult problem. For example, multiplying a 9-digit number by a 9-digit number is difficult in the sense that rarely would a person get the correct answer given the number of possible computational errors involved. Yet few would maintain that such an item assesses a deep and thorough understanding of multiplication. Assessing a "deep understanding" of mathematics entails the use of questions that reveal how students see mathematics as a connected whole and not as isolated bits of information. Further, it requires a demonstration of reasoning and the ability to communicate one's thinking. For example, we can ask students, "Three fifths of what number is 15?" but we can't be sure how connected their knowledge is to the more general topic of equivalent fractions. The simplest way to gain this information is to require students to "explain your reasoning." Other techniques that teachers find useful is to consider general questions such as the following.

What's wrong with this?
One person says this and another person says that (a contradiction). Who is correct and why?

The following questions illustrate these two types of general questions.

1. Without referring to a textbook or another person, how could you convince someone that the following statement is false?
   The general solution to $ax^2 + bx + c = 0$, $a \neq 0$ is

$$x = \frac{b \pm \sqrt{b^2 - 4ac}}{2a}$$

2. Fred maintains that as the perimeters of rectangles increase, their areas also increase. Alisha claims Fred is wrong. Who is correct and why?

Assessment should provide a wide range of contexts for students to demonstrate their mathematical understanding. Problems that have only single number answers are not likely, by themselves, to provide that range.

Some teachers find the incorporation of open-ended questions or items into their teaching a real challenge. A reasonable first step toward using such items is to engage students in a kind of "Jeopardy" game show. That is, instead of asking for an answer, have students imagine what a possible question might be if they are given a particular answer. Another is to make use of real or imagined disagreements that might occur naturally in class discussions. Below are two efforts in that direction by a teacher who originally had difficulty incorporating open-ended items into her assessment of students' understanding.

"Old" Item	*"New" Item*
Round each of the following to the nearest tenth:	Create a number that would round to be each of the following:
a. 48.128	a. 54.32
b. 1399.92435	b. 853.8
c. 4.2378	c. 91.998
Categorize each of the following numbers as prime or composite: 81, 2, 53, and 111.	Buddy thinks that 91 and 93 are prime because they end in an odd digit. Pete says that Buddy is wrong. Who is correct and why?

The teacher was impressed with the information she gained from her students. From her perspective the more open-ended items gave her an entrée into her students' thinking that had not previously been revealed when using the more traditional items.

An important part of the assessment process is to decide how to score students' responses. Developing a scoring "rubric" is an important part of the assessment process. If students' responses tend to be scored as either "right" or "wrong" then the item is unlikely to assess students' understanding in a deeper or more connected way. Consider the following item given by a secondary teacher and the scoring system he used.

Item: Is it possible for an equilateral triangle to have a right angle? If so, give an example. If not, why not?

Level One: Yes. Sides are straight at a right angle.

Level Two: Yes, as long as all of the sides are the same length.

Level Three: No, because all sides must be equal.

Level Four: a. No, because there must be one side of the triangle (hypotenuse) that is longer in a right triangle and an equilateral has all sides the same.

b. No, all the angles have to be the same and all three have to equal 180 degrees.

Level Five: a. No, you can't have 3 right angles because the sum of the angles would be 270 degrees and it must equal 180. The angle measures are all the same in an equilateral triangle.

b. No, because an equilateral triangle has all the same angles. If you had a triangle with 3 right angles, you would have 3/4 of a square but the sides would not connect.

His five-point scale was based on his analysis of what constituted different levels of understanding and on actual students' responses. It is interesting to note that the response classified as Level 4a is based on side length whereas other responses are based on angle measure. How would you respond to this student? How would you have scored the different responses?

It is important to remember that what we assess communicates to students what we value and, in all likelihood, what they will learn. Our tests, quizzes, examinations, and other means of grading students communicate to them what we believe mathematics to be. In a real sense, it defines what they ought to be doing mathematically.

. . . .

Exploration 11

Analyze the following problems in terms of the extent to which you think they give students an opportunity to communicate a deeper understanding of mathematics.

Ms. Barker's Item:

Ellen says that it is impossible for the composition of two reflections not to be a translation. Mike says that she is wrong. Who is right and why?

Mr. Walker's Item:

Find the length of the longest umbrella that can fit inside of a suitcase whose interior dimensions are 6" by 24" by 30".

Ms. Burn's Item:

For what value(s) of b will the graph of $f(x) = x^2 + bx - 12$ be tangent to the x-axis?

Mr. Klein's Item:

Ms. Jackson is having a concrete driveway put into her new home. The original plan calls for the driveway to be 8 feet wide and 50 feet long with a depth of 3 inches. If she changes the dimensions to 10 feet wide and 60 feet long (same depth), how much more should the bigger driveway cost compared to the original estimate?

Mr. Murphy's Item:

Mr. Allen is going to invest $1,000 in either stocks or a certificate of deposit. What questions and what information should Mr. Allen obtain in order to make an informed decision?

As you read other portions of *Mathematics, Pedagogy, and Secondary Teacher Education*, notice that the authors make use of assessment in many nontraditional ways. It is rare that you will be asked to engage in an activity with a right or wrong answer. Frequently, the authors suggest ways of reexamining and consolidating what you have learned via strategies other than those associated with paper and pencil tests. For example, you will find activities involving group work, interviews with your classmates, essay writing, problems, and reflective situations—all of which contain important elements of assessment built in.

WHAT DOES IT MEAN TO BE A "PROFESSIONAL TEACHER OF MATHEMATICS"?

As either a preservice teacher or an experienced teacher, you are at a particular stage of development in your professional career. You might wonder what it means for you to be a professional in the first place. After all, we don't refer to everyone as a professional. While many definitions exist, we generally think of professional teachers as those who have a certain knowledge base about teaching and learning that sets them apart from those engaged in other aspects of education. We think it is important for teachers to develop a knowledge base that makes them the experts in revising and shaping curricula for their students. Some call this *empowerment* in that teachers have the ability and the responsibility to create learning environments that encourage students to see connections within mathematics and between mathematics and the real world. This ability has to do with seeing the connectedness and the structure of mathematics and how that structure can be related to activities for students. It has to do with the means by which we engage students in the act of reflecting on their own learning and how they can develop self-generative activities so that they can explore mathematical ideas on their own. It has to do with understanding psychological principles that underlie the teaching and learning of mathematics. Foremost, we believe that it has to do with the notion of integrating content and pedagogy so that students learn mathematics in a way that is consistent with the processes of reasoning, communication, and problem solving.

More than fifteen years ago Fletcher (1979) raised the question, "Is the teacher of mathematics a mathematician or not?" His response was affirmative, using the following reasoning process. Mathematicians have a generalized knowledge of mathematics and a specialized knowledge in a particular area of mathematics. Similarly, Fletcher argues, teachers of mathematics should have a generalized knowledge of mathematics and a specialized knowledge that allows them to adapt and modify existing curricula to better accommodate their students' learning of mathematics. The very purpose of *Mathematics, Pedagogy, and Secondary Teacher Education,* is to help teachers develop this kind of knowledge so that they can become flexible and adaptive teachers in their classrooms.

As you read through these pieces, see if you can identify qualities that you associate with being a professional mathematics teacher. In "Developing a Topic Across the Curriculum," you will encounter Ms. Lopez. Not only does she provide a context for students to see mathematical functions as a vehicle for modeling real-world phenomena, but she has also acquired ways of listening to students and of encouraging them to learn from each other. Her colleague, Mr. Washington, maintains that the primary purpose of teaching mathematics is to enable students to see the logical structure of mathematics. In what ways is his professional orientation different from Ms. Lopez's? Other teachers you will meet include Mr. Kubiack, who teaches his students explicit techniques for using functions to model real-world phenomena, and Mr. Black and Ms. Waters, who not only share a common vision of teaching mathematics but also work together in a variety of contexts, including the development of a proposal to the National Science Foundation. Consider how these teachers might have responded to the questions posed in the sections above and how their responses might be similar to or different from yours. You will be introduced to students such as Dirk and Stefan, who are interviewed about their understanding of the Pythagorean theorem, and Carola and Andrea, who are engaged in the process of solving intriguing counting problems. If these students were in your classes, how would you assess their understanding of mathematics? Stories and anecdotes about these teachers and students are offered to invite you to define what mathematics means to you and how you can use your knowledge about mathematics and pedagogy in an integrated way. We offer them to assist you in your professional development.

Return now to Reflective Problem 3. Consider your responses and complete the following activity.

Reflective Problem 5

Revisit your response for Reflective Problem 3. Do you think your earlier response still captures your view of mathematics? Why or why not?

We conclude with the following reflective problem.

Reflective Problem 6

Thumb back through the chapter and identify those ideas that you think represent the biggest challenge you will face in the teaching of mathematics.

Write a two- to three-page paper on why you see these ideas as challenging as you think about your role as a teacher of mathematics.

You may want to save the paper and revisit it at a later time in your teaching career.

REFERENCES

Cuevas, G. (1990). Increasing the achievement and participation of language minority students in mathematics education. In T. J. Cooney (ed.), *Teaching and learning mathematics in the 1990s*. (pp. 135–143) Reston, VA: National Council of Teachers of Mathematics.

Damarin, S. (1990). Teaching mathematics: A feminist perspective. In T. J. Cooney (ed.), *Teaching and learning mathematics in the 1990s*. (pp. 144–151) Reston, VA: National Council of Teachers of Mathematics.

Fletcher, T. (1979). Is the teacher of mathematics a mathematician or not? In H. Steiner (ed.), *The education of mathematics teachers*. (pp. 185–199) Bielefeld: Institut fur Didaktik der Mathematik der Universität Bielefeld.

Furinghetti, F. (1993). Images of mathematics outside the community of mathematicians: evidence and explanations. *For the Learning of Mathematics* v. 13, n. 2, pp. 33–39.

Mathematical Sciences Education Board. (1993). *Measuring what counts.* Washington, D.C.: Author.

National Council of Teachers of Mathematics. (1989). *Curriculum and evaluation standards for school mathematics.* Reston, VA: Author.

————. (1990). *Teaching and learning mathematics in the 1990s.* T. J. Cooney, Editor. Reston, VA: Author.

————. (1991a). *Professional standards for teaching mathematics.* Reston, VA: Author.

————. (1991b). *Mathematics assessment: Myths, models, good questions, and practical suggestions.* Jean Kerr Stenmark, Editor. Reston, VA: Author.

————. (1993). *Assessment in the mathematics classroom.* N. Webb, Editor. Reston, VA: Author.

Stiff, L. (1990). African-American students and the promise of the *Curriculum and evaluation standards.* In T. J. Cooney (ed.), *Teaching and learning mathematics in the 1990s.* (pp. 152–158) Reston, VA: National Council of Teachers of Mathematics.

Thompson, A. G. (1992). Teachers' beliefs and conceptions: a synthesis of the research. In D. A. Grouws (ed.), *Handbook of research on mathematics teaching and learning.* New York: Macmillan.

Wilson, P. & Padron, J. M. (1994). Moving towards culture-inclusive mathematics education. In M. Atwater, K. R. Adzik-Marsh, & M. Strutchens, *Multicultural education: Inclusion of all.* (pp. 39–63) Athens: GA. The University of Georgia Press.

Developing a Topic Across the Curriculum: Functions

Introduction

Mathematical functions has long been a topic of both interest and controversy in school mathematics. Long ago, Breslich (1928) expressed the view that many teachers were reluctant to teach functions except to the more advanced students. Wells and Hart (1929) introduced what they called "functional relationships" into school mathematics. Betz (1931) emphasized the importance of recognizing functional relationships wherever they existed. Yet other authors failed to emphasize functions in any significant way as they emphasized the more symbolic nature of mathematics. May and Van Engen (1959) emphasized that the concept of function is one of the most important concepts in mathematics—perhaps as important as number itself. Textbooks in the 1960s and 1970s (and some into the 1980s) emphasized functions as sets of ordered pairs, basing such an approach on the structure and rigor of mathematics. Some authors took issue with this approach, claiming that such an orientation gave students a "static" view of functions rather than the richness of functional relationships that they considered more important. Today we have the advantage of technology and the many ways we can explore the behavior of functions using graphing calculators and various types of computer software. If not today, then very shortly, the teaching of functions will involve extensive use of various types of technologies. Our focus here is not the historical precepts of teaching functions per se but rather various pedagogical issues in the context of studying functions. We strive here to integrate content and pedagogy by examining the ways in which mathematics and pedagogy are intertwined and inseparable when one begins to teach functions.

We begin by asking you to examine why it is that we should teach functions in the first place. We will then visit Ms. Lopez's class as she teaches a lesson involving functions but encounters a number of difficulties as the lesson unfolds. We then examine the way that functions are, perhaps implicitly, involved in communication in our everyday conversations as well as in the media. Subsequently we engage the reader in card sort activities that classify functions based on their characteristics, consider various activities that can promote students' learning of functions, and consider the potential advantages of using these activities, along with the historical development of the function concept.

We then revisit the world of Ms. Lopez and one of her fellow teachers, Mr. Washington, as they engage in a debate about the value and expectations of teaching functions. Readers are invited to position themselves in this debate to reexamine, again, their reasons for teaching functions. The following section encourages us to consider the relationship between the mathematical behaviors of functions and their graphical representations. Finally, a context is provided in which readers can take their enhanced view of functions and use that knowledge to conduct interviews with students to see what meanings and interpretations secondary or middle school students hold about functions. In some sense, this is the most important section in that it addresses the issue of how students think about functions, consequently raising the issue of how, then, we should teach functions.

This piece as a whole is intended to broaden our perspective about mathematical functions and to reveal issues related to the teaching of functions that might otherwise be concealed in the presentations of functions in textbooks. The hope is that we will think more deeply about issues of teaching and mathematics that are sometimes left isolated in our rush to engage students in the doing of mathematics. We are asked to look "inside" our own heads and consider what we know and believe about functions and how to teach them. The various sorts of reflective situations that are presented provide numerous contexts for us to consider what we know and believe as a precursor to understanding how others come to know functions. We encourage readers to consider the possible symmetry between their own thinking about functions and that of their students who are learning about mathematical functions. It is our intent that the accumulation of reflective situations, activities, and problems posed here will enable the teacher, beginning or experienced, to envision functions and their teaching in a way that is consistent with the NCTM *Standards* and with other reform-minded documents as well. Let us begin by considering the various rationales teachers use for their teaching of mathematical functions.

EXAMINING OUR REASONS
FOR TEACHING FUNCTIONS

Before we begin our venture into the world of the teaching and learning of functions, stop and ask yourself, "Why should we teach functions as a topic in school mathematics?" The question may seem strange given that every secondary school textbook and most middle school textbooks treat functions in some way and that almost every teacher of mathematics teaches some topic having to do with functions. In what sense, then, does it make sense to ask the question, "*Why* should functions be taught?" What is it that is important about the teaching and learning of functions? How can we justify spending a considerable amount of the school year on this topic? What is it that we want to accomplish with our students? We could say to the first question, "Because it's there." But such a simplistic answer masks the richness of issues that present themselves when we study and teach functions.

There are many answers to the question about why functions should be taught. While there is no single right answer, we want you to consider various reasons teachers give as the most important ones for teaching functions and to consider which reasons make the most sense to you. In some sense we are asking you to begin developing a philosophy on why you should teach this critically important topic. As a means of addressing what you think is important, consider the following positions raised by five different teachers. As you consider the various positions keep in mind that there is no single right answer. Your response should reflect what you consider to be important. We will revisit this exercise later.

Reflective Problem 1

Each of the following teachers have a different perspective on what they considered important about the teaching of functions. Allocate a total of 100 points to the various teachers' positions according to the extent to which you agree with each position. You may distribute the points in any size increments. For example, you may assign all 100 points to a single position and 0 to the remaining positions or you may assign any number of points between 0 and 100 to a position. The sum total of the points must be 100 points, however.

We encourage you to share your "scores" with those of other students in the class. With respect to which positions did you tend to agree? Disagree? What reasons did others give for their distribution of points? How did these reasons compare to your reasons?

MARK: I think functions are important because they provide a context for developing basic skills such as solving equations and graphing. Let's face it, if students aren't proficient in these basics, they just aren't going to go very far in mathematics. Functions provide an ideal context for developing these skills.

DANA: I think functions are important because they give students an opportunity to deal with mathematical language and representations including the symbolism of mathematics. It is important for students to realize that functions can be represented in various ways, including formulas, sets, mappings, and graphs. They should have experience translating among these different representations.

JIM: I think functions are important because they give students an opportunity to see how mathematics can describe real-world phenomena. My students study functions such as the relationship between Fahrenheit and Celsius temperature scales and other functions that represent real-world phenomena.

GWEN: I think functions are important because they are so basic to the rest of the topics in secondary school mathematics. If students understand what a function is in general, then they can better appreciate specific functions such as linear, quadratic, exponential, logarithmic, or trigonometric functions.

JUANITA: I think functions are important because they give students an opportunity to study functional relationships, that is, to see how one variable changes when another variable changes. The study of relationships is central to the study of mathematics. Functions provide an excellent opportunity for students to study various relationships.

Assign points for each of the teachers. Write a brief explanation on why you assigned the points as you did for the teachers above. File your response for reference later.

_____ points MARK

_____ points DANA

_____ points JIM

_____ points GWEN

_____ points JUANITA

VISITING MS. LOPEZ'S CLASS

Let us now visit Maria Lopez's classroom to further explore various issues related to the teaching of functions. Ms. Lopez is in her second year of teaching secondary school mathematics. On the day we visit Ms. Lopez, she is presenting the "biggest box" problem in order to show students how technology can be used to solve problems. She realizes how much progress she has made professionally from her first year of teaching, which was frustrating for her and the students. She had struggled with the advanced algebra content, not to mention how to teach it. She had made the usual "rookie" mistakes of trying to cover too much material with her students. Now she understands what is meant by the phrase "Less is more." This, her second year of teaching, has gone much better. She feels more comfortable having the students work in cooperative learning groups and using problem solving and discovery lessons in her teaching. Most important, she finds herself more willing to listen to what the students are saying rather than just rehearsing what she is going to say next as students engage in classroom discussions. Too, the students have gotten to know her better; some of the students in her present class were in her geometry class the previous year.

The following lesson, which emphasizes exploration, illustrates the insights Ms. Lopez has developed from her teaching experience. In this lesson, she uses the "biggest box" problem to demonstrate the role technology can play in solving problems and to motivate students. Her grand ambition is to create a "mathematical community" in her classroom—an idea she gained from the NCTM *Standards*. As you study the lesson, consider the following questions.

1. How effective do you think the "biggest box" problem would have been in motivating you when you studied secondary school mathematics?

2. How effective do you think the problem will be in motivating the students you will be teaching?

3. How effective would the problem have been in encouraging you to consider different ways of solving problems?

4. How would you describe Ms. Lopez's overall teaching style? Do you think it was effective?

5. As you read about Ms. Lopez's lesson, note how many methods for solving the "biggest box" problem are given, particularly those involving technology.

6. How comfortable would you be in teaching the class as Ms. Lopez taught the class?

These questions will be revisited at the end of the story as a variety of issues about mathematics and teaching are considered.

The "Biggest Box" Problem

As the lesson unfolds Ms. Lopez has organized the class into groups of four students to consider the problem of how the "biggest box" can be made by cutting squares out of the corners of a 20 cm by 20 cm sheet of cardstock and then folding the resulting piece into a box without a top. Ms. Lopez has asked the students to cut out several different-sized squares in order to help the students develop an intuitive notion about the relationship between the cut-out squares and the volume of the box.

As we begin the story, Ms. Lopez is asking the students to describe the effect on the volume of the boxes as they cut out the squares (see Figure 1).

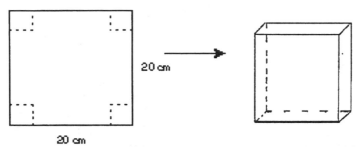

Figure 1

Ms. Lopez: Okay. Does each group now have several different boxes formed? Hold them up for everyone to see. Which boxes do you think would hold the most water if we could fill the box with water? Francis?

Francis: I'm not sure. It doesn't look like it's mine. The square I cut out was kind of small. I don't think my box would hold very much water.

Juanita: I don't think it's mine either. Look. My squares are kind of big. I didn't have much stuff left. I don't think my box would hold much water, either. It's kind of funny-looking.

Ms. Lopez: Do you think the volume of the box will keep getting bigger when the cut-out square gets bigger and bigger?

Holly: I don't think so. Look at the box we made. The square that we cut out is big—7 cm on a side—but it is kind of tall and skinny.

Ms. Lopez: How could we find out what the connection is between the size of the square and the volume of the box? [*Silence*] Could we make a table of values?

Hector: Yeah. We could measure the size of the cut-out squares. But how do we figure out the volume? We can't really put water in these things.

Monica: Can't we just figure out the dimensions of the box and then multiply the numbers together to get the volume? That seems like the simplest way. So if we cut out a 3 cm square the dimensions will be 3 by 14 by 14.

Jeff: How did you get the 14?

Monica: We cut out two 3 cm from each side. So 20 minus 3 minus 3 is 14.

[*Class agrees this method will work.*]

Ms. Lopez: These are good suggestions. Let's make up a chart that gives us the size of the square and the volume.

Hector: Well, my idea is that you don't need the whole square. You just need the length of the cutout.

Ms. Lopez: Good idea. Let's make our table for values of 1 cm, 2 cm, 3 cm, and so on. What is the largest cutout we could have?

Henry: As large as we want. Oh, wait a minute. This sheet is only 20 cm wide. So I guess 20 cm.

Ms. Lopez: Okay. So should we make our table from 1 to 20?

Ronnie: It can't be 20 because we have to cut out two of them on a side. So the largest is 10 cm but that really doesn't make sense, because nothing would be left.

Ms. Lopez: So what is the largest whole number we could use?

Lynn. Nine. So should we make our table for values of 1 through 9?

Ms. Lopez: That sounds good. Let's get started.

After some false starts the students finally come up with the following table.

Side length of cut-out square (cm)	*Volume of box (cm³)*
1	1 × 18 × 18 = 324
2	2 × 16 × 16 = 512
3	3 × 14 × 14 = 588
4	4 × 12 × 12 = 576
5	5 × 10 × 10 = 500
6	6 × 8 × 8 = 384
7	7 × 6 × 6 = 252
8	8 × 4 × 4 = 128
9	9 × 2 × 2 = 36

The students note that the maximum volume occurs when the cut-out square measures something around 3 cm on a side. The class discussion continues.

Ms. Lopez: How could we determine more precisely what the maximum volume is?

Denise: I don't think it's a good idea to cut out more squares. That takes too long. Besides the answer probably isn't a whole number.

Jim: Why can't we figure out the exact formula? That's not so hard. The dimensions are just like we did before only we use x instead of an actual number. So the dimensions are x, 20 minus x, and 20 minus x.

Ms. Lopez: Is everybody sure this is correct? Or do we see a problem with it?

Francis: I don't get it. I don't know what we're doing.

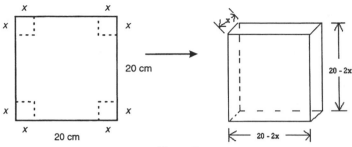

Figure 2

Samantha: Well, I think Jim is wrong. He forgot to subtract out two of the squares.

Jim: Explain what you mean, Samantha.

Samantha: Let me draw a picture and then you'll see (Figure 2).

Corey: So then the volume will be x times $20 - 2x$ times $20 - 2x$.

Ms. Lopez: Jim, what do you think? Is Corey correct?

Jim: Yeah. I just messed up. I forgot there were two squares.

Ms. Lopez: Okay, good. I'm glad we got that straightened out. Let's write down what Corey said. We'll let V be the volume and x be the side of the square that is cut out. Then, as Corey said, we have,

$$f(x) = x\,(20 - 2x)(20 - 2x) = 4x^3 - 80x^2 + 400x$$

Now I would like you to use your graphing calculators to graph the function. Let's use a domain of 1 to 9 and a range of 0 to 600.

Marianna: What increments should we use?

Ms. Lopez: What would you suggest?

Marianna: Well 1 for the domain and, well, [*pause*] maybe 50 for the range.

Ms. Lopez: Sounds good. Let's do it.

At this point in the lesson the students use their graphing calculators to graph the function and use the tracing function to determine that the maximum value of the function is a little more than 592 when the x value is about 3.33. Some of the students use the zoom-in function and determine that the value approximating the maximum value seems to get closer and closer to 3.3333—. They ponder whether the maximum occurs when the x value is actually 3⅓. Ms. Lopez poses a few questions for the students to consider in trying to determine the exact value of x that produces the maximum value.

Ms. Lopez: Let's consider a simpler problem. Suppose we had two numbers x and y whose sum is 12. What values of x and y gives us the maximum product?

Elizabeth: That's easy. It's 6 and 6. We did that last month.

Ms. Lopez: Good. Now suppose we had three numbers x, y, and z whose sum is 12. What values would give us the maximum product in this case?

Elizabeth: Well, it would be 6, 3, and 3. You would just split the one 6 into two equal parts.

Hector: I don't think so. Because that gives us 54. But if I take 5 times 3 times 4, I get 60, which is bigger.

Beverly: Yeah but 4 times 4 times 4 is even better.

Ms. Lopez: That is very interesting. Can anyone conjecture what has to happen to make the product of the three numbers be a maximum?

Juanita: They all have to be equal?

Ms. Lopez: Let's try some other numbers. Try 18. (After a few examples the students conclude that the maximum product occurs when the three numbers are equal.)

Francis: What has this got to do with anything? Why are we messing around with this stuff? I thought we were trying to find the maximum size of the box?

Ms. Lopez: [*Ms. Lopez realizes now that Francis and several other students are confused. She wants to get closure on the discussion but there is only a few minutes left in the period.*] Exactly. [*Speaking hurriedly*] Okay, I think what we need to do, let's see if I can remember this now [*pauses*]. Okay, we have three factors x, $20 - 2x$, and $20 - 2x$. Is there some way we can get the sum of these three expressions to be a constant? If so, then we could get them to be in equal parts and we could solve the problem. Let's see, if we add the three numbers we get $40 - 3x$, which is not a constant. [*Francis and other students pack up their books and other materials. They cease to pay attention.*] How could we change the numbers so that the sum would be a constant—then we could divide each number by three. [*The bell rings, ending the class period.*] Okay. I gave you the homework assignment earlier in the period. Let's think about this extra problem. I know it is difficult but we can figure it out. See you tomorrow. [*Students are leaving the class.*]

Francis: Boy did she go off the deep end or what!

Juanita: Like all I have to do tonight is extra problems. If she doesn't know it, what hope do we have of figuring it out! Unreal! Hey Jim. Did you hear what happened to William in his history class?

Elizabeth: I think it's kind of neat. I wonder how we can rewrite the expressions so that they sum to a specific number. Right now the sum is $40 - 3x$. If we could get rid of the x, we could do it.

Hector: Yeah, but what has that got to do with finding the maximum? If you get something worked out give me a call tonight and I'll do the same. The homework looks pretty easy so I'll probably work on it a little bit.

Denise: I get out of basketball practice about six o'clock. I'll ask Louise if she can help. She is really good at math.

That evening Ms. Lopez worked on the problem that was discussed at the end of the period in her Algebra II class. She regretted that the lesson had gone awry at the end when the rest of the lesson had seemed to go so well. She knew some of the students got lost but wasn't sure how she should have handled the situation. Frankly, she admitted to herself, she had forgotten how to solve the problem. It was more complicated than she had originally thought when the problem was raised in class. She remembered that if three numbers sum to a constant, then the maximum product of the three numbers occurs when the three numbers are equal, that is, each is one third of the sum. She also realized that the three expressions x, $20 - 2x$, $20 - 2x$ should sum to a constant. She reasoned that if the x were actually $4x$ then she would have $4x + (20 - 2x) + (20 - 2x) = 40$. Ms. Lopez figured out that she could get $4x$ in the following way.

$$\text{Since } V = x\,(\,20 - 2x\,)\,(20 - 2x),$$
$$\text{then } V = \frac{1}{4}\,[4x\,(20\text{-}2x)\,(20 - 2x)]$$

Hence, the maximum value occurs when $4x = \dfrac{40}{3}$ or when $x = 3\dfrac{1}{3}$. It was an interesting problem to work out. She enjoyed the challenge of solving it. Now she was faced with the problem of how to engage her students in solving the problem tomorrow in class. How was she going to get Francis and the other students interested? She began to think about this problem as well.

Reflecting on the Lesson

Consider the following questions. Discuss your responses with your classmates.

1. Revisit the questions posed at the beginning of the story.

2. How would you describe the students' role during the lesson?

3. In what way did the end of the lesson seem to vary from the rest of the lesson? What factors probably contributed to this difference?

4. Identify two instances in which the teacher apparently failed to respond to students who were experiencing difficulty. Discuss how the teacher might have handled the situations differently.

5. What do you think the students likely learned about functions as a result of the lesson?

6. How could the teacher have used spreadsheets effectively to determine a more precise x value that maximized the volume?

7. Do you think Ms. Lopez should not have started to solve the problem of finding the maximum value of the function until she was sure how to solve it herself? What advice would you have offered Ms. Lopez?

8. React to Juanita's comment that if the teacher "doesn't know it, what hope do we have of figuring it out!"

9. Why does the method Ms. Lopez worked out in the evening for maximizing the function work?

10. Suppose a student solves the box problem in the following way.

$$V = x\,(20 - 2x)\,(20 - 2x)$$

$$V = 16x \left(\frac{20 - 2x}{4} \right)\left(\frac{20 - 2x}{4} \right)$$

Since $x + (5 - \frac{x}{2}) + (5 - \frac{x}{2}) = 10$, the maximum volume will occur when $x = 5 - \frac{x}{2}$ or $\frac{3x}{2} = 5$ or $x = 3\frac{1}{3}$. Was the student's approach correct or was it a "lucky" approach? Explain your reasoning.

11. Ms. Lopez seems to be using the following logic.

    If each of the three terms is equal in value and if the sum is a constant, then the volume is maximized.

    Is there anything wrong with Ms. Lopez's logic? Explain.

12. What advice would you give Ms. Lopez as she plans to revisit the problem the next day?

13. Suppose Ms. Lopez decides to have the students work in groups the next day. What kind of preparation is needed to help ensure that the experience will be worthwhile for the students? What kinds of organizational problems do you think she would be wise to anticipate?

THINKING AND COMMUNICATING ABOUT FUNCTIONS

In the previous section we encountered Ms. Lopez and her teaching of the biggest box problem. Some students, for example, Samantha, seemed facile with the idea of representing the volume of the box as a function. Others, such as Francis, seemed confused about creating a general formula to represent the volume. That is, Samantha seemed able to think conceptually about making a functional representation of the problem whereas Francis did not. An important aspect of teaching is to create activities that build on what students know. This requires that we, as teachers, understand *what* they are thinking and *how* they are thinking about the mathematics being studied. In some sense, this requires us to "get inside the head" of the students to comprehend their understanding. An interview with Samantha and Francis would likely indicate that they hold quite different conceptions of function. Our task here is to get "inside our own heads" in an effort to reflect on our understanding of functions and to consider the implications of that reflection for teaching others. In a later section, we will consider getting "inside the heads of students."

Reflective Problem 2

1. Complete the following statement: A function is

   _____ .

2. Describe an incident that stands out in your mind when you were studying some aspect of mathematical functions. Why does it stand out in your mind?

3. Suppose someone asked you if there was any connection between mathematics and the real world. How would you respond to them *with respect to the topic of functions* ?

Share your responses in Reflective Problem 2 with your classmates. In what way are their responses similar to or different from yours?

As teachers of mathematics we should realize how mathematics affects our thinking and the language we use. Many people see mathematics as a subject separated from their daily lives, that the only real utility of mathematics is computational in nature, for example, when they balance their checkbook. But mathematics is much more than that. Many of the decisions we make require quantitative, logical, or spatial reasoning, which is basically mathematical in nature. Consider, for example, the problems of deciding how we want to invest our money given rates of interest and anticipated rates of inflation or how furniture in a room can be arranged for efficiency and esthetic value. Indeed, mathematicians and computer scientists develop mathematical models that shape decisions relative to ensuring quality control of various products, to marketing products, or to determining the effectiveness of certain drugs in combating disease.

Mathematics also influences our daily language, some in precise ways, some in metaphorical ways. The following statements illustrate some of the ways mathematical ideas creep into our language.

I like that wallpaper. It has a certain symmetry to it.
Does White Street run parallel or perpendicular to Hull Street?
He has a multidimensional personality.
Her salary is proportional to the amount of merchandise she sells.
The equation of human values makes the conflict difficult to resolve.
The circular arrangement of flowers is very beautiful.

We can see that some uses of mathematical terms are relatively precise as, for example, when we talk about streets being parallel or perpendicular. In other contexts we may be using a mathematical term from a more metaphorical perspective, as in talking about the "equation of human values."

Consider the following two vignettes and how the discussion involves the concept of function even though the term is not used.

Vignette 1

Mr. Simpson had an appointment with his physician for his annual checkup. He was particularly interested in having his cholesterol count checked because of the recent emphasis on reducing one's cholesterol. When he discussed its importance with Dr. Jackson, his physician, the following exchange took place.

Mr. Simpson: I have read so much about cholesterol count. The last time I had it checked it was about 250 and the chart said that 250 was high. To what extent is cholesterol count related to heart disease?

Dr. Jackson: Well, generally speaking, the lower the cholesterol count the better. If we could get your count below 200 I would feel better about it.

Mr. Simpson: Is a count of 250 something I should worry about?

Dr. Jackson: Our best evidence is that the probability of having a heart attack is related to the cholesterol count, although there are other factors to be considered as well. There is no "safe" number. But for the population in general, the higher the number, the greater the risk of having a heart attack. So, yes, I think your cholesterol count is something to be concerned about.

Vignette 2

In an economics class, the students are discussing the effect of advertising on sales.

Jim: It's clear to me that the more you spend on advertising, the more you sell.

Gwen: Well, that can only be true to a point. If a company spends every dollar they had, that wouldn't mean that their sales would keep increasing. There must be some point at which the amount of money you spend doesn't affect sales. There must be some kind of ceiling effect.

Maurice: I don't think there is a ceiling effect. I think the sales will always increase but at a slower rate as the amount of money for advertising increases. There is a sort of diminishing return effect.

Harriet: I don't think there is any connection. You have to spend a little to make the public aware of the product but beyond that it's whether people like or need the product. If they really like it, spending more money on advertising won't make any difference. If they don't like it, then it doesn't make any difference how much money they spend on advertising.

Teacher: Could each of you please draw a graph to illustrate what you think the relationship will be?

Exploration 1

Consider Vignettes 1 and 2 and answer the following questions.

1. Identify the quantities being related and indicate which one is the independent variable and which one is the dependent variable.

2. Write a sentence and use the word *function* to describe the relationship between the quantities being discussed.

3. Draw a graph to indicate what the relationship might look like; label the axes to indicate the two quantities that vary. Let the horizontal axis represent the independent variable and the vertical axis the dependent variable.

Another way that functions are used, either explicitly or implicitly, to communicate is in the media. For example, in a recent newspaper article, a corporation involving public utilities reported that their first-quarter earnings were down 5 percent from last year. The decline was attributed in part to rate reductions ordered by state and federal regulators. In another newspaper article, the columnist argued that the earlier one starts looking for a summer job the better the chance one has of getting a summer job. In both of these articles there is an implicit notion of function being used, that is, decreased earnings as a function of rate reductions and the probability of getting a job as a function of the time-line for beginning the search. In yet another example, National Public Radio recently reported that the Federal Reserve Board had lowered the discount lending rate. Commentary that followed suggested that other lending rates would decrease, borrowing would increase, spending would increase, and the unemployment rate would go down. That is, these outcomes were, in part, a function of the lowering of the discount lending rate. In each case, the independent-dependent relationship is at least implied between two factors.

> ## Exploration 2
>
> Find an item from either the printed or electronic media that reflects a functional relationship between two factors. Write a two- or three-page essay describing the situation and how the situation represents a functional relationship. Pay particular attention to the idea of dependent and independent variables and the effect one variable has on the other.

CLASSIFYING FUNCTIONS AND THEIR REPRESENTATIONS

Thus far we have talked about functions as a single entity as we have emphasized the concept of function. But we should also realize that there are many different types of functions and several ways of representing them. In this section we will use a card sort activity to explore various types of functions and their representations. This activity can be adapted for any level of mathematics student and for many mathematics topics.

Before we introduce the activity, a comment about the role of classification in mathematics is appropriate. One of the important characteristics of mathematics is the way its structure permits various mathematical entities to be categorized. Entities such as number, sets, geometric shapes, axioms, theorems, and definitions are categories of objects that make up the content of mathematics. We can categorize numbers as complex or real, rational or irrational, positive or negative. Two-dimensional polygons can be classified as convex or concave; triangles can be categorized by the length of their sides or by the measure of their angles; quadrilaterals can be categorized according to the characteristics of their sides, angles, or lines of symmetry; fractions can be classified as common, mixed, improper, or decimal. Indeed, textbooks organize various topics by categorizing mathematical concepts and procedures as indicated by chapter titles, for example, sequences and series, similarity, or solving linear equations. Thus the very notion of categorization is an exceedingly important idea in mathematics in general and secondary school mathematics in particular.

The notion of categorization applies to mathematical functions as well. As you reflect on your experiences in learning functions, you no doubt remember studying different types of functions. You may also recall that functions can be represented in different ways including tables, graphs, formulas, and verbal descriptions. In this section, examples of twenty-eight different functions will be presented representing seven different categories of functions and four different representations for each category. The following tasks are designed to focus your attention on different ways of categorizing functions and their representations. Each function has a number associated with it as indicated on the

following pages where the functions are displayed. You will be asked to determine different ways of sorting the functions. What is important to consider is
the criteria you used for the sorting task. Consider the following examples.

Example 1. Sort cards 17, 22, and 27 into two piles based on the type
of representation used.

Solution. Since cards 17 and 22 are graphical representations and
card 27 is a verbal representation, cards 17 and 22 should be classified
together.

Example 2. Sort cards 1, 6, and 7 into two piles based on the type of
functions involved.

Solution. Since cards 6 and 7 represent quadratic equations and card
1 represents an exponential function, cards 6 and 7 should be classified
together.

Exploration 3

Before you begin this activity you may want to copy the 28 cards in figures 3 and 4 (pages 18–19), cut them out, and paste them on 3 × 5
cards for ease of use.

1. Consider cards 1, 12, and 27. What is the easiest way to sort
   these 3 cards into two piles? What criterion would be used?

2. If you were to sort 28 cards into four piles, which criterion makes
   the sorting easiest?

3. Sort cards 3, 15, and 19 into two piles. In what sense is your sorting
   criterion different from the criterion used in exercises 1 and 2?

4. In what sense are cards 10, 12, and 27 alike?

5. In what sense are cards 6, 8, and 21 alike?

6. Sort cards 9, 13, 17, and 22 into two different piles, two different
   ways. Place the cards into the following 2 x 2 matrix; C_1 and C_2
   represent one type of criterion and D_1 and D_2 represent a different
   type of criterion.

	C_1	C_2
D_1		
D_2		

7. Sort cards 1, 6, 12, 16, 17, 21, 25, and 28 into two piles. Describe
   carefully the criterion you used to sort the cards.

8. Sort cards 1, 6, 7, 16, 18, 20, 21, 26, and 28 into three piles *two different ways using two different criteria for sorting.*

9. Select a card that satisfies the following "analogies."

   a. Card 25 is to card 21 as card 11 is to what card?

   b. Card 4 is to card 3 as card 16 is to what card?

   c. Card 5 is to card 14 as card 27 is to what card?

10. Mary has sorted cards 6, 12, and 26 into one pile and cards 7, 10, and 20 into another pile. What criteria did Mary likely use to sort the cards?

11. Ikie has sorted cards 5, 13, and 14 into one pile and cards 2, 10, and 27 into another pile. What criteria did Ikie likely use to sort the cards?

12. What are the 7 different types of functions involved in the card sorting activities? What are the 4 different representations? Form an 7 x 4 matrix using the numbers of the functions as entries that organizes the functions and their representations.

13. Check several contemporary secondary school mathematics textbooks. How do the authors of these textbooks categorize functions as evidenced by chapter titles? How well do the categories that emerged in these exercises match the categories used by the authors of the textbooks you examined?

14. Create a "card sort" activity that you could use with students who are studying a. linear functions b. quadratic functions.

15. Create a "card sort" activity that you could use with students who are studying different types of polygons.

USING FUNCTIONS TO MAKE CONNECTIONS

Recall that during the card sort activities there were seven different types of functions involved. These seven types of functions are the ones most likely encountered in secondary school mathematics. What is the value of studying different types of functions? Many reasons can be given. One has to do with studying the behavior and characteristics of different types of mathematical entities. Another, and the one we will emphasize here, is that it takes different types of mathematical functions to model and describe real-world phenomena. Quadratic functions can model the flight of balls when thrown. Exponential functions can model certain types of population growth. What follows are four different activities each involving different types of functions. These activities can be used to make connections between mathematics and real-world phenomena as suggested in the NCTM *Standards*.

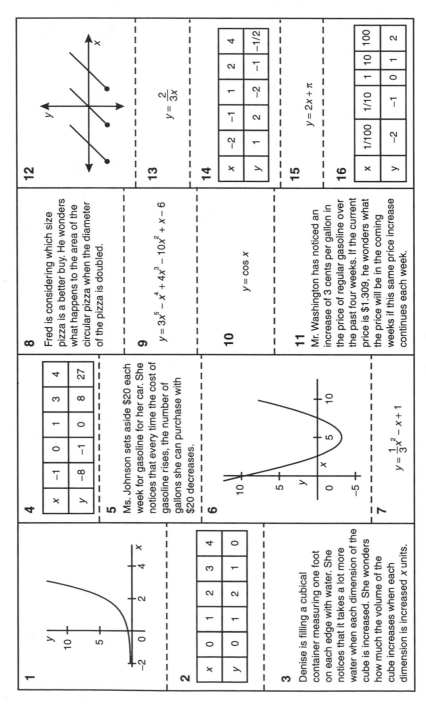

Figure 3

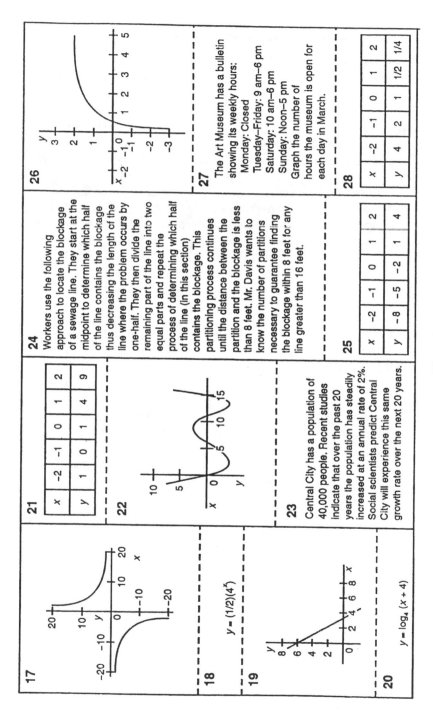

17

18 $y = (1/2)(4^x)$

19

20 $y = \log_4 (x + 4)$

21

x	-2	-1	0	1	2
y	1	0	1	4	9

22

23

Central City has a population of 40,000 people. Recent studies indicate that over the past 20 years the population has steadily increased at an annual rate of 2%. Social scientists predict Central City will experience this same growth rate over the next 20 years.

24

Workers use the following approach to locate the blockage of a sewage line. They start at the midpoint to determine which half of the line contains the blockage thus decreasing the length of the line where the problem occurs by one-half. They then divide the remaining part of the line into two equal parts and repeat the process of determining which half of the line (in this section) contains the blockage. This partitioning process continues until the distance between the partition and the blockage is less than 8 feet. Mr. Davis wants to know the number of partitions necessary to guarantee finding the blockage within 8 feet for any line greater than 16 feet.

25

x	-2	-1	0	1	2
y	-8	-5	-2	1	4

26

27

The Art Museum has a bulletin showing its weekly hours:
Monday: Closed
Tuesday–Friday: 9 am–6 pm
Saturday: 10 am–6 pm
Sunday: Noon–5 pm
Graph the number of hours the museum is open for each day in March.

28

x	-2	-1	0	1	2
y	4	2	1	1/2	1/4

Figure 4

Activities with Functions

Ms. Lopez takes seriously the importance of making connections between mathematics and real-world phenomena. She encourages the notion that mathematical functions can be used to model relationships in which two quantities vary. She believes that the notion of a "functional relationship" between two quantities, represented by variables, is central to understanding the nature of mathematical functions. In an effort to demonstrate functional relationships, Ms. Lopez uses the following four activities or experiments in her classes: the viewing tube, pendulum, investment, and Ferris wheel activities. She found the viewing tube activity in an article by Wilson and Shealy (1995).

She got the idea for the Ferris wheel activity from pages 164–165 of the *Curriculum and Evaluation Standards for School Mathematics* published by the National Council of Teachers of Mathematics (1989). She was thankful for these different references so that she didn't feel that she always had to "reinvent the wheel."

So that you might appreciate the value of these activities or experiments and to better understand what Ms. Lopez is trying to accomplish, try the following experiments/activities yourself. It might be advisable to work in groups of three or four to facilitate the data gathering and analysis activities. Note the types of functions that each activity involves. We will reflect on the value of these activities later in this section.

The Viewing Tube
The "viewing tube experiment" involves seeing through cylindrical tubes. The "viewing tubes" can be made from cardstock stapled together as shown below. Each part of the viewing tube should be about 25 cm long so that the shortest tube is approximately 25 cm long and the longest tube is about 50 cm long. Each part of the tube should be about 3 cm in diameter. Two different lengths of the tube are shown in Figure 5.

Figure 5

The focus of the experiment is to consider the relationship between the length of the tube and the vertical height that can be seen through the tube.

Place a meter stick on a wall 5 meters from where you will be standing with the tube. Place the meter stick so that the bottom of the stick is essentially at eye level (see Figure 6).

Observe how many centimeters on the meter stick can be seen through the viewing tube. As the length of the tube changes, record the values in a table similar to the one below. Let the length of the tube vary in increments of 5 cm or whatever seems reasonable given the construction of the tube. The ac-

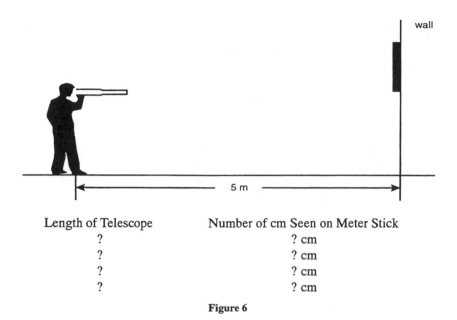

Length of Telescope	Number of cm Seen on Meter Stick
?	? cm
?	? cm
?	? cm
?	? cm

Figure 6

tual values in your table may vary according to how you constructed your tube. Take six readings if at all possible.

Based on your measurements, what type of function seems to exist between the length of the viewing tube (l) and the number (n) of centimeters seen? That is, how would you classify $n = f(l)$? As best you can determine, write an expression that represents the function.

Suppose instead of standing 5 meters from the stick, you stood 10 meters or 15 meters from the stick. How would the expression representing the function change? Would the type of function change? How would its graph change?

Suppose the length of the viewing tube remained constant but the distance from the meter stick varied—say 1 meter at a time. What type of function would be defined between the distance from the meter stick and the number of centimeters read on the stick? What would its graph look like?

Suppose you remained 5 meters from the meter stick but the diameter of the tube increased from 3 cm to 6 cm. How would the expression representing the function change? Would the type of function change if the diameter of the tube varied? What would its graph look like?

The Pendulum

The period of a pendulum may be defined as the time required for the pendulum to swing from one extreme to the other and back again. Think about the action of the pendulum. What factors would change the period? Length of the pendulum? Mass of the pendulum? The initial angle at which the pendulum is released? Of the factors that would have an effect, what type of relationship exists between that factor and the period? Linear? Quadratic? Inversely related? In the following activity, investigate and attempt to answer these questions by collecting data and organizing it in tabular and graphical form. You will need the following materials:

Five pendulums of various lengths (0.3m, 0.5m, 0.75m, 1m, 1.25m)—the pendulums may be constructed by attaching string to ring stands or a meter stick supported by ring stands. The string should have a slip knot or hook on the end to receive the masses.

Five masses: 200g, 400g, 600g, 800g, and 1000g (1 kg)

Protractor

Stopwatch

Measuring the period: Have one person release the pendulum and say "Go" and then count five periods, "One . . . two . . . three . . . four . . . stop." The person with the stopwatch starts timing on "Go" and stops the watch on "Stop." The period is then the recorded time divided by five.

1. Varying the mass.
    Construct a pendulum that is 1 meter long with different weights that vary from 200 grams to 1000 grams (1 kilogram) in increments of 200 grams. Hold the masses at about a 30-degree angle as shown in Figure 7, let go, and determine the period. (It is suggested that the 30-degree angle be maintained every time to help ensure accurate results.) Average three readings and use that average for your data.

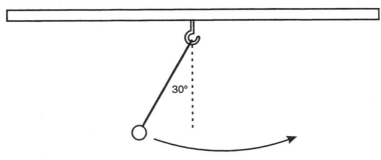

Figure 7

Construct a table that has 5 entries (ordered pairs), one for each of the 5 different weights, and the corresponding "average" for the 5 periods. Plot the points on a graph and determine the type of function that is represented. What conclusions can you draw regarding the impact of the weight on the period of the pendulum?

2. Varying the length.
    Repeat the process but this time use the pendulums of different lengths. Use a single weight in each case. (Does it matter which weight?) Construct a table that has 5 entries (ordered pairs), one for each of the 5 different lengths and the corresponding "average" for the 5 periods. What conclusions can you draw regarding the impact of the length of the pendulum on the period of the pendulum?

3. Varying the initial angle.
    Repeat the process again using a pendulum of 1 meter and one of the weights. However, this time use the protractor to vary the initial angle. Use 10, 30, 45, 60, and 90 degrees for the initial angles. Construct a table that has 5 entries (ordered pairs), one for each angle and the corresponding average for the 5 periods. Plot the points on a graph. Does the graph appear to represent either of the two functions represented in parts 1 or 2 of this experiment? Describe the relationship represented in the graph.

The Investment
The regular growth or decline of a quantity by a percentage of the initial amount has many applications. Growth of an investment, price increases due to inflation, interest owed while repaying loans, population growth, and radioactive decay are common examples. In this activity you will consider questions involving a simple investment. Through data collection and graphing try to characterize the function that models this situation.

Suppose you invested $1000 at a 7 percent annual rate of interest. Assume that the interest is compounded annually. Make a table showing how much money (to the nearest dollar) you would have after 5, 10, 15, 20, 25, and 30 years. Do you earn the same amount of money every five years? During what five-year period did the money grow the most? The least? How would you describe the relationship between the time and the amount of money you have? Plot the points on a set of axes (time × money) and draw the curve that best represents your data. What are some of the characteristics of the graph? What does the graph suggest will happen to the money in years 30, 35, and 40? What function might be represented by this graph?

Often when someone makes an investment it is for some specific purpose such as buying a car or a house or saving money for a college education. In this case the investor would want to know how long it would take for the investment to grow to a certain amount. Again, suppose you invested $1000 at a 7 percent annual interest rate. Make a table that shows when (in fractional parts of years) you would have $3000, $5000, $7000, and $9000. How long does it take to earn the next $2000? How does this time frame compare to the time for each of the previous $2000 increments? Plot the points and sketch a graph illustrating the relationship. What are the independent and dependent variables in this situation? Describe the relationship between the amount of money and time. What function could be used to model this situation? Compare and contrast this relationship and the relationship in the previous investment situation.

Write explicit formulas for each of the two relationships. Check to make sure the formulas fit the data presented in the graphs. Discuss how the formulas are related.

The Ferris Wheel

Suppose Jenny is riding a Ferris wheel as illustrated in Figure 8. Given the dimensions shown, how far off the ground is Jenny? Let us consider Jenny's vertical distance from the ground as the wheel rotates in a counterclockwise direction from its present position; in particular we want to determine Jenny's distance from the ground at twelve different positions as indicated by the various "spokes" of the wheel. Using Figure 8, measure her vertical height at each of the twelve positions and construct a graph in which there are 12 units on the horizontal axis—one for each of the vertical distances measured. Plot the twelve points and draw a smooth curve through those points. What kind of function is represented?

Suppose we want to represent Jenny's position using the sine function, that is, by the equation $y = a \sin bx + c$. Given the Ferris wheel shown in Figure 8, what is the value of a? What factor affects the a value? What is the maximum value the function could assume? The sine function $y = \sin x$ contains the point $(0,0)$ and has a y value of 0 again when $x = \pi$. In our Ferris wheel problem, Jenny's original position is not at the point of origin but rather at the point $(0, r + h)$, where r is the radius of the circle. Thus our graph of Jenny's position is shifted (upward) from the sine curve $y = \sin x$. What parameter in the equation $y = a \sin bx + c$ is affected by this circumstance? What is the value that should be assigned to this parameter in Jenny's situation? Write the equation representing Jenny's case using the form $y = a \sin bx + c$ with appropriate values for a, b, and c.

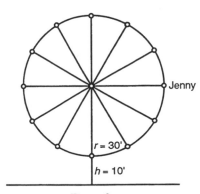

Figure 8

What angles, expressed in radian measure, are represented by these twelve positions? Substitute these values for x in the equation (of the form $y = a \sin b\,x + c$) that you previously determined. Construct a table of values for the twelve positions. Sketch a graph using these twelve points. In what way is this graph similar to the initial graph you created in which the "y values" were the vertical distances you measured?

Write equations of the form $y = a \sin bx + c$ for each of the Ferris wheels shown in Figure 9. Assume Jenny starts at the same position as was illustrated in Figure 8 and that this position corresponds to the point when $x = 0$. Describe a circumstance in which the b value would be 2 or ½ rather than 1.

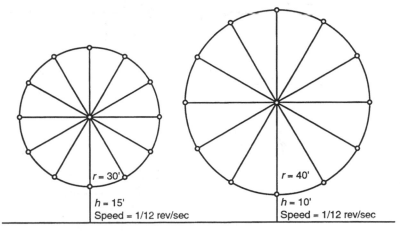

Figure 9

Reflecting on the Use of the Activities

The preceding four activities emphasize the concept of function as a relationship between two measurable quantities as they vary in some way. In the biggest box problem we related one dimension of the box to the volume of the box. We saw that as the dimension we labeled x increased, the volume increased to a certain point and then decreased. We used a third-degree polynomial to model this relationship. In the viewing tube experiment we saw two relationships. As the distance to the wall increased (keeping the tube a constant length), the diameter of the viewing area also increased at a constant rate. The graph of the relationship was linear. As the length of the tube increased (keeping the distance from the wall constant), the diameter of the viewing area decreased. But the amount of change with each unit change in the length was also decreasing. The graph was nonlinear; the relationship was an inverse variation. In the investment problem as time increased, the amount of money increased and increased at a faster rate as time elapsed. This relationship was modeled by an exponential function. In the pendulum problem,

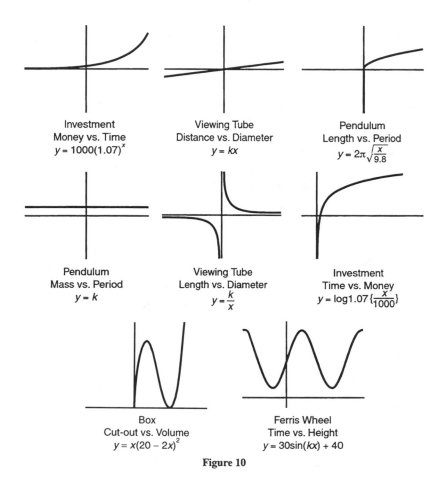

Figure 10

the relation between the length of the pendulum and the period was also increasing but the rate of increase was decreasing; it turned out to be a square root function. We also observed that the period did not change as the mass increased, thus defining a constant function. These activities emphasize the fact that a variety of functions is needed to model real-world phenomena. The graphs depicting the indicated relationships are displayed in Figure 10.

One of the important aspects of understanding functions is to be able to understand how they behave and what kinds of real-world phenomena they represent. If students can connect mathematics to real-world phenomena, they have a better chance of understanding mathematics and are also more likely to be motivated to learn mathematics, and functions in particular. The following activity asks you to transform the previous four activities into viable activities for your classroom and to consider other kinds of connections that could be made between mathematics and real-world phenomena.

Exploration 4

Suppose you were planning to use these four activities with your students where they worked in groups of three or four. Consider the following questions as you think about organizing the lessons.

1. What kind of preparation or organizational remarks do you think would be necessary for the students to have a positive experience?

2. Make up a sheet like the following that you would give to the students to guide their working through the activity. Fill in the parts marked Objectives, Directions, and Suggested Variations for each of the four activities. (Add more lines as needed.)

> Name: _____
>
> Objectives: _____
>
> _____
>
> Directions: _____
>
> _____
>
> Data Analysis: _____
>
> _____
>
> Results: _____
>
> _____
>
> Suggested Variations: _____
>
> _____

Compare your suggestions to those of your classmates.

3. In the pendulum activity, the following suggestion was made: "It is suggested that the 30-degree angle be maintained every time to help ensure accurate results." Would you consider not giving the students this directive and letting them figure out at what angle the base of the pendulum should be held? Explain your reasoning.

4. How long would you be willing to spend on teaching each of the four activities (for example, less than one period, one period but no more, two periods, three periods, or as long as it takes)? Provide a rationale for your decision.

5. Find a secondary school textbook containing the content required to do the four activities. Identify the sections in which you would use each of the activities. Describe how you would use the

activities (for example, warmup activity, class project, or end-of-chapter task).

6. Consider the following relationships. Indicate the type of function involved and how it could be used to help students see connections between real-world phenomena and mathematical functions.

    a. The total cost of buying gasoline and the number of gallons purchased.

    b. The speed at which we drive and the miles per gallon for each of the different speeds (at 10 mph intervals).

    c. The tip one leaves and the cost of different meals.

    d. The volume of a tree trunk (assume it's a perfect cylinder) and the radius of the tree trunk.

7. Create an activity that could be used to help students make connections between mathematical functions and the real world.

Using the History of Functions to Make Connections

Mathematical connections can also be made using the history of mathematics. The history of mathematics is filled with stories of real-life drama about mathematicians and their struggles to make their work known. Too, some of the issues that have arisen in the development of mathematics have implications for the teaching of mathematics as well; for example, when and for what purpose notation should be developed. In this section we will provide a brief review of the history of the development of the function concept and consider how this historical development can be used as a basis for generating classroom activities for students.

Reflective Problem 3

1. Did any of your previous mathematics teachers emphasize a historical development of mathematical ideas? If so, describe the situation or approach. Did you find it interesting or not?

2. What do you think would be particularly important in order for students to be interested in the historical development of functions?

Ms. Lopez is one of those teachers who likes making historical connections whenever she can. As it turns out, later in the year she attended an NCTM regional meeting. One of her colleagues had mentioned an interesting speaker who usually talked about how the history of mathematics could be used to motivate students. Ms. Lopez decided to attend the speaker's session. As luck would have it, the speaker emphasized the historical development of functions and how that development could be translated into viable classroom activities. Ms. Lopez was really excited about the speaker's ideas. She felt that, in addition to her use of activities to promote connections, she could now use the history of functions to make additional connections for her students. She recognized that many of her students had considerable difficulty with abstract thinking. This was why she liked the use of activities such as the ones previously described. She felt it made mathematics less abstract for her students. She felt that she could use ideas gained from the talk to make mathematics even more palatable for her students.

She had tried to introduce historical anecdotes in her classes before, as she knew that the concept of function had strong historical precepts involving descriptions of physical phenomena. However, she felt that this historical orientation was often lost in her zeal to develop students' skills in performing algebraic manipulations. The speaker had reminded her, again, that the function concept developed, at least in part, out of a need to describe and represent physical phenomena. In many ways, the previous activities illustrate how functions can be used to describe physical phenomena, an approach that honors the historical development of function. While she wanted her students to develop the necessary skills, she also wanted them to appreciate mathematics as a human invention—created by real people. She felt committed to using some of these ideas on the history of functions in her classes.

She had taken copious notes at the session. When she went home that evening, she translated her notes into a form that would be helpful when she developed lecture notes, activities, or resource materials for students who were interested in doing projects. The material that she wrote follows. (Appreciation is expressed to Dr. Joao Ponte, University of Lisbon, Portugal, for his helpful comments in reacting to this section.)

> The concept of function did not appear in mathematics by chance. It arose as a necessary tool for the quantitative study of natural phenomena. For example, Galileo (1564–1642) studied the concept of gravity and Kepler (1571–1630) studied the movement of planets. The development of the function concept was facilitated by the modern algebraic notation developed by Viète (1540–1603), and, more specifically, by the analytic geometry introduced by Descartes (1596–1650) and Fermat (1601–1665).
>
> Reacting to the verbalistic traditions of medieval scholastic thinking, Galileo emphasized that mathematics was the most appropriate language for

the study of nature. To understand a given phenomenon, it was necessary to measure quantities, identify regularities, and obtain relationships represented by mathematical descriptions as simply as possible. The study of the movement of falling bodies, of the motion of planets, and, more generally, of curvilinear motion, led to the consideration of direct and inverse proportionalities, as well as of polynomial and trigonometric functions. Mathematics and physics were at this point closely interconnected. Newton, rightly regarded as one of the greatest mathematicians of all time, was also a prominent physicist. Many other mathematicians, such as Bernoulli, Euler, Lagrange, and Fourier, were also very interested in physical problems.

Early in the development process, functions were recognized as excellent tools for studying variation. For example, one of the most extraordinary discoveries of Newton was that the motion of a body of mass m is not linearly related to the force f acting upon that body. Neither does a simple relationship exist for the velocity. However, such a relationship exists for the acceleration of the body, and it is expressed by the function commonly known as Newton's second law of motion: $f = ma$.

The origin of the function concept is rooted in the study of natural phenomena, although recent developments are not as closely tied to the physical sciences. Nevertheless, mathematical functions play an increasingly significant role in the study of the biological sciences, human and social sciences, business, communications, engineering, and technology. Functions constitute an essential means of describing, explaining, and predicting real-world phenomena.

While all of the richness of the history of the evolution of the function concept cannot be communicated in a single activity, or even in a series of activities, it is the case that teaching functions through the use of activities is quite consistent with what people have historically considered significant about the function concept. The learning of mathematics can be greatly facilitated by enabling students to see functions, and mathematics more generally, as connected to issues related to real-world phenomena and to not see mathematics as a subject separated from human activity.

It is important that functions be represented through verbal, tabular, graphical, and algebraic means. Students should construct and analyze tables, compute numerical values, develop a quantitative sense, acquire a notion of what are acceptable and unacceptable approximations, and envision the effects on graphs by changing the parameters in the algebraic representation of the function in order to develop a deep understanding of functions. Just as mathematicians have historically used functions to describe and make predictions, so should students have these kinds of experiences when studying functions. They should also be able to construct curves that approximate relationships for empirically obtained data and have an idea of the nature of the relationship between two variables. These outcomes, too, have historical precepts in the development of the concept of function. Formulas from geometry, physics, and other sciences can serve as examples for student exploration.

Exploration 5

Use the references below to answers questions 1 and 2 that follow.

References

    Kleiner, I. (1989). Evolution of the function concept: A brief survey. *College Mathematics Journal* 20(4), 282–300.

    Malik, M. A. (1980). Historical and pedagogical aspects of the definition of function. *International Journal of Mathematical Education in Science and Technology* 11, 489–494.

    Markovits, Z., Bat-sheva, E., & Bruckheimer, M. (1986). Functions today and yesterday. *For the Learning of Mathematics* 6(2), 18–28.

1. Determine the roles that Galileo, Newton, Leibniz, Descartes, Euler, d'Alembert, Fourier, Dirichlet, Cauchy, Weierstrass, Baire, and Dedekind played in the development of the function concept.

2. When did the function concept begin to be defined in terms of a set-theoretic approach? Approximately when was the language *domain, range, image,* and the notation *f(x)* introduced?

3. Find four textbooks representing the following periods: 1900–1940, 1945–1960, 1960–1980, 1990–present. How are functions defined in each of these texts? How do the exercises differ? Speculate on what might have accounted for these differences.

4. What do the NCTM *Standards* say about using the historical development of mathematics in the teaching of secondary school mathematics?

TEACHING ABOUT FUNCTIONS

We have seen that Ms. Lopez tends to emphasize mathematical connections as suggested in the NCTM *Standards*. But not all teachers share her view of teaching mathematics, nor should they necessarily. There are many facets to mathematics, one of which is to examine the structure of mathematical functions. Teachers who place value on this perspective consider it important for students to understand the algebra of functions. Consider the following debate between Ms. Lopez, who favors an emphasis on functional relationships, and Mr. Washington, who emphasizes the algebraic structure of functions. Let's listen to their discussion.

The Debate

Ms. Lopez: I want my kids to see that functions can be used to describe many of the things they encounter in their lives. If they don't see that, why should they want to study mathematics?

Mr. Washington: That's fine and dandy, but at some point, for example, when they get to calculus, they are going to have to understand how these different functions are related to one another. Take the experiments that you do. Don't you think kids should understand what the basic functions are that represent the outcomes?

Ms. Lopez: Sure. But I don't want them to think that that is the beginning and the end of functions. I think it is more important that they develop a feel for the behaviors of functions and not just manipulating symbols.

Mr. Washington: So as you see it, it's one side or the other. I don't see it that way. We can do a little of both. I like my kids to make a chart like the one here that Tammy created. [*Pulls chart out of a stack of papers.*] I thought she did a really great job.

Basic Building Blocks of Function	
Component	*Examples*
x^n; where n is a whole number	$y = x^2$; $y = 4$; $y = x$
x^m; where m is an integer	$y = x^{-3}$
x^q; where q is a rational number	$y = x^{1/2}$
a^x; where a is a real number constant; $a > 0$	$y = 2^x$
$\log_a x$; where a is usually a natural number constant greater than 1 or the irrational number e	$y = \log_2 x$; $y = \ln x$
$\cos x$; $\sin x$	$y = \sin x$

Ms. Lopez: Yes, I agree that's neat. I'm sure Tammy learned a lot. But my point is this. The other day in class, I posed a problem about what kind of function would represent the relationship between the money spent on advertising and the money generated from sales. We came up with these six graphs (Figure 11) and debated which one was most likely to represent the actual situation.

    I had them write a paragraph arguing why each of these different representations could or could not be a reasonable graph of that relationship. To me, this kind of activity is what mathematics is all about.

Mr. Washington: Isn't that relationship represented by a logistical curve of some sort? Won't the kids want to know what that curve looks like?

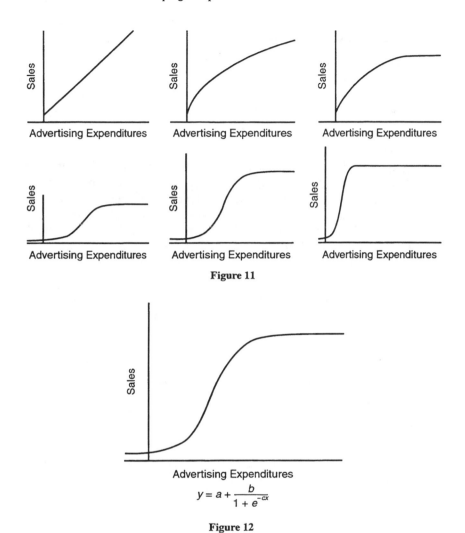

Figure 11

Figure 12

$$y = a + \frac{b}{1 + e^{-cx}}$$

Ms. Lopez: Sure, the equation given to us by Dr. Stam in the business school over at the university is this (Figure 12).

Mr. Washington: Okay. But now where do you go from there? On to another application? When will the kids dig deeper into the mathematical structure of the functions?

Ms. Lopez: Well, I thought we did dig pretty deep in trying to figure out the behavior of different kinds of functions. They had to consider what kinds of functions were increasing or decreasing or what kinds of functions had rates of change that increase or decrease.

Mr. Washington: While I applaud what you do, I find it necessary to spend some time helping my students understand the basic building blocks of functions.

Ms. Lopez: Such as?

Mr. Washington: I want students to understand that building blocks like what Tammy did can be used to generate other functions by adding, subtracting, multiplying, dividing, or composing functions to generate most of the functions that we typically study.

Ms. Lopez: So what is it that you want your students to learn? What is important to you?

Mr. Washington: How these different functions are connected. I want them to see that if terms of the form x^n, assuming n is a whole number, are multiplied by a constant coefficient and added, you know, like a linear combination, we have functions that are called polynomial functions, for example, like $y = 3x^2 + 2x - 1$ and $y = 5x + 3$. We can then classify these functions into their different types, for example, linear, quadratic, and cubic. This kind of connects up to your card sort activity, which I think is a really neat activity.

Ms. Lopez: Thanks very much. I will admit that you are doing some good mathematics there too. I suppose you encourage the kids to think about different kinds of exponents. Do you define rational functions as functions of the sort where the terms consist of things like x^m where m is an integer?

Mr. Washington: Exactly. For example, $y = 3x^{-1} + 6$ and $y = 2x^{-3} - x^{-1}$ are rational functions. The function

$$y = \frac{x+1}{x+2}$$

is also a rational function. Here, this is the kind of chart that I use when I try to get them to see how different functions are related. [*Reaches into a lesson plan book and pulls out the following chart.*]

Families of functions

Family	Description	Examples
Polynomial	Linear combinations of terms x^n where n is a whole number	$y = 2x^5 - 3x^2 + 6$ $y = 5 - 7x$ $y = 4$
Rational	Involves quotients of polynomials and/or integer exponents	$y = 3x^{-3} + 2x^{-1} - 5x^2$ $y = \dfrac{x^2 - 3x + 1}{5x - 2}$
Algebraic	Involves rational functions raised to rational powers	$y = 3x^{1/4} - 2x^3$ $y = \sqrt[3]{x^2} - 3$

Family	Description	Examples
Exponential	Involves functions with variable exponents	$y = 3(1.07)^x$ $y = -3e^x + 2$
Logarithmic	Functions in which the exponent is the dependent variable	$y = 5 - 3\log_z x$ $y = 7\ln x$ or $x = e^{y/7}$ $y = \ln\left(\dfrac{x^2 - 1}{1 - 3x}\right)$
Trigonometric		$y = 3\sin x$ $y = 4 - 2\cos(4x - \pi)$ $y = \tan(x^2 - 2)$

Ms. Lopez: I'll admit that there is some neat mathematics there. But I still put my money on kids understanding the nature of the behaviors of functions. Here's a chart that I use with my kids. I expect them to identify functions that fit into the different cells.

Function characteristics

<table>
<tr><td rowspan="2"></td><td rowspan="2"></td><td>Constant function</td><td>Always increasing or decreasing function</td><td>Sometimes increasing and sometimes decreasing function</td></tr>
<tr></tr>
<tr><td rowspan="3">Rate of change in function with each unit change in the independent variable</td><td>Constant</td><td></td><td></td><td></td></tr>
<tr><td>Always increasing or decreasing</td><td></td><td></td><td></td></tr>
<tr><td>Sometimes increasing and sometimes decreasing</td><td></td><td></td><td></td></tr>
</table>

Mr. Washington: Your kids can do that? Wow. I'm impressed.

Ms. Lopez: Well, some can. Others get lost. But it is the kind of thing that I like to emphasize when we talk about different kinds of functions.

Mr. Washington: Was that the bell?

Ms. Lopez: I'm afraid so. Got to go. See you at the faculty meeting this afternoon?

Exploration 6

1. Place yourself on the following continuum depending on which position you value the most. How does your reaction compare to those of other students?

   |_____|
   Washington   **Lopez**

2. As you reflect on your own learning experiences, which position comes the closest to describing your experiences in learning functions? Explain.

3. For the functions given in the chart developed by Tammy, the domains for *n, m,* and *q* are given. What is the domain for *x*?

4. Logarithmic, exponential, and trigonometric functions are examples of what are called *transcendental functions.* Check several secondary school textbooks and see whether this term is used. Find examples of these types of functions in the texts. Are these functions developed more from Ms. Lopez's perspective or more from Mr. Washington's perspective? Explain.

5. Examine the connection made in secondary school textbooks between logarithmic functions and exponential functions. Describe the nature of these connections.

6. Is Mr. Washington correct or incorrect in saying that "For example, $y = 3x^{-1} + 6$ and $y = 2x^3 - x^{-1}$ are rational functions"? If you were teaching students about rational functions, how precise would you want your language to be? Why?

Thinking About Ms. Lopez's Approach

During the conversation between Ms. Lopez and Mr. Washington, Ms. Lopez mentioned a chart that she used with her students in which they had to identify functions that were on the one hand increasing, constant, or decreasing, and, on the other hand, their rate of change was increasing, constant, or decreasing. Let us explore these characteristics in an effort to better understand the behavior of functions.

In the four activities presented earlier, we saw relationships between variables that gave rise to different types of functions. Modeling a phenomenon as a relationship between two variables (for example, the length of a pendulum and its period) with a mathematical function requires understanding the characteristics of that relationship and matching these characteristics with those of a particular function (for example, $P = 2\pi\sqrt{\dfrac{l}{9.8}}$). In some cases this process is performed analytically and in other cases it is done by trial and error. In any case, the question of what characteristics are central to a function becomes important. One characteristic involves whether the function value or dependent variable increases, decreases, or remains constant as the values of the independent variable increase.

Revisiting some of the activities will help illustrate this idea. We saw in the activities, for example, that the period of the pendulum increased as the length of the pendulum increased. The diameter of the area on the wall that we could see through our viewing tube decreased as the length of the tube increased. The volume of Mrs. Lopez's box increased and then decreased as the size of the corner cuts increased. Each of these activities modeled a different type of function. It would be helpful, then, to classify our families of functions in terms of whether they increase, decrease, do both, or remain constant.

We run into a problem, however, if this characterization is the only scheme we use. Consider, for example, three functions that were developed in the activities. The relationship between the length of the pendulum and the period, the relationship between what could be seen through the tube and the distance from the wall, and the relationship between the amount of money and time in the investment activity were all modeled by increasing functions, but all three of these relationships are different in other ways.

One way of thinking about this difference is to consider the amount of change in the function for each unit increase in the independent variable. The part of the wall that could be seen through the viewing tube increased the same amount for each unit increase in the distance from the wall. In the investment problem, the amount of money increased more rapidly as time (the independent variable) increased. The period of the pendulum, however, increased less with each successive unit increase in the length of the pendulum (the independent variable). The graphs in Figure 13 illustrate these characteristics.

Matching a relationship to a function would be easier if we could characterize that function. We can consider whether the function is increasing, decreasing, constant, or mixed (sometimes it increases, sometimes it decreases). We can also consider the rate of change. For example, the function $y = 3x + 5$ is an increasing function that increases at a constant rate. The function $y = x^3$ is

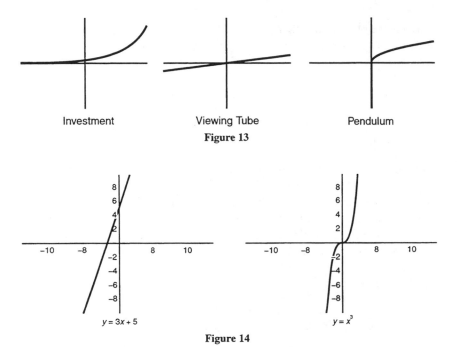

Investment   Viewing Tube   Pendulum

Figure 13

$y = 3x + 5$ $y = x^3$

Figure 14

also an increasing function but the amount of increase as x changes decreases and then increases (that is, mixed) (see Figure 14).

Ms. Lopez's chart provides a model for organizing functions. Note that $y = 3x + 5$ would fit in the first row, second column while $y = x^3$ would fit in the third row, second column.

Exploration 7

1. Fill in the chart developed by Ms. Lopez. If it is not possible to find a function that satisfies the given characteristics, explain why no such function exists.

2. Once you have completed the chart, answer the following questions.

   a. What cells, if any, contain only one type of function?

   b. What types of functions fit into only one cell?

   c. What types of functions fit into more than one of the cells?

Extending Mr. Washington's Approach

Mr. Washington was interested in students generating certain functions based on other types of functions. He wanted his students to see that rational functions consisted of the division of two polynomial functions. He would also like his students to appreciate that some functions may be composed of more than one of the basic functions listed earlier, for example, $y = x + \sin x$.

One way to think about a function that is composed of simpler functions is to look at the characteristics of the component functions. This analysis could be done with a polynomial function like $y = x + x^2$ as well as with a function like $y = x + \sin x$. Since it more natural to think of $y = x + \sin x$ as the sum of two functions, let us begin with it. Consider the function $y = \sin x$. How would you describe its characteristics? Stop and think before you read on. One might say that it is periodic. It oscillates back and forth between an upper and lower bound. Now think about the function $y = x$. How does this function behave? It is a linear function that steadily increases; its graph is a straight line. So how do the characteristics of the component functions ($y = x$ and $y = \sin x$) contribute to the function defined by the equation $y = x + \sin x$? It may make sense to think that the function will have some oscillating behavior but should also steadily increase in some way. In light of this reasoning it may not be surprising that the graph looks as it does in Figure 15.

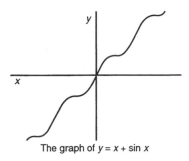

The graph of $y = x + \sin x$

Figure 15

One may also think of $y = x + x^2$ as the sum of two different functions, $y = x$ and $y = x^2$. Most students familiar with the behavior of $y = x$ and $y = x^2$ will think about them graphically. Consider the graphs of $y = x$ and $y = x^2$ which are given in Figure 16. Describe the contribution of $y = x$ and $y = x^2$ to the function $y = x^2 + x$. Note that the contribution of $y = x$ is not as easy to describe as that of $y = x^2$. Also note that the shape of the graph of $y = x^2 + x$ is much more like $y = x^2$ than $y = x + \sin x$ was like $y = \sin x$. Why is this the case? A possible explanation is that the graph of $y = x^2$ falls and then rises much more rapidly than that of $y = x$. Thus, the squared term eventually dom-

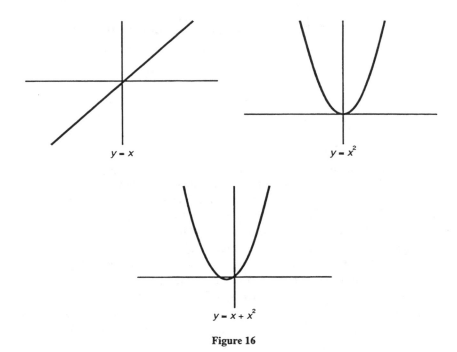

Figure 16

inates the combined function, which helps explain why its graph is a parabola. For negative numbers close to zero the two component functions are close in magnitude but have opposite signs; so the two functions almost cancel each other out in the combined function, which explains the translation of the curve to the left and down.

Composition of functions is another important way to build new functions. Take for example the polynomial function $g(x) = x + x^2$ and the rational function $f(x) = x^{-1}$. The composition of f and g, denoted $f(g(x))$ or $f \circ g$, would result in the rational function $y = (x + x^2)^{-1}$. Would you expect that this new function would have some of the characteristics of $y = x^{-1}$ as well as those of $y = x + x^2$? Compare the graph of $y = (x + x^2)^{-1}$ to that of $y = x + x^2$ and decide which, if any, of the characteristics are the same (see Figure 17).

The function $y = (x + x^2)^{-1}$ behaves in some ways the opposite of $y = x + x^2$. Where $y = x + x^2$ is increasing without bound, $y = (x + x^2)^{-1}$ is approaching zero. Where $y = x + x^2$ is approaching zero, $y = (x + x^2)^{-1}$ is increasing or decreasing without bound. If one considers the graph of $y = x + x^2$ and what happens when one divides by small or large numbers it is possible to get an intuitive idea of the behavior of $y = (x + x^2)^{-1}$.

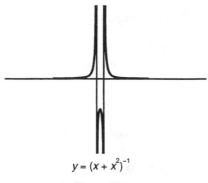

$$y = (x + x^2)^{-1}$$

Figure 17

Consider $y = \cos(x^2)$. We have already considered the behavior of $y = x^2$; the graph of $y = \cos x$ is similar to $y = \sin x$ with a translation or phase shift. How might these functions be related to $y = \cos(x^2)$? The cosine function is periodic, so would $y = \cos(x^2)$ be periodic? The cosine function is bounded by 1 and -1, so would $y = \cos(x^2)$ be bounded? The quadratic function increases more rapidly as x increases. Would you expect the period of the cosinelike curve to be decreasing as rapidly as x^2 increases? Consider the graphs in Figure 18.

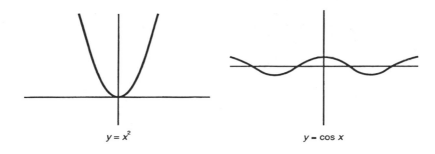

$$y = x^2 \qquad\qquad y = \cos x$$

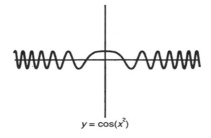

$$y = \cos(x^2)$$

Figure 18

In what way do the two component functions contribute to the composite function?

The line of reasoning we used with the addition of two functions and the composition of two functions could also be used when subtracting, multiplying, and dividing two functions to build a new function.

Exploration 8

1. Consider the following functions:

$$y = \log x + x \qquad y = x\sin x \qquad y = \frac{x+1}{x} \qquad y = \sin(\ln x)$$

$$y = x^2 - x \qquad y = 0.1x^2 + \sin x \qquad y = x^2\sin x \qquad y = \ln(\sin x)$$

Consider the characteristics of the individual components of each of these functions. Predict the expected behavior of the more complex function. Compare the graphs of the individual component functions and the more complex function. How well did your prediction turn out?

2. A common misconception in the composition of functions $f(g(x))$ is that one may apply the second or outside function, $f(x)$, to the individual parts of the first or inside function, $g(x)$. For example, this line of reasoning would give us the following equation:

$$(x + x^2)^{-1} = (x)^{-1} + (x^2)^{-1}.$$

How would you convince a student that this was false?

3. What kinds of examples would you use to convince students that $f(a + b) = f(a) + f(b)$ either holds or doesn't hold for functions in general?

4. What kinds of examples would you use to convince students that $f(ab) = f(a)f(b)$ either holds or doesn't hold for functions in general?

5. Consider the grid below and generate functions that satisfy the indicated conditions.

Cell I: $f(a) + f(b) = f(a + b)$

Cell II: $f(a) + (b) = f(ab)$

Cell III: $f(a)f(b) = f(a + b)$

Cell IV: $f(a)f(b) = f(ab)$

	$f(a + b)$	$f(ab)$
$f(a) + f(b)$	I	II
$f(a)f(b)$	III	IV

6. Test each of the following functions for each cell in the grid in Question 5 and determine which functions, if any, fit into the cells.

$y = 3x$ $y = 3x + 2$ $y = x^2$

$y = e^x$ $y = \log x$ $y = 6$

$y = \dfrac{1}{x}$ $y = x^2 + 2$ $y = \sin x$

7. Consider the graph of the function in Figure 19 and write three different equations for the graph each using a different type of function.

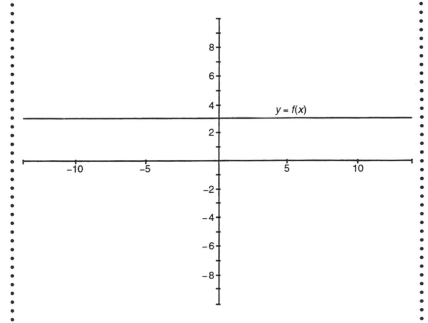

Figure 19

EXTENDING OUR NOTIONS OF GRAPHICAL REPRESENTATIONS OF FUNCTIONS

In the previous sections we have examined various activities or experiments that model different types of functions and the behaviors of a wide range of functions. What we have implicitly accepted is the fact that those functions are represented on a coordinate system consisting of orthogonal axes. Such axes form what we call the Cartesian coordinate system, named after the French mathematician René Descartes (1596–1650). It is the standard coordinate system that we use to graph functions. While it is the standard system because of its characteristics, it need not be the only system we can use to represent different types of functions. Indeed, the type of coordinate system we use is quite arbitrary. Consider the following activity, which raises questions about functions graphed on an oblique coordinate system.

Exploration 9

We know that in a coordinate system with perpendicular axes the graphs of $y = -x + 2$ and $y = -x - 2$ are parallel and the graphs of $y = -2x + 2$ and $y = x/2 + 4$ are perpendicular as shown in Figure 20.

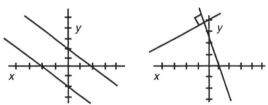

Figure 20

Suppose the axes intersected a 60° angle rather than a 90° angle (Figure 21). What would the pairs of lines look like in this coordinate system? Would the respective pairs be parallel and perpendicular in this system?

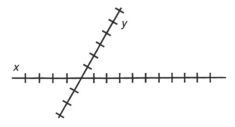

Figure   21

In the Cartesian coordinate system the graph of $y = x^2$ is symmetric about the y axis. In a 60° coordinate system would the graph of $y = x^2$ have any symmetry? If so, about what line? If not, why not?

Essentially there are two common ways of representing points in the plane: 1. By ordered pairs on the Cartesian (orthogonal) axes system and 2. by polar coordinates in which an angle and distance from the origin are given. These representations were created because they facilitated the development of mathematics. In some cases the Cartesian coordinate system is an advantage, as, for example, if you were graphing an exponential function. On the other hand, a graph of a pedal is more easily represented in polar coordinates. The unit circle can be represented relatively easily in both systems; $x^2 + y^2 = 1$ in the Cartesian coordinate system and $r = 1$ in polar coordinates. We will now explore graphs in a polar coordinate system.

Polar Coordinate System

Reflective Problem 4

What do you recall from your study of polar coordinates? Do you remember the topic being easy or difficult? Interesting or uninteresting? Based on your experiences in learning polar coordinates, what will be important to you when you teach polar coordinates?

The means by which we represent mathematical phenomena is basically a choice we can make. As suggested in Exploration 9, our representations could involve nonorthogonal axes. While it may be the case that orthogonal axes are the most convenient in many situations, there may be some contexts in which they are not convenient. In this section we will explore situations in which another coordinate system is useful, namely, polar coordinates. As you read the following discussion, keep in mind that the creation of representational systems is a creation of human ingenuity. Students should understand that representational systems are created to meet specific mathematical needs.

Most real-world problems or situations have several methods of solution or several ways of representing the situation mathematically. One example is the graphical representation of an equation based on a real-world situation. Given a certain relationship we may use a Cartesian coordinate system, an oblique system, parallel coordinates, or polar coordinates. Each system carries certain advantages and disadvantages. The context dictates which system provides the most useful information. The following specific example illustrates this idea.

Planetary motion provides one area of study that has motivated many mathematicians over the centuries. Newton found that orbiting bodies travel elliptical paths. An ellipse is considered to be a conic section that can be represented by the following general equation:

$$\frac{(x-h)^2}{a^2} + \frac{(y-k)^2}{b^2} = 1.$$

Equations of this form do not represent functions, but they are still useful in that the point (x, y) gives us the position of a planet in some Cartesian coordinate system. To keep our numbers manageable we will consider the path of the moon around the Earth (Figure 22). The moon travels around the Earth in an elliptical path with the Earth at one of the foci of the ellipse. If we also place the Earth at the origin of our coordinate system we have the following equation describing the path of the moon around the Earth using kilometers as our units:

$$\frac{(x-19,700)^2}{(387,000)^2} + \frac{y^2}{(386,5000)^2} = 1.$$

Given this equation, let us consider what information it provides us. Since 387,000 is half the major axis and 19,700 is the distance from the cen-

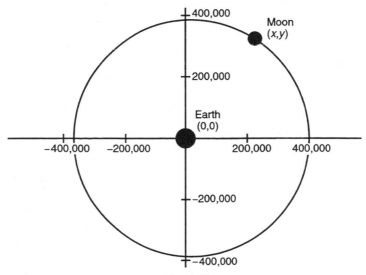

Figure 22

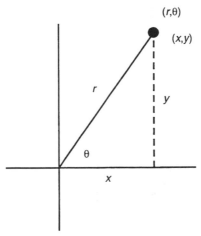

Figure 23

ter of the ellipse to the foci, we can determine that 387,000 km + 19,700 km = 406,700 km is the greatest distance (apogee) between the Earth and the moon. Similarly, 387,000 km − 19,700 km = 367,300 km is the closest (perigee) the moon comes to the Earth. If we want to know how far the moon is from the Earth at any other point in its orbit we need to know the point (x, y) to determine the distance $\sqrt{x^2 + y^2}$.

If, instead of using a Cartesian representation, we use polar coordinates, the computations required become easier. In a polar coordinate system, the coordinates $(r, \emptyset)$ give us the distance from the origin, r, in the direction of the angle, $\emptyset$, with the positive x axis as illustrated in Figure 23. If $\emptyset > 0$, we measure the angle counterclockwise, and if $\emptyset < 0$, the angle is measured clockwise. If $r > 0$, we measure the distance from the origin in the direction of the angle. If $r < 0$, the distance is measured in the opposite direction of the angle, that is, $\emptyset - \pi$. Figure 24 provides several examples of points plotted using polar coordinates. As with Cartesian coordinates, any set of ordered pairs names a unique point in the plane. With the polar coordinate system, however, note that any point in the plane may have several names. For example, $(3, \frac{\pi}{4})$, $(3, \frac{9\pi}{4})$, $(3, \frac{-7\pi}{4})$, and $(-3, \frac{5\pi}{4})$ are all names for the same point. This phenomenon makes sense in the context of an elliptical orbit since the orbiting body periodically passes through each point. The previous figures motivate the relationship between coordinate systems. If we want to maintain a particular graph we may use the following relationships to transform systems:

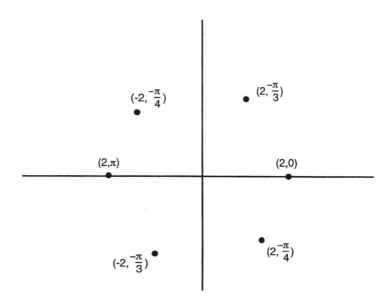

Figure 24

$$x = r\cos\phi,$$
$$y = r\sin\phi,$$
$$r^2 = x^2 + y^2,$$

and

$$\phi = 2k\pi + \arctan\left(\frac{y}{x}\right).$$

Returning to our problem of interest, in polar coordinates, an ellipse (Figure 25) has the form

$$r = \frac{ep}{1 - e\cos\phi'}$$

where e and p are constants. For our particular case, $e = \dfrac{19700}{387000}$ or $e = 0.0509$ to three significant digits. Thus, the equation representing the moon's orbit about the Earth is given by

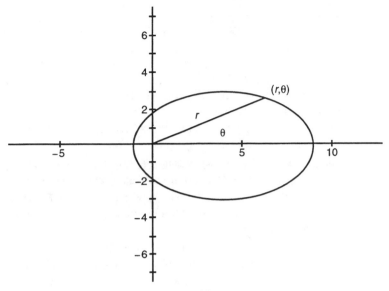

Figure 25

$$r = \frac{(386{,}000)}{1 - 0.0509\cos\phi'}.$$

In this equation, if we wish to know the distance from the Earth to the moon at any angle we simply substitute the appropriate value for ø and calculate the distance. This relationship between the angle and distance seems to be a more natural description of the motion than a relation between x and y coordinates. Another nice feature of the polar representation is that the relation is a function.

In general, any body in motion that is acted on by an inverse-square force directed toward a fixed point (gravity) travels along a path that may be described as a conic section. Furthermore, any conic section may be written in the form

$$r = \frac{ep}{1 \pm e\cos\phi}$$

where e and p are constants. Thus, motion affected by gravity provides an example where a polar coordinate system gives us a more powerful representation than the Cartesian coordinate system.

Exploration 10

1. The constant e is called the eccentricity of the ellipse and is found by dividing the distance from the center of the ellipse to a focus by half the length of the major axis. The constant p may be found by letting $(r, ø)$ be some known point on the path and solving for p. Given the following information find the equation describing the path of the body in motion.

   a. The planet Mercury travels an elliptical orbit with the sun at one of the foci. Seventy million km and 46,000,000 km are the farthest and closest points Mercury comes to the sun. Find the eccentricity of the ellipse. Find the equation that models the motion of the planet.

   b. On May 30, 1974, NASA launched the satellite ATS-6. Its low point over the surface of the Earth is 35,759 km and the high point is 35,820 km. Find the eccentricity of the elliptical path the satellite follows. Find the equation modeling the orbital path.

2. Select three different secondary school mathematics textbooks and determine how the texts treat the topic of polar coordinates.

   a. To what extent are the three texts consistent or different in their approach to the topic of polar coordinates?

   b. What kinds of problems, if any, are used to motivate the learning of polar coordinates?

Functions in the Polar Coordinate System

Constant Functions and First Order Degree Functions

Let us use the polar coordinate system to study the graphical representations of some very basic functions to see what stereotypes we have from the Cartesian coordinate system that should be broken. In the following, we say that r is a function of $ø$, that is, $ø$ is the independent variable and r is the dependent variable.

First, $r = c$ $(c > 0)$. In a Cartesian coordinate system, $y = c$ refers to a line that is parallel to the x-axis, and $y = c_1$ and $y = c_2$ $(c_1 \neq c_2)$ are parallel lines. But $r = c$ is a circle in polar coordinates! This is because no matter what $ø$ is, the point $(r, ø)$ is a fixed distance c from the origin. Accordingly, $r = c_1$ and

$r = c_2$ are concentric circles. In a Cartesian coordinate system we have no way to represent a circle as a function, but in a polar coordinate system we can! Another interesting comparison is to consider the relationship between $r = c$ and $r = -c$. Compare the result to that of $y = c$ and $y = -c$.

As a second step, consider the function $r = a\emptyset$. Select various values for a, graph the curves, and determine that the graphs constitute a spiral. One particular graph is called an Archimedes' spiral, which has applications to engineering. By changing the magnitude of the parameter a, you will obtain different, but similar, spirals. Compare this to obtaining different lines when the slope a of $y = ax$ is varied in a Cartesian coordinate system. Now, what about a "linear" function $r = a\emptyset + b$? Assign different values to a and b, graph, and determine what the graphs look like. Do any of them form a line? A shortcut to answering this question is to convert a line $y = ax + b$ into the form of $r = f(\emptyset)$, that is, $r\sin \emptyset = a\, r\cos \emptyset + b$. But in doing so, ask yourself: Have I found a general rule to represent any line in the polar coordinate system? If so, how? If not, what lines cannot be represented? Why?

Trigonometric Functions

It is natural to think that since an angle q is involved in the relationship between two arguments we should study the trigonometric functions in the polar coordinate system. By plotting points on the plane, you might soon guess that $r = \cos \emptyset$ is a circle. In fact it is. To verify your conjecture use your knowledge of geometry. By tracing the point moving around the circle twice, you can show that this trigonometric function is periodic. Find out other facts that could be verified using this graph.

Recall that $y = \cos x$ and $y = \sin x$ are closely related. In the Cartesian coordinate system, a shift of the graph of $y = \cos x$ will enable you to get the graph of $y = \sin x$, or vice versa. How can you obtain the graph of $r = \sin \emptyset$ in the polar coordinate system by manipulating the graph of $r = \cos \emptyset$? Is it also a circle?

We have experience with changing the parameters in a trigonometric function such as changing a and b in $y = a \sin (x + b)$. We know that the changing of a will induce the change of the amplitude of the graph while changing of b will result in a shift of the graph. In the case of $r = a \sin (\emptyset + b)$, what kinds of changes will happen if you are going to change the parameters a and b?

Now, let us study the relationship between $r = \sin \emptyset$ and $r = \sin \emptyset/2$, $r = \sin \emptyset$ and $r = \sin 2\emptyset$. You know that the periodicity of $r = \sin \emptyset/2$ is 4π, that is, twice that of $r = \sin \emptyset$ and that the periodicity of $r = \sin 2\emptyset$ is π, that is, half that of $r = \sin \emptyset$. How would you interpret these phenomena when you are plotting $r = \sin \emptyset/2$ and $r = \sin 2\emptyset$? Refer to Figure 26 and give your ideas.

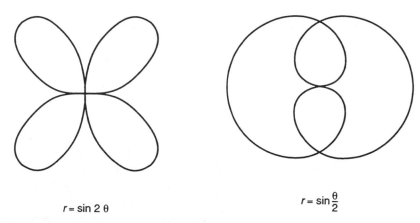

$r = \sin 2\,\theta$

$r = \sin \dfrac{\theta}{2}$

Figure 26

In the Cartesian coordinate system, $y = 1 + \cos x$ is one unit above $y = \cos x$. Is this the case for $r = 1 + \cos \o$ and $r = \cos \o$? Would $r = 1 + \cos \o$ be a circle with its radius one unit larger than that of $r = \cos \o$? The answers are no, $r = 1 + \cos \o$ is not even a circle! The new curve is called a *cardioid* because it looks like a heart. The change of the shape of the curve happens because $r = \cos q$ is not a circle with the origin as its center. Do the plotting yourself to see what is going on each time 1 is added to r. This is another example for reminding ourselves that we should be aware of the changes that the new system brings. Conveying this awareness, consider what $r = a + b\cos \o$ would look like with different parameters a and b. Are they also cardioids? If not, when are they cardioids?

Exploration 11

1. Consider $r = a/\o$ and discuss the issues of the monotonic property, maximum or minimum values, and the existing of asymptotic lines.

2. Identify a function for which you think there are some advantages or some interesting points by using the polar coordinate system to represent it.

3. Consider the vertical line test for functions in the Cartesian coordinate system. Would this test have a counterpart in the polar coordinate system? If so, what would it be? If not, why not?

4. In this section you have already seen that circles in this system could be represented as different functions. Do you think that all circles in the polar coordinate system plane could be represented

in the form of $r = f(\emptyset)$? If the answer is yes, show how. If the answer is no, give a counterexample.

5. Consider the graphs in Figure 27 illustrating $r = a\emptyset + b$. Generate a series of questions that you could ask students to assess their understanding of the nature of these graphs and the influence of changes in the parameters a and b on the graphs. Compare your questions with those of others in the class.

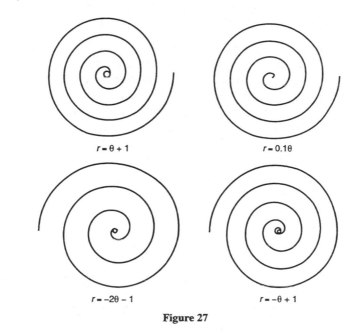

$r = \theta + 1$ $r = 0.1\theta$

$r = -2\theta - 1$ $r = -\theta + 1$

Figure 27

MS. LOPEZ'S LESSON ON PATTERNS OF GRAPHICAL REPRESENTATIONS

Mathematics has sometimes been defined as the study of patterns. One of the ways that teachers can help students determine patterns is through the use of inductive reasoning, by which students recognize a common characteristic over a set of examples and then generalize that characteristic to a larger set of examples. With respect to graphing functions, one way to accomplish this is to ask students to use graphing calculators and graph sets of linear or quadratic equations and determine common characteristics of the graphs. For example, beginning algebra students can graph equations such as $y = 2x + 3$, $y = 2x - 4$, $y = 2x - 5$, and $y = 2x + 1$, observe that the lines are parallel, and generalize that graphs represented by $y = mx + b$ will be parallel when the m values are equal.

Let us return now to Ms. Lopez's classroom as she is trying to help her students see the effect of different parameters on graphs. She has two goals for the lesson. First, she wants the students to become comfortable using their graphing calculators. Second, she wants them to recognize the effects on the graphical representations for functions of the form $y = a f(x + b) + c$ when the parameters a, b, and c take on different values. She decides to begin with quadratic functions since the students are familiar with these kinds of functions and then consider the graphs of the natural log function. As we can see, this kind of activity is confusing to some students.

Ms. Lopez: Okay. One type of pattern can be observed when we consider the effect of changing values for parameters a and c in a general equation $y = ax^2 + c$. If we consider a variety of equations of the form $y = ax^2$ with different values for a or equations $y = x^2 + c$ for different values of c, we can begin to recognize a pattern of behaviors for the graphs of these equations. I want each of you to graph these equations: (i) $y = x^2$, (ii) $y = x^2 + 1$, (iii) $y = (x - 1)^2$, and (iv) $y = 2x^2$ on your graphing calculator. Note that these can be expressed in the general form $y = a(x - b)^2 + c$.

[Students obtain the graphs in Figure 28.]

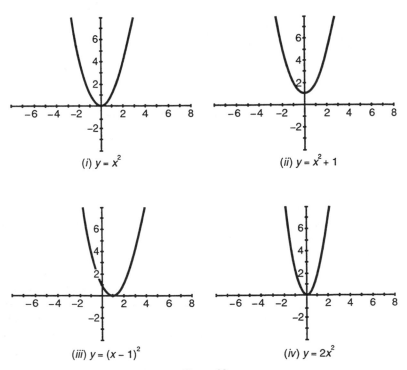

(i) $y = x^2$

(ii) $y = x^2 + 1$

(iii) $y = (x - 1)^2$

(iv) $y = 2x^2$

Figure 28

Hector: [*Under his breath*] She always gets carried away with that general stuff. What do your graphs look like?

Francis: I got these. [*Shows Figure 28.*] Looks like we got the same thing.

Ms. Lopez: If we were to draw these graphs on paper and cut them out, which ones would fit exactly on top of each other?

Elizabeth: It looks like they all would.

Samantha: No, I don't think so. I think the graph of *d* is skinnier than the rest of them.

Monica: Yeah. I agree. But I am not so sure about the third one either.

Ms. Lopez: Well, Samantha is right. Graph four is skinnier. Why do you think this is the case? What is there about the equation that makes it skinnier?

[*Pause*]

Jim: I think it's the 2 in front. Except it seems like it should be ½ if the graph is skinnier.

Holly: It is the 2. I remember we did this before once in algebra one. The two means the *x* values are multiplied by 2, which means the graph goes up faster and so it looks thinner.

Lynn: If you squared the $(x - 1)$ out in number three, the number in front would be 1. So I think all of them except number four have the same thickness.

Ms. Lopez: Okay. The number in front that Lynn is referring to is called the coefficient. What effect does the 1 have in the second equation?

Juanita: That's easy. Everything just moves up. You added 1. So for every *x* squared value, you have one more.

Ms. Lopez: Very nice, Juanita. And what about the minus one in number three?

Jeff: Well, obviously it shifted the curve to the right. But I'm not sure why.

Jim: I think of it this way. Since you subtract one from *x*, it just takes the *x* an extra unit to get to the value it would have had otherwise. So in order for $x - 1$ to equal *x* it has to get one bigger.

Marianna: Huh? How can $x - 1$ equal *x*?

Ms. Lopez: I think Jim has the right idea in that the number we square will be one less because of the $x - 1$ term. So it shifts the graph to the right. So the effect of the 1 in cases two and three is to translate the curve up or to the right. But the 2 in case four has the effect of making a vertical stretch or a horizontal shrink, depending on how you think about it. Now I want you to graph the following functions, but before you do, guess what the curve will look like. Draw a sketch before you get it on your calculator: (i) $y = x^2 + 1$, (ii) $y = x^2 + 3$, (iii) $y = (x - 3)^2$, and (iv) $y = (x + 4)^2$.

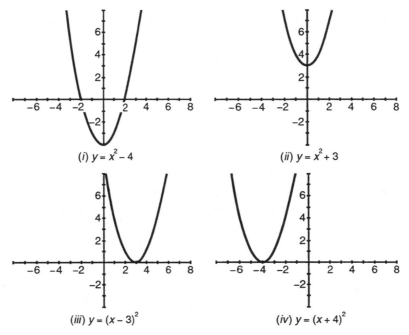

Figure 29

[*The students do this and obtain the graphs in Figure 29 on their graphing calculators.*]

Ms. Lopez: I see that we all got the same graphs. What do these graphs tell us? I want you to talk to me in terms of the general form $y = (x - b)^2 + c$. Corey?

Corey: Well. (*Pause*) If the c part is positive, it makes the graph shift up. If it is a negative, it makes it shift down. If the b part is negative, it shifts it to the right. If it's positive, it shifts to the left.

Ms. Lopez: Okay, but the graph itself remains the same size. Is that correct?

Corey: It did for these cases anyway.

Ms. Lopez: Do we agree with Corey?

Lynn: Well, by the c part I assume he means the whole thing after the x squared term and by the b part he means everything inside the parentheses. Is that what you mean?

Corey: Yes.

Lynn: Then I agree.

Ms. Lopez: Okay. Now when the parameter a in $y = ax^2$ is changed, the graph is not shifted, but stretched in some way. We saw this in our first set of graphs. Now consider these graphs. Again, draw a sketch before you graph them on your graphing calculator: (i) $y = 2x^2$, (ii) $y = \frac{1}{2}x^2$, (iii) $y = -4x^2$, and (iv) $y = -\frac{1}{3}x^2$.

[Students graph these and determine the effect of the coefficient of the x^2 term on the graph.]

Ms. Lopez: Very good. So the effect of the *a* value in $y = a\,x^2$ is to determine whether the graph opens up or down and whether the basic graph, $y = x^2$, gets stretched or shrunk. If $|a| < 1$, the graph gets shrunk. If $|a| > 1$, it gets stretched. Now we are going to consider functions in general. Now we are going to consider these kinds of effects but using the natural log function.

Ronnie: Oh man. I knew it. Off the deep end again.

Ms. Lopez: Now, now. I am not going to abuse you too much, you poor things. Let's think about it this way. In each case, I want you to determine the effects of changing the parameters *a*, *b*, and *c* in the general case of $y = a \ln (x - b) + c$. We will assume that the coefficient of the *x* term remains 1. Work in groups of three or four and create your own examples. Write a statement about the effects of changing each of the parameters *a*, *b*, and *c* once you have discovered the pattern. You can work on this the rest of the period and then finish it for homework. Tomorrow we will compare the set of examples each group used and compare the statements that the different groups came up with.

Monica: Can we take the graphing calculators home?

Ms. Lopez: Oh yes, of course. I want you to use the graphing calculators.

Exploration 12

1. Design a sequence of examples that Ms. Lopez's students might use to discover the effect on the graphs of $y = a \ln x$ when the parameter *a* takes on different values. Include values of *a* that are greater than 1, less than 1, positive, and negative. Graph your equations on your graphing calculator and observe the effect.

2. Design a sequence of examples that Ms. Lopez's students might use to discover the effect on the graphs of $y = \ln(x - b)$ when the parameter *b* takes on different values. Be sure and include both positive and negative values for *b*. Graph your equations on your graphing calculator and observe the effect.

3. Ms. Lopez asked her students to keep the coefficient of the x term as 1 for the equation $y = a \ln (x - b) + c$. Would you have made this stipulation or would you have varied the coefficient of x as well? Explain your reasoning.

4. Suppose Ms. Lopez decided to have students vary the coefficient of x in the equation $y = \ln bx$. Design a sequence of examples that could lead her students to discover the effect on the graphs of $y = \ln bx$ when the parameter b takes on different values. Be sure and include values of b that are greater than 1, less than 1, positive, and negative. Graph your equations on your graphing calculator and observe the result.

5. One of the advantages in helping students discover patterns of the sort we are discussing here is that they can develop a "sense" of what a graph looks like and can then draw a reasonable sketch of it. To test your ability to sketch graphs, sketch each of the following graphs and then graph them on a graphing calculator. How accurate were your sketches?

   a. $y = 3 \ln(x - 2) + 1$

   b. $y = \ln \left(\dfrac{1}{2} x + 4\right) - 1$

   c. $y = 3 - \dfrac{1}{2} \ln(2x - 1)$

6. On last year's chapter test, Ms. Lopez posed the following problem. Solve the problem yourself and then critique the problem as a possible test item for advanced algebra students.

   Match the following equations and their graphs given in Figure 30.

   a. $y = 2 \ln(-x) + 3$

   b. $y = - \ln x - 2$

   c. $y = 3 \ln(x - 3)$

   d. $y = \dfrac{1}{2} \ln(x - 1) + 2$

   e. $y = \ln\left(\dfrac{1}{3} x + 1\right) - 2$

7. Create an activity for advanced algebra students in which they consider 4–6 graphs that would help them determine the effects of changing the parameters a, b, and c in the equation $y = a x^b + c$.

8. Repeat Activity 7 using the equation $y = a \log b x + c$.

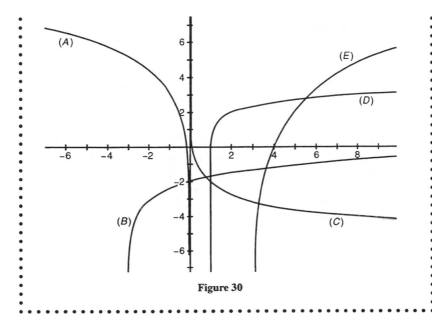

Figure 30

Reflective Problem 5

Do you recall any experiences in your high school mathematics classes where you were asked to search for mathematical patterns of the sort presented here? If not, do you think searching for these kinds of patterns would have helped you learn more mathematics?

UNDERSTANDING STUDENTS' UNDERSTANDING OF FUNCTIONS

One of the primary reasons for working through the topic of functions is to provide a foundation for understanding what difficulties students experience in learning functions. We have considered how functions are classified, the various characteristics of functions, the graphs of different types of functions, and how functions can be represented graphically. This section is designed to assist you in conducting an interview with one or more students. Tasks are suggested that include students' interpretations and meanings of graphs, their interpretations and meanings of functions per se, their understanding of the graphs of linear functions, the connections they make between graphs and equations, and their ability to recognize different types of functions. There is more material here than can reasonably be covered in a single interview. You will need to select what seems reasonable for you and the students you will interview. After the interview you'll write a report on your students' understanding of functions. But first, let us consider some general techniques for conducting interviews.

Interviewing Students

When someone mentions "conducting an interview," what comes to your mind? Often we think of two individuals interacting in a context in which one person asks questions and the other person responds. But a good interview is more than just one person posing questions for another. It involves listening and constructing questions based on what the interviewee says. It has a dynamic quality to it. The following activity is an introduction to conducting interviews.

Exploration 13

Select a classmate (say Rod) and consider the following statement:

Every secondary mathematics teacher should have experience teaching mathematics at the elementary school level before teaching at the secondary level.

One of you should construct an argument in favor of the proposition and the other should construct an argument to the contrary. Suppose you and Rod decide that Rod will start. The rules are as follows.

1. Rod can make only one point at a time. If he starts to make a second point, he should be stopped.

2. Once Rod is finished making his first point, you *must* summarize what Rod said. You *cannot* begin to make a counterargument unless your summary of Rod's point has been *completed* and *confirmed* by him. (But in confirming that the summary is correct, Rod *cannot* amplify his argument.)

3. Once you have completed the summary process, you can then present your first point of the counterargument (but no more than one point).

4. Similarly, Rod must then summarize your point and you must confirm that his summary is correct. But you cannot amplify your argument. Once this summary process is complete, and only then, Rod can present his second point in his argument.

This process should continue for several "rounds."

Note what happens during the dialogue. You *had* to listen carefully to your partner in order to present the summary. You could not be "rehearsing" your next point while your partner was talking, for otherwise you could not provide an accurate account of what your partner said. The value of this activity is to emphasize the importance of listening in conducting an interview. A good interviewer listens carefully to what the interviewee is saying in order to ask appropriate questions during the interview process.

In the next section we will provide a structure for you to consider in planning for your interview with a secondary student. While a structure is provided, it is important for you to maintain an atmosphere of "give and take" throughout the interview in which your questions are based on the student's responses. The interview should be conducted more as a conversation than as a list of activities or questions to check off. Listen carefully to your student's responses and base your follow-up questions on those responses.

Your task is to design, conduct, and report on an interview with a high school student to find out what he or she knows about functions. The interview should last no longer than thirty minutes. It is important that you keep the interview focused—you will not be able to determine everything the student knows based on one interview. The purpose of the interview is *not* to teach the student per se but rather to assess the student's understanding of functions. The following *suggested* tasks can be included in your interview depending on the level of student you are interviewing. They are not intended to be exhaustive, but it should give you some ideas to help plan your interview.

Interpreting Graphs
The graph of a function is one way of communicating how two quantities are related. Some students, however, are not able to meaningfully interpret a graph. Find out if your student can interpret the graph in Figure 31.

Graph 1: Age Versus Average Weight (in kg)
Present the graph in Figure 31 to the student.

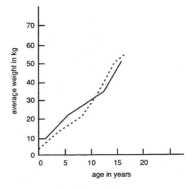

Figure 31

Consider asking the following questions.

> Which graph do you think best describes boys? girls? Why?
> At what age do boys weigh 40 kg?
> When do girls and boys weigh about the same?
>
> When do boys weigh more? When do girls weigh more?
> When do girls gain weight the fastest?
> If you extended the graph for another 15 years, what would it look like?

Graph 2: Plant Height Versus Pot Size
Present the following information to the student:
(Encourage the student to extend the graph.)

A horticulturist wanted to find out if a certain plant grows better in larger pots. She planted seedlings in ten different pots of varying sizes, then measured the plants' heights after one month. Ask the student to draw a graph illustrating what (s)he thinks the results might be for this experiment and to explain the graph that (s)he has drawn. Then present the four graphs in Figure 32 and ask the student to describe what information each of these graphs is communicating.

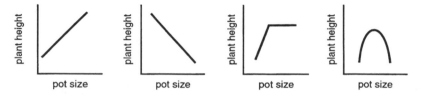

Figure 32

Ask the student if it matters which axis (vertical or horizontal) represents pot size. Encourage the student to explain his or her reasoning.

Examining Students' Meaning of Functions
Ask the students what comes to mind when you say "function." Do they tend to focus on a formula, a rule, a relationship between two quantities that vary, or some other meanings? Ask them if they can think of two quantities that vary. If they can, explore with them which one would be the independent variable and which one would be the dependent variable—although you probably want to avoid using these terms. If they have trouble identifying two quantities that vary, introduce the relationship between the cost of gasoline and the number of gallons purchased. In particular, focus on whether the students understand that as one of the quantities varies (the independent variable) this affects the values of the second quantity (the dependent variable). For exam-

ple, the more gasoline we purchase, the more the total cost of the gasoline.

Examining Functions Containing Given Points
Some students have little understanding of functions beyond linear functions. Many also believe that all functions can be described by a formula or equation. Even some advanced students tend to believe that all functions can be represented by "smooth" and continuous curves.

The following tasks can provide a basis for determining a student's understanding of function and whether they hold these more limited views of functions or whether they hold a broader perspective about functions.

Show the student the diagram in Figure 33.

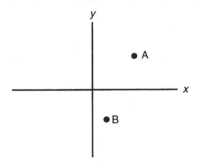

Figure 33

Ask:

Can you draw the graph of a function that contains points A and B?
Can you give an equation describing your function?
Is there a second function that contains these points?
Could you add another point C making it impossible for someone
else to draw a function containing all three points?
Add a third point, C, in various places (like somewhere in quadrant
II) and ask questions similar to those above.

Graphing Linear Functions
Many students think of functions as operations rather than as mathematical objects that describe processes. For example, they may think a function is represented by a formula, as an activity of generating a table, plotting points and connecting them, or manipulating the formula so it is in "standard form" (for example, $y = mx + b$), rather than as a representation of the relationship between two varying quantities. Students may be capable of identifying specif-

ic points on the graph but not interpreting the process described by the graph.
Write each of the following equations on a separate card.

1. $y = 2x - 7$
2. $y = -(2/3) x + 1$
3. $2x + 5y = 10$
4. $y = 1$

While showing the student the cards, ask,

What does this equation mean to you?
Can you draw a graph of the equation?

If the student responds "Yes" to the second question, ask,

What will the graph look like?

Let the student describe what the graph will look like and then draw it.
Encourage the student to explain how he/she is graphing the equation. Identify the method used to graph the equation. Ask,

Why does that method work? or,
Why did you use that method?

If the student graphs the function by plotting points and connecting them
with a line, ask,

How are the points you plotted related to the equation?
Why did you connect the points with a line?
Are those the only points on the graph?
Is there a point on the graph with x-coordinate 25?
How are the graph and equation related?
Does the graph of this equation tell you anything that the equation
does not?
Could you graph this equation by any other method?

If the student identifies the y-intercept and slope in constructing the
graph, ask,

What do you mean by "slope"?
What do you mean by "y-intercept"?
How are the graph and equation related?
Could you graph this equation by any other method?

If the student uses some other method, probe his or her thinking with
questions similar to those above. If the student cannot draw the graph, ask
him/her to tell you anything else he/she can about the equation. Ask her if she
can construct a table or if she knows the slope or y-intercept of the graph.
Keep in mind that all of these questions are to be couched in a discussion for-

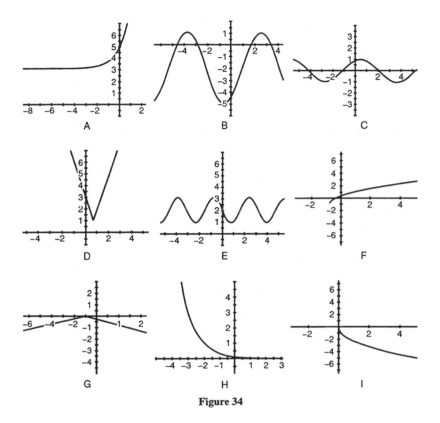

Figure 34

mat designed to indicate the student's understanding about functions.

Connecting Graphs and Equations

If the student is an advanced algebra student, consider the following tasks to see if he/she can relate the equation representing a function to its graph. Ask the student to match the following equations to the corresponding graphs shown in Figure 34. Ask the student to indicate his/her thinking process when making selections.

6. $y = -\dfrac{1}{4}|x+1|$

1. $y = \sqrt{x+2} - 1$

7. $y = 3\sin(x-1) - 2$

2. $y = -\sqrt{2x}$

8. $y = 3 - x - 2$

3. $y = \cos(x - \dfrac{\pi}{6})$

9. $y = 3x + 4$

4. $y = -\sin(2x) + 2$

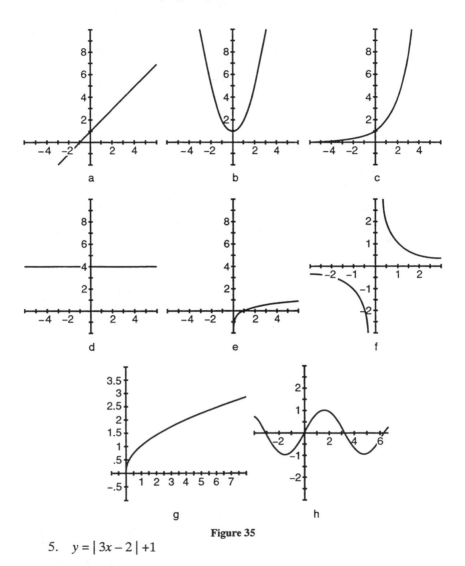

Figure 35

5. $y = |\,3x - 2\,| + 1$

Identifying Types of Functions (Graphs to Equations)
The tasks here require students to recognize the type of function represented in a given graph. Provide the students with the graphs (each on a separate card) shown in Figure 35 (You could select other graphs if you wish.). For each case, ask them what type of function is represented. If they can successfully identify the type of function, then ask them to give their best guess as to which equation represents the graph of the function. The correct equations are given in the following chart. Note for which graphs the students can identify the functions and for which ones the students seem to have difficulty identi-

Case	Type of function	Equation
a	linear	$y = x + 1$
b	quadratic	$y = x^2 + 1$
c	exponential	$y = 2^x$
d	constant (linear)	$y = 4$
e	logarithmic	$y = \log x$
f	rational	$y = \dfrac{1}{x}$ or $y = x^{-1}$
g	rational/algebraic (square root)	$y = \sqrt{x}$ or $y = (x)^{\frac{1}{2}}$
h	trigonometric (periodic)	$y = \sin x$

fying the function or creating a reasonable equation. In some cases you may need to provide guidance or help to the students.

Identifying Types of Functions (Equations to Graphs)
Based on your own ability to recognize functions, what do you consider to be the most troublesome aspect of students' ability to understand the behavior of different types of functions? Sometimes students focus only on the particular function that they are studying and they see the function as essentially a symbolic representation to be manipulated in some uncertain way. It is not likely that these students will develop an understanding about the behaviors of different functions. One of the purposes of conducting this part of the interview is to explore further students' ability to differentiate different types of functions.

Present the following equations to the student(s).

$y = xn$, n a whole number
$y = xq$, q a rational number
$y = \log a\ x$, a a natural number
$y = xz$, z a negative integer
$y = ax$, a a natural number
$y = \sin x$

Ask the students if they can identify the type of function represented, for example, polynomial, rational, exponential, trigonometric. Ask them to create a specific (simple) equation that represents the family of functions represented. For example, $y = x^2$ is an example of the first class of functions given. Then ask them to draw a graph of the specific function just created. Note the accuracy of their sketch. Determine how many graphs they can create for the different equations represented. You may need to provide some hints if the students experience difficulty with the task.

Connecting Interviewing and Teaching

An important aspect of teaching is assessing students' understanding of mathematics. A characteristic of good teaching is obtaining this information by conducting "interviews" with students throughout classroom discussions. This can be done, not by focusing on a single student for thirty minutes, but rather by listening to what students are saying and asking follow-up questions that require the students to elaborate on their responses.

Let us now revisit Ms. Lopez's class for the last time and the lesson that was presented at the beginning of the chapter (pp 5–10). What opportunities might she have had to conduct "in class" interviews? Which of the students' responses did you find the most interesting or perplexing? What follow-up questions might you have posed for the student? Note Juanita's response, "They all have to be equal?" What do you think was her understanding at that point? What questions might you have asked her? Following Ms. Lopez's subsequent response, Francis seems quite confused when she says, "What has this got to do with anything?" What do you think is the source of her frustration? How would you have responded to her?

• •

Exploration 14

Identify an exchange between one of the students and Ms. Lopez where there seems to be some confusion or misunderstanding. Write your own dialogue in which Ms. Lopez poses additional questions and the student seems to respond in a reasonable way. Consider what you think a high school student might say and how a good teacher might respond.

• •

A FINAL REFLECTION ON THE IMPORTANCE OF TEACHING FUNCTIONS

Let us return now to Reflective Problem 1 (page 3). Repeat the activity again, assigning the 100 points to the five different positions. Compare your present scoring with the one you completed at the beginning of the chapter. On which positions did your responses remain the same? For which ones did the responses change? If there were changes, to what would you attribute the change? Were there specific topics covered here that influenced your thinking

Exploration 15

Suppose you wanted to convey to your students why it is important for them to study functions. What type of activity would you create in order to convince them that the study of functions is important? With which of the five teachers' positions did your activity seem best to match? Would any of the activities or questions explored here serve the purpose for which you are designing the activity?

Exploration 16

Write a short essay on what you think is the single most important reason for teaching functions. Indicate how your teaching would reflect this reason.

In this chapter we have presented a number of situations for reflection in the hope that you will find them intriguing and that they will enable you to begin or continue to develop your own philosophy of teaching mathematics. This is an important consideration for teachers. Once various proclamations come down from professional organizations or from local school districts it is important for teachers to interpret those proclamations in light of their own situation and teaching philosophy.

In closing, here is one final reflection problem for you to consider regarding your professional development as a teacher of mathematics. You might save your response to this reflective situation for future reference in your teaching career.

Reflective Problem 6

Thumb back through the preceding pages and identify those ideas that you think represent the igges chall nge you will face in the teaching of functions.

Write a two- to three-page paper on why you see these ideas as challenging as you think about your role as a teacher of mathematics.

REFERENCES

Betz, W. (1931). *Algebra for today: Second course.* Boston: Ginn.

Breslich, E. R. (1928). Developing functional thinking in secondary school mathematics. In National Council of Teachers of Mathematics (ed.), *The third yearbook* (pp. 42–56). New York: J. J. Little and Ives.

May, K. O. & Van Engen, H. (1959). Relations and functions. In National Council of Teachers of Mathematics (ed.), The 24th Yearbook: *The growth of mathematical ideas grades K–12* (pp. 65–110). Washington, DC: National Council of Teachers of Mathematics.

National Council of Teachers of Mathematics. (1989). Curriculum and evaluation standards for school mathematics. Reston, VA: Author.

Wells, W. & Hart, W. W. (1929). *Modern second course in algebra.* Boston: D. C. Heath.

Wilson, M. R., & Shealy, B. E. (1995). Connecting students' formal and informal understanding: Experiencing functional relationships with a viewing tube. In P. House & A. Coxford (eds.), *Connecting mathematics throughout the curriculum.* Reston, VA: National Council of Teachers of Mathematics. pp. 219–24.

Designing Teaching:
The Pythagorean Theorem

INTRODUCTION

Here we consider a fundamental activity of teachers that has to be based on an integrated view of mathematics and pedagogy in order to be successful: namely, the design of teaching. As expressed in the title, a well-known topic of geometry, the Pythagorean theorem, is used for illustrating this integrative approach to student teachers. In other words, the emphasis of the paper is *less* on the Pythagorean theorem per se but *more* on general principles of a teacher's "design kit" that can be applied to other topics as well.

The design of teaching lies at the very heart of a teacher's professional activities. That is why some authors conceive of teaching as a *design profession* and correspondingly of mathematics education as a *design science* (Clark/Yinger 1987, Wittmann 1984, 1995). For this reason the paper can also be understood as an example of how to organize research and development in mathematics education along the lines of design.

Accordingly there are four sections that follow. The first section is to make the reader think about the Pythagorean theorem within the context of school by remembering personal experiences from school and university; by solving textbook problems; by looking at the treatment of the Pythagorean theorem in textbooks; and by interviewing students on what they have retained from teaching.

The second section introduces the reader to the framework of mathematical concepts behind and around this theorem and its proofs; problem contexts from which the theorem naturally arises; and research on students' psychological development in understanding and using these concepts.

The third section will demonstrate how the mathematical, heuristic, and psychological strands from the second section have to be related and tuned to one another, that is to be *integrated,* in the design of teaching units. The section contains teaching plans of introductory teaching units for the Pythagorean theorem.

The final section explains some key concepts that can be generalized from the three strands of section 2: the notion of "informal" proof; the heuristic strategy "specializing"; and the so-called operative principle.

All three principles will also be illustrated by subject matter different from the Pythagorean theorem in order to stimulate the transfer of these key concepts to other topics.

THINKING ABOUT THE PYTHAGOREAN THEOREM WITHIN THE SCHOOL CONTEXT

But neither thirty years, nor thirty centuries, affect the clearness, or the charm, of geometric truths. Such a theorem as "the square of the hypotenuse of a right-angled triangle is equal to the sum of the squares of the sides" is as dazzlingly beautiful now as it was in the days when Pythagoras first discovered it, and celebrated its advent, it is said, by sacrificing one hundred oxen—a method of doing honour to science that has always seemed to me *slightly* exaggerated and uncalled for. One can imagine oneself, even in these degenerate days, marking the epoch of some brilliant scientific discovery by inviting a convivial friend or two, to join one in a beefsteak and a bottle of wine. But *one hundred* oxen! It would produce a quite inconvenient supply of beef.

C. L. Dodgson

In any right triangle the area of the square described on its longest side (the hypotenuse) is equal to the sum of the areas of the squares described on the other two sides (the legs).

This theorem is named after the Greek philosopher Pythagoras, who died around 500 B.C. and was the spiritual leader of a kind of philosophic-religious sect (the Pythagorean brotherhood, see van der Waerden 1978). Historians are certain that the fact stated in the theorem was already known to the ancient Babylonians and Egyptians. So Pythagoras did not discover it, but might have been one of the first to give a proof.

The Pythagorean theorem enables one to compute the length of the third side of a right triangle if the lengths of the other two sides are given. In elementary geometry and its applications this situation arises very frequently when information about lengths of segments is near at hand and right triangles can easily be identified or introduced.

Because of its richness in mathematical relationships and applications, the Pythagorean theorem and its generalizations form a cornerstone of geometry. Mathematicians do not hesitate to rank the theorem among the top ten theorems of all time. Without any doubt the Pythagorean theorem is *the* outstanding theorem of school mathematics. Generations of students have learned it, willingly or unwillingly, and many of them have kept the "Pythagorean" in their minds throughout their lives as the incarnation of a mathematical theorem.

Before interacting with the views expressed in this paper it is absolutely necessary for you first to mobilize your knowledge about the Pythagorean theorem and to get some fresh firsthand experiences about the Pythagorean theorem, its teaching and, most important, about the learners. The following six explorations are intended as catalysts for "jumping in."

Hints to solutions can be found in the Appendix, but first try them yourself.

Exploration 1

Write down your own "memories" of the Pythagorean theorem both from high school and college. Do you remember how the theorem was introduced, proved, applied? Did you encounter the theorem later on? Discuss your notes with your fellow students.

Exploration 2

Figure 1 shows a cartoon from the nineteenth century. Discuss it in terms of the Pythagorean theorem: What special case is represented and how can it be proved from the two shapes?

Pythagoras

before   and   after

the discovery of his theorem

Figure 1

Exploration 3

The following three problems may serve as a test for your feeling about the appropriate use of the Pythagorean theorem.

Solve the problems, and record whether or not you used the Pythagorean theorem.

1. How long is the spatial diagonal *s* in a rectangular solid with edges *a*, *b*, *c* (see Figure 2)?

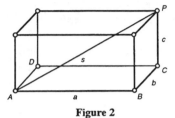

Figure 2

2. The vertices of a square and the midpoints of its sides are connected as shown in Figure 3. What part of the area is formed by the shaded figure?

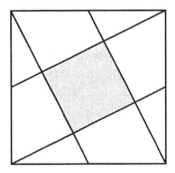

Figure 3

3. A car is jammed in a parking lot. Under which conditions is it possible for the car to move out of the lot? Represent cars by pieces of cardboard, do some tests and devise a geometric model (see Figure 4).

Figure 4

Exploration 4

Because of its prominent role in school mathematics the Pythagorean theorem provides a rich source for collecting data on what "remains" in students after they have been taught the Pythagorean theorem in school.

   The following interview form (Figure 5) may give you an idea of how to probe students' thinking about the Pythagorean theorem. The interview starts with questions that scratch only the surface of the Pythagorean theorem and from there goes on to questions that test understanding.

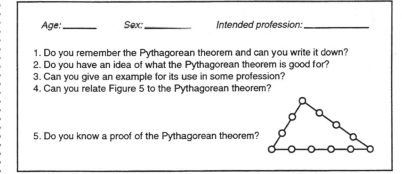

*Age:*_____   *Sex:*_____   *Intended profession:*_____

1. Do you remember the Pythagorean theorem and can you write it down?
2. Do you have an idea of what the Pythagorean theorem is good for?
3. Can you give an example for its use in some profession?
4. Can you relate Figure 5 to the Pythagorean theorem?

5. Do you know a proof of the Pythagorean theorem?

Figure 5

1. Use the above interview form (or make your own form) and interview some students from grades 9 to 12. You may also ask some students to give written responses.

2. Analyze your data. Are there recurring patterns in students' responses?

Exploration 5

Select a sample of textbooks for grades 7 to 10 and investigate if and how the Pythagorean theorem is introduced, proved, and applied. Which approach do you find most convincing? Discuss your choice with your fellow students.

Exploration 6

If you had to design a teaching unit for introducing the Pythagorean theorem on the basis of your present knowledge about the Pythagorean theorem, what basic idea would you choose and why?

UNDERSTANDING THE STRUCTURE
OF THE PYTHAGOREAN THEOREM

The design of teaching units requires a thorough understanding of the subject matter and of the psychological premises for learning it as teaching is a continuous process of mediating between the mathematical structure of the subject matter and the cognitive structures of the learners.

The best way to understand the *mathematical* structure of the Pythagorean theorem consists of examining proofs of and heuristic approaches to it. In order to get information about the *psychological* structures on which the teaching of this theorem can be based we have to look into developmental research on students' thinking about basic notions relevant in this context.

Although the mathematical, the heuristic, and the psychological strands of the Pythagorean theorem will be investigated separately in this section and their proper integration is to be attacked in the next section within the design of teaching units, relationships between them will become apparent quite naturally without taking special effort.

Different Proofs of the Pythagorean Theorem

> The main goal of all science is first to observe and then to explain phenomena. In mathematics the explanation is the proof.
>
> D. Gale

The richness of the Pythagorean theorem in conceptual relationships is clearly demonstrated by a multitude of different proofs. Lietzmann (1912) lists about 20 proofs, Loomis (1968) in his classic "The Pythagorean Proposition" even 370, most of which, however, are obtained from a few basic proofs by slight variations. It is interesting to realize that the Pythagorean theorem is rooted in all cultures. A particularly nice ethnomathematical approach based on a special decorative motif was developed by Gerdes (1988).

The following four proofs and their variations are interesting for both historic and educational reasons, and they cover also the essential approaches to the Pythagorean theorem found in textbooks. These four proofs are presented here as they are typically met in the mathematical literature. Taken as they stand they certainly cannot serve as a model for lively teaching, and the reader might wonder why they have been included here. However, the proofs display the conceptual relationships behind and around the Pythagorean theorem in the most effective way, and so analyzing and comparing them is indispensable for integrating content and pedagogy. Moreover, it will be instructive for the reader to compare the "lecture style" of this section with the process-oriented style of the next section and to see by what means life can be brought into seemingly "dead" content.

Proof 1: Euclid's proof (Euclid, Book I, § 47)

Euclid's famous *Elements of Mathematics* (1926) represents the first systematic mathematical treatise ever written. The thirteen books develop elementary geometry and arithmetic through a deductively organized sequence of theorems and definitions starting from basic concepts and axioms. The *Elements* has been the most influential mathematical textbook of all times and up to the twentieth century has also determined the teaching of geometry at school.

At the end of Book I we find the Pythagorean theorem (Proposition 47, see Figure 6):

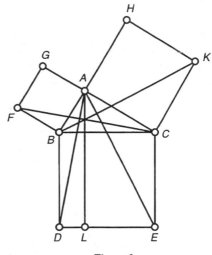

Figure 6

> In right-angled triangles the square on the side subtending the right angle is equal to the squares on the sides containing the right angle.

> Let ABC be a right-angled triangle having the angle BAC right; I say that the square on BC is equal to the squares on BA, AC.

> For let there be described on BC the square BDEC, and on BA, AC the squares GB, HC; through A let AL be drawn parallel to either BD or CE, and let AD, FC be joined. Then, since each of the angles BAC, BAG is right, it follows that with a straight line BA, and at the point A on it, the two straight lines AC, AG not lying on the same side make the adjacent angles equal to two right angles; therefore CA is in a straight line with AG.

For the same reason BA is also in a straight line with AH. And, since the angle DBC is equal to the angle FBA: for each is right: let the angle ABC be added to each; therefore the whole angle DBA is equal to the whole angle FBC.

And, since DB is equal to BC, and FB to BA, the two sides AB, BD are equal to the two sides FB, BC respectively; and the angle ABD is equal to the angle FBC; therefore the base AD is equal to the base FC, and the triangle ABD is equal to the triangle FBC.

Now the parallelogram BL is double of the triangle ABD, for they have the same base BD and are in the same parallels BD, AL.

And the square GB is double of the triangle FBC, for they again have the same base FB and are in the same parallels FB, GC. (But the doubles of equals are equal to one another.)

Therefore the parallelogram BL is also equal to the square GB.

Similarly, if AE, BK be joined, the parallelogram CL can also be proved equal to the square HC; therefore the whole square BDEC is equal to the two squares GB, HC.

And the square BDEC is described on BC, and the squares GB, HC on BA, AC. Therefore the square on the side BC is equal to the squares on the sides BA, AC.

Therefore etc.

Q.E.D.

Proof 1: Dynamic Version of Euclid's Proof*

In order to seek a more palatable way of understanding a proof whose diagram is as complicated as Euclid's proof, it is necessary first of all to understand the essence of the proof. What is Euclid trying to do? He has two squares, BAGF and ACKH, on the sides of the right triangle ABC. He wants to show that the sum of the areas of these squares is equal to square BCED, the one on the hypotenuse. How does he do that? We can reduce the number of lines considerably for the purpose of demonstrating what he is trying to show. That is, look at the sketch in Figure 7.

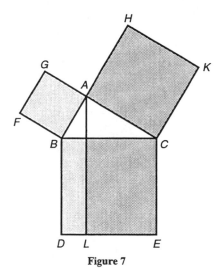

Figure 7

He is trying to demonstrate that the area of square BDEC can actually be decomposed into two pieces, one equal in area to square BAGF and the other equal in area to ACKH. He demonstrates that the two darker regions are equal in area and the two lighter regions are equal in area.

Once you have convinced yourself that the above description is an accurate rendition of Euclid's proof, then you are in a position to create a proof that has more visual appeal. One such proof involves transforming each of the small squares on the sides of the original triangle into something more dynamic than the triangles as intermediaries. We can actually imagine the original small squares being transformed progressively into several parallelograms before actually forming the shaded rectangles that compose square BCDE.

Once we have the essence of the proof, we are still left with the pedagogically interesting task of transforming something quite technical and nonintuitive into something that is dynamic and intuitive. Euclid's proof shows that the two lighter regions are equal in area by introducing an intermediary figure: Δ FBC. He shows that the two darker regions are equal in area by introducing another intermediary figure: Δ BCK. Each member of the pair of similarly shaded regions is equal to twice the area of that corresponding triangle.

Below is a description of the stages of successive transformation (see Figure 8).

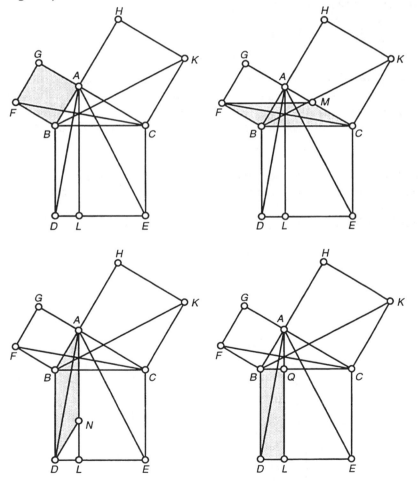

Figure 8

1. Square BAGF is sheared into parallelogram BCMF.

2. Parallelogram BCMF is rotated into parallelogram BDNA.

3. Parallelogram BDNA is sheared into rectangle BDLQ.

All three transformations preserve area. Therefore square BAGF and rectangle BDLQ have equal areas. In an analogous way square ACKH is transformed into rectangle QLEC. As a consequence the area of CBDE is equal to the sum of the areas of squares ACKH and BAGF.

It is tempting to reduce the whole argument to a film simply "showing" the equality of areas. However, this would give a distorted view of proof. A visual demonstration can certainly support, but not replace, a proof. The proof hinges upon a conceptual framework that explains *why* these transformations can be applied and *why* they lead to the properties in question.

Exploration 7

Compare proofs 1 and 1*. Which parts of proof 1 correspond to which parts of 1*? Are there details in proof 1 that are missing in proof 1*? What are the advantages and the disadvantages of the formal language of "signs" in proof 1 and the informal language of "pictures" in proof 1*?

While proofs 1 and 1* employ transformations, the following proofs 2 and 3 depend on dissecting figures and rearranging the parts in clever ways.

Proof 2: Indian Decomposition Proof
This proof comes to us from the ancient Indians. It gives a direct solution of the problem to construct a square whose area is equal to the sum of the areas of two given squares.

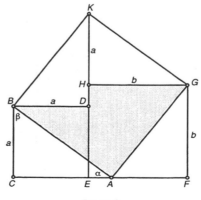

Figure 9

Construction (Figure 9):   Draw right triangle ABC with sides *a* = BC, *b* = AC, *c* = AB. Describe square CEDB on side BC, extend CA and draw square EFGH (side *b*). Extend EH such that HK = *a* and draw quadrilateral AGKB.

Statement: The sum of the areas of squares CEDB and EFGH is equal to the area of square AGKB.

Proof: Let α and β be the acute angles in the right triangle ABC. As the sum of angles in all triangles is 180° we have the basic (and frequently used!) relation α + β = 180°–90°=90°.

   By construction AF = CE + EF – CA = a + b – b = a and DK = EH + HK – ED = b + a – a = b.Therefore all triangles ABC, GAF, GKH, and KBD have sides *a,b* subtending a right angle and so are congruent. As a consequence all sides of AGKB have equal length *c* and all angles have measure α + β = 90°, that is, AGKB is a square.

   The area *c*² of AGKB is equal to the sum *a*² + *b*² as AGKB is composed of the shaded polygon and two triangles and the original squares are covered by the same polygon and two congruent triangles.

Proof 3: Geometric-Algebraic Proof

This proof relates the Pythagorean theorem to the binomical formula $(a + b)^2 = a^2 + 2ab + b^2$, another fundamental topic of school mathematics.

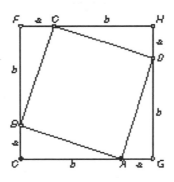

Figure 10

Construction (Figure 10):   Given lengths *a,b* we construct a square with side *a* + *b* and inscribe a quadrilateral ADCB which is a square (why?). As the area of each of the right triangles surrounding ADCB is $\frac{1}{2} \cdot ab$ we get

$$c^2 = (a + b)^2 - 4 \cdot \frac{1}{2} ab = a^2 + 2ab + b^2 - 2ab = a^2 + b^2.$$

Exploration 8

Cut a square frame (side $a + b$) and four right triangles with legs a,b out of a piece of cardboard. The triangles can be put into the frame in different ways (see Figures 11a, 11b, and 11c).

1. Derive the Pythagorean theorem from Figures 11a and 11b and also from Figures 11c and 11b without using algebra. Compare these geometric proofs with proof 3.

2. Compare Figures 11b and 11c with Figure 9 (proof 2). Can you extend Figure 10 such that both Figure 11b and Figure 11c are visible in the extended figure?

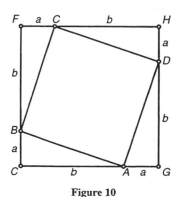

Figure 10

Figure 11

Proof 3*: Bhaskara's Proof
This proof is credited to the Hindu mathematician Bhaskara, who lived in the twelfth century, but it is much older and likely to have been known to the Chinese before the time of Christ.

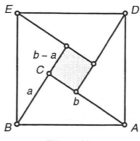

Figure 12

The "Bhaskara" Figure 12 arises from Figure 10 (proof 3) by folding the four right triangles inside the square. A careful check of lengths and angles reveals that the small quadrilateral inside is a square with side $b - a$.

Therefore $c^2 = 4 \cdot \dfrac{1}{2}\, ab + (b - a)^2 = 2ab + b^2 - 2ba + a^2 = a^2 + b^2.$

In this case there is no *immediate* purely geometric interpretation as before. However, we will come back to this problem later.

Proof 4: Similarity Proof
It is an interesting question for historians which proof might have been given by Pythagoras himself. Van der Waerden (1978) concludes from the context in which the Pythagoreans lived and worked that they might have used the self-similarity of a right triangle, that is its decomposability into two triangles similar to it. This proof runs as follows (see Figure 13):

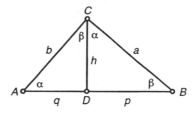

Figure 13

The altitude dropped from vertex C divides the right triangle ABC into two right triangles with angles equal to the original triangle (why?). Therefore BCD and CAD are similar to ABC. This gives the proportions

$$\frac{p}{a} = \frac{a}{c}, \frac{q}{c} = \frac{b}{c}$$

that can be transformed into

$$p = \frac{a^2}{c}, \quad q = \frac{b^2}{c}.$$

As $p + q = c$ we get $c = p + q = \dfrac{a^2}{c} + \dfrac{b^2}{c}$ and finally $c^2 = a^2 + b^2$.

Note that area doesn't play any role in this proof. The geometric basis is provided by proportions of *lengths* arising from similarity. The squares are the result of a purely algebraic manipulation of symbols standing for lengths. However, it is possible to interpret Figure 13 in terms of area. This leads us to

Proof 4*: Similarity/Area Proof

Consider Figure 13 once more. Triangles BCD and CAD are small copies of triangle ABC. Therefore the lengths of the sides of BCD and CAD can be obtained by reducing the lengths of the corresponding sides of ABC by the factor $\dfrac{a}{c}$ and respectively the factor $\dfrac{b}{c}$. So we have

$$\text{Area (BCD)} = \frac{a^2}{c^2} \cdot \text{Area (ABC)}$$

$$\text{Area (CAD)} = \frac{b^2}{c^2} \cdot \text{Area (ABC)}.$$

As the sum of the areas of BCD and CAD is equal to the area of ABC we arrive at

$$\frac{a^2}{c^2} \cdot \text{Area (ABC)} + \frac{b^2}{c^2} \cdot \text{Area (ABC)} = \text{Area (ABC)}$$

$$\left(\frac{a^2}{c^2} + \frac{b^2}{c^2}\right) \cdot \text{Area (ABC)} = \text{Area (ABC)}$$

$$\frac{a^2}{c^2} + \frac{b^2}{c^2} = 1$$

$$a^2 + b^2 = c^2.$$

Note: If a dilatation with scale factor k is applied, areas are transformed by the *square* k^2. For example, area is multiplied by 4 if lengths are doubled, and multiplied by $\dfrac{1}{4}$ (that is, divided by 4) if lengths are halved.

Exploration 9

Compare proofs 4 and 4*: in both proofs each of the two small triangles is first related to the big triangle separately. How? Then all three triangles are brought together. What is the crucial relation combining the three triangles and leading to the Pythagorean theorem in each proof? In other words: the Pythagorean theorem expresses an equality of areas. On what relationship is this equality based in each proof?

Reflective Problem 1

Analyze the proofs in this section: Where in the proof is the existence of a right angle crucial?

On which geometric or algebraic concepts is each of them based? Which geometric transformations are used? How do these affect area, length, measure of angles? Which algebraic formulae are used? Which step establishes the "equals" sign inherent in the theorem?

Evaluate the proofs: Which of them do you find easiest, which one most demanding? List them in order of increasing difficulty. Do you find them equally sound? If not, why? Which proof do you find most convincing, which one most interesting? Why? Do you prefer the algebraic or the geometric proofs?

Discuss your views with your fellow students; in particular compare your "difficulty" lists.

Heuristic Approaches to the Pythagorean Theorem

We should orientate our teaching more on problems than on theories; a theory should be taught just as far as necessary for framing a certain class of problems.

G. Prodi

From the point of view of mathematical learning the mere study of proofs is not satisfactory, as it presents mathematics as a corpse laid down for an autopsy. Certainly logical analyses have their merit for recognizing conceptual relationships. However, in order to design teaching units that stimulate students to explore, describe, explain, and apply patterns we have to go back to the source of mathematical activity, that is, to *mathematical problems* inside and outside of mathematics. It is of central importance that students are offered the opportunity to experience mathematical concepts, theorems, and techniques as *answers to problems* and as starting points for new problems. Otherwise it will be almost impossible for them to grasp the meaning of mathematics and to develop confidence in the use of it.

Our next task will be to find appropriate problems that can lead to the discovery of the Pythagorean theorem and to explanations, that is proofs, of it.

The general direction of the search is clear: we have to investigate situations in which the Pythagorean theorem is naturally used and examine whether the context is strong enough in order to "generate" the theorem and to establish a proof.

Two approaches are offered below.

Approach 1: Clairaut's Approach (Clairaut 1741, sections 16, 17)
A. C. Clairaut (1713–1765) was one of the most famous French mathematicians of the eighteenth century. He was a mathematical prodigy and wrote his first published mathematical paper on four spatial curves he discovered as a twelve-year-old. Another paper of his attracted the attention of members of the French Academy of Science, who at first couldn't believe that a sixteen-year-old had written such an ingenious and profound paper of 127 pages. By special order of the king, Clairaut was appointed a member of the Academy at the age of eighteen. It remained the only exception ever made to admit a person under twenty to the Academy.

Clairaut was also very much interested in teaching mathematics, and as he strongly objected to the formalistic style of the textbooks used at his time, including Euclid's *Elements of Mathematics,* he set out to write books on elementary geometry and algebra in a quite different style. In the preface of his *Eléments de Géometrie* (Clairaut 1743) he explains his views on learning and teaching as follows:

> Although geometry is an abstract field of knowledge, nobody can deny that the difficulties facing beginners are mostly due to how geometry is taught in elementary textbooks. The books always start from a large number of definitions, postulates, axioms and some preliminary explanations that appear to the reader as nothing but dry stuff. The theorems coming first do not direct the students' mind to the interesting aspects of geometry at all, and, moreover, they are hard to understand. As a result the beginners are bored and rejected before they have got only the slightest idea of what they are expected to learn.
>
> In order to avoid this dullness attached to geometry some authors included applications in such a way that right after the theoretical treatment of the theorems their practical use is illustrated. However, in this way only the applicability of geometry is shown without facilitating the learning of it. As any theorem precedes its applications the mind is brought into contact with meaningful situations only after having taken great pains in learning the abstract concepts.
>
> Some thoughts on the origins of geometry made me hope to avoid these unpleasant difficulties and to take students' interests seriously into account.

It occurred to me that geometry as well as other fields of study must have grown gradually; that the first steps were suggested by certain needs, and that these could hardly have been too high as it were beginners who made them for the first time. Fascinated by this idea I decided to go back to the possible places where geometric ideas might have been born and to try to develop the principles of geometry by means of a method natural enough to be accepted as possibly used by the first inventors. My only addendum was to avoid the erroneous attempts these people necessarily had to make.

Exploration 10

Compare Clairaut's view on problem-oriented teaching with statements on "Mathematics as Problem Solving" in the NCTM *Curriculum and Evaluation Standards for School Mathematics* (1989, pp. 7, 66, 75–77, 125, 137–139). What arguments are put forward in favor of problem-oriented teaching?

The problem chosen by Clairaut for introducing the Pythagorean theorem was this:

Determine the side *c* of a square whose area is the sum of the areas of two given squares with sides *a* and *b*.

In section 16 of his book he considers first the special case $a = b$ by asking how to construct a square whose area is twice the area of a given square.

The solution of this special case is fairly easy if one takes two copies of the given square, draws the diagonals, and rearranges the four triangles (see Figures 14a and b). In concrete form four congruent isosceles triangles can be cut from cardboard and arranged in two ways corresponding to Figures 14a and 14b ("square puzzle").

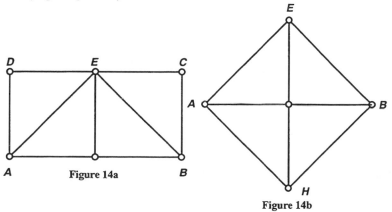

Figure 14a

Figure 14b

In section 17 of his book Clairaut addresses the general case:

How to construct a square whose area is the sum of the areas of two different given squares?

The straightforward transfer from the special to the general case (see Figure 15) is not successful, however, at least not immediately. Figure 16 does not "close."

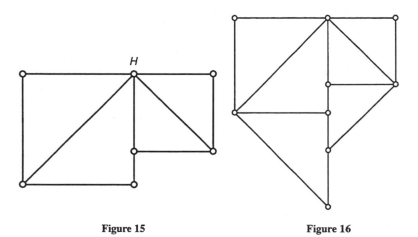

Figure 15   Figure 16

But the construction can be adapted. If one dissects Figure 16 by starting from a different point H (see Figure 17) the new Figure 18 is an "improvement."

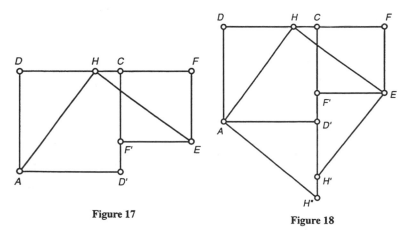

Figure 17   Figure 18

Clairaut continues: "Following this idea it is quite natural to ask if it is possible to find a point H on DF such that

1. the triangles ADH and EFH if rotated around A resp E into the positions AD'H' and EF'H' meet in H',

2. the four sides AH, HE, EH', and H'A are equal and form right angles.

It is easy to see that H is determined by DH = CF(= b) or HF = DC(= a). (See Figure 19.)

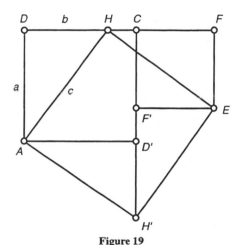

Figure 19

The problem is now solved and all that remains to do is to introduce the sides a,b,c and to state that by construction $c^2 = a^2 + b^2$. The figure is determined by the right triangle AHD and can be drawn by starting from an arbitrary right triangle AHD. Therefore $c^2 = a^2 + b^2$ holds for the sides of *any* right triangle.

Figure 19 is well known to us: It is nothing but Figure 9 of the "Indian decomposition proof" (proof 2). While this figure came out of the blue in section 1 it appears here *within the solution of a problem,* and the Pythagorean theorem gives the answer to this problem. We have in this example a good illustration of the difference between a proof embedded solely into a net of logical relationships and a proof embedded into a meaningful context.

Exploration 11

Use the software The Geometer's Sketchpad for representing Clairaut's approach in a dynamic way.

Special case: First draw figure 14a. Rotate AED around A by 270° and triangle BCE around B by −270° (or 90°). You get a combination of Figures 14a and 14b.

General case: Draw Figure 17 starting with segment DF and choose H as a (moving) point on DF. Rotate AHD around A by 270° and EFH around E by –270° (or 90°). You get Figure 18. By moving H on segment DF, points H' and H" move on line CD', and you can easily find the position of H when the figure "closes" (see Figure 19).

Approach 2: The Diagonal of a Rectangle
Our second approach starts from the following problem:

How long is the diagonal of a rectangle with sides *a* and *b*?

This problem is interesting from the mathematical point of view, but it also has a reasonable real interpretation: *A rectangular frame with sides* a, b *is to be stabilized by means of a diagonal lath. How long should the lath be (see Figure 20)?*

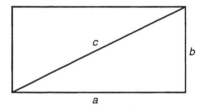

Figure 20

If the Pythagorean theorem is known the answer is obvious: $c = \sqrt{a^2 + b^2}$.

However, our aim is again to use this problem for "generating" the Pythagorean theorem.

How can we approach this problem? For example, we can compare *a*, *b*, and *c* and find that *c* is longer than both *a* and *b* and smaller than *a* + *b*. We also can draw rectangles of different shapes, measure *c*, and establish a table.

a in cm	10	8	4	8	7.5	9	•
b in cm	5	5	3	6	7.5	7.5	•
c in cm	11.2	9.4	5	10	10.6	11.7	•

But how to *calculate c*? The heuristic strategy "specializing" used by Clairaut is a reasonable strategy here, too. So let us consider first the *special case of a square* (see Figure 21).

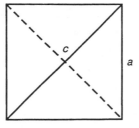

Figure 21

How is the diagonal c of a square related to its side a?

Reflective Problem 2

Think about this problem. Note that one diagonal divides the square into two congruent right triangles with hypotenuse c and altitude $c/2$. So there are two ways of calculating the area that can be used to derive the relationships $c^2 = 2a^2$ and $c = \sqrt{2 \cdot a}$.

$c^2 = 2a^2$ "cries" for a geometric interpretation. It is provided by the "square puzzle" from approach 1. Four congruent right isosceles triangles can be put together to form either one big square or two small squares (see Figures 22a and b).

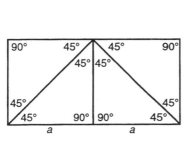

Figure 22a

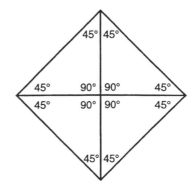

Figure 22b

As before we try to generalize this result to rectangles, that is, we look for a generalized "puzzle" establishing the Pythagorean theorem for arbitrary right triangles.

Is it possible to recombine the four halves of two congruent rectangles to make a square whose side is the diagonal of the rectangle?

Exploration 12

Cut four congruent right triangles from cardboard (see Figure 23) and think about this problem first for yourself. Can you make a square shape with these pieces?

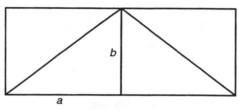

Figure 23

A first attempt leads to Figure 24, which, however, is *not* a square but only a rhombus: all sides are equal, but the angles are different—two of them are 2α and two of them are 2β.

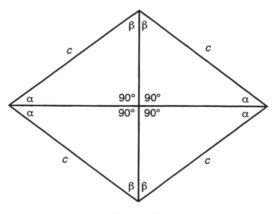

Figure 24

However, because of the basic relation $\alpha + \beta = 90°$ we could try to combine the four right triangles in a slightly different way (see Figure 25).

Does the fourth triangle really fit in? The dotted line indicates a square "hole" with side $a - b$. Because of $a - (a - b) = b$ and $b + (a - b) = a$ the gap is exactly filled indeed by the fourth triangle. So we get a square with side c but, alas, with a square hole inside (see Figure 26).

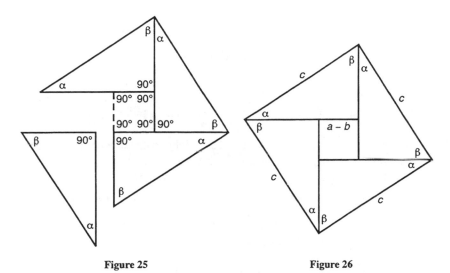

Figure 25   **Figure 26**

Nevertheless we can calculate c:

$$c^2 = 4 \cdot \frac{1}{2} ab + (a-b)^2$$

$$c^2 = 2ab + a^2 - 2ab + b^2$$

$$c^2 = a^2 + b^2$$

$$c = \sqrt{a^2 + b^2}$$

This is the formula we were looking for: The side c is expressed as a function of a and b.

Again, Figure 26 is well known to us: It is exactly Figure 12 used by Bhaskara (proof 3*). In marked contrast to that presentation, the figure appears here within the solution of a problem. So we have another illustration of the difference between a formal proof within a deductive structure and an informal proof arising from a meaningful context.

As in the special case we want to understand $c^2 = a^2 + b^2$ in purely geometric terms.

The square with side c can be formed by means of a puzzle consisting of five pieces ("Bhaskara puzzle"): four congruent rectangular pieces with sides

a, b and a square piece with side $a - b$. Can these five pieces be recombined to form a shape composed of a square with side a and a square with side b?

Exploration 13

Cut the five pieces of the "Bhaskara puzzle" from cardboard and show geometrically that $c^2 = a^2 + b^2$. You have to arrange the five pieces such that they cover the union of a square with side a and of a square with side b.

    Hint: It is not necessary (and not possible) to cover each of the two squares separately. The line separating the squares runs across the pieces of the puzzle.

Exploration 14

Reexamine the logical line in approaches 1 and 2: At what places is the assumption of right angles crucial?

Exploring Students' Understanding of Area and Similarity

Concepts are the backbone of our cognitive structures. But in everyday matters concepts are not considered as a teaching subject. Though children learn what is a chair, what is food, what is health, they are not taught the *concepts* of chair, food, health. Mathematics is no different. Children learn what is number, what are circles, what is adding, what is plotting a graph. They grasp them as *mental objects* and carry them out as *mental activities*. It is a fact that the concepts of number and circle, of adding and graphing are susceptible to more precision and clarity than those of chair, food, and health. Is this the reason why the protagonists of concept attainment prefer to teach the number concept rather than number, and, in general, concepts rather than mental objects and activities? Whatever the reason may be, it is an example of what I called the anti-didactical inversion.

Hans Freudenthal

The mathematical and heuristic structure of subject matter forms only two of the three strands that have to be twisted in the design of teaching. The third, equally important one is knowledge of the students' cognitive structures as far as they are relevant for the topic to be learned.

Our mathematical analyses have shown that the Pythagorean theorem is fundamentally related to the concepts of area and similarity. Therefore it is necessary to provide data on the psychological development of these concepts. We cannot give a systematic and coherent review of research here. Instead we concentrate on a few interesting studies that give a first orientation and—what is even more important—also provide a basis for doing similar studies. The central part of this section is "Clinical interviews on area and on doubling a square," where the reader is stimulated to do some study of his or her own.

The basic message of this paper is this: mathematical concepts are neither innate nor readily acquired through experience and teaching. Instead the learner has to reconstruct them in a continued social process where primitive and only partly effective cognitive structures that are checkered with misconceptions and errors gradually develop into more differentiated, articulated, and coordinated structures that are better and better adapted to solving problems. For teachers this message is of paramount importance. Concepts must not be presupposed as trivially available in students nor as readily transferable from teacher to student. On the contrary, the teacher must be aware that students often will misunderstand or not understand what he or she is talking about. To have a feeling for students' misconceptions, to be able to dig into students' thinking until some solid ground appears that may serve as a basis for helping the students to reconstruct their conceptual structures on a higher level, to interact with students particularly in seemingly hopeless situations— that is the supreme mark and criterion of a competent teacher.

Doubling a Square: Plato's Dialogue Meno

The Greek philosopher Plato (ca. 428–348 B.C.) is an important figure for mathematics education. Mathematics played a fundamental role in his philosophic system. Relevant for teaching and learning and therefore frequently referred to is his dialogue *Meno*, which centers around the fundamental questions of whether virtue can be taught and where knowledge comes from.

One part of this dialogue is particularly interesting as perhaps the oldest recorded lesson in mathematics. Socrates teaches, or better interviews, a boy on how to double a square (Plato 1949).

The structure of the interview is as follows:

1. A 2 × 2 square is presented and the boy is asked to find a square of double size (see Figure 27).

Figure 27

2. Although the boy predicts the area of this new square as 8 square feet, nevertheless his first suggestion is to double the sides. This leads to the 4 × 4 square (see Figure 28) that turns out to be four times as big instead of twice as big—a cognitive conflict for the boy!

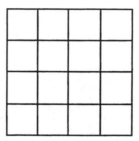

Figure 28

3. In order to correct his mistake the boy offers the 3 × 3 square (lying between the 2 × 2 and the 4 × 4 square) as the solution (see Figure 29). Again Socrates arouses a cognitive conflict by having the boy calculate its area: to his own surprise the boy finds 9 square feet instead of the expected 8!

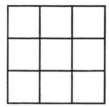

Figure 29

4. Finally, it is Socrates who returns to the 4 × 4 square (see Figure 30), introduces the diagonals and guides the boy to discover that the square formed by the diagonals has the required area of 8 square feet and therefore is the solution to the problem.

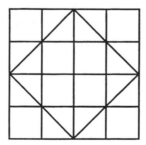

Figure 30

Clinical Interviews on Area and on Doubling a Square

Plato's dialogue is interesting in our context not only because it deals with a special case of the Pythagorean theorem, the doubling of a square, but also because it can be considered as the ancient version of a psychological method that was fully developed by the great Swiss psychologist and philosopher Jean Piaget (1896–1980) in the thirties and is now widely used in research: the "clinical interview" (see 1964, Chapter 7 and the detailed description in Ginsburg 1983, 10–14). However, there is a basic difference in the views of Plato/Socrates and Piaget as far as the origin of knowledge is concerned. These Greek philosophers believed that knowledge was already *innate* in human beings. So they compared the teacher's task to that of a midwife: with a definite goal in mind the teacher has to make the student "remember" and bring his or her knowledge to light. In sharp contrast with this view, Piaget sees knowledge not as something prefabricated inside or outside the learner but as the continued personal construction and reconstruction of the learner while interacting with and trying to adapt to the natural and social environment. Therefore the Piagetian interviewer, unlike Socrates in Plato's dialogue, is anxious *not* to guide the student to a definite end. The aim of the clinical interview is to uncover the student's authentic mental structures, not to subject him or her to any kind of "teaching." Therefore the interviewer must be open to what the student has to offer, to try as far as possible to put him- or herself in the student's place and make sense of the student's thinking—also in case of strange and contradictory answers. He or she must not be content with just listening to students, but has to stimulate them to express their mental processes with words or actions, always following their fugitive thoughts. Questions like "How do you know?" or "Why do you think so?" and cautious counterarguments for arousing cognitive conflicts like "But some other child told me . . ." are essential elements of clinical interviews. In short, the clinical interview is a kind of "mental auscultation" analogous to the physical auscultation in medical checkups. For this reason it was called *clinical*.

It is important for student teachers to realize that the clinical method is valuable not only from the psychological but also from the pedagogical point of view: in conducting clinical interviews the student teacher acquires insight into children's thinking and becomes familiar with essential habits of good teachers—introducing children into a mathematical situation with parsimonious means and with clear explanations, showing interest in what they are doing, observing them without interrupting, listening to them, accepting their intellectual level, giving them time to work and to think, stimulating their thinking by sensitive questions and hints, and so forth (Wittmann 1985).

Of course, the clinical method is also extensively used in Piaget/Inhelder/Szeminska (1964), one of the major studies of children's geometric thinking. That book contains a chapter on doubling area and volume (Chapter XIII).

The following study done by student teachers was inspired by both Plato and Piaget. It may give a feeling for both Piaget-like studies into students' thinking and the clinical interview as a research method.

The following setting was used:

Material: 16 congruent squares (3 cm × 3 cm) and 32 right triangles (half of one 3 × 3 square), made of cardboard.

Technique: Students were interviewed individually according to the following scheme:

1. Involve the student in an informal chat as a kind of warm-up.

2. Show the student the geometric forms and ask: *What different figures can you build with these?*

3. After phase 2 is finished, take four squares, form a 2 × 2 square, tell the student the following story, and conduct some "mental auscultation" on his or her understanding of area:

Imagine that this is a pasture surrounded by a fence. It is just big enough to provide grass for exactly eight cows. Now the farmer buys eight more cows and wants to fence off a pasture that is twice as big. As he likes squares, the bigger pasture should be a square as well.

Can you help the farmer and make a square of double size?

The above scheme is "half-standardized" in the sense that only some key information and questions are prescribed that have to be reproduced in all interviews and so form the common core. All other interactions depend on the student's responses.

The following two interviews with eleven-year-old Dirk and with fifteen-year-old Stefan give an impression of the wide range of students' abilities and thinking.

Dirk

1. While playing around with the forms and laying out a variety of figures Dirk explicitly states that four triangles can be arranged to make a larger triangle (see Figure 31).

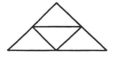

Figure 31

2. In order to solve the pasture problem Dirk adds four squares and produces Figure 32:

Figure 32

Dirk: Oh, no, that doesn't work. That gives me nine squares, but I need eight.

Next he tries to attach a triangle to a square (see Figure 33a).

When seeing that this is possible he builds Figure 33b and adds another triangle (see Figure 33c).

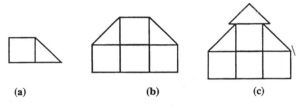

(a)   (b)   (c)

Figure 33

Dirk: Oh, no, that doesn't fit!

His next figure is Figure 34.

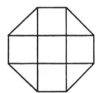

Figure 34

He counts the squares. There are only seven squares. Must all sides be equal?

Interviewer: Yes. Do you think you can do it?

Dirk's next step is Figure 35, a figure with an area equivalent to eight squares, but not a square.

Figure 35

Dirk, after thinking for a while: I could try it with triangles.
He first makes the original square (Figure 36a).
Then he supplements eight more triangles (Figure 36b).

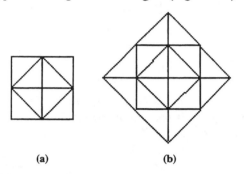

(a)   (b)

Figure 36

Dirk: I think that's it!

Interviewer: Why do you think it is twice as big as the old square?

Dirk: Inside you have the old square with eight triangles, and in addition eight new triangles.

Interviewer: How did you hit upon the idea to arrange the triangles this way?

Dirk: I saw that two triangles make a larger triangle (Figure 37) that can be added to the square.

Figure 37

Stefan

1. Stefan builds only a few figures, for example a rectangle and a "house" (Figures 38a and b).

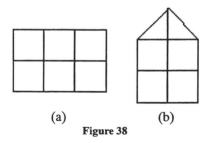

(a)   (b)

Figure 38

2. Stefan immediately lays a 3 × 3 square (Figure 39).

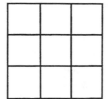

Figure 39

Interviewer: Do you think this is right for twice as many cows? Is it really double the size?

Stefan: Yes.

Interviewer: How do you know that?

Stefan: These are four [*he points to the original square*] and these are . . . five—there is room for more cows.

Interviewer: Can you also build a pasture for exactly sixteen cows?

Stefan: I do not see how.

He adds two squares to the original square (Figure 40).

Figure 40

Stefan: No. In this way I again get one more . . . It is not possible.

Interviewer: What about using these triangles?

Stefan: No. Two triangles make a square again.

Interviewer: So you think it's not possible?

Stefan: No, it's not possible. Either you have to take one square more or you must build a rectangle.

Exploration 15

Analyze Figures 33c, 34, and 35 in the interview with Dirk. How far are they away from the solution? Keep in mind that the solution has to meet two requirements: it has to be a square *and* it has to have an area of 8 unit squares.

Figure 34 can be extended to a square in two ways: 1. By adding four given triangles to the four longer sides of the octagon one gets a 3 × 3 square. 2. But compare Figure 33c with Figure 34. Obviously Dirk tries to add triangles to the *smaller* sides of the octagon. The given triangles are too big, as Dirk recognizes: What triangles would be necessary to extend the octagon to a square in this second way? How many unit squares would this second square have?

Do a similar analysis with the second interview. What is the biggest block in Stefan's thinking?

The main findings of some thirty interviews with students in the age range eleven to fifteen were the following:

1. Only a few students built first the 4 × 4 square and they were aware *at once* that it was too big, that is, the first misconception in Plato's dialogue was not observed.

2. However, almost all students arrived at the 3 × 3 square somewhere in the interview, either taking it for the solution (as did the boy in Plato's dialogue) or using it as a step toward the solution.

3. Students who flexibly operated with forms (like Dirk) had a much higher chance of finding the solution than students who were "fixed" to certain tracks (like Stefan). The variable "age" was of minor importance.

Reflective Problem 3

Form pairs or triples and conduct clinical interviews with secondary students on doubling a square by using the material and the technique described above. One of you should conduct the interview, the other one or two should act as observer(s) and take written notes or use a cassette recorder or video camera. Don't forget to change roles.

In retrospect you can also examine how far you have fulfilled the requirements for clinical interviews listed at the beginning of this subsection or in Ginsburg 1983.

• •

Exploration 16

Show secondary students the "Bhaskara puzzle" (Exploration 13) and ask them to form "different figures." If they do not hit upon the square by themselves ask them to make one.

• •

Student Conceptions and Misconceptions About Area Measure and Similarity
Piaget's research on area formed the starting point for many investigations that share the following general framework: The student is offered a series of items where figures are to be constructed and transformed in various ways—cut from paper, moved around, reflected, decomposed, rearranged, enlarged, and reduced. The student is always asked to describe, predict, and explain how area "behaves" under these transformations. The answers indicate how well he or she has attained the concept of area.

We will see in the section called "The Operative Principle" that in Piaget's theory of cognitive development the flexible use of "operations" is considered as the cornerstone of intelligent behavior in mathematics and beyond. Of course the nature of operations differs from domain to domain: in arithmetic we deal with number operations, in calculus we use transformations of functions, in combinatorics we operate with combinatorial formulae, and so forth. Nevertheless in all these fields there is an operative structure of knowledge. The following analysis of operations connected to area and similarity has therefore far-reaching importance as an instructive special case.

The present subsection tries to give an idea of research that clearly follows the Piagetian paradigm and covers the age range from eight to fifteen. The aim is just to establish a feeling for area as a concept *developing in students' minds*.

In clinical interviews with eight- to eleven-year-olds Wagman (1975) used the following tasks that directly reflect the basic properties of the concept of area: 1. Existence of unit squares, 2. Invariance under rigid motions, 3. Additivity.

Unit Area Task. The investigator presents three polygons that can be covered by unit squares and asks the child to find out how many squares are needed in each case. The necessary squares are piled beside each polygon. In the second part the child is given a large number of triangular tiles, each of which is equal to one half the square tile. The child is asked to find out how many of these triangular tiles are needed to cover the polygons.

Congruence Axiom Task. The investigator presents the child with two congruent isosceles right triangles, one blue, the other one green. The child is asked how many white triangles (of half linear dimensions) are necessary for tiling the blue triangle. After discovering the answer (4) the child is asked to guess without trying how many white triangles will be needed to tile the green triangle.

Additivity-of-Area Tasks

1. The child is presented with two polygonal regions a. with equal areas, b. with different areas. Given a set of smaller shapes the child is asked to cover each of the two polygons and to decide if they have the same or different amounts of space.

2. Polygons are decomposed and the pieces are rearranged to form another polygon. The child is asked to compare the areas.

In all these tasks the investigator encourages the child to work on the materials and to give explanations: "How do you know?" "Why do you know?" "Are you sure?"

As we shall see, these tasks test the children's ability to operate flexibly and effectively with shapes and their understanding of the concept of area.

In her study with 75 children from eight to eleven years, Wagman found that 6 of them were still in a "pre-measurement" stage, 31 showed some first understanding of area, 35 could use all properties of the area concept in simple cases, and only 4 displayed full mastery (Wagman 1975, 107).

In a study with large numbers of secondary students (twelve to fourteen years), Hart (1981, 14–16) used the following tasks, which are similar to some of Wagman's tasks and also test the mastery of the properties *invariance* and *additivity*:

1. A machine makes holes in two equal squares of tin in two different ways (see Figure 41 A, B). Students are asked to compare the amount of tin in A and B.

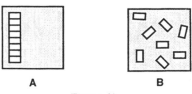

A   **B**

Figure 41

2. A square A is cut into three pieces and the pieces are arranged to make a new shape B (see Figure 42). Students are asked to compare the areas of A and B.

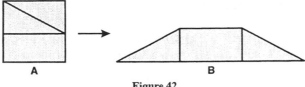

Figure 42

The results revealed that about 72 percent of the total population could successfully answer both questions. There were no major differences between the age groups.

In comparing Wagman's findings with these results we recognize a substantial increase in understanding the concept of area for the majority of students. However, the concept of area is by no means mastered by all secondary students.

In the past decade research on the development of the similarity concept has been intensified. A typical problem used in the International Studies of Mathematical Achievement in 1964 and in 1982 for eighth graders is the following one:

> On level ground, a boy 5 units tall casts a shadow 3 units long. At the same time a nearby telephone pole 45 units high casts a shadow the length of which, in the same units, is
>
> A. 24
>
> B. 27
>
> C. 30
>
> D. 60
>
> E. 75

The results are remarkable: 56 percent of the students chose the correct answer (27) at the end of the school year 1963–64, whereas only 41 percent did so at the end of the school year 1981–82.

In examining students' thinking on ratio and proportion, Hart (1981, 97–101) used a battery of items, among them the following task:

> The students are shown a 3 cm × 2 cm rectangle (Figure 43) and a base line of 5 cm (Figure 44) that is to be completed "so it is the same shape but larger" than the given rectangle.

Figure 43   **Figure 44**

This task requiring an enlargement in ratio 5:3 belongs to the highest level of difficulty. Hart (1981, 99) found that only 5 percent of the thirteen-year-olds, 9 percent of the fourteen-year-olds, and 15 percent of the fifteen-year-olds achieved this level and stated:

> Similar triangles appear early in the introduction to ratio in most secondary textbooks and children are expected to recognize when triangles are similar to each other and the properties they possess. On interview it was found that the word "similar" had little meaning for many children. In everyday language the word is used in a non-technical sense to mean "approximately the same." There was particular difficulty with the word when similar triangles or rectangles were under discussion. The test items dealing with similar figures (not triangles or rectangles) were some of the hardest on the test paper. Using ratio to share amounts between people "so that it is fair" seemed to be much easier than dealing with a comparison of two figures. In enlarging figures there is the danger of being so engrossed in the method to be used that the child ignores the fact that the resulting enlargement should be the same shape as the original. . . . The introduction of non-whole numbers into a problem does not make the question a little harder but a lot harder.

These findings are confirmed by a series of other papers (see, for example, the review by Lappan/Even 1988).

Summary

Psychological research on the concepts of area and similarity suggests the following conclusions for teaching the Pythagorean theorem:

1. A satisfactory treatment of the Pythagorean theorem can only be reached within a long-term perspective of the curriculum. For coming to grips with the concepts of congruent and similar figures as well as those of linear and area measure students need rich opportunities to operate with figures within meaningful contexts. Work has to start in the early grades with concrete materials, it has to be continued with concrete materials and drawings in the middle grades, and should gradually be extended to more symbolic settings in higher grades. It is only in this way that students can understand the properties of area and relationships between figures based on area and exploit them with mental flexibility for solving problems as well as for proving theorems.

2. The approach to the Pythagorean theorem via similarity is conceptually much more difficult for students than the approaches via area preserving dissections and recombinations of figures. Therefore similarity is not appropriate for introducing the Pythagorean theorem. However, it is a good context for taking up the Pythagorean theorem at a more advanced level. Because of the fundamental importance of the Pythagorean theorem the first encounter with this theorem should take place at the latest in grade

7 or 8. In each of the subsequent years the students should meet the theorem in ever-new contexts and with new proofs.

Exploration 17

The psychological findings on children's thinking as illustrated in the present section show that students of a given age range differ considerably in their understanding of basic concepts. The teacher is therefore confronted with the following fundamental problem: How to cope with this wide spectrum of student abilities?

List the major measures that are recommended to teachers in the *Curriculum and Evaluation Standards for School Mathematics* (NCTM 1989) for addressing this problem.

DESIGNING TEACHING UNITS ON THE PYTHAGOREAN THEOREM

The mathematical and psychological analyses and activities in the preceding sections have set the scene for attacking the central problem of this paper: the design of teaching units on the Pythagorean theorem.

From what has been said so far the following boundary conditions for designing introductory teaching units on the Pythagorean theorem should be clear:

1. Students should be faced with a *problem* that is typical for the use of the Pythagorean theorem and rich enough to derive and explain (prove) the theorem.

2. The conceptual underpinning of the unit should be as firmly rooted in students' basic knowledge as possible.

3. The setting should be as concrete as possible in order to account for different levels in the mastery of basic concepts, to stimulate students' ideas, and to facilitate checking.

It is typical for all kinds of design that the designer cannot derive his "products" by means of logical chains of arguments from a scientific basis. Instead he or she has to *invent* them, relying on his or her imagination and using the scientific basis for checks of validity, reliability, and effectiveness. Therefore the above boundary conditions do not determine one teaching unit but leave room for the designer's preferences. It is important to keep this in mind and to interpret the following units as suggestions, not as dogmatic prescriptions.

Exploration 18

Before analyzing the following teaching units resume Exploration 6 and do some brainstorming on ideas for how to introduce the Pythagorean theorem. Which mathematical or real problem situations do you think appropriate at which school level? What approaches are chosen in textbooks?

Two introductory teaching units on the Pythagorean theorem are offered below. One of them is based on ideas developed in the section on heuristic approaches (pages 15–24), the other one is taken from a Japanese source and puts strong emphasis on technology.

Approaching the Pythagorean Theorem via the Diagonal of a Rectangle

The problem of determining the diagonal in a rectangle with sides a,b ($a \geq b$) seems to be an appropriate context for introducing the Pythagorean theorem in grade 8. Students can explore this problem by first measuring diagonals, then considering the special case $a = b$, and finally trying to transfer the idea from this case to the general case. The solution and the proof depend on dissecting and recombining figures. These area-preserving operations can easily be illustrated by using two puzzles made of cardboard:

1. The "square puzzle" consisting of four semi-squares with side a.

2. The "Bhaskara puzzle" consisting of four right triangles (semi-rectangles) with legs a,b and a square of side $a - b$ (where $a > b$).

The language of puzzles is very powerful and allows for expressing proof 3 of the Pythagorean theorem in the following way that seems to be a good orientation for work with students (for other approaches to the Pythagorean theorem using puzzles see Eaves (1953), Spaulding (1974), Engle (1976), and Beamer (1989)). We take an arbitrary square piece of cardboard with side a and cut it along one of its diagonals (length c) into two isosceles right triangles (see Figure 45).

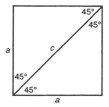

Figure 45

We repeat this process with a second congruent square piece of cardboard and arrive at four isoceles triangles with legs a and acute angles of 45° (see Figure 46). These triangles are pairwise congruent as the right angles and the legs are equal. The four pieces can be recombined to make a square with side c as the four right angles form one full angle at the midpoint and adjacent legs of lengths a fit together.

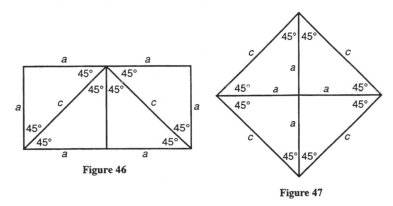

Figure 46

Figure 47

All angles at the four vertices are right angles as 45° + 45° = 90°. Figure 47 is really a square.

Obviously, the area of the square with side c is equal to the sum of the areas of two squares with side a: $c^2 = 2a^2$.

In a similar way we dissect two congruent rectangular pieces of cardboard with sides a and b ($a > b$) into four right triangles with legs a and b (Figure 48).

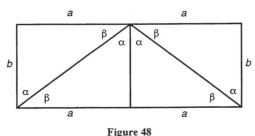

Figure 48

All four triangles are congruent as they coincide in the right angles and the legs a and b. The sum of the acute angles α and β is 90°(= 180° − 90°).

The four triangles can be recombined to make a square with a small square hole. At each corner the triangles fit perfectly as $\alpha + \beta = 90°$ (see Figure 49).

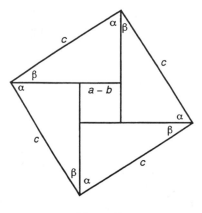

Figure 49

The square inside has four right angles and equal sides of length $a - b$. Hence it is a square.

We fill the hole with a square piece of cardboard and recombine the five pieces as in Figure 50.

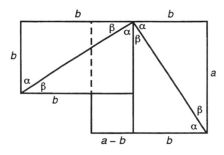

Figure 50

The resulting figure consists of two rectangles with sides a,b and a square with side $a - b$. The dotted line decomposes the figure into two quadrilaterals: As $(a - b) + b = a$, $a - (a - b) = b$ and all angles are right angles, the quadrilaterals are squares with sides a and b. Now the square with side c is composed of the same five pieces as the two squares with sides a and b. Therefore we have proved that $c^2 = a^2 + b^2$.

This description may sound a little clumsy, but it describes a procedure students can perform and comment on *orally* quite easily, and this procedure explains *why* the relationship $c^2 = a^2 + b^2$ must be true: the line of arguments is a sound proof in an informal setting centered around the solution of a problem.

It appears as instructive to round out the unit by comparing the measurements in the table with the values calculated by means of the formula. Also the heuristic use of the Pythagorean theorem should be derived from this special context: given the lengths of two sides of a right triangle the length of the third side can be calculated.

As a result we arrive at the following plan for a teaching unit. The plan is presented in a "half-standardized" way directly analogous to the scheme used in conducting clinical interviews (see pp. 25–37). The unit is divided into "episodes." At the beginning of each episode the teacher has to take the initiative. His or her crucial interventions (and only these!) are explicitly described. The further moves to be taken depend on students' ideas and therefore they have to be left open.

Teaching Plan

1. Presenting the guiding problem

Rectangles of different shapes are drawn on the blackboard (Figure 51).

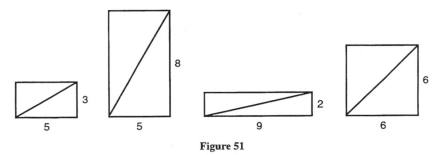

Figure 51

The teacher explains the problem of finding the length of the diagonal. As an example making a lath for stabilizing a rectangular frame is mentioned.

It is only natural that the students will also suggest measuring the diagonals. The teacher recommends drawing a variety of rectangles, measuring the diagonals, and fixing the results in a table (Figure 52).

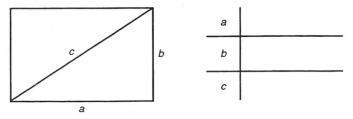

Figure 52

At the end of this episode some data are collected in a common table on the blackboard.

2.   Redefining the problem

The teacher redefines the problem as the typically mathematical problem of finding a formula for computing the diagonal c from the sides a and b. The advantage of a formula should be plausible to students.

Students are stimulated to guess what such a formula could be like. The suggested ideas are written up and tested against the values in the table.

At the end of this episode the students are informed about the steps to follow: receiving some hints from the teacher they should try to discover and prove the formula as far as possible by themselves.

3.   Specializing the problem: Diagonal of a square

Material: Congruent paper squares. As a first hint the teacher suggests studying squares as an easier special case.

Each student gets some congruent paper squares and diagonalizes them. The task is to find an arrangement of squares such that a relationship between diagonal c and side a can be deduced.

Figure 53 is almost inevitable and leads to the relationship $c^2 = 2a^2$, from which $c = \sqrt{2} \cdot a$ can be derived.

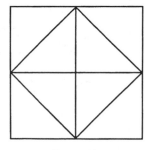

Figure 53

The episode is concluded by a guided informal proof of the relationship $c^2 = 2a^2$ based on the transformation in Figure 54.

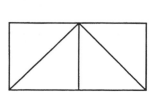
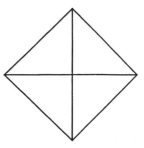

Figure 54

4. Generalizing the solution: Diagonal of a rectangle

Material: Congruent paper rectangles. The teacher suggests adapting the solution from squares to rectangles.

Each student gets two paper rectangles, diagonalizes them and tries to make a square. Students are guided to discover the Bhaskara solution and to give an informal proof of the Pythagorean theorem (Figure 55).

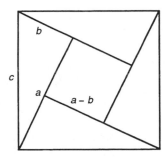

Figure 55

$$c^2 = 4 \cdot \frac{ab}{2} + (a-b)^2 = a^2 + b^2$$

$$c = \sqrt{a^2 + b^2}$$

5. Discussing the formula

The teacher informs students about the history of the Pythagorean theorem and about its importance. Students check the formula by comparing the measured values (episode 1) with the values obtained from the formula.

A Japanese Approach to the Pythagorean Theorem

The Japanese volume *Mathematics Education and Personal Computers* contains a case study on the Pythagorean theorem as an example for improving the traditional format of teaching (Okamori 1989, 155–61). Instead of treating the whole class as one body the class was split up into small groups (four or five students) according to interests, academic abilities, and social relationships. The idea was to offer students different approaches to the subject matter that might better serve their individual needs and preferences.

Each group was provided with a microcomputer that had been loaded with interactive software allowing for three different contexts to investigate and prove the Pythagorean theorem:

1. "Geometric-algebraic": The screen shows squares and dissections as presented in proofs 3 and 3* (see Figures 10 and 11a).

2. "Euclid dynamized": The screen shows a movie acccording to proof 1* (see Figure 8).

3. "Experimental": The screen shows a right triangle and the squares described on its sides. The medium-size square is dissected according to Figure 73 (see the dissection proof derived from problem 2 of Exploration 3 on page 4).

Teaching Plan

1. General information

The class is divided into small groups. Students are told that they are expected to do a geometric investigation by means of the computer. Then they receive some instructions on how to use the system and how to interact within the groups. The three contexts for approaching the theme are explained in general terms, and the groups are asked to decide for themselves which context they would like to choose.

2. Introducing the task

When the students start the program three triangles appear on the screen: an obtuse one, a right one, and an acute one. The sides of each triangle carry squares: the longest side a square colored red, the smaller sides squares colored green. The students are stimulated to discuss the relationship between the area of the red square and the sum of the areas of the green squares in all three cases. The teacher suggests drawing the squares on graph paper and estimating the area. The discussion within the groups and with the whole class should lead to the conjecture of the Pythagorean theorem for right triangles.

3. Defining the task

The groups are given the following task: Try to find out from the figures and tranformations offered by the computer program why the conjectured relationship must hold. Give a written account of your reasoning. Use the prepared worksheets.

The groups are handed out worksheets that present the essential figures and give some hints for the solution. Groups that have finished their task may switch over to another context.

Context (1): The group has to express the lengths of the relevant segments and the areas of the relevant figures by means of letters and to derive the Pythagorean theorem by means of algebraic formulae. The worksheet for this context is shown in Figure 56.

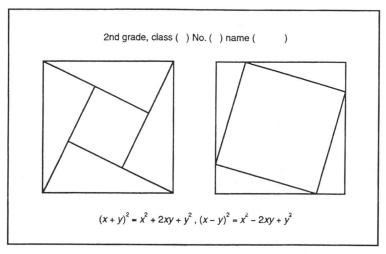

Figure 56

Context (2): The group has to describe and to explain the dynamic version of Euclid's proof (proof 1*). The worksheet for this context is shown in Figure 57.

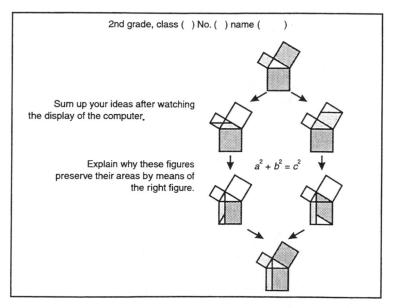

Figure 57

Context (3): Students are asked to fit the four parts of the medium-size square and the small square into the big square and to prove that the five parts fill the big square exactly. The worksheet for this context is shown in Figure 58.

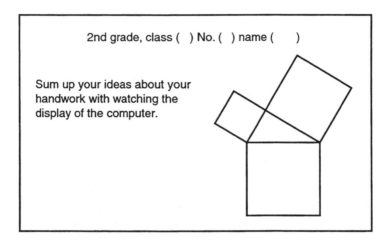

2nd grade, class ( ) No. ( ) name (   )

Sum up your ideas about your handwork with watching the display of the computer.

Figure 58

4. *Consolidation*

The results of the groups are corroborated. The teacher asks some questions that test students' understanding.

Reflective Problem 4

Compare the two teaching units. Discuss the advantages and disadvantages of

- elaborating one idea versus presenting a variety of ideas
- introducing the Pythagorean theorem in a problem context versus guiding the students quickly to a conjecture
- using concrete materials versus using dynamic pictures on a screen
- formulating a proof orally versus fixing it on a worksheet

Reflective Problem 5

Tom Apostol made a videotape called *The Theorem of Pythagoras* that is available from the NCTM. The three main ideas are:

1. Lengths of corresponding sides of similar triangles have the same ratios.
2. Shearing a triangle does not change its area.
3. If the scale for measuring distances is multiplied by a factor k, the area of a figure is multiplied by k^2.

If you have access to this videotape: analyze it in terms of the proofs discussed in this chapter. How are the conceptual relationships represented that are essential for sound proofs but cannot be replaced by pictures? In which grade would you use the videotape? How would you use it? As an introduction, as an illustration during learning, or as a summary?

REFLECTING ON THE UNITS: SOME KEY GENERALIZABLE CONCEPTS

The outlines of each of the units on the Pythagorean theorem given in the preceding section are restricted to a short description of a sequence of phases. They state what is "on" in each phase, but no information is given about how to interact with the students *within* each phase.

It might be tempting for student teachers to fill these holes with a step-by-step script promising control and a reduction of the uncertainties of teaching. This, however, would run counter to the conditions of effective teaching and learning as described in the introduction. Instead of a *straitjacket* the teacher needs a *concept* for his or her teaching, and this can be provided only by a professional tool kit consisting of appropriate general principles. By their very nature these principles go beyond individual teaching units. They ensure that present learning is rooted in past learning and oriented toward future learning, and thus they provide teaching and learning with a direction, locally and globally.

The present section will examine three general principles that are rooted in the analyses and explorations on pages 6–37 above: the notion of informal proof, heuristic strategies, and the "operative principle."

Informal Proofs

> A proof becomes a proof only after the social act of "accepting it as a proof."
> This is as true for mathematics as it is for physics, linguistics or biology. The
> evolution of commonly accepted criteria for an argument's being a proof is
> an almost untouched theme in the history of science.
>
> Y. I. Manin

A proof of a theorem is a pattern of conceptual relationships linking the statement to the premises in a logically stringent way. In an earlier section we have
met a number of proofs of the Pythagorean theorem that vary in the conceptual
relationships employed and—even more important for mathematics education—also in their representations. Some of them consist mainly of a text and
use a figure just for supporting the text. Others rely heavily upon figures and
transformations and contain only a few explaining lines. The proof aimed at in
the first teaching unit even uses pieces of cardboard, real displacements and
rearrangements of these pieces, and a comment that may be given only orally.

It is of paramount importance for appreciating new developments in the
teaching of proofs to understand that the evaluation of different types of proof
has been controversial in mathematics *and* in mathematical education over
history, particularly in the twentieth century.

For almost two thousand years Euclid's *Elements of Mathematics* domi-
nated mathematics and the teaching of it, and the notion of mathematical
proof established in this book was the celebrated peak of mathematical activity. In mathematics education, too, it was admired, emulated as far as possible, and hardly ever questioned, apart from a few outsiders (see, for example,
Clairaut 1743).

At the end of the nineteenth century the situation changed fundamentally. Mathematicians and a growing minority of mathematics teachers became
dissatisfied with the Euclidean standard for quite different reasons and initiated opposing developments. Mathematicians working in the foundations of
mathematics discovered that Euclid unexpectedly had used intuitive assumptions in his logical chains of arguments—for example, the assumption that
any line intersecting a side of a triangle also intersects at least one other
side—and they set out to establish a purported level of "absolute" rigor that
was to reduce reasoning to a manipulation of symbols and statements according to formal rules. No room was left for intuition. Hilbert's famous book,
Foundations of Geometry, became the model for the new standard that is perfectly described, for example, in MacLane (1981, 465):

> This use of deductive and axiomatic methods focusses attention on an ex-
> traordinary accomplishment of fundamental interest: the formulation of an
> exact notion of *absolute rigor.* Such a notion rests on an explicit formula-
> tion of the rules of logic and their consequential and meticulous use in de-

riving from the axioms at issue all subsequent properties, as strictly formulated in theorems. . . . Once the axioms and the rules are fully formulated, everything else is built up from them, without recourse to the outside world, or to intuition, or to experiment. . . . An absolutely rigorous proof is rarely given explicitly. Most verbal or written mathematical proofs are simply sketches which give enough detail to indicate how a full rigorous proof might be constructed. Such sketches thus serve to convey conviction—either the conviction that the result is correct or the conviction that a rigorous proof could be constructed. Because of the conviction that comes from sketchy proofs, many mathematicians think that mathematics does not need the notion of absolute rigor and that real understanding is not achieved by rigor. Nevertheless, I claim that the notion of absolute rigor is present.

In mathematics education, on the contrary, a growing number of teachers, supported by a few eminent mathematicians like F. Klein and H. Poincaré, recognized the educational inadequacy of formal systems in general and looked for more natural ("genetic") ways of teaching. Although this movement brought about very nice pieces of "informal" geometry, its influence remained quite limited as it failed to develop a global approach to the teaching of geometry comparable in consistency and systematics with the usual programs derived from Euclid. The main difficulty was to conceive a notion of an informal and at the same time sound proof, convincing the mass of teachers.

While up to the 1950s extreme forms of mathematical formalism were mitigated by the pedagogic sensitivity of many teachers who used informal proofs in their teaching, and if only as a didactic concession to their students, the movement of New Maths, influential around the world from the late fifties to the early seventies, sought to introduce mathematical standards of rigor into the classroom without any reduction (see, for example, the excellent analysis in Hanna 1983). This program eventually failed, not only because it proved impracticable, but also, and even more, because mathematical formalism and the idea of "absolute" rigor turned out to be mere fictions. Mathematicians became more and more aware that a proof is part of the social interaction of mathematicians, that is of human beings, and therefore not only the discovery but also the checking of proofs greatly depends on shared intuitions developed by working in a special field (Davis and Hersh, 1983, chap. 7). The validity of a proof does not depend on a formal presentation within a more or less axiomatic-deductive setting, and not on the written form but on the logical coherence of conceptual relationships that are not only to *convince that* the theorem is true, but also to *explain why* it is true. Informal representations of the objects in question are a legitimate means of communication and can greatly contribute to making the proof meaningful.

In a letter submitted to the working group on proof at the 7th International Congress on Mathematical Education, Québec 1992, Yuri Manin, a leading Russian mathematician, described the new view on proof very neatly:

Many working mathematicians feel that their occupation is discovery rather than invention. My mental eye sees something like a landscape; let me call it a "mathscape." I can place myself at various vantage points and change the scale of my vision; when I start looking into a new domain, I first try a bird's-eye view, then strive to see more details with better clarity. I try to adjust my perception to guess at a grand design in the chaos of small details; and afterwards plunge again into lovely tiny chaotic bits and pieces.

Any written text is a description of a part of the mathscape, blurred by the combined imperfections of vision and expression. Every period has its own social conventions, and the aesthetics of the mathematical text belong to this domain. The building blocks of a modern paper (ever since Euclid) are basically axioms, definitions, theorems and proofs, plus whatever informal explanations the author can think of.

Axioms, definitions and theorems are spots in a mathscape, local attractions and crossroads. Proofs are the roads themselves, the paths and highways. Every itinerary has its own sightseeing qualities, which may be more important than the fact that it leads from A to B.

With this metaphor, the perception of the basic goal of a proof, which is purportedly that of establishing "truth," is shifted. A proof becomes just one of many ways to increase the awareness of a mathscape. . . .

Any chain of argument is a one-dimensional path in a mathscape of infinite dimensions. Sometimes it leads to the discovery of its end-point, but as often as not we have already perceived this end-point, with all the surrounding terrain, and just did not know how to get there.

We are lucky if our route leads us through a fertile land, and if we can lure other travellers to follow us.

The consequences of this new view for mathematics education can hardly be overestimated (Wittmann/Müller 1990, 36–39). While in the past unjustified emphasis was put on the formal setting of proofs, mathematics education is now in a position to exploit the rich repertoire of informal representations without distorting the nature of proof.

In this new framework the use of puzzles in proving the Pythagorean theorem as suggested in the first teaching unit is quite natural. However, it is essential for the soundness of the proof that the decomposition of figures into parts and their rearrangement is accompanied by explanations of *why* the figures fit together in different ways and *what* this means for area. It is the task of the teacher to ensure that the necessary questions are asked and answered by the students. For this interaction with the students the teacher needs a clear understanding of what an informal proof is about.

The use of informal proofs is by no means restricted to geometry. In order to illuminate the difference between formal and informal proofs a bit more we consider the famous theorem on the infinity of primes.

Formal proof:
Let us assume that the set of prime numbers is finite: $p_1, p_2, \ldots, p_r$.
The natural number

$$n = p_1 \cdot p_2 \cdot \ldots \cdot p_r + 1$$

has a divisor p that is a prime number, that is, n is divisible by one of the numbers $p_1, \ldots, p_r$. From $p|n$ and $p \mid p_1 \cdot \ldots \cdot p_r$ we conclude that p also divides the difference $n - p_1 \cdot \ldots \cdot p_r = 1$. However, $p|1$ is a contradiction of the fact that 1 is not divisible by a prime number. Therefore our assumption was wrong.

Informal proof:
We start from the representation of natural numbers on the number line and apply the sieve of Eratosthenes (Figure 59). The number 2 as the first prime number is encircled, and all multiples of 2 are canceled as they certainly are not prime numbers. The smallest number neither encircled nor canceled is 3. The number 3 must be a prime as it is no multiple of a smaller prime. Therefore 3 is encircled and again all multiples of 3 are canceled. For the same reason as before the first number neither encircled nor canceled, namely 5, is a prime number. Thus 5 is encircled and all multiples of 5 are canceled. This procedure is iterated and yields a series 2, 3, 5, 7, 11, ... of prime numbers.

Figure 59

The infinity of prime numbers will be demonstrated if we can explain why the iterative procedure does not stop. Assume that we have arrived at a prime number p. Then p is encircled and all multiples of p are canceled. The product $n = 2 \cdot 3 \cdot 5 \cdot 7 \cdot 11 \cdot \ldots \cdot p$ of all prime numbers found so far is a common multiple of all of them. So it was canceled at every step. As no cancellation can hit adjacent numbers the number $n + 1$ has not been canceled so far. Therefore numbers must be left and the smallest of them is a new prime number.

If we compare the two proofs we see that both are based on similar conceptual relationships. In particular a product of prime numbers increased by 1 plays the crucial role in both proofs. Contrary to the formal proof that works with symbolic descriptions of numbers, the informal proof is based on a *visual* representation of numbers on the number line and on operations on it. In this way the *formal* apparatus can be reduced as some of the necessary conceptual relationships are built into this representation.

In the past concrete and visual representations of mathematical objects were almost exclusively used for the formation of concepts and for illustrating relationships. Our analyses have shown, however, that appropriate representations are powerful enough to carry sound proofs. This fact opens up to mathematics education a new approach to the teaching of proofs: instead of postponing the activity of proving to higher grades where the students are expected to be mature for some level of formal argument, informal proofs with concrete representations of numbers and geometric figures can be developed from grade 1. Students can gradually learn to express conceptual relationships more and more formally.

Exploration 19

The sequence in Figure 60 indicates a transformation of the squares described on the smaller sides of a right triangle into the square described on the hypotenuse and is sometimes offered as a "proof without words." The reader is only invited to look at the figure ("Behold!"). Of course, without any explanations the transformation is nothing but an experimental verification. Elaborate an informal proof by describing the transformations, explaining why they are possible and why area does not change. Hint: See proof 1* for comparison.

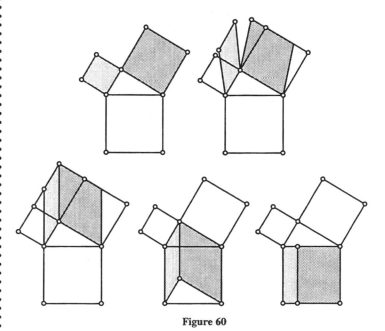

Figure 60

Exploration 20

Give two proofs of the formula $1 + 3 + \ldots + 2n - 1 = n^2$: an *informal* one based on Figure 61 and a *formal* one based on mathematical induction.

Figure 61

"Specializing"—A Fundamental Heuristic Strategy

When we study the methods for solving problems, we notice a different face of mathematics. Actually, mathematics has two aspects; it is the rigorous science of Euclid, but it is also something else. According to Euclid mathematics appears as a systematic, deductive science; but mathematics in the making appears as experimental and inductive. Both aspects are as old as mathematics itself.

G. Polya

The heart of our teaching unit, stimulating and controlling all activities, is a mathematical problem: *How long is the diagonal of a rectangle?*

The essential step in solving this problem consists of considering a special case—*How long is the diagonal of a square?*—and in generalizing the special solution. It is important to understand this approach not just as a clever trick in the context of the Pythagorean theorem but as a fundamental heuristic strategy widely used in solving mathematical problems.

We owe to G. Polya (1887–1985), the great master of mathematical discovery in this century, a basic revival of *heuristics*, the study of means and methods of problem solving (Polya 1981). Polya's work was taken up and extended by mathematics educators (Mason 1982, Brown/Walter 1983, Schoenfeld 1985) and is clearly visible in curriculum developments all over the world (for example, the items "mathematics as problem solving and as reasoning" in the NCTM Standards).

Heuristic strategies operate on two levels: They serve to generate new problems out of given ones, and they help to construct solutions to problems out of known results. The two levels, however, are inseparably intertwined: the art of problem posing and the art of problem solving are sides of one and the same medal.

Schoenfeld (1985, 76, 80–81) describes and differentiates the strategy "Specializing" (Strategy S) as follows:

> To better understand an unfamiliar problem, you may wish to exemplify the problem by various special cases. This may suggest the direction of, or perhaps the plausibility of, a solution . . . the description of Strategy S given above is merely a summary description of five closely related strategies, each with its own particular characteristics:

> Strategy S_1:   If there is an integer parameter n in a problem statement, it might be appropriate to calculate the *special cases* when $n = 1, 2, 3, 4$ (and maybe a few more). One may see a pattern that suggests an answer, which can be verified by induction. The calculations themselves may suggest the inductive mechanism.

> Strategy S_2:   One can gain insight into questions about the roots of complex algebraic expressions by choosing as *special cases* those expressions whose roots are easy to keep track (e.g., easily factored polynomials with integer roots).

> Strategy S_3:   In iterated computations or recursions, substituting the particular values of 0 (unless it causes loss of generality) and/or 1 often allows one to see patterns. Such *special cases* allow one to observe regularities that might otherwise be obscured by a morass of symbols.

> Strategy S_4:   When dealing with geometric figures, we should first examine the *special cases* that have minimal complexity. Consider regular polygons, for example; or isosceles or right or equilateral rather than "general" triangles; or semi- or quarter-circles rather than arbitrary sectors, and so forth.

> Strategy S_{5a}: For geometric arguments, convenient values for computation can often be chosen without loss of generality (e.g., setting the radius of an arbitrary circle to be 1). Such *special cases* make subsequent computations much easier..

> Strategy S_{5b}: Calculating (or when easier, approximating) values over a range of cases may suggest the nature of an extremum, which once thus "determined," may be justified in any of a variety of ways. *Special cases* of symmetric objects are often prime candidates for examination.

The heuristic pattern related to "specializing" can be described as follows:

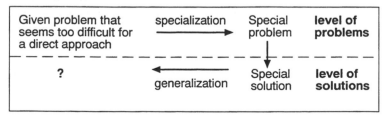

For further illustration of Strategy S_4, which obviously has been applied in our proof of the Pythagorean theorem, let us consider another example from geometry, Viviani's theorem. This theorem states that the sum of distances of an arbitrary point inside or on the boundary of an equilateral triangle from the three sides has a constant value independent of the position of P (Figures 62a–c).

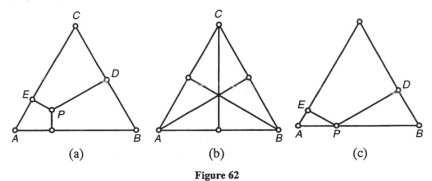

(a)   (b)   (c)

Figure 62

Students asked to measure the distances and to add them for different points will quickly conjecture this fact. As a direct proof is not near at hand a heuristic approach using Strategy S_4 seems natural.

The complexity is least if P is one of the vertices as then two of the three distances are 0 and the third distance is an altitude of the triangle. In an equilateral triangle all altitudes have equal length h (case 1, Figure 62b).

The next level of complexity (case 2) is provided by points P on one of the three sides as in this case one distance is 0 (Figure 62c).

Our goal is to show that the two other distances add up to h.

If P is the midpoint of the side the two distances are equal by way of symmetry (Figure 63).

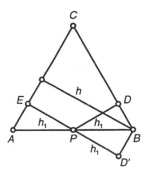

Figure 63

The reflection at line AB maps PD onto PD'. The 30° angles around P ensure that D' is on line PE. Because of the right angles at E and D resp. D' lines BD' and AC are parallel and $D'E = 2h_1$ is the distance between them. But this distance is also h. Therefore $2h_1 = h$.

This line of arguments holds also if P is an arbitrary point on a side (Figure 64).

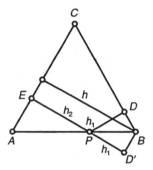

Figure 64

The general case (P inside of ABC) can be reduced to case 2 (Figure 65): A'B' is the line through P parallel to AB.

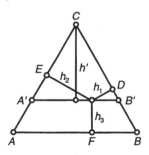

Figure 65

As the angles at A' and B' are equal to the angles at A and B, triangle A'B'C is equilateral and, according to case 2, $h_1 + h_2 = h'$ = altitude of A'B'C. Obviously h' and h_3 add up to h, the altitude of ABC. Therefore $h_1 + h_2 + h_3 = h$. (For an alternative approach following the "What if not . . .?" strategy, see Jones/ Shaw 1988.)

Our example shows that "specialization" at the level of problems and "generalization" at the level of solutions can be performed in steps: the solution of the problem for an extremely special case is step-by-step transferred to less special cases up to the general case.

The interaction between "specialization" and "generalization" is often used to generate new knowledge in the following way: One tries to generalize a problem that has been solved (possibly in different ways). If a reasonable generalization has been found one attempts to generalize the solution(s).

Pattern of generalization:

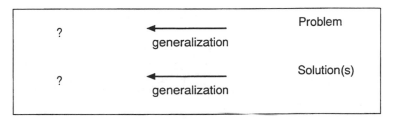

This heuristic strategy is particularly fruitful for the Pythagorean theorem and leads to the discovery of two important generalizations:

Law of cosines:
The sides a,b,c and the angles a,b,c of an arbitrary triangle are related by the following formulae:

$$a^2 + b^2 = c^2 + 2ab \cos\gamma$$
$$b^2 + c^2 = a^2 + 2bc \cos\alpha$$
$$c^2 + a^2 = b^2 + 2ca \cos\beta$$

General Pythagorean theorem:
If similar figures are described on the sides of a right triangle then the sum of the areas of the two smaller figures is equal to the area of the third figure.

For an excellent heuristic analysis of these generalizations the reader is referred to *The Art of Problem Posing* by Stephen Brown and Marion Walter (1983, 44–61, 112–16).

Exploration 21

The midpoints of the sides of an arbitrary quadrilateral are the vertices of a new quadrilateral. What do you conjecture about the shape of this midpoint-quadrilateral? How long are its sides?

Prove your conjecture by applying the strategy "specialization."

Exploration 22

Generalize Problem 2 of Exploration 3.

The Operative Principle

> It would be a great mistake, particularly in mathematics education, to neglect the role of operations and always to remain on the level of language. . . . The initial role of operations and logico-mathematical experience, far from hindering the later development of deductive thought, constitutes a necessary preparation.
>
> J. Piaget

In discovering the Pythagorean theorem and in establishing a proof as envisaged in the teaching unit, students have to "play around" with figures: squares and rectangles are dissected, the pieces are arranged in various ways, a hole is filled, and so forth.

The teacher of mathematics must be aware that this activity offers by no means just an ad hoc approach to the Pythagorean theorem but that it reflects the natural functioning of our cognitive system. According to the constructivist view of learning, knowledge neither is received from environmental sources (that is from structures considered as inherent in reality or structures offered by the teacher) nor unfolds simply from inside. Knowledge is *constructed* by the individual through interacting with the environment: the individual operates upon the environment and tries both to assimilate the environment to his or her mental structures and to accommodate the latter to the external requirements.

Let us illustrate this goal-directed "playing around" by means of some examples.

Episode 1: During a Christmas party a $1\frac{1}{2}$-year-old is sitting on the legs of his father at a table with candlelights. He gazes at a candle burning in front of him, but out of his reach. Suddenly a child on the other side of the table bends over the table and blows the candle out. The boy observes the event carefully and notes how somebody else lights the candle again. Now it is he who wants to blow the candle out: he hisses—the candle is still burning, he reinforces his hissing sound, again without success, he growls, he moves his body, first toward the candle, then aside, he hits the table with his hands and moves them around and so forth. All cognitive schemas available to him are tested, however, without success. After fifteen minutes the boy loses his interest.

Episode 2: Two twelve-year-olds play the following game of strategy (Figure 66).

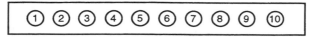

Figure 66

One of the players has red counters, the other blue ones. They take turns to fill the row from 1 to 10 successively with counters. Each player may add one or two counters of his color. The player first arriving at 10 is the winner.

First the students play more or less randomly. Then they discover that 7 is a favorable position: the player arriving at 7 can also arrive at 10: If the opponent adds 1 counter, then 2 counters lead to 10. If the opponent adds 2 counters, then 1 counter is sufficient to cover 10. By trying out different moves and by evaluating them the students discover that 4 and 1 are also favorable positions, and that the player starting the game has a winning strategy.

Episode 3: A student teacher tries to solve the following geometric problem by means of The Geometer's Sketchpad: Given lines *g*, *h*, and circle *k* construct a square *ABCD* such that *A* lies on *g*, *B* and *D* on *h*, and *C* on *k* (Figure 67).

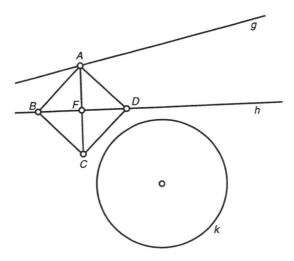

Figure 67

First she draws *g*, *h*, and *k*. Then she chooses A on *g* as a moving point. She recognizes that the choice of A determines B and D on *h* as the foot F of the perpendicular *l* dropped from A to *h* must be the midpoint of the square. The student constructs points B and C as images of A under rotations with center F and angles 90° and –90°. Next she recognizes that A is mapped to C by means of a rotation with center F and angle 180°. But C does not lie on circle k. In order to fulfill this requirement the student moves A along g, back and forth. B, C, and D move correspondingly and it is easy for her to maneuver C on k. Actually, there are two solutions in this case. When performing the movement a second time the student suddenly observes that A and C move symmetrically with respect to h (Figure 68). This leads her to the following solution of the problem: Line g is reflected on h into g'. The intersections of g' and circle k are possible positions for vertex C. Dropping the perpendicular from C to h and intersecting it with g gives the corresponding vertex A. B and D can be constructed as above.

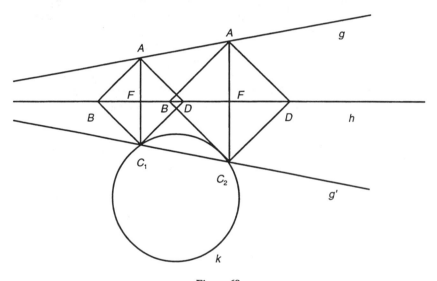

Figure 68

Each of the three episodes illustrates an important aspect of Piaget's view: The searching individual acts upon objects and observes the effects of his or her actions (episode 1). Known effects are used for anticipating paths to certain goals (episode 3). Knowledge is not a ready-made matter, but it is constructed by the individual through interaction with reality (episode 2).

This "operative" approach ranges from everyday situations to more and more abstract and complex mathematical situations, from concrete objects to symbolically represented objects, and thus it is essential for the whole mathematical curriculum.

For illustration, again a few examples.

Example 1 (Primary Level): **Addition and Subtraction**

Problem: The sum of two numbers is 32, the difference is 8. Which are the numbers?

To solve this problem the numbers are represented by counters of different colors (Figure 69).

Figure 69

Here 16 red and 16 blue counters make 32, but the difference is 0. Replacing a blue counter with a red one leads to $17 + 15 = 32$, $17 - 15 = 2$. Repeating this operation two more times gives

$$19 + 13 = 32, 19 - 13 = 6, 20 + 12 = 32, 20 - 12 = 8$$

Example 2 (Secondary Level): **Symmetric Figures**

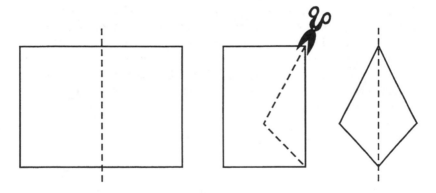

Figure 70

A rectangular piece of paper (Figure 70) is folded along a line of symmetry and cut along the dotted lines. The shaded triangle is unfolded and leads to a special quadrilateral, a kite.
    Questions:

       Which properties are imprinted into the kite by this generating process?
       Which forms can a kite have?
       How to cut in order to make all sides equally long?
       Can a square be generated in this way?

To answer these questions students will have to fold, cut, check, vary the attempts, check again until they arrive at the answers.

Example 3 (Secondary Level): **Quadratic Functions**
The graph of a quadratic function is typically derived from the standard parabola, the graph of the function $y = x^2$, by means of four basic *geometric* transformations that model *algebraic* transformations of the functions:

Algebraic transformation			Geometric transformation
$y = x^2$	into	$y = ax^2$	Affine dilatation of the standard parabola with factor a along the y-axis
$y = ax^2$	into	$y = -ax^2$	Reflection at x-axis
$y = ax^2$	into	$y = a(x - c)^2$	Translation by c along the x-axis
$y = a(x - c)^2$	into	$y = a(x - c)^2 + d$	Translation by d along the y-axis

Of course, the ideal device for studying (quadratic) functions and their graphs is the computer.

Example 4 (College): **Derivative**
The software program Supergraph developed by David Tall allows—among other interesting things—for representing graphs of functions on the screen and for pursuing the tangent on its way along the graph. The computer also fixes the slope of the tangent step by step (derivative). By observing this "movie" for various functions the student can find out how basic properties of a function are reflected in the derivative (domains of increase and decrease, maxima, minima, etc.).

The common kernel of these examples has been termed the *operative principle* and described as follows (Wittmann 1987, 9):

> To understand *objects* means to explore how they are *constructed* and how they *behave* if they are subjected to *operations* (transformations, actions, . . .).
>
> Therefore students must be stimulated in a systematic way
> (1) to explore which *operations* can be performed and how they are related with one another,
> (2) to find out which *properties* and *relationships* are *imprinted* onto the *objects* through construction,
> (3) to observe which effects properties and relationships are brought about by the operations according to the guiding question "What happens with . . ., if . . .?"

In this formulation the nature of the "objects" has deliberately been left open. Therefore the operative principle has a wide range of applications.

It is not by chance that examples 3 and 4 employ the computer. In fact the computer, if properly used, is the ideal device for making the operative principle practical.

Through the lens of the operative principle the concept of area appears in the following operative setting:

The "objects" in question are geometric figures. These figures can be changed by a great variety of "operations," for example, reflections, translations, rotations, dilatations, shearing motions, decompositions, extensions, reductions. . . .The standard questions are: *What happens* with the area of a figure *if* the figure is reflected, translated, decomposed, extended . . .?

Answers:

Area behaves   *invariant* under rigid motions,
                additive under decompositions,
                monotone under extensions,
                quadratic under dilatations and
                invariant under shearing motions.

In other words:

Congruent figures have the *same* area.
The area of a composite figure is the *sum* of the areas of its parts.
If a figure F_1 is contained in figure F_2, the area of F_1 is *not bigger than* that of F_2.
If figure F is mapped on to F' by means of a dilatation with factor k, then Area (F') = $k^2 \cdot$ Area (F).
Shearing motions do *not change* the area.

In retrospect the reader will see that the tasks for studying the development of the concept of area mentioned earlier involved exactly the above operations. The reader is perhaps surprised that the clear emphasis on psychology at the beginning of this section has given way to quite mathematical considerations. However, this change of perspective has not happened by chance. In Piaget's view cognitive *psychology*, that is, the study of the growth of knowledge in individuals, is strongly related to *epistemology*, that is, the study of the growth and structure of scientific knowledge.

The "operative" perspective on cognition, learning, and teaching is also strongly related to the notion of proof. Earlier it was stated that a proof is a logical chain of conceptual relationships. Now we can put it a little more precisely: In a proof objects are presented and introduced that are *constructed* in characteristic ways, and these objects are subjected to certain *operations* such that known effects arise. It is from these constructions and operations that the essential conceptual relationships flow on which the proof is based.

For illustration let us consider proof 2 of the Pythagorean theorem. The proof starts with constructing an appropriate figure (Figure 71). Then certain parts of the figure are analyzed whereby at some places operations appear.

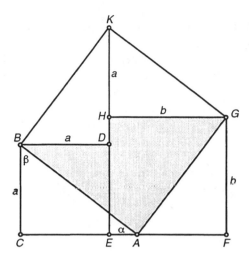

Figure 71

Objects	*Relationships imposed on the objects by construction or by operation*
Triangle ABC:	$\alpha + \beta = 90°$
Segment AF:	$AF = a$
Segment DK:	$DK = b$
Triangles ABC, GAF, GHK, KBD:	all congruent (triangle ABC can be laid upon the others)
Quadrilateral AGKB:	square
Hexagon BCFGHD (consisting of squares BCED and EFGH) and square AGKB	equidecomposable, and therefore of equal area (three parts covering the hexagon can be rearranged to cover the square)

Exploration 23

What are "objects," "operations," and "effects" in

1. the Bhaskara puzzle proof of the Pythagorean theorem (see page 12),

2. Clairaut's approach (see Figures 15 to 19 and Exploration 11),

3. the three episodes and the four examples of the present section?

Acknowledgment. The author is greatly indebted to Thomas J. Cooney for valuable suggestions in preparing and finalizing this paper and to Jerry P. Becker, Phares O'Daffer, Douglas Grouws, and Barry Shealy for critical comments on a first draft.

APPENDIX:
SOLUTIONS TO THE PROBLEMS IN
EXPLORATION 3

Problem 1

This is a typical example for using the Pythagorean theorem. First, the diagonal d of the rectangular base ABCD is calculated, $d^2 = a^2 + b^2$. Then the Pythagorean theorem is applied once more: the triangle ACP with sides c, d, and s is also right. Therefore $s^2 = d^2 + c^2 = a^2 + b^2 + c^2$, or $s = \sqrt{a^2 + b^2 + c^2}$.

Problem 2

The problem seems to call for the Pythagorean theorem, and in fact it is possible to solve it by calculating the side of the shaded square in several steps by means of the Pythagorean theorem and similarity arguments. However, the Pythagorean theorem is not necessary. The figure can be embedded into a square lattice (why?). By comparing the parts of the resulting dissection (see Figure 72) one sees that the original square is five times the area of the shaded square.

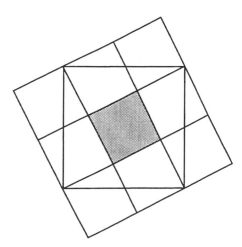

Figure 72

The new figure, however, is close to figures related to the Pythagorean theorem, for example to the figures in proof 3 and in Exploration 8. If we combine the parts of the original square in an appropriate way (see Figure 73), we touch the idea of a new dissection proof of the Pythagorean theorem: by starting from the midpoints of its sides a big square can be dissected into a small square and four congruent rectangles. The latter can be recombined to make a square whose sides are twice the length of the small square (see Figure 74).

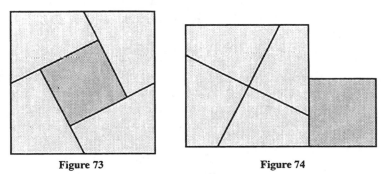

Figure 73   Figure 74

The transition from Figure 72 to Figure 74 can also be made with arbitrary squares. All one has to do is to decompose the sides of the larger square into two segments whose difference is the side of the smaller square. Check it and you have the idea of a new proof of the Pythagorean theorem! Explain Figure 75, which is used by the Japanese teaching unit mentioned earlier (worksheet (3)).

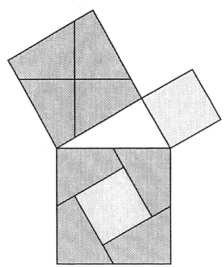

Figure 75

Problem 3

Assume that the car is 4.60m long and that the distances to the adjacent cars are 0.30m each. Then the "length" available for the car is 4.60m + 2 × 0 .3m = 5.20m. In order to move the car out of the lot without too much trouble the diagonal d of the car should be a little bit smaller than the available length 5.20m (see Figure 76).

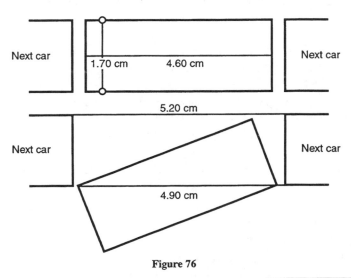

Figure 76

Application of the Pythagorean theorem leads to $d = \sqrt{(4.60)^2 + (1.70)^2}$ m $\approx$ 4.90m. 4.90m is 30 cm smaller than the available length. So it is possible to move the car out.

REFERENCES

Beamer, J. E. (1989). Using puzzles to teach the Pythagorean theorem. *Mathematics Teacher* 82 336–41.

Brown, St. I. & Walter, M. I. (1983). *The Art of Problem Posing.* Philadelphia: The Franklin Institute Press.

Clairaut, A. C. (1743). *Eléments de Géometrie.* Paris.

Clark, N. & Yinger, R. J. (1987). Teacher planning. In Calderhead, J., *Exploring Teachers' Thinking.* London: Cassell.

Davis, Ph. J. & Hersh, R. (1983). *The Mathematical Experience.* Boston: The Harvester Press.

Eaves, J. C. (1953–54). Pythagoras, his theorem and some gadgets. *Mathematics Magazine* 27, 161–67.

Engle, J. A. (1976). A two-square one-square puzzle: The Pythagorean theorem revisited. *Mathematics Teacher* 69 112–13.

Euclid (1926). The thirteen books of Euclid's *Elements,* translated from the text of Heiberg by Th. L. Heath. Cambridge: University Press.

Gerdes, P. (1988). A widespread decorative motif and the Pythagorean theorem. *For the Learning of Mathematics* 8, No. 1, 35–39.

Ginsburg, H. P. (1983). Protocol methods in research on mathematical thinking. In Ginsburg, H. P., *The Development of Mathematical Thinking.* New York: Academic Press.

Hanna, G. (1983). *Rigorous Proof in Mathematics Education.* Toronto: OISE Press.

Hart, K. M. (ed.) (1981). *Children's Understanding of Mathematics: 11 to 16.* London: John Murray.

Jones, D. L. & Shaw, K. L. (1988). Reopening the equilateral triangle problem: What happens if? *Mathematics Teacher* 81, 634–38.

Lappan, G. & Even, R. (1988). Similarity in the Middle Grades. *Arithmetic Teacher* 35, 32–35.

Lietzmann, W. (1912). *Der Pythagoreische Lehrsatz.* Leipzig/Berlin: Teubner.

Loomis, E. S. (1968). *The Pythagorean Proposition.* Washington, D.C.: NCTM.

MacLane, S. (1981). Mathematical models: A sketch for the philosophy of mathematics. *Am. Math. Monthly* 88, 462–72.

Mason, J. H. (1982). *Thinking Mathematically.* London: Addison-Wesley.

National Council of Teachers of Mathematics. (1989). *Curriculum and Evaluation Standards for School Mathematics.* Reston, VA: Author.

Okamori, H. (ed.) (1989). *Mathematics Education and Personal Computers.* Tokyo: Daiichi Shuppan.

Piaget, J., Inhelder, B. & Szeminska, A. (1964). *The Child's Conception of Geometry.* New York: Harper & Row.

Plato, *Meno,* transl. by B. Jowett with an introduction by F. H. Anderson. (1949). Indianapolis/New York: Bobbs-Merrill.

Polya, G. (1981). *Mathematical Discovery.* New York: John Wiley & Sons.

Schoenfeld, A. H. (1985). *Mathematical Problem Solving.* New York: Academic Press.

Spaulding, R. E. (1974). Pythagorean Puzzles. *Mathematics Teacher* 67, 143–146.

Wagman, H. G. (1975). The child's conception of area measure. In Rosskopf, M. F. (ed.) *Children's Mathematical Concepts.* New York: Teachers College Press.

van der Waerden (1978). *Die Pythagoreer.* Zürich: Artemis.

Wittmann, E. Ch. (1984). Teaching units as the integrating core of mathematics education. *Educational Studies in Mathematics* 15, 25–36.

———. (1984, 1985). Clinical interviews embedded in the "Philosophy of Teaching Units"—A means of developing teachers' attitudes and skills. In Christiansen, B.

(ed.) *Systematic Cooperation Between Theory and Practice in Mathematics Education,* Mini-Conference at ICME 5 Adelaide. Copenhagen: Royal Danish School of Education, Dept. of Mathematics, 18–31.

———. *(1987).* Objekte-Operationen-Wirkungen: Das operative Prinzip in der Mathematikdidaktik. *mathematik lehren* 11, 7–11.

———. (1989). The mathematical training of teachers from the point of view of education. *Journal für Mathematik-Didaktik* 10, 291–308.

———. (1995). Mathematics education as a "design science." *Educational Studies in Mathematics* 29, 355–74.

———. & Müller, G. N. (1990). When is a proof a proof? *Bull. Soc. Math. Belg.* 42, 16–42.

Analyzing Subject Matter: Fundamental Ideas of Combinatorics

*What is wanted is not the will to believe, but the will to find out,
which is the exact opposite.*

Bertrand Russell

COMBINATORICS EVERYWHERE

Combinatorics is a topic that is becoming increasingly important in the secondary school curriculum. In essence it involves different ways of counting, some of which are simple and some of which are exceedingly complex.

Reflective Problem 1

Write a page that describes what you can remember from your learning of secondary school mathematics that involves the topic of combinatorics. What kinds of problems do you remember solving? Share your description with others. In what way are your remembrances the same? Different?

As an introduction to the topic of combinatorics, consider the following dialogue, which focuses on combinatorial problems that occur in our daily lives. As you read the dialogue, think about the mathematical structure that underlies the questions being addressed.

Anna: I had a wonderful weekend. Saturday was my birthday. Look at my new necklace. It's a birthday present from my younger sister. She combined eight black and six white pearls. Isn't it beautiful?

Teacher: Tell us about your birthday. Had you invited some friends?

Anna: Of course, I had a party with my friends. We played a lot, had a good dinner, listened to music, and danced. And best of all, there was no mathematics to spoil my birthday!

Teacher: I think we all would like to hear more about your party. What exactly were you and your friends doing?

Anna: Well, my friends were supposed to come about three o'clock. At that time I had already prepared the tables. There were dishes for each guest and the cakes were ready. There were six girls and five boys—moreover, there were my parents and my two sisters and of course myself.

Teacher: When your guests arrived, did they shake hands with each other?

Anna: Not really. Two of the boys and three of the girls came together. Of course they did not shake hands with each other when they arrived.

Teacher: Okay, go on!

Anna: After all my guests had arrived my parents went to another room, leaving us alone. We all sat down at two tables. There was one table for eight persons and the other one for six persons.

Teacher: Did all the boys sit together?

Anna: Of course not. Three of the boys took places at the large table and two at the smaller one. We had three cakes, twelve pieces in each one, and I imagine that we finished them all. After that we played games in different groups. I had a lot of different games and puzzles available: Playing cards, dice, chess, nine-men-morris; games called Triangle, Mastermind, the Tower of Hanoi, and even some more. Some of the boys even tried to make big money—they filled out some Lottery forms.

Teacher: I know most of these games, but what is Triangle?

Anna: It's a kind of puzzle. It consists of several equilateral triangular tiles. The corners of each tile are colored red, blue, or green. The task is to build up geometrical forms like bigger triangles or hexagons from the triangular tiles, such that the colors of adjacent corners always are the same.

Teacher: Seems to be a nice game! What did you do in the evening?

Anna: We had dinner—just hamburgers, potato salad, and orange soda. Then we listened to music and danced. Some of my friends brought discs of their favorite groups. It was about eleven o'clock when everybody went home.

Teacher: I see you had a really enjoyable weekend. Nevertheless, I think mathematics can be detected almost everywhere. Perhaps we can derive some mathematical problems even from your birthday activities.

Exploration 1

State as many mathematical questions as you can from the above episode that you think are interesting questions. Compare your questions with those of your classmates. Make a list of the three most interesting questions that you think were created.

In real life, problems usually do not emerge in mathematical terms. Problems arise anywhere and sometimes they can be formulated—more or less precisely—mathematically. It is an essential part of mathematical competence to recognize mathematical structure in real-world happenings. The awareness of students about mathematics in their environment should be promoted by your teaching style and it should be part of the students' evaluation. Moreover, teaching experience proves that students like to deal with problems they have developed from their own experiences.

Exploration 2

Observe your environment with "mathematical eyes." Identify or create situations in which mathematics might be involved. Find patterns, arrangements, relations, numbers, geometrical forms, etc. Create your own dialogue similar to the above one.

Exploration 3

Do you know all the toys and puzzles Anna had available at her birthday party? Most of them you can buy but it is more fun to construct some of them by yourself. Identify mathematical problems that may arise when you are playing.

Exploration 4

Cut some square tiles from cardboard. Divide the top side of each tile into four congruent smaller squares and color them red, blue, green, and yellow, all squares of a tile with different colors. (See Figure 1.)

1. What is the maximum number of such tiles that can be distinguished by the arrangement of colors?
   (What does it mean to say that two tiles can (not) be distinguished?)

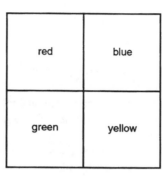

Figure 1

2. Does it make a difference if both sides of the tiles are colored?
   Consider the two cases:
   a. The coloring is such that the four squares of each tile are of the same color on both sides.
   b. Both sides are independently colored red, blue, green, and yellow.

3. Take six differently colored tiles as in #1 and try to build the following patterns. The adjacent corners of the tiles you put together must always be of the same color. (See Figure 2.)

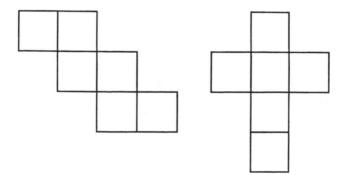

Figure 2

4. The above patterns can be folded to form a cube. Try to arrange the six tiles in such a way that at each corner of the cube adjacent colors are identical.

Exploration 5

The six faces of cubes are to be colored red, blue, green, yellow, pink, and white—each color for one face. How many differently colored cubes could be produced? Consider the same problem if the same color can be used for more than one face.

Exploration 6

1. Opposite faces of a die sum up to 7. How many different numberings of such a kind exist? Try to find differently (with respect to the arrangement of numbers) manufactured dice.

2. Five dice are piled up. You have a short glance at the top die. How could you immediately determine the sum of the numbers on the nine hidden faces?

Dealing with problems in Explorations 4–6 you should do much more than just try to solve them. More important than getting the correct answer is to observe your own solution process and to reflect on the way you approach the problems. Monitor yourself! What are you doing and why?

Here are some questions of the type you might ask yourself: How do you start the process of problem solving? Is the problem familiar to you? Did you solve similar problems before? Might a model or a drawing be helpful? Could you formulate an algebraic equation connected to the problem or do you know a formula that applies? Could you perform experiments to get additional insights, perhaps to discover regularities? Would it possibly be helpful to consider special cases? Could the problem be generalized? Could you formulate similar but maybe easier problems? (Struggling with such slightly changed problems might give you helpful ideas of how to attack the original problem.) What are the mathematical tools you are applying? Are there common features in the different problems?

Discuss these and similar questions with your fellow students. Compare their solutions to your own try to understand and to appreciate their approaches.

EXPLORING STUDENTS' THINKING

How do you understand how a student is thinking about mathematics? One way is to observe students struggling with well-chosen problems and make them explain what's going on in their minds. To take maximal advantage of the situation the observer should be able to interrogate and make the candidate clarify what he is doing and why. To be able to analyze thoroughly what happened during the problem-solving process there should be a detailed documentation of the interview. Such documentation may be done best using a video camera. Here we will present parts of the written protocols of two actual interviews.

Two students, Carola and Andrea, have been asked to solve some problems of Exploration 4 by "thinking aloud." The interviews have been transcribed to document the way these students handled the problems. Of course a transcript is only an incomplete documentation. The gestures, the handling of the manipulatives, the expressions in the students' eyes when they got a sudden insight cannot be recorded this way. Nevertheless, transcripts are excellent tools in educational research. Here the two interviews should demonstrate the quite different approaches the two students realized.

For preservice teachers it is extremely instructive to plan and to accomplish similar experiments themselves.

Interview with Carola

Carola is a thirteen-year-old eighth grader. She is high-spirited and impulsive. As a fifth grader she had solved some combinatorial problems using the multiplication principle (see Fundamental Counting Principles, p. 21) and tree diagrams.

T = Teacher   C = Carola

(The teacher gives Carola a set of ten cardboard squares and colored pencils.)

T: It is your task to mark the corners on the front side of these tiles with four different colors—red, blue, green, and yellow. I would like to know how many different-colored tiles you can create.

(Carola starts immediately to color the first square.)

C: Blue, green, yellow, red. For the next square I leave blue and rotate the remaining colors counterclockwise. So the next tile is blue, red, green, yellow. The next one is blue, yellow, red, green. (See Figure 3).

b	g	b	r	b	y
y	r	g	y	r	g

Figure 3
(Carola has fixed the position of the blue colored corner.)

Now I have all the patterns with blue in this position.

Next I will fix the position of the yellow corner and rotate the other three colors.

Yellow, green, blue, red. Then yellow, red, green, blue. (See Figure 4.)

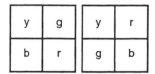

Figure 4

Oh no!

(She notices that there are two equal patterns as in Figure 5.)

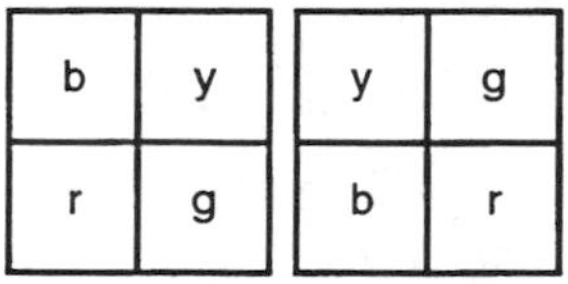

Figure 5

I think I have rotated the colors in the wrong direction.

(She alters the second one of the duplicates in Figure 5 as shown in Figure 6.)

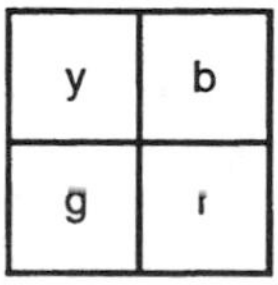

y	b
g	r

Figure 6

Next I fix red. (See Figure 7.)

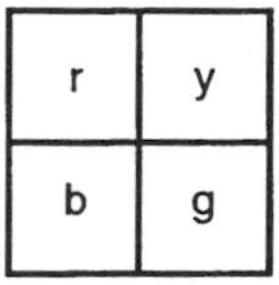

r	y
b	g

Figure 7

No! There is a new duplicate! That's stupid!

(She scratches her head and tries to find out what was wrong.)

Okay, I will make a new start.

(She cuts some new cardboard squares.)

I am going to complete what I found so far in some way.

Here I have in clockwise order red, yellow, blue, green. (See Figure 8.)

Figure 8

I got an idea! I start with this one. Then I first interchange colors at opposite corners and then at opposite edges.

The next one then is blue, yellow, green, red. (See Figure 9.)

Figure 9

Now on the basis of the first one I leave red and blue fixed. (See Figure 10.)

b	y
g	r

Figure 10

No, that's the same as before!

(In the meantime Carola has produced a lot of tiles and apparently lost control.)

Here again I have two identical tiles. That's impossible! Next I interchange yellow and red. (See Figure 11.)

b	g
r	y

Figure 11

T: How many different tiles do you have?

C: Five.

T: Do you think that's all?

C: I don't believe that. No—I know another one.

Wouldn't you tell me how many there are in total?

T: No. What do you think is the reason that some of your patterns are equal?

(As Carola's approach comes to a dead end, the teacher tries to stimulate a new start.)

C: It's because you can rotate them. I will start completely new.

(She puts away all the colored squares and cuts new ones.)

Here I have red, blue, yellow, green. (See Figure 12.)

Figure 12

(She talks as she colors the tile.)

If I keep one color fixed and change the others then I will get new patterns.

I fix green. Green, yellow, blue, red. (See Figure 13.)

Figure 13

(She marks a second tile and puts the first one on top of the new one as in Figure 14.)

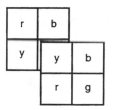

Figure 14

Now it's clear that both are different.

(Carola colors a third tile and piles them up so that they are overlapping at the green corner as in Figure 15.)

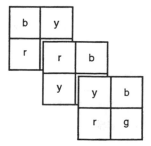

Figure 15

If I interchange blue and red at the top tile I get something new. I can do the same with the two other tiles.

(She constructs three additional tiles.)

T: Are they all different?

C: Sure!

T: How can you be sure?

(Instead of an answer Carola piles up all six tiles as in Figure 16.)

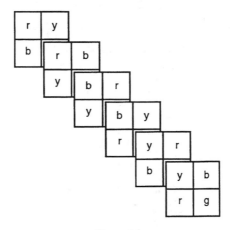

Figure 16

C: Here I have two with yellow corners while the other two colors have been swapped. It's the same with blue and red.

T: So all are different?

C: Yes?

T: Did you find all possible patterns?

C: Yes. There are just two patterns such that green and yellow are at opposite corners. The same holds for green-blue and green-red.

(She got it!)

T: That's excellent!

(Second problem.)

Now let's vary the problem. You may color the tiles on both sides, such that at each corner they have the same color on the front side as on the back side. How many patterns do you find now?

C: There cannot be more than six.

T: Why is that?

C: Well, there are only six patterns on the front side. And the back is the same.

T: That's really good. But are these six tiles all different?

C: Okay, we will see.

(She colors the back sides of the six different tiles she has assembled so far. Then she notices that two of them cannot be distinguished although they have different front sides as in Figure 17.)

b	y
g	r

y	b
r	g

Figure 17

What's that? I don't understand.

Do you mean because on both sides—what do you want?

T: Are your six tiles all different?

C: No.

(She divides the set of tiles into three pairs as in Figure 18.)

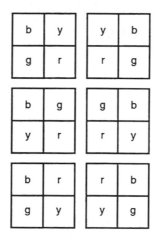

Figure 18

(With the help of the concrete colored tiles Carola could give the final argument.)
If I turn these top-side down then they are equal. So in this case there are only three different patterns.

Interview with Andrea

Andrea is a fifteen-year-old tenth grader. She has basically the same background in combinatorial mathematics as Carola, that is, she has learned to apply the multiplication principle solving simple problems. Andrea is a reflective student with the ability to argue on a high level of abstraction.

A= Andrea   T = Teacher

T: Andrea, here you have ten tiles cut out from cardboard. The top side shall be colored so that the corners are red, blue, green, and yellow. Each color must occur exactly once. How many different tiles of this kind can be assembled?

(Andrea immediately sees the essential point.)

A: I start coloring with green—or any other color—the lower left corner of each square. Because you can always rotate the square so that the color comes to this place.

(She colors the green section of three tiles and stops as in Figure 19.)

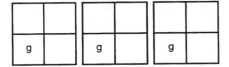

Figure 19

Next I color the opposite corner red and the remaining colors blue and yellow can be swapped (Figure 20).

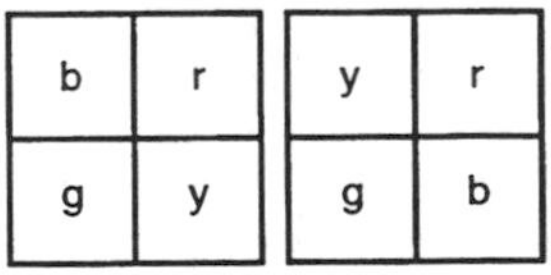

b	r		y	r
g	y		g	b

Figure 20

Then I bring blue in the opposite corner and swap red and yellow. The same with the third color.

(She does not color the tiles but writes down the six patterns on a piece of paper.)

These are all possible patterns. Any other pattern can be rotated to coincide with one of these six.

T: Excellent. *(Second problem.)* Next let us color both sides of the tiles so that each corner is the same color on the front as on the back side.

(Andrea thinks for a while. She seems to "see" the solution in her mind.)

A: I believe in this case there are fewer patterns. Let me think about it. Yes, there are only three instead of six.

T: Why is that?

(The teacher wants an argument.)

A: Is it wrong what I said? I don't know how to explain it. Look here.

(She marks two of the squares as in Figure 21.)

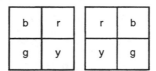

Figure 21

This one is the back side of the other one. So both cannot be distinguished.

(Again Andrea got the point.)

(She marks three pairs as in Figure 22.)

b	r		r	b
g	y		y	g

b	y		y	b
g	r		r	g

b	y		y	b
r	g		g	r

Figure 22

First we had six patterns, now only three are left over.

T: That's a very good solution. Thank you!

Exploration 7

Study thoroughly the two interviews to understand the approaches of Carola and Andrea. When did they use erroneous arguments and when did they get helpful insights and ideas? If you were to provide Carola with some hints when she experienced difficulties, what kind of hints would you give? Try to characterize Carola's and Andrea's abilities and their mathematical styles.

Exploration 8

Use the same tasks and interview several students. Analyze and compare the different approaches the students use. Are their approaches similar to or different from those of Carola or Andrea?

Exploration 9

Construct other appropriate tasks, share them with your fellow students, and select the best activities to conduct further interviews.

Exploration 10

Create and solve variations of Carola's and Andrea's problems. For example: How many patterns can be distinguished if front and back sides of the squares are colored independently? What about cutting and coloring rectangles instead of squares?

Exploration 11

Write an essay on the value of interviews and what you can learn about students' thinking as a result of conducting interviews.

COMBINATORICS AND SCHOOL MATHEMATICS

Before reading this section, consider the following problems.

Reflective Problem 2

Consider the following problems:

1. Alfredo has three pairs of pants and six shirts. How many combinations of outfits does he have?
2. In how many ways can you arrange a round table for three men and three women if you want males to be sitting next to females?

3. How many possibilities are there to choose 6 of 44 lottery numbers?

4. To represent an integer in the programming language PASCAL, 16 binary positions (two bytes) are made available by the computer. One position is used to define the sign of the integer. What range of integers can be represented in this way?

To what extent did your study of combinatorics involve these kinds of problems? With which one of these four problems are you most familiar? Have you ever encountered these types of problems in contexts outside of a school setting?

Reflective Problem 3

Consider the following two positions regarding the importance of teaching combinatorics in school mathematics.

Margo: Combinatorics is an important topic because it involves practical problems that involve counting. It leads into discrete mathematics, which is a very important topic.

Zell: Baloney. The most important thing we can do for students is get them ready for calculus. Combinatorics has little or nothing to do with calculus. It is a waste of time.

With whom do you agree and why? Compare your position and rationale with those of a classmate.

Combinatorics deals with finite sets and is a central part in the wide field of discrete mathematics. Discrete mathematics problems may roughly be categorized corresponding to three types of questions: How many elements exist in a certain set? Are there any elements at all? What element would give an optimal solution to a particular problem?

Corresponding to these questions we distinguish three types of problems in discrete mathematics: counting problems, existence problems, and optimization problems. Let us consider one problem of each type:

1. Anna has a combination padlock with three dials ranging from 0 to 9. She remembers the first digit 6 to open the lock but forgot the second and third digit. How many positions must she check in the worst possible case to open the lock?

2. Figure 23 is the well-known 15 puzzle (or Boss puzzle).

3	7	12	5
14	11	10	1
2	15		9
8	4	6	13

Figure 23

You can change the arrangement of numbers interchanging the empty field with one of its neighbors.

Among the arrangements you can produce in this way is the one in Figure 24.

1	2	3	4
5	6	7	8
9	10	11	12
13	14	15	

Figure 24

3.   Find the shortest way from *A*-town to *Z*-town in Figure 25. (Numbers in the map indicate distances.)

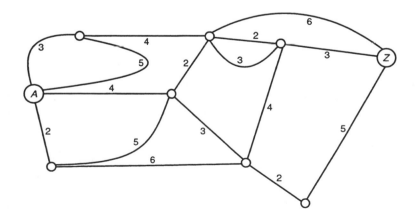

Figure 25

This section will concentrate on mathematical and pedagogical issues related to combinatorial counting, that is, to the first of the above questions. It provides a variety of techniques to determine the number of elements of a finite set when an exhaustive enumeration is not possible (or is too boring).

Counting is at the heart of mathematics and therefore combinatorial problems have arisen almost everywhere in mathematics since ancient times. Combinatorics may be considered as an established part of mathematics since the seventeenth century, when such eminent mathematicians as B. Pascal, G. E. Leibniz, A. de Moivre, and J. Bernoulli systematically studied combinatorial problems. It was Leibniz who first used the name *ars combinatoria*. (For earlier testimonies of combinatorial techniques in mathematics see Biggs, 1979, and David, 1962.)

Counting problems often arose (and arise) in the context of mathematical puzzles and entertainments. A large part of the terminology in combinatorial mathematics refers to this origin. There is an officer problem (proposed by L. Euler, 1779), the problem of schoolgirls (proposed by T. P. Kirkman, 1892), the problem of the bridges of Koenigsberg (solved by L. Euler, 1736), the problem of the Tower of Hanoi (an invention of E. Lucas, 1883), the chessboard problem of the eight nonattacking queens (enunciated by F. Nauck, 1850), etc. So the "play" feature of mathematics is especially present in combinatorics. At the same time combinatorics is a fast-growing area with serious applications in many fields. A major reason for its rapid growth is its wealth of modern applications, to computer science, communications, transportation, genetics, experimental design, scheduling, and so on (see Roberts, 1984). Even some of the above-mentioned puzzle problems gained practical importance as they were connected to modern applications. The famous officer problem, for example (at the end of this section), is strongly related both to the design of statistical experiments and to the foundations of finite geometries. Many questions arising in the context of this problem have only recently been solved or are still the object of intensive research.

Exploration 12

Find several books that discuss combinatorics and determine the extent to which the books address the kinds of problems suggested in the previous paragraph.

In traditional curricula only little attention has been paid to combinatorics, perhaps for the following two reasons.

1. In contrast to subjects like algebra, geometry, or calculus, there is no systematic theory that provides standard solutions to a wide range of prob-

lems. If your students have to solve a quadratic equation or if they have to determine the extreme values of a differentiable function, you and (hopefully) your students know the conventional path to the solution. There are even computer programs that solve almost all exercise problems in algebra or calculus (for example, Derive, Maple, and Mathematica) and even some calculators have the power to do this job. The situation is quite different in combinatorial mathematics. Typically for combinatorial problems there are no prefabricated solutions available. Instead the use of appropriate tools calls for creativity and intuition. For this reason—in contrast to the usual curriculum—combinatorial problems are frequently discussed in mathematical clubs and used in contests. The teacher dealing with combinatorial problems in the classroom may find himself or herself in an unusual—perhaps uncomfortable—position. A strong theoretical background does not provide standard solutions to combinatorial problems. So the teacher has to struggle with these problems in essentially the same way as his students. To handle this situation, the teacher needs general experience in solving mathematical problems, knowledge of heuristic strategies, and familiarity with fundamental combinatorial principles. This peculiarity might offer a pedagogical opportunity: to give up an authoritative style of teaching and to practice teamwork in the classroom in such a way that the students are respected partners in the process of problem solving. The teacher can no longer be the source of all knowledge. He or she should be able to say "I don't know." Some teachers may find this role threatening because they feel it could undermine their authority. In fact the reverse is true: Students have a good feeling for real competence. They do not expect the teacher to have an answer at hand for every question. Their respect and their interest will grow if the teacher allows them to make genuine contributions to the progress of the class.

2. As combinatorial problems frequently appear as mathematical puzzles, the practical importance of combinatorics often is not fully recognized. Thus, combinatorics has the reputation of recreational mathematics. Many teachers have a repertoire of combinatorial problems that they use as brain teasers at special occasions—at the end of a school year or when they are substituting for the regular teacher. But even combinatorial problems presented in the form of mathematical puzzles involve the same ideas as serious applications. Indeed, real-life applications comprising combinatorial issues are usually rather complex, so an interesting puzzle might be a good motivation to study combinatorial concepts at school.

During the past decade a certain amount of combinatorics became part of the mathematical curriculum because of its importance in calculating elementary probabilities. But independent of its role in courses on probability and statistics, there are a number of good reasons to study the power of combinatorics as an integral part of the mathematical curriculum (see Kapur, 1970):

1. Since combinatorics does not depend on calculus, its problems can be taken up at an early stage in the school curriculum. There are motivating and challenging problems for all grades—from K to 12—and for all levels of ability.

2. Combinatorial problems can be used for a wide range of activities in accordance with the NCTM *Standards*: to educate students in concepts of enumeration, to practice problem-solving strategies, to communicate and reason mathematically, to make reasonable use of computers and calculators, to deal with questions of existence and optimization, and to make important mathematical connections.

3. Many problems encourage students to use a computer. Students can learn to appreciate the power and limitations of mathematical thinking as well as the power and limitations of computers and calculators.

4. Combinatorics can help to develop fundamental concepts and notions of mathematics like mapping, equivalence classes, and isomorphisms.

5. Many combinatorial problems and their applications have emerged only recently. There are many unsolved problems that can be easily stated. Thus the need for creation of new mathematics can be discussed with students.

6. Combinatorial problems occur in almost all fields of mathematics. Moreover, there is a wide range of applications to physics, chemistry, biology, social sciences, engineering, computer science, communications, and business.

7. Due to the availability of powerful computers, discrete methods in mathematics are growing in importance. Combinatorics is an essential and indispensable part of discrete mathematics.

Moreover, many combinatorial problems have a rich mathematical structure which allows one to construct local theories around these problems. This gives students a realistic opportunity to develop mathematics as a professional mathematician does: asking questions, making mathematical experiments, posing conjectures, developing suitable notions and models, proving theorems, and generalizing questions and concepts. Such activities can help the student to avoid or to overcome common misconceptions about the nature of mathematics. She or he may experience that mathematics is an open man-made universe. *Doing* mathematics this way clearly supports the "New Goals for Students" as they are formulated in the NCTM *Standards* (1989): learning to value mathematics, becoming confident in one's own ability, becoming a mathematical problem solver, learning to communicate mathematically, learning to reason mathematically.

You may ask, "Where is the place for combinatorial mathematics in an already overloaded curriculum, and what shall we give up if we include combinatorics?" This question is indeed crucial and there are no definitive answers. But clearly we don't need additional courses on combinatorial mathematics.

Combinatorial questions arise everywhere in the mathematical curriculum: in elementary mathematics as well as in algebra, geometry, calculus, and probability. It is up to the competent teacher to decide whether and to what degree it is appropriate to consider such problems in the classroom. However, it is certainly important that a thorough study of paradigmatic combinatorial problems and projects takes place repeatedly in the school mathematics curriculum.

In 1779, Euler expressed the officer problem for 6 × 6 officers as follows:

Is it possible to arrange 36 officers, each having one of six different ranks and belonging to one of six different regiments, in a square formation of six by six, so that each row and each column contains just one officer of each rank and just one from each regiment?

Euler conjectured that the answer is no, and this was proved by G. Tarry 121 years later. Moreover Euler made the conjecture that the analog problems for formations of order 10 × 10, 14 × 14, etc., were all unsolvable. This conjecture stood firm until it was disproved in 1960 by R. C. Bose, E. T. Parker, and S.S. Shrikhande.

Exploration 13

1. Try to solve the officer problem for $n \times n$ formations where $n = 2, 3, 4, 5$.

2. Identify books that discuss the officer problem. In what contexts is the problem presented?

Exploration 14

The following problems were taken from textbooks for middle school and secondary school students. Solve the problems and record the means by which you solved them.

1. Telephone area codes consist of three digits. The first digit must be chosen from 2 to 9. The second digit must be 0 or 1. The third digit cannot be 0. How many area codes are possible?

2. Combination locks have 36 numbers used in three-number combinations. How many different numbers are there? (Assume that the same number cannot be used twice in a row.)

3. Suppose points are arranged in a plane so that no three of them are collinear.

a. Find the number of segments that can be drawn using the given number of points as endpoints. Record answers in a table.

b. How many segments can be drawn using eight points?

c. Write an expression that gives the number of segments that can be drawn using *n* points.

Compare your solution strategies with those of your classmates and address the following questions:

1. To what extent did people use the same or different strategies to solve the problems?

2. To what extent did you have to rely on your own creativity rather than recall a particular formula to solve the problem?

Exploration 15

Describe what you consider to be the role of the teacher in helping students to learn how to solve problems like the ones above.

Exploration 16

Take one or two of the problems and give them to high school students or to friends who are not mathematics majors. Notice how they try to solve the problems. Are their solution methods similar to yours? Describe their approaches.

FUNDAMENTAL COUNTING PRINCIPLES

In this section we will study some simple but basic ideas of combinatorial mathematics which we call "fundamental counting principles" because each one of them has a wide range of applicability. Almost any enumeration problem—at least on the level of school mathematics—can be solved by skillful application of these principles.

Reflective Problem 4

Mrs. Thompson, a junior high school mathematics teacher, has given her seventh graders four problems to practice fundamental counting principles. As homework every student has to choose one of the problems and work on it.

The next day before discussing the homework Mrs. Thompson confronts her students with a different problem: "In our class there are seventeen students. What do you think, how many possibilities are there to choose one problem for each of you?"

There is some murmur. After a while Mara speaks.

Mara: I had four possibilities to select my problem. The same is true for Tom, for Carol, and for everybody in our class. So there is a total of $17 \cdot 4 = 68$ possibilities for the seventeen of us to make our choices.

Teacher: Do the others of you agree or are there different opinions?

There is some nodding in agreement to Mara's answer. Fred seems to disagree.

Fred: I think we have to multiply by 4 for every student. So there are 4^{17} ways for us to select the problems. I just figured out using my calculator that this number equals 17,179,869,184.

Wow, that's about three times the number of all people living on earth!

Don: I found an even different solution. Any of the seventeen of us can get the first problem, the same way anyone can get the second or the third or the fourth problem. So there are —oh help me, there are either $17 \cdot 4$ or $17 \cdot 17 \cdot 17 \cdot 17$ possibilities. The correct answer must be 68 or 83,521. Maybe we can test it. I think Mara is right—68 is the solution.

Teacher: So it's 68 or 83,521 or 17,179,869,184—that's quite a difference. What do you think, who is right?

How should the teacher react in this situation to help her students?

Exploration 17

Try to solve the following problems. Identify one or more key ideas in each of your solutions. Are there some ideas or techniques that are helpful for solving several of the problems? Write down such ideas that may be useful beyond the special problem.

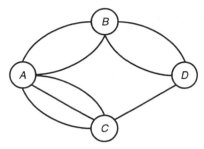

Figure 26

1. What is the number of different ways from which you can select to go from A-town to D-town in Figure 26? (It is not allowed to return to A from B or C.)

2. If you write down all numbers from 1 to 999, how often would you write the digit 5?

3. Find the number of regions into which a plane is divided by *n* straight lines if every pair of lines intersect, but no three lines meet at a common point. How many of these regions are finely bounded?

4. How many integers between 1 and 1,000,000 are palindromes, that is, read the same from left to right as from right to left? (For example: 30703.)

5. How many integers between 1 and 1000 contain the digit 9?

Return to these problems after you have studied this section and compare your own collection of important ideas to the list of fundamental counting principles as presented here.

The analysis of many examples like those above led us to the following list of principles. One or even several of the ideas assigned by these principles can be identified in almost all enumeration problems.

Fundamental counting principles:
> The principle of indirect counting
> The addition principle
> The multiplication principle
> The principle of inclusion and exclusion
> The shepherd principle
> The Fubini principle
> The recurrence principle.

A short description together with a simple example shall illustrate the idea behind each of these principles.

The Principle of Indirect Counting

If there are two finite sets A and B and a one-to-one (bijective) mapping $f: A \longrightarrow B$ then A and B have the same number of elements. So the order of A can be determined counting B instead of A.

The fact that two finite sets are representatives for the same number if there is a one-to-one mapping is basic for the concept of natural numbers. The principle is often used unconsciously when the one-to-one correspondence is obvious. For example, to find out how many people came to a concert one may count the number of sold tickets. It is less obvious that the number of subsets of an n-set is the same as the number of 0,1-strings of length n which can easily be counted.

As an example let us consider a set A consisting of three elements:

$$A = \{a_1, a_2, a_3\}.$$

Subsets of A	0,1-strings of length 3
$\emptyset$	0 0 0
$\{a_1\}$	1 0 0
$\{a_2\}$	0 1 0
$\{a_3\}$	0 0 1
$\{a_1, a_2\}$	1 1 0
$\{a_1, a_3\}$	1 0 1
$\{a_2, a_3\}$	0 1 1
$\{a_1, a_2, a_3\}$	1 1 1

(Explain the above correspondence between subsets and 0,1-strings!) The principle may be generalized:

If the number of elements of a set A *is a known function of the number of elements of a set* B, *one may enumerate the elements of* B *to determine the order of* A.

We will explicitly refer to this principle only if it is used in a non-trivial way, helping to replace a particular problem by an equivalent but easier one.

The Addition Principle

Suppose that there are n disjoint sets with k_1 elements in the first set, k_2 elements in the second set, etc. Then the number of elements in the union of the sets is $k_1 + k_2 + \ldots + k_n$.

At an international conference there are participating 8 American, 4 German, 6 Japanese, and 5 Russian scientists. The total number of conference members then is $8 + 4 + 6 + 5 = 23$.

The Multiplication Principle

Suppose in a procedure consisting of k steps, the first step can be performed in n_1 different ways, the second one in n_2 different ways (no matter what the first step was), etc. Then the entire procedure can be performed in $n_1 \cdot n_2 \cdot \ldots \cdot n_k$ different ways.

At a combination lock a number is entered by selecting one of the digits 0 to 9 for each of three positions. There are $10 \cdot 10 \cdot 10 = 1000$ different numbers that can be entered.

The application of the multiplication principle can depend on the way we transform the original problem into a dynamic process. This aspect will be clarified by the next example:

How many four-digit numbers with all different digits are odd ?

Here are some numbers of this type:

$$3\ 4\ 5\ 7$$
$$6\ 9\ 2\ 3$$
$$4\ 3\ 2\ 1$$

Apparently we can construct each such number selecting the digits from left to right.

1. Step: 9 possible choices for the first digit (no zero!).

2. Step: 9 possible choices for the second digit (no matter what the first choice was).

3. Step: 8 possible choices for the third digit.

4. Step: Now the trouble begins. The fourth digit must be an odd one. So the number of available choices depends on the number of odd digits selected in the previous steps.

So the multiplication principle does not apply—at least not this way!

Now let us reorganize the construction of the four-digit numbers working from right to left:

1. Step: 5 possible choices for the first (rightmost) digit.

2. Step: 9 possible choices for the second digit.

3. Step: 8 possible choices for the third digit.

4. Step: Again we are in trouble. If all the digits selected so far have been different from 0 then there are still 6 possible choices for the leftmost digit. If one of the previously selected digits has been 0 then there remain seven choices.

Once again the presuppositions of the multiplication principle are not fulfilled. Nevertheless the problem can be solved by the multiplication principle if we first select the rightmost digit, then the leftmost digit, and then in some order the remaining digits. For example we can make the selection of the digits in the following order:

                2. Step   3. Step   4. Step   1. Step

1.   Step: 5 possible choices.
2.   Step: 8 possible choices.
3.   Step: 8 possible choices.
4.   Step: 7 possible choices.

Now the number of possible choices at each step is independent of the previously made selections and we can apply the multiplication principle. There are $8 \cdot 8 \cdot 7 \cdot 5 = 2240$ odd numbers consisting of four different digits.

   In many textbook problems the multiplication principle applies in an obvious and natural way. But sometimes as the above examples demonstrate it is not easy and needs some creativity to find a proper representation of a problem so that the principle can be applied.

The Principle of Inclusion and Exclusion

For any finite sets $A_1, A_2, \ldots A_r$, define n_s for $1 <= s <= r$ to be the sum of the sizes of all possible intersections of s sets chosen without repetition from among $A_1, A_2, \ldots A_r$. Then $|A_1 \cup A_2 \cup \ldots \cup A_r| = n_1 - n_2 + n_3 - n_4 + \ldots + (-1)^r n_r$.

   This principle generalizes the addition principle. How many integers between 1 and 1000 are multiples of 3 or 5 or 8? This principle generalizes the addition principle. (See Figure 27.)

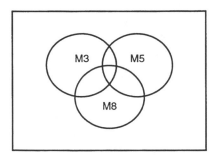

Figure 27

There are $[1000/3] = 330$ multiples of 3, $[1000/5] = 200$ multiples of 5, and $[1000/8] = 125$ multiples of 8. Using the above terminology we have $n_1 = 655$.

Further there are $[1000/15] = 66$ multiples of 3 *and* 5, $[1000/24] = 41$ multiples of 3 *and* 8, and $[1000/40] = 25$ multiples of 5 *and* 8. So we have $n_2 = 132$.

Finally there are $[1000/120] = 8$ multiples of 3 *and* 5 *and* 8. That means $n_3 = 8$.

So the number n of integers between 1 and 1000 that are divisible by at least one of the numbers 3, 5, or 8 is $n = 655 - 132 + 8 = 531$.

The Shepherd Principle

Let L and S be two sets with finite cardinalities l and s. If there is a mapping f from L onto S (f: $L \rightarrow S$, surjective) such that $|f^{-1}(y)| = c$ for all $y \in S$ then $l = c \cdot s$. (See Figure 28.)

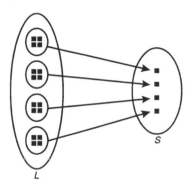

Figure 28

This principle also describes a way of indirect counting.

The name "shepherd principle" was introduced by N. Bourbaki (1963). It may be illustrated by the following anecdote: A shepherd was asked how he would manage to determine the number of sheep in his flock. He answered: "That's easy: I count the legs and divide the result by four."

In combinatorics sometimes situations occur where it is easier to count the "legs" than the "sheep."

A dodecahedron has twenty vertices. Exactly three edges meet at each of the vertices. How many edges has a dodecahedron?

We know that each edge has two endpoints and there is a total of $3 \cdot 20 = 60$ such points. So the number of edges is $60/2 = 30$.

In this example the edges are the "sheep" and the endpoints of the edges are the "legs."

The Fubini Principle

When you count (correctly) a finite set in different ways you will always get the same result.

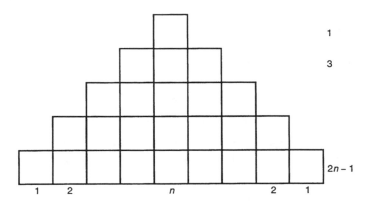

Figure 29

Suppose the number of rows in the above pattern is n. Counting the squares row by row gives $1 + 3 + 5 + ... + 2n - 1$. Counting column by column gives $1 + 2 + ... + (n-1) + n + (n-1) + ... + 2 + 1$. So for any n yields $1 + 3 + 5 + ... + 2n - 1 = 1 + 2 + ... + (n-1) + n + (n-1) + ... + 2 + 1$.

Many combinatorial identities can be deduced, developing two different formulas for the same number of elements. The general strategy emerging from the Fubini principle can be formulated as follows:

Count objects in two (or more) different ways and use the counts obtained to reach conclusions.

The name "Fubini principle" is due to S. K. Stein, who introduced it (1979, p. 62). It honors Guido Fubini (1879–1943), an Italian mathematician who is well known for "Fubini's theorem," which states fairly general conditions when the order of counting (or integrating) does not affect the result.

The Recurrence Principle

Let $a(1)$, $a(2)$, ... be a finite or infinite sequence of numbers. If some initial values $a(1)$, $a(2)$, ... $a(k)$ are known and if for all $n>k$ there is a rule which defines $a(n)$ in terms of $a(1)$, $a(2)$, ... $a(n - 1)$, then every element of the sequence can be calculated according to this rule.

The rule that defines $a(n)$ in terms of $a(1)$, $a(2)$, ... $a(n - 1)$ is called a recurrence relation. The sequence is said to be defined recursively. (More generally a recurrence relation is a way to define a function by an expression involving the same function.)

A well-known example is the sequence of Fibonacci numbers, which may be defined and calculated according to

$$F(n) = \begin{cases} 1 & \text{for } n = 1 \text{ or } 2, \\ F(n-2) + F(n-1) & \text{for } n \geq 3. \end{cases}$$

$F(1) = 1$ and $F(2) = 1$ are the initial values.
$F(n) = F(n-2) + F(n-1)$ is the recurrence relation.

The idea of recurrence is of fundamental theoretical and practical importance both in mathematics and in computer science. Combinatorics provides us with many motivating problems to introduce this idea at an early stage of students' development.

$F(n) = F(n-1) + F(n-2)$ is an example of so-called difference equations—the discrete counterparts of differential equations studied in courses on calculus. The theory of difference equations enables us to find explicit solutions for the corresponding recursively defined functions. For example:

$$F(n) = \frac{1}{\sqrt{5}} \left(\frac{1+\sqrt{5}}{2} \right)^n - \frac{1}{\sqrt{5}} \left(\frac{1-\sqrt{5}}{2} \right)^n.$$

Exploration 18

Test this formula for some values of n. Notice what kind of number results. State a conjecture for what you found. Test your conjecture by trying other values of n.

A treatment of difference equations—which is beyond our scope here—can be found in almost every book on discrete mathematics (see for example Dossey, 1993).

The above principles are landmarks that may be helpful to keep an orientation in the diversity of combinatorial problems. All these principles describe very simple and intuitive ideas. There is no need to teach them explicitly and to ask students to memorize them. Instead students should internalize the ideas, using them in well-designed problems. For the teacher, however, being aware of the principles may be helpful in planning lessons, as well as understanding what is going on and possibly going wrong in students' minds.

Exploration 19

Solve each of the following problems. Identify the various principles that you used in solving these problems. Share your solution methods with your colleagues. Did they use the same counting principles as you did?

1. A single domino shows a pair of numbers both between 0 and 6. A complete set of dominoes consists of a certain number of dominoes such that every pair of this kind occurs exactly once. How many dominoes make a set?

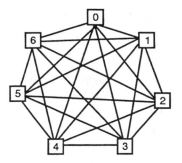

Figure 30

Figure 30 is called a "domino graph." Explain how it is related to a set of dominoes. How can the just-stated problem be solved by means of the domino graph?

2. Suppose you want to pave the bottom of a box of size 2 × 10 with 1 × 2 dominoes. In how many ways can this be done? (See Figure 31.)

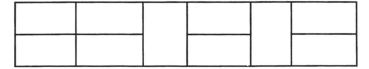

Figure   31

Hint: Let $B(n)$ be the number of ways a 2 × n box can be filled. For example $B(1) = 1$, $B(2) = 2$, and $B(3) = 3$.

3. Each integer between 2 and 100 that is not a multiple of 2, 3, 5, or 7 is prime. Explain why! Use this statement to determine the number of primes smaller than 100.

4. How many different strings can be created rearranging the letters of the word MISSISSIPPI?

5. Six chips are used to represent the number 231 in the abacus of Figure 32. How many different numbers can be represented

   a. using exactly six chips?

   b. using at most six chips?

   c. using exactly six chips, if each column of the abacus contains at least one chip?

100	10	1
o o	o o o	o

Figure 32

6. *The Tower of Hanoi*

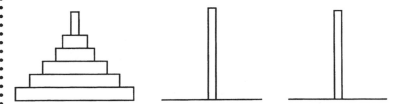

Figure 33

   Suppose that *n* rings are placed on a peg, the rings increasing in size from top to bottom. Two initially empty pegs are also available. We wish to move the rings one at a time from peg 1 to peg 3 (using peg 2 for storage), under the constraint that no ring can ever be placed on a smaller one. (See Figure 33.)

   If $T(n)$ is the minimum number of moves required, set up and solve a recursive equation to find $T(n)$.

   (Hint: When the largest ring is ready to be moved to peg 3, where must the other $n-1$ rings be?)

   A legend tells that the monks in a Vietnamese monastery are moving 64 golden rings according to the above rules and that it will be Doomsday when their task is accomplished. Suppose that the monks are working day and night moving one ring every five seconds. How many years will they need to come to the end? Compare the number to other large numbers, for example the estimated age of our universe.

   The complete story about the monks and the golden rings may be found in the book of Ball and Coxeter (1974, p. 317).

PERMUTATIONS AND THE FIFTEEN PUZZLE

Earlier, the so-called Fifteen puzzle (also known under the name Boss puzzle) was described. This puzzle, which is sold in many stores, was invented about 1870 by Sam Loyd, a great American problematist who created a large number of puzzles and challenging mathematical problems. Apparently Sam Loyd was also an excellent public relations manager. He sold the puzzle proposing the problem to begin with the starting arrangement indicated in Figure 34 and to obtain the pattern in Figure 35 by sliding the tiles either horizontally or vertically.

1	2	3	4
5	6	7	8
9	10	11	12
13	14	15	

Figure 34

1	2	3	4
5	6	7	8
9	10	11	12
13	15	14	

Figure 35

He offered a $1000 prize to the first person submitting a correct solution.
The following editorial footnote about the puzzle was published in a research paper in 1879 in the *American Journal of Mathematics*.

The "15" puzzle for the last few weeks has been prominently before the American public, and may safely be said to have engaged the attention of nine out of ten persons of both sexes and of all ages and conditions of the community. But this would not have weighed with the editors to induce them to insert articles upon such subject in the *American Journal of Mathematics*, but for the fact that the principle of the game has its root in what all mathematicians of the present day are aware constitutes the most subtle and characteristic conception of modern algebra, viz: the law of dichotomy applicable to the separation of the terms of every complete system of permutations into two natural and indefeasible groups, a law of inner world thought, which may be said to prefigure the polar relation of left- and right-handed screws or of objects in space and their reflections in a mirror.

(Quotation from Sherman K. Stein, 1969.)

Of course Sam Loyd knew that there was no risk of losing the $1000. Our problem is to confirm that the Fifteen puzzle cannot be solved. More generally one may ask when two arrangements are equivalent in the sense that one arrangement can be transformed into the other.

To simplify the notation, let us represent the empty place in the puzzle by the number 16. Then, reading the puzzle row by row, the arrangement of numbers is a *permutation* of the numbers 1 to 16. So, let us first deal with permutations in general.

Suppose that there are n objects $a_1, a_2, \ldots a_n$. Each linear arrangement of these objects is called a permutation. We will especially deal with permutations of natural numbers 1, 2, ...n. That is not really a restriction, as the elements of an arbitrary finite set may be denoted 1, 2, ...n. Obviously there are 6 permutations of the numbers 1, 2, 3, namely:

$$1\,2\,3 \qquad 1\,3\,2 \qquad 2\,1\,3 \qquad 2\,3\,1 \qquad 3\,1\,2 \qquad 3\,2\,1.$$

How many permutations of n objects do exist?

By P_n we denote the number of permutations of n objects. Systematic construction of all permutations for small values of n gives

n	1	2	3	4	...
P_n	1	2	6	24	...

Reflective Problem 5

Describe your method of listing systematically all permutations for a special n!

A common way to write down all order n permutations is to do it in *lexicographic* order. For example, the permutations for $n = 3$ in lexicographic order are: 123, 132, 213, 231, 312, 321. If there are two permutations $P1$ and $P2$ listed in lexicographic order then $P1 < P2$ (that is, $P1$ is listed before $P2$) if in the first position, in which both permutations differ, $P1$ has a smaller value than $P2$. (Compare this order to the way words are ordered in a dictionary.)

To count the number P_n of all permutations of order n one can apply the principle of multiplication: There are n ways to first select the number for the first position of a permutation, $n-1$ ways to select the number for the second position next, etc. So there are $n(n-1)(n-2) \ldots 1$ ways to construct order n permutations. (See Figure 36.)

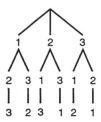

Figure 36

Using the common notation $n(n - 1) \ldots 1 = n!$ (read "factorial n") we get P_n $= n!$ By convention we define $P_0 = 0! = 1$.

Exploration 20

Look at your calculator to see if it has a function for getting factorials. Whether it does or not, calculate $n!$ for $n = 1, 2, \ldots 15$. What is the largest n for which you obtain an exact value for $n!$ on your calculator?

Exploration 21

Justify the following recursive definition:

$$P(n) = \begin{cases} 1 & \text{if } n = 0, \\ nP_{n-1} & \text{otherwise} \end{cases}$$

Next we study a two-person strategy game, which will lead us to an analysis of the Fifteen puzzle.

Swap

In the game Swap, any game position is given by a permutation of the numbers 1, 2, ... n. (For example: 6 2 8 3 7 1 5 4.) Two players alternately take turns selecting a pair of numbers from the permutation, such that the larger one of the two numbers is found at the left of the smaller one. These two numbers are then swapped to produce a new permutation. The game stops when the numbers are in their natural order 1 2 . . . *n*. The player who made the last move wins.

. . . .

Exploration 22

Write down an initial position and then play the game several times. What do you observe? Try several other initial game positions and play each several times. State a conjecture about your observations.

. . . .

Let us consider two different runs of the game that started with 8 7 6 5 4 3 2 1.

First run	*Second run*
8 7 6 5 4 3 2 1	8 7 6 5 4 3 2 1
8 7 2 5 4 3 6 1	1 7 6 5 4 3 2 1
1 7 2 5 4 3 6 8	1 2 6 5 4 3 7 8
1 2 7 5 4 3 6 8	1 2 3 5 4 6 7 8
1 2 6 5 4 3 7 8	1 2 3 4 5 6 7 8
1 2 3 5 4 6 7 8	
1 2 3 4 5 6 7 8	

In the first run it took six moves to reach the end position while the second run came to an end after only four turns. Each time the second player (that is, the player having the second turn) won.

Play some more games starting with this same permutation. You will notice that the second player always wins. The number of turns is always even for this starting position.

Have you noticed that whether the first player or the second player wins is determined by the starting position, no matter what moves the two players make?

Even and Odd Permutations

To find an explanation for the just-stated observation let us consider the number of pairs in a permutation such that the larger number precedes the smaller one. Each such pair is called an *inversion*. Thus for example the permutation 1 4 3 2 5 contains three inversions, namely (4,3), (4,2), and (3,2). 5 4 3 2 1 contains $4 + 3 + 2 + 1 = 10$ inversions. (Which ones?)

A permutation is said to be *even* if it contains an even number of inversions. It is said to be *odd* otherwise. Thus 1 4 3 2 is an odd permutation, while 5 4 3 2 1 is an even one.

Exploration 23

How many inversions are there in each of the following permutations? Which permutations are even, which are odd?

a) 3 7 4 2 1 5 6   b) 3 7 5 2 1 4 6   c) 6 5 4 3 2 1
d) 6 1 5 2 4 3   e) 7 6 5 4 3 2 1   f) 8 7 6 5 4 3 2 1

When a new permutation is produced from an old one by swapping two numbers, how is the number of inversions affected?

To answer this question, we first consider what happens if two neighboring numbers in a permutation are interchanged. So let us assume that a permutation $a_1 a_2 \ldots a_i a_k \ldots a_n$ is changed to $a_1 a_2 \ldots a_k a_i \ldots a_n$.

If $a_i < a_k$, then the new permutation contains an additional inversion (a_k, a_i) that the original permutation does not have. Similarly, if $a_k < a_i$, then the original permutation has an inversion that is not contained in the new one. The position of all the other numbers relative to a_i and a_k and relative to each other number remains unchanged. Thus the two permutations differ by exactly one inversion. So, interchanging two neighboring numbers transforms an odd permutation into an even one and vice versa.

Next let us study what happens if two arbitrarily selected numbers of a permutation are swapped. (See Figure 37.)

Figure 37

If there are r numbers between the two numbers a and b which we will swap, the exchange may be realized moving the right standing number b step by step to the left, switching places with its neighbor until it is left to a, and then moving a step by step to the right, until it is on the place originally occupied by b.

Try it before you read on! How is the number of inversions affected?

The total number of switches between adjacent numbers has been $2r + 1$. At each step the *parity* (odd or even) of the permutation has been changed. So, if the original permutation was an even one, interchanging two arbitrary numbers leads to an odd permutation, and if the original permutation was odd, we get an even one if we exchange two numbers.

The theorem, then, is that interchanging any two numbers in a permutation gives a new permutation of different parity.

Now we are ready to analyze the Fifteen puzzle.

Reading the puzzle row by row, the arrangement of the sixteen numbers of the puzzle (remember that we denote the empty place by 16) forms a permutation of the numbers 1 to 16. Switching the empty place with one of the adjacent squares makes a new permutation such that the number 16 has been interchanged with one of the other numbers. So the new permutation and the old one have different parities. Thus, each permutation we get after an even number of moves has the same parity as the starting permutation, while a permutation produced by an odd number of moves has a different parity.

If there are two different arrangements of numbers then the number of switches needed to proceed from one arrangement to the other is even or odd, depending only on the two patterns and not on the intermediate positions of the empty square. To verify this statement suppose that the squares of the puzzle are colored black and white like a checkerboard. (See Figure 38.)

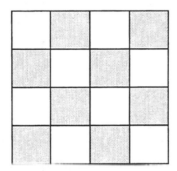

Figure 38

Each switch on the puzzle moves the empty square from white to black or from black to white. Thus, to bring the empty place from a black field to another black field or from a white field to another white field takes an even number of moves. To transfer the empty square from black to white or from white to black requires an odd number of moves.

So, if two arrangements of the puzzle have the empty square both on black or both on white, then both corresponding permutations must have the same parity. On the other hand, if one arrangement has the empty field on white, while the other arrangement has the empty field on black, then one permutation must be even and the other one odd. As a consequence, an arrangement *cannot* be transformed into another one, if one of the following conditions is fulfilled:

1. Both arrangements have the empty square on fields of the same color, while the corresponding permutations have different parities.

2. One arrangement has the empty square on a black field while the other arrangement has the empty square on a white field and both permutations have the same parity.

If none of these two conditions is fulfilled for two arrangements, then indeed it is possible to transform one into the other. A technique for doing this is sketched in Stein (1969). It is fun to convince yourself by practicing.

Exploration 24

1. Which of the arrangements in Figure 39 can be transferred to each other?

1	2	3	4
5	6	7	8
9	10	11	12
13	14	15	

a

1	2	3	4
5	6	7	8
9	10	11	12
13	15	14	

b

7	15	9	12
8	6	13	10
2	5	11	1
14	3	4	

c

1	7	11	13
4	9	2	8
15	10	3	6
5	12	14	

d

6	15	9	
10	1	7	11
5	12	2	4
14	3	8	13

e

3	9	11	13
4		2	8
10	7	15	6
5	14	12	1

f

Figure 39

Exploration 25

Prove that one half of all permutations of order *n* is even and the other half is odd.

(Hint: What happens if you have a list of all the permutations and you switch the first with the second number in each permutation?)

Exploration 26

In this section we used a checkerboard like black and white cells of the Fifteen puzzle for reasoning. Skillful coloring sometimes provides proofs of striking elegance and simplicity. Try the following examples:

1. Assume that a domino is exactly big enough to cover two neighboring cells of a checkerboard. Of course a complete 8 x 8 checkerboard can be covered by 32 of these dominoes. Now, if two diagonally opposite cells have been removed from the board, is it possible to cover the remaining 62 cells by 31 dominoes?

2. A straight tromino (a figure looking like the one in Figure 40 is assumed to be just the right size to cover three cells of a checkerboard. Is it possible to cover all but one cell of an 8 x 8 checkerboard? Cut trominoes from cardboard and try to cover a checkerboard. (Hint: For means of reasoning color the checkerboard white, black, and red in such a way that each tromino covers cells of all three colors.)

Figure 40

BINOMIAL COEFFICIENTS AND PASCAL'S TRIANGLE

Part I

Exploration 27

Two students, Andrea and Bill, alternately flip a coin—ten times in total. If "H(eads)" shows up, Andrea gets a point; if "T(ails)" shows up, Bill gets a point.

Try several such games in the classroom. Let students record the coin-flipping series. Represent the games graphically by a diagram showing how far Andrea is ahead (or behind) Bill while the game goes on.

For example:

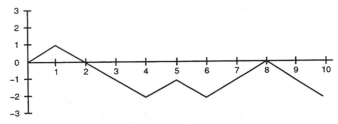

Figure 41

Discuss the experiment and the results.

Some questions to discuss:

- What are the possible outcomes? (Make a list of the numbers of points that Andrea and Bill can get in total.)

- How often does it occur during your games that Andrea and Bill have an equal number of points? How often is Andrea ahead and how often is Bill?

- What is the total number of different series (or strings) of length *n* consisting of H's and T's—or of 0 and 1? (Make a list for small values of *n*.)

- How many different series can occur consisting of *k* H's and (10-*k*) T's? (Try to find answers for some simple cases—for example, *k* = 0, 1, 2, 8, 9, 10.) What are the probabilities for these results?

- If only one student—Bill or Andrea or a third person—flips the coin, does it make a difference for Andrea's or Bill's chances to win?

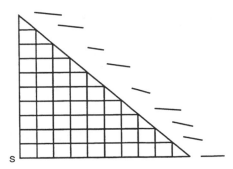

Figure 42

- Compare the records of the games to walks in Figure 42 from S to the river. (At each block the traveler flips a coin to decide if he goes east or north.)
- Suppose that the player who first scores five points gets twelve candies. If the game must be stopped when Andrea has four points while Bill has three points, how should the two fairly divide the twelve candies? (What does it mean to be fair in this situation?)

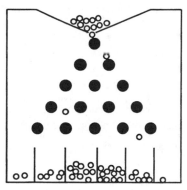

Figure 43

A *Galton board* (see Figure 43) is a mathematical tool that motivates lots of activities in combinatorics and probability. Small balls fall from a reservoir at the top of the board through an array of pins to collect in the compartments at the bottom. The probability for a ball to go either left or right is ½ at each obstacle. The board was designed by the British anthropologist Sir Francis Galton (1822–1911) to visualize the frequency curve of binomial distributions.

A Galton board should be part of the collection of mathematical manipulatives at every secondary school. If it is not available, it would be a nice project to build a Galton board with your students. There are also computer programs that allow experiments with the Galton board on the screen. Some of these programs include the option to change parameters and thereby the probabilistic behavior of the board. Nevertheless, it is much more fun to experiment with the real board.

Exploration 28

Observe the running balls and how they are collected in the slots at the bottom. If you don't have a Galton board at hand, simulate the path of a ball by flipping a coin five times. In which slot does the ball fall? Repeat

this fifty times and study the distribution of the balls into the slots. Try to
explain what you observe! You may also simulate the running balls with
a simple computer program.

We will use the Galton board to answer some of the above questions motivated by the coin-flipping game. This time, instead of flipping coins Andrea and Bill make a ball run through a Galton board with ten rows. Each time the ball goes R(ight) at a junction point, Andrea gets a point, and if it goes L(eft), Bill gets a point.

Exploration 29

Compare this game to the game of flipping coins. Is it necessary to observe the route the ball takes to find out the scores of Andrea and Bill?

It should be quite clear that any series of H's and T's realized by flipping a coin ten times may be substituted by a random path on a Galton board with ten rows and vice versa. If the path from the top to the bottom of the Galton board is recorded by a list of L(eft)'s and R(ight)'s, then clearly each such list corresponds in a one-to-one way to a record of a coin-flipping experiment— as may be seen for example by interchanging R's and H's and equally L's and T's. In this sense both games are equivalent.

We identify the junction points on the Galton board, numbering the rows from top to bottom by $0, 1, 2, \ldots$ and in each row we number the positions of the pins by $0, 1, 2, \ldots$. (At this point it may seem strange that we start the enumeration with 0 and not with 1. The reason will become obvious later in this section.) So each such point can be identified by a pair (n, k) of coordinates, where n is the number of the corresponding row and k is the position in that row.

To determine the number of possible routes a ball may take to reach position (n, k) we use the fact that a ball bouncing at (n, k) must be coming either from $(n-1, k-1)$ or from $(n-1,k)$. So, if we denote by $C(n, k)$ the number of paths from the top to position (n, k) we get the recursive definition

$$C(n,k) = \begin{cases} 1 & \text{if } k = 0 \text{ or } n, \\ C(n-1, k-1) + C(n-1,k) & \text{if } 0 < k < n. \end{cases}$$

Entering these numbers into the corresponding positions results in the famous triangle of Pascal.

						1						
row 0						1						
row 1					1		1					
row 2				1		2		1				
row 3			1		3		3		1			
row 4		1		4		6		4		1		
row 5	1		5		10		10		5		1	
etc.												

The name "Pascal's Triangle" is due to Pascal's paper "Traite du Triangle Arithmétique" (A Treatise on the Arithmetic Triangle), written in 1653
and published posthumously in 1665. It describes many of the properties of
this triangular pattern. However, the Italian mathematician Niccolo Fontana
(1499–1557)—better known by his nickname Tartaglia (the Stammerer)—already was familiar with it. (Tartaglia is famous for his discovery of the formula to solve cubic equations.) In 1527 the triangle was printed on the title page
of an arithmetic text by Petrus Apianus, an astronomer at the University of
Ingolstadt (Germany). Moreover, there are testimonies proving that the pattern was long ago known to Arabian and Chinese mathematicians. Detailed
historical information may be found in Edwards (1987).

Pascal's triangle is an inexhaustible treasury for mathematical activities
and discoveries. It provides a laboratory for students to conduct mathematical experiments: looking for patterns, formulating from their observations
some general statements, and then trying to prove them (see Peter Hilton and
Jean Pedersen, 1987). A book full of activities around the Pascal triangle is
Green and Hamberg (1986).

• •

Exploration 30

What is the total number of paths from the top of the Galton board to its
tenth (nth) row?

• •

At each junction point a ball may go left or right. So by the multiplication
principle there are $2^{10} = 1024$ (2^n) such routes. As $C(n, k)$ paths run through
position (n, k) we calculate the probability that a ball passes (n, k) as being
$C(n,k)/2^n$. So, for $n = 10$ we get the following list:

k	0	1	2	3	4	5	6	7	8	9	10
$C(10, k)$	1	10	45	120	210	252	210	120	45	10	1
$P(10, k)$	.001	.01	.044	.12	.20	.25	.20	.12	.044	.01	.001

Exploration 31

If in the coin-flipping game Andrea has 4 points while Bill has 3 points, what is the corresponding position on a Galton board? What is the probability that Andrea gets 5 points first? Make use of the Galton board to explain your argument!

Exploration 32

Look together with a group of fellow students for patterns in Pascal's triangle. Share what you find. Try to explain what you detect. Here are some interesting items you may look for:

- The sum of numbers in one row.
- The sum of two adjoining numbers in the second column, that is, $C(n, 2) + C(n+1, 2)$ for some n.
- What kind of numbers do you find in the second row?
- Add the squares of the entries for each of the rows 1, 2, ... Where can the results be found in the triangle?
- Add all the elements in the triangle up to the nth row for $n = 1, 2,$ . . . . What kind of numbers do you find?

Exploration 33

A family has six children. What is the probability that three of them are boys and three are girls?

    (Make a guess, then simulate the problem with a Galton board or by coin flipping, and finally give an argument and calculate!)

Part II

A different context where the numbers of Pascal's triangle appear is the expansion of binomials. (A binomial is an expression of the type $(a + b)^r$.)

$$(a + b)^0 = 1$$
$$(a + b)^1 = 1a + 1b$$
$$(a + b)^2 = 1a^2 + 2ab + 1b^2$$
$$(a + b)^3 = 1a^3 + 3a^2b + 3ab^2 + 1b^3$$

Calculate $(a + b)^4$, $(a + b)^5$, and $(a + b)^6$. Do you find a pattern? The examples motivate the guess

$$(a+b)^n = \sum_{k=0}^{n} C(n,k)a^{n-k}b^k.$$

To prove this conjecture let us denote by $B(n, k)$ the coefficient of $a^{n-k}b^k$ in the expansion of $(a + b)^n$. Obviously $B(n, 0) = B(n, n) = 1$. For $0 < k < n$ we get a recurrence relation from

$$
\begin{aligned}
(a + b)^n &= (a + b)^{n-1}(a + b)\\
&= (a^{n-1} + ... + B(n-1, k-1)\, a^{n-k}\, b^{k-1} + B(n-1, k)\, a^{n-1-k}b^k + ... + b^{n-1})\, (a +b)\\
&= (a^n + ... + B(n, k)\, a^{n-k}b^k + ... + b^k).
\end{aligned}
$$

Comparing the last two rows shows that $B(n, k) = B(n-1, k-1) + B(n-1, k)$. So $B(n, k)$ satisfies the same initial conditions and the same recurrence relation as $C(n, k)$. It follows $B(n, k) = C(n, k)$.

Because of this relationship the numbers $C(n, k)$ are called the *binomial coefficients*.

Part III

Next let us deal with a seemingly different type of problem:

How many possibilities are there to select 3 (or k) persons out of 20 (or n) to form a committee?

What is the number of different ways to choose 6 numbers out of 44 to fill out a lottery form?

Before you read on try to establish a one-to-one correspondence between the set of 0,1-strings of length n consisting of k 1's and $(n-k)$ 0's on one hand and the set of k-subsets of a set of order n on the other hand. As an example choose $n = 5$ and $k = 2$.

Consider a set A with n elements and number the elements $a_1, a_2, \ldots a_n$ (Figure 44). Then a k-subset of A may be identified by an 0,1-string such that position i of the string has the entry 1 if the ith element of A is a member of the subset and 0 otherwise.

a1	a2	a3	a4	a5	a6	a7	a8	a9	a10
0	1	1	0	1	0	0	0	1	0

Figure 44

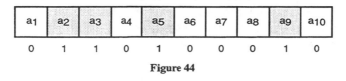

0 1 1 0 1 0 0 0 1 0

This correspondence between the subsets of A and 0,1-strings is apparently one-to-one and you can apply the principle of indirect counting. So according to Part I of this section the number of k-subsets is $C(n, k)$.

The binomial coefficient $C(n, k)$ – read "n choose k"—is the number of subsets consisting of exactly k elements which can be chosen from a set of n elements. Another common notation for this number is $\binom{k}{n}$.

Binomial coefficients are the most important and prominent combinatorial entities. They are involved whenever we count the number of subsets of a given finite set containing a specified number of elements. Thus the solution of the Lotto problem above is the binomial number $C(44,6)$. We could find this number extending Pascal's triangle up to row 44. But apparently that's a tedious method. It would be much nicer to have a formula to calculate $C(n, k)$ directly.

There are several ways to get such an explicit formula. Two of them are presented here:

First let us compile some facts we have developed so far or that are obvious from the definition of "n choose k":

1. $C(n, k) = 0$ if $n < k$,
2. $C(n, 0) = C(n, n) = 1$,
3. $C(n, 1) = C(n, n - 1) = n$,
4. $C(n, k) = C(n, n - k)$ (there is an obvious one-to-one correspondence between the k-subsets and $(n - k)$-subsets of a set of order n),
5. $C(n, 2) = (n - 1) + (n - 2) + ... + 1 = n (n + 1)/2$.

To prove statement 5, bring the n elements of a set in any order. The first element can be combined with $n - 1$ elements to form a subset of order two. The second element can be combined in $n - 2$ ways with one of the remaining elements and so on.

Now let us consider the general case with $0 < k < n$.

Method 1
There are $n(n - 1) .. (n - k + 1)$ ordered k-tuples that can be formed from the elements of an n-set A (multiplication principle). Each k-subset of A corresponds in a one-to-one way to the class of the $k!$ ordered k-tuples that are formed from the elements of the subset. So corresponding to the shepherd principle we get

$$k! \cdot C(n, k) = n(n - 1) ... (n - k + 1) \text{ and}$$
$$C(n, k) = n(n - 1) ... (n - k + 1)/k! = n!/(k! \cdot (n - k)!).$$

Method 2
Suppose there are *n* persons in a group of people who want to select a *k*-person committee including a chairman. This selection can be done in two different ways:

1. The *k* persons of the committee are selected first. Then one member of the committee is selected to be the chairman.

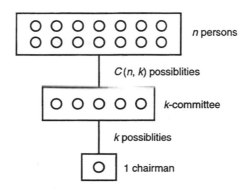

Figure 45

In this way according to the multiplication principle $C(n, k) \cdot k$ different committees can be constructed.

2. First the chairman is chosen and thereafter the remaining $k - 1$ members of the committee.

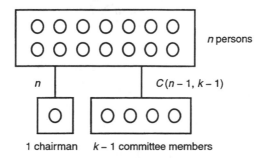

Figure 46

Apparently there are $n \cdot C(n - 1, k - 1)$ possibilities to choose the committee in this way.

By both methods we have counted all possible groupings for the committee. So, making use of the Fubini principle we get

$$C(n, k) \cdot k = n \cdot (C(n - 1, k - 1), \text{ which gives}$$
$$C(n, k) = n / k \cdot C(n - 1, k - 1).$$

Applying the same recurrence relation to $C(n - 1, k - 1)$, $C(n - 2, k - 2)$, etc., we get

$$C(n, k) = n / k \cdot (n - 1) / (k - 1) \cdot \ldots \cdot (n - k + 2) / 2 \cdot (n - k + 1) \cdot C(n - k, 0)$$

or

$$(Cn, k) = n (n - 1) \cdots (n + 1 - k) / k! = n! / (k! \cdot (n - k)!)$$

Some numerical considerations:
1. Above formula gives us $C(100, 97) = 100 \cdot 99 \cdot \ldots \cdot 4/(97 \cdot 96 \cdot \ldots \cdot 1)$.
    But we also know $C(100, 97) = C(100, 3)$. So we get a much simpler term to calculate $C(100, 97)$, namely $(100 \cdot 99 \cdot 98)/(3 \cdot 2 \cdot 1) = 161700$. Whenever $k > n-k$ it is easier to calculate $C(n, n-k)$ instead of $C(n, k)$.
2. Because of its interpretation, "n choose k" must be a natural number. You should avoid unnecessarily large numbers. So to evaluate $C(44, 6)$ do not calculate $44 \cdot 43 \cdot 42 \cdot 41 \cdot 40 \cdot 39/(6 \cdot 5 \cdot 4 \cdot 3 \cdot 2)$ in this order.
    If you try $(44/6) \cdot (43/5) \cdot (42/4) \cdot (41/3) \cdot (40/2) \cdot 39$ instead, the intermediate results will not be excessively large, but you are leaving the domain of integers. On a calculator this may give round-off errors.
    If we enter $39 \cdot (40/2) \cdot (41/3) \cdot \ldots \cdot (44/6)$ the intermediate results are $C(39,1)$, $C(40,2)$, ... $C(44,6)$, which are all integer values.
3. To calculate $C(44,6)$ or some other binomial coefficient by hand, cancel the denominator so that the calculation is reduced to simple multiplication. (Try it!)

. . . .

Exploration 34

Here are three problems that may be used to introduce the concept of binomial coefficients. Prove the equivalence of all three problems.

1. What is the number of k-subsets in an n-set? (For example: How many different committees of 5 persons can be selected from a group of 20 persons?)

2. How many 0,1-strings of length n are there containing k 1's and
   $n-k$ 0's? (Example: A family has seven children, four girls and
   three boys. How many sequences are there to give birth to four
   girls and three boys if you distinguish only between boy and girl?)

3. Figure 47 shows a section of the map of a town. The town
   consists of m x k rectangular blocks separated by $m-1$ horizontal
   and $k-1$ vertical streets. A traveler wants to get on a shortest
   route from A to B, which is $n = m + k$ blocks away. In how many
   ways can he do so?

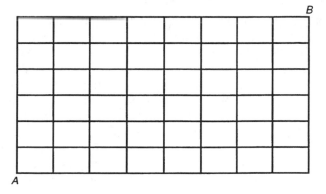

Figure 47

Exploration 35

In how many ways can you read HAPPY BIRTHDAY in the following array if you start at the top left position and go on reading to the right and
downward?

H	A	P	P	Y	B
A	P	P	Y	B	I
P	P	Y	B	I	R
P	Y	B	I	R	T
Y	B	I	R	T	H
B	I	R	T	H	D
I	R	T	H	D	A
R	T	H	D	A	Y

Exploration 36

There are simple arguments to prove $\sum_{k=0}^{n} C(n,k) = 2^n$ and $\sum_{k=0}^{n} C(n,k)2^k = 3^n$.

Confirm and generalize these results!

ONE PROBLEM—MANY APPROACHES

It is a common belief that there is exactly one way to solve each mathematical problem, because that is the way textbooks traditionally used to present mathematics. Of course this belief is wrong. If you give a nonroutine problem to different people, students or professional mathematicians, they typically will come up with quite different ways of solving it. For a teacher it is not enough to have just one solution for each problem in mind. To appreciate students' ideas it is necessary to listen carefully and to try to understand. To competently guide students who are struggling with a problem it is helpful to anticipate several strategies—even if it is impossible to foresee all approaches that students will find. Comparing different solutions to one problem can help to develop a feeling for the power and elegance of mathematical ideas. The NCTM *Standards* (1989) are focusing on multiple approaches to problems, and today there are textbooks on the market that have excellent development related to this idea.

Exploration 37

What is the number of possibilities to select three elements from a list of ten, such that no two of the three elements are adjacent?

To deal with a more stimulating setting let us replace this problem with an equivalent one.

The Unfriendly Customers

Sam's café has ten counter seats in a straight line. Each morning there are three grouchy people who have their morning coffee in Sam's and none of them feels like socializing until after that first coffee. How many different ways can the three unfriendly customers occupy these ten seats so that no two of them are sitting adjacent? (In this form the problem has been published by J. M. Shaughnessy, 1984, p. 30.)

J. M. Shaughnessy comments: "If this problem is assigned in a class that has just looked at counting techniques, the overwhelming problem solving 'technique' is to 'find the right formula.' Fortunately this problem is just non-routine enough so that none of the standard formulas are helpful. So, it was very refreshing for me to give this problem to a class full of preservice teachers and watch them come up with a multitude of approaches en route to successful solutions, while a senior level class in probability and statistics stumbled around for the right formula."

The reformulation of our problem not only has the advantage of being more attractive because it stimulates our imagination, it also suggests certain operations—taking some of the seats out of the line and rearranging them—that do not come to mind so easily when dealing with our original setting of the problem.

I will give three different solutions for the problem. But before reading on, you should try to solve the problem yourself, or—even better—solve it cooperatively with others. Maybe you will find solutions quite different from those that follow.

To generalize the problem let us assume that there are n seats in a line and k unfriendly customers, such that $k > 0$ and $n \geq 2k - 1$. The number of possible ways to choose k seats such that no two of them are sitting adjacent we denominate by $A(n, k)$.

Solution 1
If the number n of seats is small enough, an obvious solution is to make a list of all the ways the customers can sit down. Of course it is helpful to develop a procedure to write down this list systematically to make sure that no solution is missed.

Write down some examples and show a system!

Using such an approach, most students can be—at least partially—successful.

Solution 2
For less than $2 \cdot k - 1$ seats apparently there is no way for k customers to sit down in an unfriendly way. If the number of seats is $2 \cdot k - 1$ then the customers have exactly one possibility to choose the chairs to sit down in.

If $k \geq 1$ and $n \geq 2 \cdot k$ we can distinguish two types of choosing the seats: either the first seat in the line is taken by one of the customers or this seat remains free. If the first seat is occupied by one customer then the remaining $k - 1$ guests must choose among $n - 2$ seats. If the first seat stays free then all k guests have to sit down selecting among $n - 1$ seats. Let us consider an example with 7 seats and 3 customers.

```
XOXOXOO      OXOXOXO
XOXOOXO      OXOXOOX
XOXOOOX      OXOOXOX
XOOXOXO      OOXOXOX
XOOXOOX
XOOOXOX
```

A   B

Figure 48

In Figure 48A shows in systematical order all patterns such that the first seat on the left is occupied while B represents those patterns with the leftmost seat staying free.

Applying the "addition principle" yields the recurrence relation $A(7, 3) = A(5, 2) + A(6,3)$ and generally $A(n, k) = A(n-2, k-1) + A(n-1, k)$.

If there is only one guest, he or she may take any seat. So $A(n, 1) = n$. If the number of seats is $2 \cdot k - 1$ the only way to sit down is X O X . . . O X. If $n < 2k - 1$ there is no way to place the unfriendly customers.

With these starting conditions we get the general solution

$$A(n,K) = \begin{cases} 0 & \text{if } n \le 2(k-1), \\ n & \text{if } k-1, \\ A(n-1, k) + A(n-2, k-1) & \text{otherwise.} \end{cases}$$

From this we can construct a table for $A(n, k)$ (Figure 49).

n/k	1	2	3	4	5
1	1	0	0	0	0
2	2	0	0	0	0
3	3	1	0	0	0
4	4	3	0	0	0
5	5	6	1	0	0
6	6	10	4	0	0
7	7	15	10	1	0
8	8	21	20	5	0
9	9	28	35	15	1
10	10	36	56	35	6

Figure 49

For example, if there are 10 seats then there are 56 ways to select places for three unfriendly customers.

The above table can easily be constructed by hand. It is also a good example to make use of a spreadsheet program.

Compare the table to Pascal's triangle! Can you guess how $A(n, k)$ may be expressed as a binomial coefficient?

Solution 3
This solution reduces the problem to a similar, already solved problem. Suppose there are 3 unfriendly customers and 10 seats. To choose their seats at

the counter the guests take 3 chairs away, leaving 7 there. Then the guests return, each one carrying a chair, and place them in the spaces between the other chairs or at either end of the line.

$$O_\wedge O_\wedge O_\wedge O_\wedge O_\wedge O_\wedge O$$

Figure 50

So the customers have to choose 3 of 8 possible places for their chairs, which can be done in $C(8, 3)$ ways. The generalization is obvious: $A(n, k) = C(n + 1 - k, k)$.

Our third approach gave the result

$$A(n, k) = C(n + 1 - k, k) \text{ if } k > 0 \text{ and } n \geq 2k - 1 \quad (1)$$

while the second solution gave the recurrence relation

$$A(n, k) = A(n - 2, k - 1) + A(n - 1, k). \quad (2)$$

Replacing $n + 1 - k$ by the symbol s and combining (1) and (2) (i.e., applying the Fubini principle) yields

$$C(s, k) = C(s - 1, k - 1) + C(s - 1, k) \qquad \text{if } 0 < k < s.$$

This is again the famous recurrence relation which is used to construct Pascal's triangle.

Let us give the final word to J. M. Shaughnessy (1984, p. 32): "I have found this problem a rich source for sharing problem solving strategies, plans of attack, and for discussion in a 'look back' session with students. Tables lead to patterns. The problem can be both simplified to few people and fewer seats, or generalized to k people and n seats, and in either case more patterns arise. Triangular numbers, Pascal's triangle, finite differences, recursion formulas, and different ways to represent the problem all arise naturally in the solution process."

Reflective Problem 6

What were the most challenging ideas you learned in this chapter? Why were they challenging? What is the most important thing you learned in working through this chapter that you would like your students to learn? You might want to keep a record of your responses for future reference when you teach combinatorics.

REFERENCES

Ball, W. W. Rouse & Coxeter, H. S. M. (1974). *Mathematical Recreations and Essays.* Toronto: University of Toronto Press.

Biggs, R. L. (1979). The roots of Combinatorics. *Historia Mathematica* 6, 109–36.

Bourbaki, N. (1963). *Elements de Mathématique,* Livre 1. Paris: Hermann.

David, F. N. (1962). *Games, Gods, and Gambling.* London.

Dossey, J. A., et al. (1993). *Discrete Mathematics.* New York: Harper Collins.

Edwards, A. W. F. (1987). *Pascal's Arithmetic Triangle.* London.

Green, T. M. & Hamberg, Ch. L. (1986). *Pascal's Triangle,* Palo Alto, CA.

Hilton, P. & Pedersen, J. (1987). Looking into Pascal's triangle: Combinatorics, arithmetic, and geometrie. *Mathematics Magazine*, Vol. 60, No. 5, 305–16.

Kapur, J. N. (1970). Combinatorial analysis and school mathematics. *Educ. Stud. Math.* 3, 111–27.

National Council of Teachers of Mathematics. (1989). *Curriculum and Evaluation Standards for School Mathematics.* Reston, VA.

Roberts, F. S. (1984). *Applied Combinatorics,* Prentice-Hall Inc.

Shaughnessy, J. M. (1984). The case of the unfriendly customers. *The Oregon Mathematics Teacher,* 30–32.

Stein, S. K. (1969). *Mathematics, The Man-Made Universe.* San Francisco: Freeman.

———(1979). Existence out of chaos. In R. Honsberger (ed.), *Mathematical Plums.* Washington, D.C.: The Mathematical Association of America, 62–93.

Modeling with Functions

EXAMINING OUR UNDERSTANDING OF USING FUNCTIONS TO MODEL REAL-WORLD EVENTS

Perhaps the most important role that functions play in mathematics, at least as they are applied, is serving as models for understanding phenomena that take place in our daily surroundings. Here we focus on how linear, quadratic, logarithmic, and exponential functions serve to help us understand, predict, and control events in our lives. Along the way, we also see the power that technology provides in helping us "see" mathematics and its usefulness in our world. We begin by visiting Mr. Kubiack's class as they wrestle with an applied problem.

Visiting Mr. Kubiack's Class

What does it mean to teach mathematics? What does it mean to "do mathematics"? When you think of "mathematics" or using "mathematics" to solve real-world problems, what comes to your mind? Do you think of memorizing formulas, using the methods you practiced in the textbook, looking for patterns, using a computer to model a problem, or hiring a consultant?

To provide some points of reference about teaching mathematics, we visit the classroom of Mr. Stan Kubiack, a veteran mathematics teacher, who has taught at Kengrove High, an urban magnet school, for over twenty years. He is well known for producing students who, as others describe it, can "think mathematically." As we enter his classroom during the first week of the school year, we find him moving between groups of three or four students as they work to solve the problem below using mathematics they have learned in last year's Algebra II class.

Consider the pizza prices offered by Gumpy's Pizza and Pizza Shack shown in the tables below. How do these two companies price their various sizes of pizza? How do the two pizza businesses determine their pricing? Does it appear that they are using the same model to develop their pricing patterns?

Gumpy's Pizza		Pizza Shack Pizza	
Diameter	Cost	Diameter	Cost
20 cm	$ 6.50	25 cm	$ 7.00
30 cm	$ 9.00	35 cm	$10.75
40 cm	$12.50	45 cm	$15.50

As we look in on the class, think about the following questions:

- How would you answer the question the class is considering?
- What goals might Mr. Kubiack be trying to achieve by giving students this problem to start the year?
- What solutions do you think students might propose?
- What relationship does this problem have to the NCTM *Standards*?
- What would you listen for if you were Mr. Kubiack as you walked from group to group as the students work on the problem?
- What hints, if any, would you be prepared to give the students as they work to answer the question?

Group 1
Jack, Maria, Viva, and Chi have approached the problem via graphing the prices on a piece of graph paper. Their graphs appear in Figure 1.

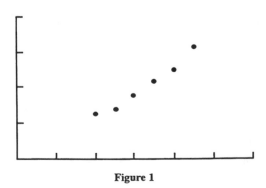

Figure 1

Jack: Look, I have graphed the six price points on my graphing calculator. It looks like they fall on a straight line.

Chi: I am not so sure, it doesn't look like that to me. There seem to be some wiggles as the diameter of the pizzas increases.

Jack: Those things happen when you graph data on a calculator; they are just normal rounding errors.

Maria: Let's draw the line that fits this data.

Chi: Does anyone remember how to do it?

Viva: Yeah, draw a line so that it goes through the average of the x's and the average of the y's and about the same number of points fall on each side of the line.

Jack: Where did you learn to do that?

Viva: In chemistry last year.

Maria: Then we want to find a line going through (32.50, 10.21)!

The students try drawing several lines through the point that Maria gave and shifting the slope of the lines to achieve the balance of points on both sides of the line that Viva mentioned.

Jack: I think that y = 0.4x – 2.8 will work well. It looks good, but it doesn't quite go through the points. Look at it! (Figure 2)

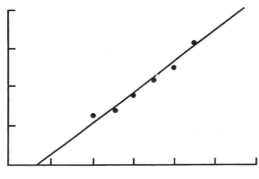

Figure 2

Viva: That's about the same thing that I got. When you plug 32.5 in for x it gives a y of 10.20 and that's pretty close. I think that this is okay.

Maria: Look, it's almost 10:45. If we don't hurry we will have to work on this after school.

Jack: What do we have to do to finish?

Chi: I think that Mr. Kubiack wants us to tell what this equation means in terms of pricing pizza. I think that we should use both companies' prices in the equation and see how much they are off what this equation would predict.

Students work independently for a period of about two minutes and then Viva seems to take control of the group.

Viva: Look at this way of doing it! I just figured out what it would cost if we use the equation to figure the prices for each company.

Diameter	Actual Price	Equation Price
20	5.20	6.50
25	7.20	7.00
30	9.20	9.00
35	11.20	10.75
40	13.20	12.50
45	15.20	15.50

Maria: Let's find the difference in the actual and equation prices for each company.

They calculate the following chart.

Diameter	Actual	Equation	Difference
20	5.20	6.50	−1.30
25	7.20	7.00	0.20
30	9.20	9.00	0.20
35	11.20	10.75	0.45
40	13.20	12.50	0.70
45	15.20	15.50	−0.30

Chi: We need to split these differences up for the two companies to answer Mr. Kubiack's questions. Look, the differences for Gumpy's Pizza are −1.30, 0.20, and 0.70, while those for Pizza Shack Pizza are 0.20, 0.45, and −0.30.

Jack: If we just add up these differences we get −.40 cents for Gumpy's and +.35 cents for Pizza Shack. So, it looks like the best deal is at Gumpy's!

Viva: Don't you have it backwards? We subtracted the value given by the equation from the actual cost, so a positive answer would give the best! The best deal would be at Pizza Shack. I think we have the models!

Bell rings ending the class.

Group 2
Bill, Christa, Earl, and Naomi approached the problem by making a separate graph for each of the two sets of diameter–cost data. Their graphs appear in Figure 3.

Bill: Look at these graphs! What kind of graphs do you think these are? They don't look like perfect lines. Do you think there is some mistake in Mr. Kubiack's numbers?

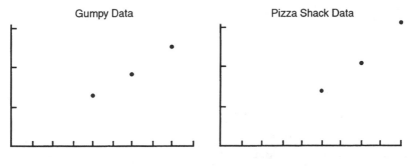

Figure 3

Christa: Things don't always work out perfect in the real world. He said he got the data from the managers of the stores.

Earl: Why don't we look at the differences between the values like we did last year in looking for the formula for a circle's area?

Bill: That's a good idea!

Naomi: That's just what I have been doing. Look at this—

I think that rules for the pizza costs are quadratic—the second differences are equal.

Christa: Yeah! The first differences would be the slopes and it's easy to see that lines won't fit either set. Quadratics look like a good guess. But I sure don't remember anything about second differences.

Earl: How about if we suppose that a quadratic will work. That means that the cost is a quadratic function of the input, or diameter. So, cost = a(diameter)^2 + b(diameter) + c. But, how can we find a, b, and c?

Christa: You've got me!

At this point the group gets off target and Mr. Kubiack drops by and gives them a nudge by asking them, if they think the relationship is quadratic, could they write equations using the ordered pairs, like (pizza size, cost), based on data from the two stores' prices.

Bill: How about if we substitute the numbers he gave us in the equations? Like $20 = a(6.5)^2 + b(6.5) + c$. Then we could look for the solution.

They try substituting in the equations as Bill suggested and work with their individual scratch work.

Christa: Wait a minute, we've put the numbers in backwards. They should be the cost and the x the diameter. We are predicting cost, not diameter. The cost is the dependent variable.

Earl: Right, that is how we graphed them.

Naomi: Here are the equations for Gumpy's:

$$6.50 = a(20)^2 + b(20) + c$$
$$9.00 = a(30)^2 + b(30) + c$$
$$12.50 = a(40)^2 + b(30) + c.$$

Earl: Here are the equations for Pizza Shack:

$$7.00 = a(25)^2 + b(25) + c$$
$$10.75 = a(35)^2 + b(35) + c$$
$$15.50 = a(45)^2 + b(45) + c.$$

All we need to do is find a, b, and c and we are done!

Bill: No! We can't use the same a, b, and c for both of the businesses. The stores might have different pricing rules. We had better call the variables for Pizza Shack r, s, and t.

The group grudgingly agrees and changes the second set of equations to

$$7.00 = r(25)^2 + s(25) + t$$
$$10.75 = r(35)^2 + s(35) + t$$
$$15.50 = r(45)^2 + s(45) + t$$

and sets about solving the sets of equations for the values that satisfy the two systems. After some work they agree that the appropriate values for a, b, and c are 0.005, 0, and 4.5 respectively and for r, s, and t are 0.005, 0.075, and 2 respectively.

Naomi: How can we use these numbers to find the prices for pizza at Gumpy's and Pizza Shack?

Earl: It looks as if they price by these models:

Gumpy's: Price $= 0.005(\text{diam.})^2 + 4.5$
Pizza Shack: Price $= 0.005 \,(\text{diam.})^2 + (0.075)\text{diam.} + 2.$
Do they check?

*The group dissolves into a calculating frenzy again and comes to a
tentative agreement that the rules apply to the respective stores.*

Christa: Look at the time. Can you write this up for us, Naomi? You always
do such a good job.

Naomi: Okay, but what do I need to write up?

Bill: We need to compare the prices that each of these rules gives for different sizes of pizza and then describe which one gives us the better deal,
that is, if we have the money to buy pizza.

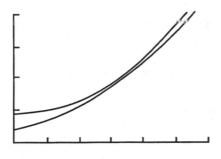

Figure 4

Here are two graphs on the same scale ([0,60] × [0,20]). (See Figure 4.)
That's Pizza Shack's graph on the bottom at the *y*-axis. Maybe this will
help.

Bell rings and the group disperses.

Group 3

*This group consists of Ila, Cynthia, Gaea, and Madhu. They start out the same
way as the first group, but decide that the shape of the curves outlined by the
data is probably quadratic in form. Ila gets out his graphing calculator and
we pick up the conversation shown.*

Ila: If each store has a quadratic rule, I can find that rule with my calculator.
Watch!

*Ila quickly opens the STAT package on his calculator and selects the
EDIT feature to enter the data from Gumpy's. He calls the x-list DIA for
diameter and the y-list CST for cost. He then quickly enters the data lists
for each variable as follows:*

$$x_1 = 20$$
$$y_1 = 6.5$$
$$x_2 = 30$$

$$y_2 = 9$$
$$x_3 = 40$$
$$y_3 = 12.5$$

He then toggles to 2nd CALC and gets the list of possible ways of fitting functions to data. Since the group thought the equations would be quadratic, Ila keys in MORE and selects the P2REG for a quadratic regression equation. The calculator gives:

$$y = 0.005x^2 + 0x + 4.5.$$

He quickly repeats the sequence of activities with the data for Pizza Shack. The resulting equation is:

$$y = 0.005x^2 + 0.075x + 2.$$

He writes the equations of the board as shown.

Gumpy's: Cost $= 0.005d^2 + 4.5$
Shack: Price $= 0.005D^2 + 0.075D + 2.$

Ila: Here are the equations that I got using my calculator. Let's see what they mean.

Cynthia: Let's substitute the values into the equations to see if the equations really work.

The group checks out the two equations and agrees that they do.

Gaea: Let's make a graph of the two equations and see what they give us.

Ila enters the two equations and gets the following graph on a [0,60] × [0,20] screen and then zooms in to their point of intersection as in Figure 5.

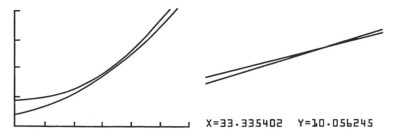

X=33.335402   Y=10.056245

Figure 5

Linking the calculator to a PC, they send the graphs to the monitor so they can investigate them a bit more.

Cynthia: So, if I understand the graphs right, we are better off to buy pizzas from Gumpy's if the diameters are less than 33½ centimeters and from Pizza Shack if the diameters are greater than that value. Right?

Gaea: Right. But, we also know that the two different stores are using different pricing guidelines. We just started studying about this in economics. I think it has something to do with supply and demand and the most frequently ordered sizes at the stores.

Madhu: Maybe Pizza Shack gets few orders for the smaller-diameter pizzas and they are selling them for less and trying to look competitive while making a larger profit on the bigger pizzas. Why don't we call the stores and see how many pizzas of each size they sell on average each week—that is, if they will tell us.

Bell rings and class is dismissed.

These three segments from the working groups in Mr. Kubiack's class provide glimpses of students' approaches to solving a problem. Unfortunately, much of the conversation that we were privy to in these groups is often missed by a classroom teacher as he or she moves from group to group helping, asking questions, and observing student progress. Fortunately, Mr. Kubiack is a strong leader in helping his students to think independently and to work problems in a variety of ways. He realizes that there is considerable difference in the ways his students have approached the problem he set for them. He was quite surprised to find that none of the groups had used the method he would have used to model the costs. However, he was pleased that the students had offered a number of innovative ways of looking at the problem. The problem now was to decide how to begin the discussion of the problem in class tomorrow.

Reflective Problem 1

As you reflect on Mr. Kubiack's lesson, consider the following questions.

1. Outline another way in which the students might have modeled the costs of the two pizza businesses.

2. How would you characterize the interpersonal interactions in each of the groups? How did they work together to solve the problem? What would you try modify about how each group works as the year progresses?

3. Why do you think Mr. Kubiack selected a problem like this to kick off the year? What criteria would you list for selecting such a problem to open the year?

4. The NCTM *Curriculum and Evaluation Standards for School Mathematics* (1989) make several recommendations for redefining the teaching and learning of mathematics. What relationships do you see between the standards for problem solving, reasoning, communication, connections, and functions and the activities in Mr. Kubiack's class?

5. Are there any places where you would have intervened as a teacher as you watched Group 2? Be specific in the actions you would have taken in terms of the points you would note, comments you would make, or questions you might ask.

6. How would you plan to start the period on the following day, knowing that each of the groups will have something put together by the beginning of the hour?

7. Is there some way in which spreadsheets might have been used to illustrate the relationships inherent in the problem noted?

8. How would you characterize each group's insight into the problem of modeling the pizza costs?

9. Describe the approach each of the groups took. Explain the strengths and weaknesses of each approach.

10. Write a similar problem that you might use to kick off an Algebra II class at the beginning of the year for a group of average students. Illustrate any graphical or tabular material you would give them and any technology you would expect them to employ. Describe at least one solution you would expect to get to your problem.

Reflecting on Applying Mathematics

The problem-solving activities in Mr. Kubiack's classroom were probably a great deal different from what took place in the mathematics classrooms of your high school days. Indeed, the discourse and operation of the secondary mathematics classroom is changing rapidly. If you are to be successful in secondary mathematics teaching, change will be a constant for the rest of your career in education. How you adapt to it and reflectively alter your teaching will say a great deal about the success and enjoyment you will derive from your teaching.

This section asks you to reflect on mathematical problems you have solved and the mathematical methods you used in solving them. Respond to each of the questions in Reflective Problem 2 with enough detail that someone else can understand the problem you describe and the process you used to solve it. Think also about how you might respond to these same questions if you were teaching a class and the same questions originated from your students.

Reflective Problem 2

1. Describe the most significant "real world" problem you have solved using mathematics. In doing so, provide some detail about the setting of the problem, the reason a solution was needed, the process you went about to "understand" the problem, how you solved the problem, and what decisions you made in implementing your solution.

2. Describe how long it took you to solve the problem. In doing so, tell how the time was allocated to formulating the problem, seeing how to solve it, computing the answer, and implementing the solution in action.

3. How, if at all, did you use technology, software, measuring instruments, or other aids in solving the problem?

4. Have you used the same method you used to solve the problem described again to solve another similar, or different, problem? In what ways?

5. How did you feel about the problem before, during, and after you solved it? Have your feelings about the problem changed today?

6. Was there anything specific in your school mathematics that suggested the methods you used to solve the problem?

7. How would you make a classroom problem for your students out of the problem you solved? Where in the curriculum would you insert this problem for students to work on it?

Consider questions 1 through 6 in Reflective Problem 2 above. These questions asked you to consider a time mathematics assisted you in solving a real-world problem. Working with another college student who is majoring in a field other than mathematics, ask the student the questions in Reflective Problem 3 and record the student's responses, reflecting on them in light of your own experiences with mathematical problem solving.

Reflective Problem 3

1. What use do you make of mathematics in and outside your studies? How have these experiences changed your view of mathematics?

2. Describe a "real world" problem you have attempted to solve using mathematics.

3. Were you able to solve the problem? If so, how?

4. Did you use any technology, for example, computers or calculators, in working on the problem?

5. Describe in writing the results of your interview with the student. Try to capture as much of the interview as possible in your summary. Then, write an analysis comparing your approach to your problem with the student's approach to his/her problem. How were the approaches different and how were they alike?

MATHEMATICAL MODELING IN THE SECONDARY CLASSROOM

Most problems individuals face are complicated and ill formed, and require all sorts of trade-offs in their solutions. Mathematical problem solving outside the classroom often requires situation simplification and the determination of whether an exact solution or a reasonable estimate is required. Developing models, like the ones for the pizza pricing in Mr. Kubiack's classroom, is rarely discussed in most secondary mathematics classrooms. However, the active involvement of students in such activities gets them *doing mathematics*. The injection of such problems into the secondary mathematics curriculum is one of the primary goals of the National Council of Teachers of Mathematics' *Curriculum and Evaluation Standards for School Mathematics* and their *Professional Standards for the Teaching of Mathematics.*

This unit will focus on assisting you in extending your knowledge of functions to represent a variety of real-world situations. In doing so, you will be called on to expand your experiences and feelings about mathematics and its uses, your knowledge and ability to use functions in a variety of settings, your facility with a graphing calculator as a problem-solving tool, and your ability to develop quality instruction appropriate for secondary school mathematics students.

Developing mathematical models to represent real-world problems is a creative task. This unit will limit itself to models that are based on polynomial, logarithmic, and exponential functions. You will see elementary and advanced approaches to the construction of function-based models in each of these areas. In each case, you will see the iterative aspect of model building—the first approximation, the testing, the tuning, and the interpretation—that goes with the application of mathematics to solving important problems.

What Is Mathematical Modeling?

The application of mathematics in the "real world" is often a tentative and intuitive process. The clarity of the problem at hand, the adequacy of the information available, the nature of the desired solution, and the support available for executing the needed data collection, calculations, and verification of results are often questionable at best. The skills required to apply mathematics in such situations differs greatly from the study of mathematics as traditionally taught in the school classroom.

The development of a function to represent, or model, a mathematical problem often calls on the problem-solver to learn new concepts on his or her own, to combine skills learned in the mathematics classroom with those coming from other disciplines in new and creative ways, and to create new frames of reference for thinking about the context at hand. Inevitably, the problem situation is translated from reality back into a realm of mathematics with which the individual is familiar—or with which they will soon become familiar. This imaging of the problem situation is the heart of mathematical modeling. This representation is then studied using known mathematics or mathematics specially created for the context. Based on an analysis of the outcomes of derived relationships, calculations, and other mathematical manipulations, the problem situation as transformed is "solved." This mathematical solution is then translated back into the context of the original problem to determine the meaning of the "solution" and what decisions it might imply. In this process, the "best" or "exact" mathematical solution may not turn out to be the best "real world" solution as the context may not allow such precision or the technology needed to enact the "solution" may not be available.

As one example of such a problem, consider the determination of how to place a home on a piece of property in order to make maximal use of solar energy to warm the home in winter without causing an unbearable temperature situation in the summertime. What are the considerations that must be taken into account? What fields other than mathematics would you draw upon? What mathematics might be useful? What geometry might enter into the design questions involved? What data would you want to know?

The process described above is known as *modeling*. The actual graph, symbolic equation, table of data, or geometric figure is the *model*. The process of developing such a model normally results from a description of some real-world *system* in mathematical terms. A system is a set of real-world objects that are bound together by a pattern of interaction or interdependence. Some exam-

ples of systems are: epidemics, national economies, air-traffic control networks, communication networks, factory assembly lines, social structures in a
small town, and temperature-pressure relationships in a sealed vessel.

One can think of a model as a parallel world portraying a real-world
system in terms of mathematical concepts, relations, and principles. The
mathematician, or the person employing the mathematician, is interested in
understanding :

- how the system functions
- what causes the system to alter its state
- how robust the system is to changes in its state.

In addition, the person involved in constructing the model is usually interested in *predicting*:

- what changes will take place in the system
- when those changes will take place
- what the impact of such changes might be.

Simply put, the two can be contrasted thus:

Real-World Situation	Mathematical Model
Observations, data, patterns, happenings representing problem situation	Representations Mathematical operations and principles Mathematical conclusions

Probably the most elementary technique for constructing mathematical
models is the "fitting" of functions to observed phenomena or data. The data,
their graphs, and related functions from science, social studies, linguistics, or
other disciplines are then applied to interpret the data and work toward the
resolution of the problem at hand.

An Example of the Development of a Function-Based Model

The general nature of mathematical models is best illustrated by Robert Fadeley's 1965 investigation of the possible relationship of the U.S. government
Hanford nuclear reactor activities to the occurrence of malignancies in Oregon. Fadeley, an environmental scientist, was concerned about the increase in
malignancy occurrences in Oregon in counties bordering the Columbia River
and the potentially dangerous storage of radioisotopes from the Hanford reactor upstream on the Columbia in Washington. In particular, he was concerned about the potential leakage of the stored reactor wastes into the
Columbia and the exposure of Oregon citizens in counties and cities adjacent
to the river and the incidence of deaths by cancer in these counties.

Fadeley began with a hypothesis that the number of deaths due to cancer in the Oregon counties and cities bordering the Columbia downstream from Hanford was probably related to the presence and storage of nuclear materials at the reactor site. The nature of such a pattern was somewhat clouded by the fact that the population levels in these locales differed and in some sites the population was massed along the shores of the river, while in other counties bordering the river, the population did not live immediately adjacent to the river. Fadeley hypothesized that there was a functional relationship between the cancer deaths in counties and major cities adjacent to the Columbia River and some expression relating the distance of a county along the river from the Hanford plant, the population of the counties, and the nature of the distribution of the population in the counties. Note that it is here that Fadeley began to build his model (Figure 6). The original situation only indicated the possibility of a problem. He then began to structure the problem in terms of potential factors that might affect outcomes in terms of data that might help explain what was happening. Here the problem was deaths by cancer. A first step might be to think of factors that could be related to the untoward death rates.

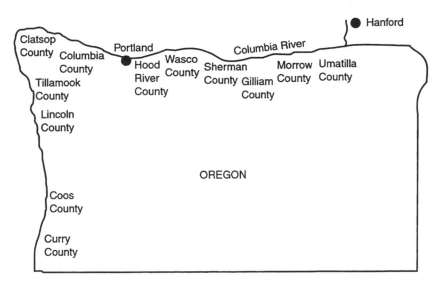

Figure 6

To deal with these variables, Fadeley surmised that exposure to the run-off wastes might be inversely proportional to the river distance from the Hanford site, as it would make sense that the danger would decrease the farther one was from the Hanford site. This idea was supported by the data. An analysis of the death rates for counties' populations suggested that the rates were inversely proportional to the square of the distance of a county's, or a city's, population center from the river. A final factor related to the death rates was the amount of river frontage a county or city had. Here the data suggested that this relationship was one of direct proportion. Again, this made sense, as the exposure should increase a fixed amount for each foot of river frontage. Based on these factors, Fadeley developed an index of exposure using these three factors. The values for this exposure index for each county and the city of Portland, as well as the deaths per 100,000 residents in each of these regions, are shown in the table.

Location	Index of Exposure	Deaths per 100,000
Umatilla County	2.49	147.1
Morrow County	2.57	130.1
Gilliam County	3.41	129.9
Sherman County	1.25	113.5
Wasco County	1.62	137.5
Hood River County	3.83	162.3
City of Portland	11.64	207.5
Columbia County	6.41	177.9
Clatsop County	8.34	210.3

It is often hard to see relationships in tables of data, so to explore for a relationship between the index of exposure and the number of cancer deaths we can make a scatterplot of the data. An analysis of the pattern of the data points in the scatterplot suggests that a linear equation could be developed to model the relationship between values of the index of exposure and the number of deaths per 100,000 population. Such a line has been sketched on the scatterplot (Figure 7).

Cancer Deaths by Exposure Index Values

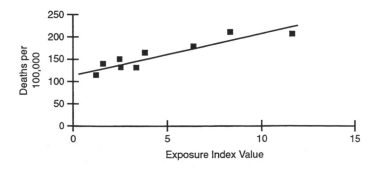

Figure 7

Using the median-line-fit to fit a line to the data, a method that will be studied later, a linear equation relating exposure index values (x) and death rates (y) can be derived. The resulting equation is $y = 10.75x + 111.51$. This linear equation provides a *model* for the situation under the assumptions Fadeley made in the development of the index of exposure. The model can also be written in function form, $d(e) = 10.75e + 111.51$, indicating that the death rate, $d(e)$, is a function of the exposure value, e, for a given site.

The slope of the line indicates that the death rate is expected to increase by 10.75 deaths per 100,000 inhabitants for each increase of 1 in the value of the exposure index. The intercept of the equation with the vertical axis suggests that a normal death rate of 111.51 deaths per 100,000 inhabitants might be expected for the region in the absence of the use of exposure index data.

To see if this linear function model for the incidence of cancer deaths could be extended, data were collected along the coastal counties of Oregon using the same assumptions. These sites are downcurrent from the mouth of the Columbia River as it empties into the Pacific Ocean at Astoria in Clatsop County.

Location	Index of Exposure	Predicted Deaths per 100,000
Clatsop County	8.34	210.3
Tillamook County	5.51	163.8
Lincoln County	6.21	170.4
Coos County	1.85	117.6
Curry County	2.81	73.6

An analysis of this data, using the same process as used above, results in the equation $D(E) = 18.73E + 20.21$. While the coefficients involved are different, it still indicates a strong linear relationship between the exposure index value and the death rate per 100,000 inhabitants for a county. This similar finding supports the story portrayed by the initial model developed.

Reflecting on the Model-Building Process

The series of steps taken in the development of the relationship between the exposure rates for the Columbia River and the death rate in various Oregon counties and the city of Portland shows the modeling process in action. The study began with the recognition of a problem involving some suspicions about the effect the radioactive waste runoff into the Columbia River might have on rate of cancer deaths per 100,000 inhabitants in counties/cities along the Columbia. A study of the data suggested a form for the exposure of individuals to the river and the death rate. Using the assumptions, the investigator formulated an exposure index to describe the potential for individual exposure.

Based on this information, a plot of the data suggested that a linear relationship existed. This relationship was developed using statistical methods for fitting a line to data. This solution was then supported by extending the process to the coastal counties of Oregon, which are also exposed as the current sweeps the Columbia River outflow down the western coast of Oregon. While the exact coefficients of the model changed, the linear relationship between the data values was substantiated.

The steps in mathematical modeling involve the following:

Step 1. Identify the problem.
Step 2. Make assumptions.
    a. Identify and classify possible variables that might explain the patterns observed.
    b. Determine interrelationships among these variables.
Step 3. Develop a functional relationship, if possible, among the variables, developing indices involving the variables if necessary.
Step 4. Verify the model.
    a. Does it address the problem?
    b. Does it make common sense?
    c. Do its predictions match real-world data?

Developing a function relationship describing relations in a situation and then using the function to understand the nature of the situation are important aspects of *mathematical modeling*. While there are many different kinds of models that can be developed to "make sense" of real-world contexts, at present we will focus on the role of mathematical functions as models. We will examine how to recognize when one of these models is appropriate and how to develop such functions from numerical data or graphical displays. Once the models have been developed, we will examine how such models can be used to analyze the situations from which they arose and make predictions or decisions in the original contexts.

The ability to create function-based models and employ them in mathematical problem solving is empowering. Often students are not given adequate opportunities to study such modeling, or even see examples of it, until they are graduate students in mathematics. As a result, many students finish their study of mathematics and other courses without ever seeing the guessing, hypothesis formation, problem solving, and applications of basic concepts and principles that go into understanding real-world problems. Mathematical models and the skills of modeling are central to the creation and application of mathematics. To study mathematics without exposure to the various types of function-based models is to give students an incomplete view of the work of a mathematician and the power of mathematics.

Exploration 1

1. Using the four-step model-building process outlined above, relate each step to an aspect of the development of the Hanford waste runoff example.

2. Graph the data for the set of data related to the Hanford waste runoff and the coastal counties of Oregon. "Fit" your own line to the data and compare the equation you get to the one given in the text. How similar are they?

3. Given the following set of ordered pairs, graph them and then find a function you think "fits" them best: (1960, 179,380), (1965, 193,223), (1970, 203,849), (1975, 214,931), (1080, 226,451), (1985, 238,207). What do you think the data represent?

In the next three exercises, consider the situations described. Define a problem inherent in the situation, collect data if necessary, and make an analysis of the problem you defined. Describe your work and the meaning of your solution.

4. Sara was working on designing smock patterns for her friends for art class. She thought that she had heard about a relationship between individuals' heights and other body measurements.

5. Latisha felt that there was an unfair relationship between lane assignments at Central High and victories in the 200-meter dash. She checked the records for 24 races during the past season and found the following data.

Lane	1	2	3	4	5	6
Victories	1	2	3	5	6	7

6. Detail an instance in which you have constructed a functional model to solve a problem. Describe the model, giving how you dealt with the steps in the modeling process.

7. In what way does modeling relate to the recommendations in the NCTM *Curriculum and Evaluation Standards* and the *Professional Standards for the Teaching of Mathematics?* How does modeling play a role in the structure of curriculum, in assessment, and in the teaching of mathematics?

MODELING LINEAR RELATIONSHIPS

Relationships that can be expressed by a linear equation are among the easiest with which to work. In this section, we examine the process for developing such linear models, as well as look at how they might be used in interpreting the relationships they portray.

The prediction of sports records into the future is a topic of interest for both fans and medical researchers. One record that has received more interest than others over the years is the world record for the one-mile run. Roger Bannister was the first person to break the seemingly impossible four-minute barrier with his run in 1954. After that unforgettable race, the psychological barrier was broken and the record was quickly pushed lower as shown in the table.

Year	Person/Country	Time	Year	Person/Country	Time
1875	Slade/England	4:24.5	1944	Andersson/Sweden	4:01.6
1880	George/England	4:23.2	1945	Haegg/Sweden	4:01.4
1882	George/England	4:21.4	1954	Bannister/Britain	3:59.4
1882	George/England	4:19.4	1954	Landry/Australia	3:58.0
1894	Bacon/Scotland	4:18.2	1957	Ibbotson/Britain	3:57.2
1895	Bacon/Scotland	4:17	1958	Elliott/Australia	3:54.5
1911	Connett/U.S.	4:15.6	1962	Snell/New Zealand	3:54.4
1911	Jones/U.S.	4:15.4	1964	Snell/New Zealand	3:54.1
1913	Jones/U.S.	4:14.6	1965	Jazy/France	3:53.6
1915	Taber/U.S.	4:12.6	1966	Ryun/U.S.	3:51.3
1923	Nurmi/Finland	4:10.4	1967	Ryun/U.S.	3:51.1
1931	Ladoumegue/France	4:09.2	1975	Bayi/Tanzania	3:52.0
1933	Lovelock/New Zea.	4:07.6	1975	Walker/New Zea.	3:49.4
1934	Cunningham/U.S.	4:06.8	1979	Coe/Britain	3:49.0
1937	Wooderson/Britain	4:06.4	1980	Ovett/Britain	3:48.8
1942	Haegg/Sweden	4:06.2	1981	Coe/Britain	3:48.5
1942	Andersson/Sweden	4:06.2	1981	Ovett/Britain	3:48.4
1942	Haegg/Sweden	4:04.6	1981	Coe/Britain	3:47.3
1943	Andersson/Sweden	4:02.6	1985	Cram/Britain	3:46.3

Exploration 2

Based on the information in the table, what do you think that the world record for the mile will be in the year 2000? When do you think that someone will first run under 3:40 for the mile run?

Based on the data in the table can you create a functional model for the world record for the one mile as a function of years? How well does your model "fit" the data given in the table?

Try this problem using all that you know about functions. In this part of the chapter, you will learn at least two ways to solve this type of problem. At the end of this part of the unit, you will have a chance to revisit this problem with more tools to solve it than you presently have.

Modeling Linear Relations by Median-Fit Line

Linear relationships are characterized by a constant rate of change, similar to that found in arithmetic sequences. For each unit of change in the independent (input) variable, there is a constant amount of growth in the dependent (output) variable. Linear relationships are noted by their shape when graphed in scatterplot form in the xy plane. The linear pattern was easily seen in the data from the Hanford reactor shown earlier.

Algorithms exist for *fitting* lines to such displays of points in an attempt to provide an interpretation of the relationship inherent in the data. One such approach is called the *median-fit line*. This approach is easy to do and makes use of very elementary algebra. It was developed and popularized by the Princeton mathematician John Tukey.

To illustrate the process, consider the following data: The *1991 Statistical Abstract of the United States* reports the U.S. population (in thousands):

1960	179,386	1975	214,931
1965	193,223	1980	226,451
1970	203,849	1985	238,207

The first step in building a model for this data is to look at ordered pairs of related data on a graph. A graph that plots such ordered pairs on coordinate axes is called a *scatterplot*. The ordered pairs (year, population) provide a look at the data distribution. It appears in Figure 8.

U.S. Population Across Time

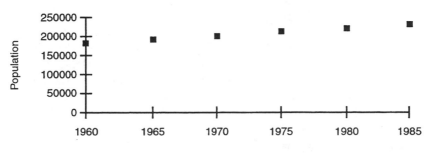

Figure 8

The points in the data set appear to fall along a straight line. Our task is to find a line $y = mx + b$ that fits these points so as little error as possible exists between the values of the actual values and those predicted by the fitted line.

We begin by dividing the ordered pairs in the data into three sets of equal size according to ascending values of their first coordinates. If the number of ordered pairs is not divisible by three, place the additional ordered pairs in the middle set. In our case the number of points is divisible by three and hence, the sets are {(1960, 179,386), (1965, 193,223)}, {(1970, 203,849), (1975, 214,931)}, and {(1980, 226,451), (1985, 238,207)}. For each of the sets, find the ordered pair whose coordinates are the median x-coordinate and y-coordinate for the x- and y-coordinates of the points in the set. For our data, the resulting three points, in ascending x-coordinate values, are (1962.5, 186,305), (1972.5, 209,390), and (1982.5, 232,329). (See Figure 9.)

U.S. Population Across Time

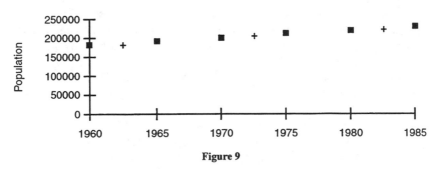

Figure 9

Plot these points, called *submedians,* on the graph of the data using small + signs. Connect the outer two submedians with a line and find its equation using the point slope form for a line. In this case we get:

$$(y - 186,305) = 2301.2 \, (x - 1962.5).$$

This simplifies to the equation $y = 2301.2 - 4,329,800$. However, this equation is built only on the basis of the four outermost data points.

To correct for the influence of the middle two data points, we evaluate the above equation for the middle submedian by substituting 1972.5 for x and computing. This gives an estimated corresponding y-value of 209,317. This y-value is lower than the middle submedian of 209,390. To give the middle two points in the original data set their fair share of determination of the position of the line, it needs to be lowered to adjust for their values. This is shown in Figure 10a below. As these two points comprise ⅓ of the data, we take ⅓ of the difference between the predicted value of 209,317 and the actual value of 209,390. This amounts to 24.$\overline{3}$. Adding this from the y-intercept of the line translates the line ⅓ of the way toward the position of the middle submedian as shown in Figure 10b. This translation is equivalent to moving the y-inter-cept up 24.3 units, resulting in $y = 2301.2x - 4,329,775.67$. This linear equa-tion could be written in an equivalent function form as $p(x) = 2301.2x - 4,329,775.67$, where $p(x)$ is the U.S. population in thousands in the year x.

When this model is used to predict the U.S. population in 1990, it gives 249,612,000 or a population of 249,612,000. The actual figure given by the 1990 census was 248,709,873. The relative error in our prediction was less than 1 percent of the actual census value. Thus it appears that our model is working well.

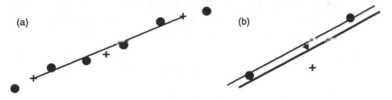

(a)

(b)

Figure 10

Another method of finding the equation of the median-fit line is to first locate the coordinates of the three submedian points. Then find the point whose coordinates are the average of the respective coordinates of the three submedians. Use this point and the slope of the segment joining the outer two submedians to write the equation of the median-fit line.

Exploration 3

Does Advertising Pay Off?

One of the questions that businesses often consider is the effect of money spent on advertising versus the amount of profit they make in a period. The data in the table at right show the money spent on adver-tising in each of the past nine years by a major firm and the amount of profit made by the firm in the same period of time. What conclusions can you draw about the relation of the two factors?

Ad $ (in millions)	Profit $ (in millions)
17	250
9	140
12	187
14	209
11	165
18	270
23	332
21	300

1. Use the data on the previous page to analyze the relationship(s) existing between money spent on advertisements and profit for the company.

2. Does it appear that a linear model will illustrate this relationship?

3. Suppose that you are the director of advertising for this firm. Write a letter to the board of directors describing what could happen if $30 million were invested in an upcoming advertising campaign.

4. Suppose $30 million was invested in the advertising campaign discussed in item #3, but the profit realized was only $400 million dollars. Using your model as a base, write a memo explaining why that outcome may have occurred.

5. A professor of business economics suggested that a model of the relationship between dollars spent on ads and profits resembled the curve in Figure 11. Explain what this model suggests. How is it different from the linear model developed earlier?

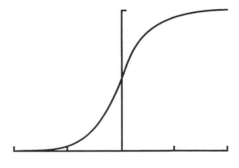

Figure 11

Exploration 4

Who Will Finally Triumph?
Try This One with Your Group

Sports fans are always comparing performances of male and female athletes in various sports. The times at the right reflect the winning times in the Olympic 400m freestyle swimming races in the years indicated. Based on this information, what predictions would you make about the future performances of the two sexes?

Year	Men's	Women's
'56	4:27.3	4:54.6
'60	4:18.3	4:50.6
'64	4:12.2	4:43.3
'68	4:09.0	4:31.8
'72	4:00.3	4:19.4
'76	3:51.9	4:09.9
'80	3:51.3	4:08.8
'84	3:51.2	4:07.1
'88	3:46.9	4:03.8

1. Develop a line of best fit for each gender's data.

2. Based on your models, what pattern of performances would you expect for both sexes in the future? Does there appear to be any validity to the claim that female performances may soon exceed those of males?

3. Were the patterns of improvement in times for men's times similar to the improvement in women's times? What times would your models predict for each group in 1924? The actual times in 1924 were men's, 5:04.2, and women's, 6:02.2. How do these times compare with your model's predictions?

4. In what year do your models predict that each gender will first swim the 400-meter freestyle in under 1 minute? Does this seem to be a reasonable use of models to interpret the data? What bounds would you put on the use of models?

5. How does the nature of your answers to item 2 affect your faith in the equation's ability to predict future performances?

Extending Line Fits with Technology

Most graphing calculators allow an extension of the modeling process to use another method of fitting a line to a set of data. This method is called the *method of least squares*. This process makes use of calculus to minimize the error between observed data points and data values predicted by a model to fit the data. The difference between an observed value y_o and the predicted value y_p, that is, $y_o - y_p$, for a given input value x is called the residual associated with the value of x. The process is also referred to as *linear regression* in many statistical textbooks.

This method was developed in 1805 by the Frenchman Adrien Legendre in his work on celestial mechanics. The method minimizes the sum of the squares of the residuals associated with the line of fit, thus the name for the process. The derivation of this method for linear and other types of data sets is beyond the scope of this work. Interested readers can consult references to the method in almost any standard elementary statistics textbook.

A graphing calculator allows one to enter a series of related data points (x,y), create a scatterplot of the data, and find a linear regression line describing the data. To do this, first clear any functions from the $\boxed{Y_i=}$ lines in the graphics display.

To enter a set of related (x,y) values, touch the $\boxed{2^{nd}}$ $\boxed{STAT}$ keys to enter the statistics menu. Use the $\boxed{>}$ key to toggle over to the DATA option. Touch $\boxed{2}$ $\boxed{ENTER}$ to clear the statistics in the data file at present. Then enter the keystrokes of $\boxed{2^{nd}}$ $\boxed{STAT}$ and toggle over to DATA again, this time entering $\boxed{1}$ to get the EDIT feature. This allows you to enter paired data into the data registers of the calculator. Touching $\boxed{ENTER}$ brings a screen like this:

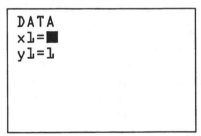

Figure 12

The blinking cursor in the $x1=$ position is waiting for you to enter the x-value from the first data pair (Figure 12). Then touch $\boxed{ENTER}$ and then enter the corresponding y-value by typing over the 1 in the $y1$ position. Touching $\boxed{ENTER}$ again will bring you to the next x-value to enter. Continue this process until all of the data has been entered.

To illustrate the method of least squares we will develop a predictive equation for entrance examination scores for a group of university students. Using the statistics feature of a calculator we enter the math and verbal score data for the college students on their entrance examinations.

math	verbal
44	45
79	72
81	82
80	78
89	79
92	90
63	55
84	77
85	81

When you have entered the nine pairs of scores into the calculator, touch ⟨2ⁿᵈ⟩⟨STAT⟩ to get back to the main statistics menu. This time use the ⟨>⟩ key to toggle over to the DRAW command. Then touch ⟨2⟩ to select the Scatter feature. Touch ⟨ENTER⟩ to get a scatter graph of the data set. If your graph does not show the points, you may need to touch ⟨RANGE⟩ to reset the boundaries of the display screen. For this set of data, the boundaries of Xmin=0, Xmax=100, Xscl=10, Ymin=0, Ymax=100, Yscl=10, Xres=1 would be appropriate. Repeating the sequence above starting with ⟨2ⁿᵈ⟩ ⟨STAT⟩ , followed by a toggle right to the DRAW feature, followed with ⟨2⟩ and ⟨ENTER⟩ , will give the scatterplot, if you didn't get it the first time (Figure 13).

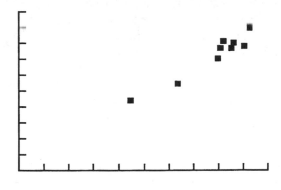

Figure 13

Clearly this is a linear set of data. To get the least squares model for the data, all we need do is stroke ⟨2ⁿᵈ⟩ ⟨STAT⟩ ⟨2⟩ to get the LinReg feature. Touching ⟨ENTER⟩ gives the screen shown below.

LinReg
$a = 8.79403022$
$b = .8663611593$
$r = .9627663178$

The output consists of the coefficients of what is called the linear regression line of best fit to the data entered. The standard statistical form for this line is $y = a + bx$. The data in the output gives the values of a and b for the equation. This indicates that the line $y = 0.866x + 8.794$ is the linear least squares regression equation minimizing the sum of the squares of the residuals for the test data.

To graph this line on the scatterplot, stroke ⟨Y_1 =⟩ followed by ⟨VARS⟩ . Then toggle with the ⟨>⟩ key to LR. Touch ⟨4⟩ to get the RegEQ feature. This enters the linear regression equation into the first graphing position ⟨Y_1 =⟩ . Touching ⟨GRAPH⟩ places the graph of the line on the scatterplot (Figure 14).

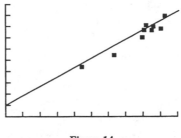

Figure 14

The value of $r = .9627663178$ given in the output on the TI-81 is a measure of the "goodness of fit" of the line to the data. In reality, this value is the *Pearson product-moment correlation coefficient* of the observed data and the data predicted by the model. A correlation coefficient is a measure of the degree of relation between variables. While there are many different forms of correlation in use, the most commonly used one is the product moment correlation developed by the English statistician Karl Pearson (1857–1936) in 1896.

The correlation coefficient for a set of observed scores and a set of related predicted scores gives a measure of the degree to which the two sets of numbers are related. If the scores increase together, then the coefficient will be 1 or near 1. If the pattern of scores is such that as one increases, the other decreases, then the coefficient will be –1 or near –1. If there is no discernable relationship between the observed and predicted scores, then the correlation coefficient will be 0 or near 0.

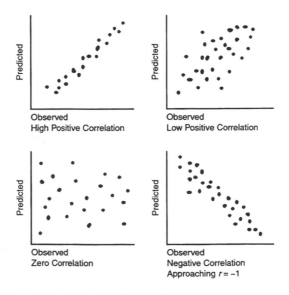

Figure 15

The graphs shown in Figure 15 show the nature of the type of correlation coefficient that is associated with different shapes of scatterplots of observed and predicted values. For our purposes, a value of r between 0.8 and 1.0 is considered to signify a "good fit." If two different types of fit are made to a set of data, the one with the higher absolute r-value is considered to "fit" the data better.

Additional Explorations

Check the Reading

1. In Exploration 3 (pages 23–24) what can you say about the rate of change in profit for each change of one million dollars in expenditures for ads?

2. How does the appearance of a line of fit depend on the value of m in the linear model $y = mx + b$? What impact does the value of b have on the appearance of the graph of the line of fit?

3. Describe a situation different from those contained in this chapter where you think a linear model may apply.

Practice and Apply the Skills

4. Use a median-fit line to
   a. develop a model based on the first eight values given,
   b. test compare your model's predicted value against the observed data value for the ninth and tenth input values

x	0	1	2	3	4	5	6	7	8	9
y	2.3	9.3	15.9	23.1	30.1	36.7	43.5	50.5	57.6	64.4

   For the following problems, use a graphing calculator to
   c. make a scatterplot of the data and determine the nature of the linear model that may fit the data,
   d. develop a model based on the first six values given,
   e. test-compare your model's value against the data value given for the seventh input given,
   f. give the correlation between the values predicted by the model and the actual reported data marks.

5.
x	26	17	23	33	26	44	12	24
y	33	17	22	54	26	40	10	22

6.

x	1	2	3	4	5	6	7	8
y	11.0	10.5	10.3	10.1	9.9	9.9	9.8	9.7

7. *Population Reconsidered.* In the reading for this section, we developed a model for the population growth for the United States. Consider this model in light of the following information. The 1989 census prediction for the U.S. population, in thousands, was 247,617. The 1950 estimate for the population, in thousands, was 151,235. Do these data fit with the model developed? Write an explanation describing the modeling process, the model, and your observations on the latter two data points.

8. *Latitude–Mean January Temperature.* The following chart gives the latitude and mean January temperatures for several U.S. cities for the period 1951–1980. Using this data, find a linear function model expressing mean January temperatures as a function of the number of degrees of North latitude.

City	°Lat	Temp	City	°Lat	Temp
Mobile, AL	30	51	St. Louis, MO	38	29
Juneau, AK	58	22	Omaha, NE	41	20
Los Angeles, CA	34	56	New York, NY	40	32
Denver, CO	39	30	Raleigh, NC	35	40
Washington, DC	38	35	Cleveland, OH	41	26
Jacksonville, FL	28	53	Rapid City, SD	44	13
Honolulu, HI	21	73	Nashville, TN	36	37
Chicago, IL	41	21	Salt Lake City, UT	40	29
Des Moines, IA	41	19	Seattle, WA	47	39
New Orleans, LA	29	52	Milwaukee, WI	43	19
Detroit, MI	42	23	San Juan, PR	18	77

9. *Water Consumption.* The data below represent the average per capita usage of water, in gallons, for every United States citizen averaged over all usages, personal and commercial, for the years 1940 to 1980. What relationship holds between the year and the per capita water usage? If we know that the value for 1985 was 1650 gallons, does this fit the model? Explain why or why not, giving a plausible explanation.

Year	40	50	55	60	65	70	75	80
Gal/Per.	1027	1185	1454	1500	1602	1815	1972	1953

10. *Student Computer Usage at Home.* A national survey compared students' access to computers at home to the household income in their homes. Examine this data and develop a model to explain the relationships in it.

Household Income	Percent with Access
Under $5,000	8.4
$5,000–$9,999	5.4
$10,000–$14,999	7.2
$15,000–$19,999	11.3
$20,000–$24,999	12.9
$25,000–$29,999	17.0
$30,000–$34,999	17.7
$35,000–$39,999	21.4
$40,000–$49,999	25.7
$50,000–$59,999	31.1
$60,000–$74,999	32.2

11. *Student Computer Usage at School.* The same national survey reported in item 10 also compared students' access to computers in the school to the household income in their homes. Examine this data and develop a model to explain the relationships in it.

Household Income	Percent with Access
Under $5,000	36.7
$5,000—$9,999	36.1
$10,000-$14,999	38.4
$15,000-$19,999	41.5
$20,000-$24,999	42.4
$25,000-$29,999	46.1
$30,000-$34,999	44.2
$35,000-$39,999	45.2
$40,000-$49,999	44.7
$50,000-$59,999	48.4
$60,000-$74,999	45.3

12. Write a short newspaper article explaining the patterns resulting from the data in items 10 and 11. Refer to the recommendations of the NCTM *Curriculum and Evaluation Standards for School Mathematics* relative to the findings.

13. *Radioactive Wastes.* In the beginning of the lesson the runoff wastes of the Hanford reactor were discussed. The data below give the exposure index and death rates for the Pacific coast counties of Oregon. Check the comment in the reading that a linear relationship also exists between the two factors for this location. Compare the features of the models for these counties with those counties that border the Columbia River.

Location	Index of Exposure	Cancer Deaths (per 100,000)
Clatsop County	8.34	210.3
Tillamook County	5.51	163.8
Lincoln County	6.21	170.4
Coos County	1.85	117.6
Curry County	2.81	73.6

Thinking, Reasoning, and Communicating About New Ideas

Problem formulation: In exercises 14 and 15 answer the following questions.

- Make up a real-world problem that can be modeled by each of the following functions.
- Describe the problem in some detail, giving the meaning of each of the variables.
- Pose a question for your classmates to answer about the behavior of the model.

14. $f(t) = .25x$

15. $g(t) = 9x + 10$

16. *Communicating About Math.* Write a paragraph that explains why a data set of 15 points is better than a data set of 6 points when one wishes to fit a line to the data.

Looking Back: Modeling with Linear Functions

Year	Person/Country	Time	Year	Person/Country	Time
1875	Slade/England	4:24.5	1944	Andersson/Sweden	4:01.6
1880	George/England	4:23.2	1945	Haegg/Sweden	4:01.4
1882	George/England	4:21.4	1954	Bannister/Britain	3:59.4
1882	George/England	4:19.4	1954	Landry/Australia	3:58.0
1894	Bacon/Scotland	4:18.2	1957	Ibbotson/Britain	3:57.2

Year	Person/Country	Time	Year	Person/Country	Time
1895	Bacon/Scotland	4:17	1958	Elliott/Australia	3:54.5
1911	Connett/U.S.	4:15.6	1962	Snell/New Zealand	3:54.4
1911	Jones/U.S.	4:15.4	1964	Snell/New Zealand	3:54.1
1913	Jones/U.S.	4:14.6	1965	Jazy/France	3:53.6
1915	Taber/U.S.	4:12.6	1966	Ryun/U.S.	3:51.3
1923	Nurmi/Finland	4:10.4	1967	Ryun/U.S.	3:51.1
1931	Ladoumegue/ France	4:09.2	1975	Bayi/Tanzania	3:52.0
1933	Lovelock/ New Zea.	4:07.6	1975	Walker/New Zea.	3:49.4
1934	Cunningham/U.S.	4:06.8	1979	Coe/Britain	3:49.0
1937	Wooderson/ Britain	4:06.4	1980	Ovett/Britain	3:48.8
1942	Haegg/Sweden	4:06.2	1981	Coe/Britain	3:48.5
1942	Andersson/ Sweden	4:06.2	1981	Ovett/Britain	3:48.4
1942	Haegg/Sweden	4:04.6	1981	Coe/Britain	3:47.3
1943	Andersson/ Sweden	4:02.6	1985	Cram/Britain	3:46.3

In the opening task of this lesson, you were asked to find a model for predicting the world record for the mile run as a function of the year. Work this problem now, using what you have learned in this lesson. Compare the results now to the results you obtained when you began this lesson.

17. How do they compare?

18. How would you answer the original questions now?

19. In developing the median-fit line, the translation made to adjust for the effect associated with the middle group's median was made to the y-intercept of the line based on the medians for the two outside groups. Why can this adjustment just be made in the y-intercept of the line?

20. How has your view of the role of linear equations changed as a function of working in this chapter on modeling so far? Does it make sense to introduce linear equations in Algebra I through scatterplots and fitting lines? How might that change students' views about Algebra I?

MODELING NONLINEAR RELATIONSHIPS
Quadratic Relationships

In this section we consider the development of models that employ quadratic and exponential models to develop our understanding of a number of situations. We begin with the consideration of a forestry application.

Plant specialists in the U.S. Forest Service maintain careful records of the rate of first-year growth, in inches (i), of redwood trees. They are interested in using this data to model the rate of reforestation of areas that have been overcut in past years. One of the most promising predictive bits of data appears to be the number of inches (r) of rainfall per year. Consider the data in the table to the right and attempt to develop a model that will predict the growth of trees in inches on the basis of inches of rainfall per year.

r	i
0	1
3	4
5	6
12	9.5
17	10.8
22	10.9
34	6
35	5.3
50	1

Exploration 5

Based on the data, what model will represent the growth of the redwood tree in terms of the amount of annual rainfall? What is the maximal growth that can be expected for a young redwood in its first year? What rainfall amount is associated with this value?

Using Your Model: Make a graph of your data and compare the graph of your function with the graph of the data. Are there points on the graph that do not make sense in terms of the data generated by the model? What accounts for this?

Try this problem using all that you know about functions. In this part of the unit, you will learn at least two ways to solve this type of problem. At the end of this part of the unit, you will have a chance to revisit this problem with more tools to solve it than you presently have.

Modeling Quadratic Relations by Median-Fit Line

Dealing with data that produce *nonlinear* graphs requires some ingenuity. In this section of the unit, we will be considering the development of models to represent situations where the data seem to take the shape of a parabola. From algebra, we know that these situations may be represented by quadratic functions, that is, functions of the form $f(x) = ax^2 + bx + c$. Assuming that a quadratic function fits the data in Exploration 6, give it a try.

Exploration 6

What Is the Rocket's Path?

The Walnut Grove Rocket Club keeps records on the launches of its new models. The new Hornet model achieved a velocity of 49m/sec at the end of its burn stage. At this point the rocket was 155 meters in the air and directly above the launch point. Use the data in the table at the right to find a curve that represents the height of the rocket in terms of the number of seconds after burn ceases. How soon will the rocket reach the ground? How far will it be from the launch site?

Time	Height
0	155
1	199
2	233
3	258
4	272
5	278
6	273
7	255
8	232

Try These with a Partner

1. Make a model for this data and use your model to predict when the rocket will strike the ground, assuming that there is no deployment of its parachute.

2. How far from the launch site is the point of impact?

3. Make a graph showing the relationship between your model for the data and the actual data points given. How good was your fit?

Linearizing Data

The development of a model for quadratic situations can be approached in a number of ways. If the point (0,0) could make sense in the situation we are considering and the scatterplot appears quadratic in shape, one approach to making a model, which builds on the median-fit line, starts by reexpressing the data in the table. This is done by making a new table, replacing each of the output values by its square root. This has the effect of "undoing" the squaring associated with the hypothesized quadratic nature of the relationship. Statisticians call this *linearizing* the data. In our redwood tree-growth example, it makes sense to think of 0 rain, 0 growth for a seedling. So we proceed to take the square root of the inches of new growth.

r	i	$\sqrt{i}$
0	1	1
3	4	2
5	6	2.45
12	9.5	3.08
17	10.8	3.29
22	10.9	3.30
34	6	2.45
35	5.3	2.3
50	1	1

When the two different outcomes, i and $\sqrt{i}$, are graphed against the rainfall, the graphs in Figure 16 (left and right, respectively) result. While the shape of the graph of rainfall versus $\sqrt{i}$ is not linear, it suggests that a relation between r and i of the form $\sqrt{i} = mr + b$ can be found. Using these nine points, we can determine the median-fit line that would give the relationship between rainfall and inches of growth. The related quadratic relationship desired can be found by squaring both sides of the defining equation, that is, $i = (mr)^2 + 2mrb + b^2$.

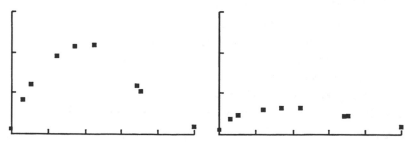

Figure 16

Exploration 7

Prisoners' Cost to Society

Try This One with a Partner

A recent survey of some county jails revealed the data shown at right in terms of the dollars required per day to keep prisoners (p) incarcerated. This cost includes the overhead for the jail, food, salaries, medical attention, special transportation to and from court, and the value of the retail sales of materials the prisoners produce for the state. Find a model that describes the real cost of keeping a prisoner in jail in one of these counties.

#p	$
5	4752.5
10	4290
22	3282
25	3052.5
40	2040
60	1040
90	290
95	252.5
100	240

1. Develop both linear and quadratic models for this data. Which one provides the better fit to the points in the data set?

2. Write a report for the county board administrators describing the relationship between the number of prisoners and the associated costs at the jail.

3. Suppose that you have heard that there was an error in collecting the data in the set for the jails having more than 60 prisoners. How might that change the model you might use in describing the relationship between number of prisoners and costs?

4. What would your original quadratic model suggest the costs to be for 10,000 prisoners? Does this make sense? Explain how you should interpret your model. What might be a more appropriate feature to model than cost/day per prisoner?

5. Do you think that an exponential model $y = ae^{-bx} + c$ for the prisoner cost data might work even better? Why or why not?

Extending Curve Fits with Technology

A graphing calculator provides some assistance in considering nonlinear data to be fit by a polynomial. It offers a *power regression* feature that allows one to find a function of the form $f(x) = ax^b$. This function is a result of a least-squares approach to fitting a single-term expression in x raised to a power to the data. In building this model, we have to omit the data point $(0,1)$, as it could not come from a pure power regression model. When b approximates 2 in value, the shape of the resulting curve approaches that of a parabola. However, the shape when b is near 0.5 is that of the square-root function. The graphing calculator also offers an option of fitting a second-degree polynomial to data with the P2REG feature. Which model (quadratic or power) do you think would provide the best model for the growth of redwood trees? The quadratic model provided is $i = -0.014r^2 + 0.628r + 2.60$. The power regression model for the same data set is $i = 9.6r^{-0.2}$.

Additional Explorations

Check the Reading

1. If the model for a set of data takes the form of $ax^2 + bx + c$, what is the effect of the value of a, b, and c on the shape of the graph associated with the data?

2. What if one tries taking the square root of the data to linearize a data set, fits a line and squares both sides when the data set does not include the origin?

3. If you guess that a data set would support a quadratic model $w = mx^2 + nx + p$ and you know three data points for the situation, explain another way besides linearization that you could solve for m, n, and p.

4. Give an example of another quadratic-based situation and its context. Develop a problem of your own based on relevant data for the situation.

Practice and Apply the Skills

For each of the following problems, use a median-fit line to

- develop a median-fit-line model based on the first nine values given,

- test-compare your model's value against the data value for the tenth input value given,

- compare your model with one generated by a graphing calculator's quadratic regression feature.

5.

x	0	1	2	3	4	5	6	7	8	9
y	49	36	25	16	9	4	1	0	1	4

6.

x	0	1	2	3	4	5	6	7	8	9
y	7	0	−11	−26	−45	−68	−95	−126	−161	−200

7. *Pizza Bargains.* Gumpy's Pizza offers a free jumbo pizza to the student who can figure out the pricing model behind their super sausage pizza. The data that is available is shown below. Figure out the model and explain how it changes as the radius of the pizza changes.

Diameter	Price
30 cm	3.92
40 cm	5.92
45 cm	7.25
50 cm	8.76
55 cm	10.10
60 cm	11.50

8. *Braking Olympics.* The distance that it takes a car to stop once the brakes have been applied is a function of the speed of the car in miles/hour. Consider the data below and find a model that predicts the distance the car travels from the time the brakes are applied. Then consider what the model would be if, on average, it takes a human being 0.23 seconds to react and apply the brakes in an emergency situation. What would the model be for this latter situation?

Speed	Distance
30 mph	64
40 mph	114
45 mph	145
50 mph	180
55 mph	216
60 mph	260

9. *Accident Prone?* The table below contains the number of accidents reported in Krinkleville over the past decade by age of the

driver at fault. Consider the table, develop a model, and write a
paragraph describing what your model tells you about the accident frequency for differing ages.

Age	Accidents
20	215
25	235
30	242
40	237
50	210
60	200

Modeling Exponential Relationships

Marketing research studies patterns people follow in reacting to advertisements, looking at products, and making purchases. The data they use is collected from total sales, surveys, and interviews. The spreadsheet gives the
percentage of people in Eureka who had purchased a box of a new cereal
Crunchies by t days after the *County Journal* ran an advertisement on the ben-
efit of eating Crunchies. Experience has shown that the data in similar studies often takes the form of $f(t) = c - e^{0.at}$, where t is the number of days since
an advertisement ran in the newspaper and a is a constant.

Days Since Advertisement	Percent Purchased
1	3
2	25
3	40
4	50
5	57
6	61
7	64
8	66
9	67
10	69

Exploration 8

Use what you know about exponential functions to find a possible function that explains the percentage of people in Eureka who have purchased a box of Crunchies. What is the maximal percentage of people who will purchase a box of Crunchies in the near future according to your function?

Using Your Model:
Based on the marketing data, explain how what you know about functions in general can be applied to the model you developed for the advertising campaign to answer the second problem posed.

Using Logarithms to Discover Functional Relationships

In your earlier study you saw the relationship between exponential and logarithmic functions. This tie has applications in fitting functions to situations where the underlying relationship may be exponential in nature. Consider the information collected during the initial years of record keeping related to cases of AIDS. The data in the spreadsheet show the rapid growth in the number of cases of AIDS given by the United States Centers for Disease Control in Atlanta. Epidemiologists, mathematicians who study the growth and spread of diseases, were interested in developing a mathematical model to describe the number of cases as some function of the year. A graph of this data is shown in Figure 17. The number of reported cases appears to be an increasing function of the year. The underlying functional relationship appears to be exponential, given the rapid increase in the cases reported.

Year	Cases
1	744
2	2117
3	4445
4	8249
5	13166
6	21070
7	31001

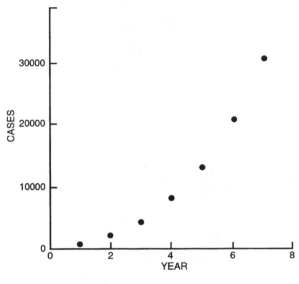

Figure 17

To see if the underlying function is exponential, epidemiologists graph the natural log of the cases against years. This is a similar approach to the square root approach used to linearize quadratic data. This results in the graph in Figure 18.

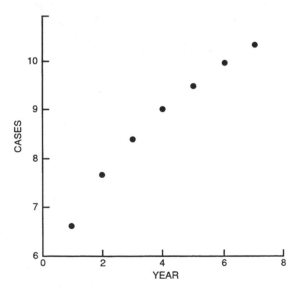

Figure 18

This method of expressing the data is called a *semi-log plot.* As the data now appear linear in form, we can use our median-line fit to find an expression for the data. Finding the appropriate medians for the first 2, middle 3, and last 2 points, the median line turns out to be ln(cases) = 0.6(year) + 6.6. This can be reexpressed to show the number of cases as a function of year by exponentiating both sides of the equation.

$$\text{cases} = e^{0.6(\text{year}) + 6.6}$$
$$\text{cases} = e^{0.6(\text{year})}e^{6.6}$$
$$\text{cases} = 735\ e^{0.6(\text{year})}.$$

The graph of this line fits the data set well, as shown.

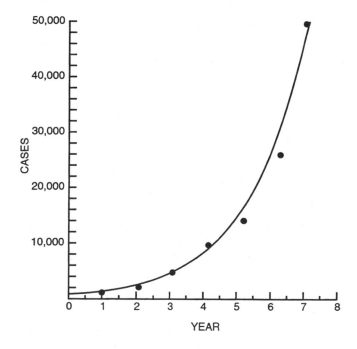

Figure 19

Looking at the graph, one can see that the graph fits the data fairly well, especially in the first years of the data. In the latter years, the model predicts more cases than were reported. This can be due to preventive measures regarding the disease by the population or to some other change in either the disease or the population.

Thus, the epidemiologists can assume that the number of reported cases of the AIDS virus in the early years of their study does appear to be increasing exponentially. This is often true in the study of a new disease, as it spreads rapidly in a population that has never built up natural or medical protection against its various forms.

Exploration 9

World Population

Try This One with a Partner

The spreadsheet at right shows the population of the world at five different times since the mid-seventeenth century. Use this information to develop a model for the growth of the world's population as a function of the year.

Year	Population
1650	0.5 billion
1750	0.7 billion
1850	1.1 billion
1980	4.5 billion
1990	5.3 billion

1. Use available technology to construct a model for the world population data. What type of model seems to fit the data best, linear, quadratic, or exponential? Describe the model you selected and explain why you selected it.

2. What does your model predict the population of the world to be in the year 2000?

3. What does your model predict over the next century? How are these predictions related to past patterns in population growth? What factors might increase or decrease the rate of population growth in the next 50 years?

In working with models, always remember to check the difference between the actual data points and the predicted data points for each of the values you consider. These differences should be small, relative to the size of the numbers involved, and portray no particular pattern of increase or decrease. The graph in Figure 20 shows the residuals for the AIDS data.

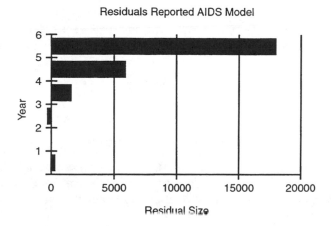

Figure 20

What does the residual graph look like for your world population model?

Exploration 10

Mystery Interest

The data at right show the values in a savings passbook that had been lost and forgotten for a period of time. Chad and his sister Shelly were wondering what rate of interest the account was paying. Shelly said that they could fit a curve to the data to find out. They had the rough idea that the initial deposit was $1,000.

Year	Value
1	smeared
2	1199
3	1314
4	1439
5	1576

1. Use the data and your calculator to make a graph of the checking account data. Based on the information available can you predict what the rate of interest might have been?

2. Use the procedures developed earlier to create a function model for the interest situation described, assuming the money was compounded annually.

3. Using the resulting model, what does it appear that the interest rate might be? Did you model given an initial deposit of $1,000? If not, can you adjust the model to $1,000 and determine the interest rate?

Additional Explorations

Consider the data sets in tasks 1 and 2. For each, make a scatterplot for the data and then fit an exponential function to the data. For each of the resulting models, make a residual plot to check the nature of your model's fit to the data.

1.

x	0	1	2	3	4	5	6	7	8
y	2.0	2.74	3.64	4.91	6.64	9.01	12.1	16.36	22.04

2.

x	0	1	2	3	4	5	6	7	8
y	5.0	4.9	4.8	4.71	4.62	4.52	4.43	4.35	4.26

3. *Dollaring Douglas.* When Doug was born 21 years ago, his grandparents invested a sum of money in an account which was to compound annually for his future college education. The data below show values in that account at various points in time.

   a. Probably, what was the initial investment?

   b. At what point did the value of the money initially invested first double?

   c. About what was the value of the account when Doug reached age 20?

   d. What is your model for the value of this account?

After t years	Value
3	$ 3814
4	$ 4475
9	$ 6163
11	$ 7232
14	$ 9195
17	$11689

4. *Eternal Glowing.* The decay of radioactive isotopes is modeled by an exponential function. The atoms of these isotopes emit radiation and then change into different forms. As they do, the amount

of the original substance present decreases. If 500 grams of radium decay to 250 grams of radium in 1600 years and further decay to half that amount, or 125 grams, in another 1600 years, etc., find an exponential model for the decay of radium.

a. When will the amount of radium first be less than 10 grams by this model?

b. How much radium will remain after 1,000,000 years?

c. Will the radium ever totally disappear?

5. *Heated Homicide*. The rate of cooling of a hot body in air is very nearly proportional to the difference between the temperature of the body and the temperature of the air. Lieutenant Smith of Homicide found a murdered body having a body temperature of 18°C in a meat locker set at 4°C. If the normal body temperature is 37°C and a comparable body is known to have cooled 5°C in one hour, approximately how long ago had the murder taken place if the body was immediately placed in the locker?

6. *Improving AIDS Reporting*. Records from the U.S. Centers for Disease Control also provide data on the number of deaths that resulted from the AIDS virus in the United States during the initial years of data collection about the disease. The data are as follows:

Year	1	2	3	4	5	6	7
Deaths	434	1416	3196	6242	10620	13933	15463

Develop a model for this data.

a. Does your model for this data fit the data better than the model for the reported cases data for AIDS given earlier? If so, why?

b. In what ways does this data compare to the data for the reported cases given earlier?

c. Which data appear to be more purely exponential in form and growth?

Extending Exponential Modeling

Exponential models are used in a variety of fields from medicine to economics to linguistics. These models take on a number of forms, from the unbounded growth, or decay, of $f(x) = ae^{bx}$ to the more constrained shapes of curves with forms like $g(x) = c(1 - e^{-bx})$; $h(x) = ae^{-bx} + c$; and $j(x) = axe^{-bx}$. In this portion of the lesson we consider additional powerful applications of exponential functions in applied mathematics.

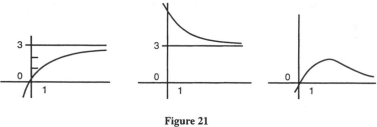

Figure 21

$$g(x) = 3(1 - e^{-0.5x}) \qquad h(x) = 3e^{-0.5x} + 3 \qquad (x) = 3xe^{-0.5x}$$

Use your graphing calculator to explore the nature of the functions $g(x)$ and $h(x)$ given above. Note that they are merely transformations of the curve $e^{-0.5x}$. Experiment with various changes in the parameters for functions of these types and see how their graphs are related to the graphs of functions of the form $f(x) = ae^{bx}$. Once the roles of the transformations are seen, these functions can be fit just like we fit the earlier functions of the form $f(x) = ae^{bx}$.

Data sets with these general forms can be fit with functions using technology to perform least-squares analyses as we did with the linear sets earlier, or by assuming the type of functions and using the points we know on the curve to develop a system of equations that we can solve simultaneously.

Exploration 11

Drug Absorption

Try This One with a Partner

A painkiller administered following surgery is absorbed into the bloodstream in a fashion that shows increased concentration of the drug followed by a gradual decrease. The decrease is a function of the time since the peak concentration following the administration of the drug. How long would you expect it to take for the level of the drug to drop below 0.1 mg/liter?

Time	mg/liter
0	1.50
1	1.25
2	1.05
3	0.87
4	0.73
5	0.61
6	0.51
7	0.43
8	0.36

1. Use the data and your calculator to make a graph of the data. Does it appear to be exponential in shape? Based on your graph, how long would you expect for the level of the drug to fall below 0.10 mg/liter?

2. Develop a model to describe the absorption process described.

3. Use your model to test your prediction for the amount of time it takes for the concentration level to drop beneath 0.10 mg/liter. How accurate were you?

Earlier we discussed the examination of the quality of the fit of a model to data via the study of the residuals and through the correlation of the observed and predicted data.

In the case of our models, we can use either our graphing calculators or a statistical package to check the value of the correlation between our observed set of data and the sets of data predicted by our models. The values of the correlation for two sets of data will range between a positive 1 and −1. The former value indicates a high agreement between the model and data, the latter indicates the values are opposite, that is, high data goes with low model value, etc. A correlation of 0 indicates that there is practically no discernible relationship between the data and the predicted model values.

Using the graphing calculator or our graphing package, we can fit an exponential curve to our data and then check the degree to which the model predicts the data values.

Exploration 12

Running the Marathon

The data table at the right shows the winning times for the Olympic marathons since 1948. The marathon race is 26 miles, 385 yards, roughly the distance that the ancient Greek warrior Phillipedes ran from the battlefield at Marathon to the square in Athens to tell the citizens of their victory over the invading Persian army.

Develop a model to fit this data. When do you think that an Olympic marathon will first be run in 2 hours or less? (Hint: Build your model in decimal portions of minutes over two hours.)

1. Based on a graph of the data, when do you expect the first Olympic marathon to be run in 2 hours or less?

2. Develop a model for the marathon data. Write a description of the processes that you used and describe in some detail the features of the model and its breadth of interpretability.

3. Why do you think that the time for the 1968 Olympic marathon fell so far off of the curve generated by the other times? What effect might this have had on your model?

Year	Time
1948	2h34m52s
1952	2h23m03s
1956	2h25m00s
1960	2h15m16s
1964	2h12m11s
1968	2h20m26s
1972	2h12m20s
1976	2h09m55s
1980	2h11m03s
1984	2h09m21s
1988	2h10m32s

Additional Explorations

Check the Reading

1. How does the shape of an exponential model $f(x) = e^{ax}$ depend on the value of a?

2. How does the shape of an exponential model $g(x) = 3(1 - e^{-0.5x})$ compare and contrast to the graph of the exponential model $f(x) = e^{-0.5x}$?

3. Can you describe a situation different from those contained in this chapter where you think an exponential model may describe the growth or decay in a situation? If so, develop a problem for the situation, complete with data and questions.

Practice and Apply the Skills

4. Use your calculator to
   - develop a model based on the first six values given,
   - test-compare your model's value against the data value for the seventh input value given,
   - describe the correlation between your model and the data,
   - use your calculator to develop a model based on the first six values given and test it on the seventh value given.

x	0	1	2	3	4	5	6	7
y	5.0	5.15	5.31	5.47	5.64	5.81	5.99	6.17

5. *Drug Absorption.* The liquid form of a certain prescription contained 400 units of a drug per milliliter when it was prepared in the
   research laboratory. The following data show the amount of the
   drug it contained per milliliter during several successive analyses.
   Assuming that the model of decomposition is somewhat predictable, find an exponential function describing the decay.

Day	3	6	7	9	11	13	17
Amount	380.1	361.2	355.1	343.25	331.8	320.7	299.6

6. *Waiting Time.* If the probability of waiting less than *t* minutes until
   an operator comes on the line to take your pizza order is approxi-
   mated by a model of the form $f(t) = 1 - e^{-t/a}$, where *a* is the average time in minutes between successive taking of orders by the
   operator, find the model that represents the following data. Then
   describe what the probability of waiting 5 minutes might be under
   this model.

minutes waiting	0	.5	1	1.5	2	2.5
probability	0	.22	.39	.53	.63	.71

7. *Learning Curve.* The training supervisor at a factory has observed
   that the maximum number of parts a new employee can be expected to produce per day is 300. The learning curve in approaching this level of production is modeled by a function $P(d) = 300(1
   - e^{.05d})$, where $P(d)$ is the number of parts that will pass quality
   control on day *d*. Build a model for this learning curve using the
   data below. How many days will it take for the employee to reach
   the production levels of 150 parts, 200 parts, 250 parts?

d	2	4	10	18	20	30
P(d)	28	54	118	178	190	233

8. *Change in a Language.* If one studies the change in word usage
   in a language over time, they find that words disappear according
   to an exponential model. Consider the data below where $R(t)$ is
   the percentage of words remaining after *t* thousand years in a language. Create a model based on the data points below to predict

the decay in a language's word set, not accounting for the addition of new words. How many years would pass before half of the words have disappeared according to this model?

t	1	2	3	4	5	6	7
$N(t)$	.47	.22	.11	.05	.02	.01	.005

Thinking, Reasoning, and Communicating About New Ideas

- Make up a real-world problem that can be modeled by each of the following functions.
- Describe the problem in some detail, giving the meaning of each of the variables.
- Pose a question for your classmates to answer about the behavior of the model.

9. $f(t) = (x + 2)^2$

10. $F(t) = 20e^{0.05t}$

Communicating About Math

11. Write a paragraph that explains why one needs more points to fit a model to a set of data representing an exponential model than to a set of data that can be represented by a linear model. Use some graphs in making your explanation.

12. Write a paragraph that explains why a data set of 15 points is better than a data set of 6 points when one wishes to fit a line to the data.

Conjecturing

13. The graph below shows the curve representing the model $b(x) = 0.5x^2 - 3$. Sketch a graph showing the curve representing the model for $c(x) = 2x^2 + 3$.

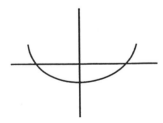

Figure 22

14. The graph below shows the curve representing the model $b(x) = e^{-0.5x}$. Sketch a graph showing the curve representing the model for $c(x) = 5 - 2e^{-0.5x}$.

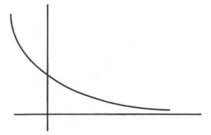

Figure 23

Looking Back: Modeling with Quadratic and Exponential Functions

In the opening task of this section on nonlinear models, you were asked to find a model for growth of redwood trees based on the amount of yearly rainfall they receive. Compare your solution now with the results you obtained when you began this section.

Plant specialists in the U.S. Forest Service maintain careful records of the rate of first year growth, in inches (i), of redwood trees. They are interested in using this data to model the rate of reforestation of areas that have been overcut in past years. One of the most promising predictive bits of data appears to be the number of inches (r) of rainfall per year. Consider the data in the table and attempt to develop a model that will predict the growth of trees in inches on the basis of rainfall.

r	i
0	1
3	4
5	6
12	9.5
17	10.8
22	10.9
34	6
35	5.3
50	1

15. How do they compare?

16. How would you answer the original questions now?

In another task in this section on nonlinear models, you were asked to find a model describing the purchase of Crunchies after an ad campaign.

Marketing research is used to study the patterns people follow in reacting to advertisements, selecting products, and making purchases. Individuals working in this field collect data via sales records, mail surveys, and interviews with customers. The spreadsheet gives the percentage of people in Eureka who had purchased Crunchies by t days after the *County Journal* ran a massive advertisement on Crunchies.

Days Since Advertisement	Percent Purchased
1	3
2	25
3	40
4	50
5	57
6	61
7	64
8	66
9	67

Experience has shown that the data in similar studies often take the form of $f(t) = c - e^{0.at}$, where t is the number of days since an advertisement ran in the newspaper.

Consider this problem again, using what you have learned. Compare the results now to the results you obtained when you began this lesson.

17. How do they compare? How would you answer the original questions now?

RELATING MODELING TO SECONDARY PROGRAMS

Building on the Process Standards

The NCTM *Curriculum and Evaluation Standards for School Mathematics* prominently features four process-related standards for each level of mathematics education. These process standards are those for problem solving, communication, reasoning, and connections. The mental abilities described by these four standards are also central features of the process of mathematical modeling. Any application of mathematics to better understand the world about us requires the productive use of these four processes.

The *Standards* state that mathematical problem solving is similar to doing mathematics. This could easily be extended to tie mathematical problem solving to modeling, as it involves:

- recognizing a problem exists,
- formulating a conjecture about how to represent that problem,
- developing a strategy for finding a solution to the problem,
- considering how to compute or determine an answer to the problem using the strategy,
- working to verify that the resulting purported solution is reasonable, and
- communicating the result in terms that are understandable by individuals who must function in the context of the situation where the problem arose.

In suggesting this, the *Standards* for grades 9–12 make several explicit mentions of mathematical modeling. In particular, the *Standards* equate modeling with mathematical thinking in providing the following model for understanding the process. In doing so, they present the following graphic for modeling modeling.

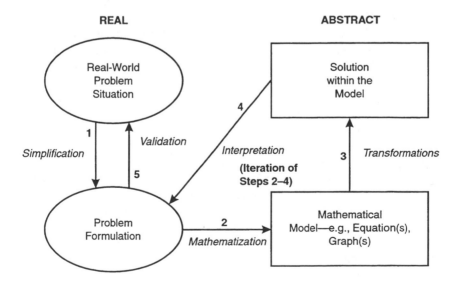

Figure 24

This graphic illustrates mathematical modeling as a dynamic activity with a number of interrelated activities. The numbering of the actions indicated by arrows in the model provides a guide to the process. Of particular importance is the triangle of actions numbers 2 through 4. The mathematization of the situation, the transformations of the tentative model, and the interpretation of the initial results may need to be iterated several times until the sophistication of the model reaches a level that provides the decision-making power desired for the real-world situation.

Such iterations of the model require the modeler to bring additional information to the process, to consult specialists in the area of content represented by the real-world problem, to employ technology in visualizing the ramifications of the models as they are extended to related problems, and to develop communications for individuals who do not have the technical background of those developing and interpreting the model.

The models that you have seen have been built in a fairly conscribed setting, with data provided to you for your use. In the real world, the mathematician, or modeler, must decide what data needs to be collected, how it should be collected, and then determine what type of model might be appropriate in the context where the problem arose. This module has provided a first look at modeling. Additional coursework can be taken to examine the finer features of modeling in less defined real-world settings.

If students are to break their long-held view that mathematics is a staid set of rules, having little to do with their world, which are to be memorized for later writing during a testing period, the components of mathematical modeling must come to play a greater role in our mathematics classrooms at all levels, especially at the secondary school level. Involving students in modeling activities in the classroom can help alter their view of mathematics from a sterile theoretical subject into one where guessing is appropriate, if testing follows; one where creativity has a role and is valued; one where there is not just one "answer" to a problem; and one where thought is more valued than computation.

The inclusion of modeling in the school mathematics curriculum moves the student from isolated practice and listening to lectures to working in groups, deciding on plans of action, collecting and analyzing information, developing hypotheses, creating equations, and communicating results. This facility with problem solving, communication, and reasoning skills, combined with the ability to represent mathematical ideas in a number of forms, is the heart of learning and actually doing mathematics. The reflection that comes with analyzing the final outcomes helps students become self-correcting in terms of their mathematical understandings, a goal often overlooked in the regular classroom.

Another outcome associated with the inclusion of mathematical modeling in the curriculum is the validation in students' eyes of studying mathematics. If the mathematical models students are involved in studying can be tied to school functions such as school sports, community activities, and other subjects they are studying, the value of mathematics increases and students become more confident that what they are doing is important and useful. These affective goals are in many ways as important, if not more important, than the content- and process-related goals we so often focus upon in planning instructional sequences for our classes.

Additional Explorations

1. Examine the NCTM *Curriculum and Evaluation Standards* with respect to the inclusion of modeling activities in the curriculum. What justification do you find for the use of modeling in the teaching of content in secondary school mathematics?

2. Examine the NCTM *Standards for the Professional Teaching of Mathematics* with respect to the teaching of modeling in the secondary classroom. What information do you find that suggests how one might teach modeling in the classroom?

3. In the NCTM *Curriculum and Evaluation Standards* there is extensive coverage given to the assessment of student learning in school settings. How might you structure an assessment of students' ability to model linear, quadratic, and exponential settings? How would you evaluate their work on the assessment that you suggest?

4. What classroom management problems might one anticipate in having students involved in group work in modeling various phenomena in a secondary mathematics classroom? How would you suggest dealing with the problems?

5. Consult past copies of the *Mathematics Teacher, School Science and Mathematics,* and similar journals from other disciplines' professional organizations to find articles containing data that might be useful for teaching modeling. Find five such data sets and develop Guided Activities for these sets. Provide a solution for each of your activities.

Looking Back: Modeling with Functions

Consider the following situations. Analyze the data provided and construct models both with the median-fit-line methods and using technology. Compare the results from the two methods and write a short paragraph detailing the model and its implications for the context described.

6. *Egg Cooler.*

   An egg is taken from the water with a temperature of 98°C and
   placed in a sink filled with water having a temperature of 18°C.
   Assuming that the water does not warm appreciably, build a
   model based on this data for the change in temperature of the egg
   as a function of the amount of time it has been in the sink of water. At what point can we expect the temperature of the egg to fall
   beneath 20° C?

Time	Temp.
0	98
1	78.5
2	63.7
3	52.2
4	44.0
5	37.9
6	33.0
7	29.4
8	26.6

7. *Boom Boxes.*

   Consumer Reports rated "boom box" stereos in 1985, establishing
   an overall rating score. The scores for several models, along with
   their prices, are given below. Find a model rating the prices and
   rating scores. Which model is the best buy according to this information? Which is the worst buy?

Type	Price	Score	Type	Price	Score
Aiwa HSP02	120	73	GE Escape II	90	55
Aiwa HSJ02	180	65	KLH Solo S200	170	54
JVC CQ1K	130	64	Sanyo Sport36D	100	52
Sanyo MG 100	120	64	Koss Box A2	110	51
Sony Walk M7	170	64	Toshiba KTS3	120	47
Sony Sport 16D	70	61	Panasonic RQJ7	50	46
Toshiba KTVS1	170	60	Sears 21162	60	45
JVC CQF2	150	59	GE Escape I	70	43
Panasonic RQJ2	150	59	Sony Walk R2	200	41
Sharp WF9BR	140	59	Sony Walk F2	220	38
Sony Walk M4	75	56	Realistic SCP4	70	37

8. *Logging for Board Feet.*

   Loggers make estimates of the number of board feet in a tree based on the age of the tree. Suppose that the following data give a set of findings from a survey of trees cut in a random survey to determine the relationship. Find a functional relationship between the age of the tree in years and the number of units of 100 board feet of finished lumber coming from the tree.

Age of Tree	100 Bd. Ft.
20	1
40	6
80	33
100	56
120	88
160	182
200	320
220	408
240	510

9. *Driving, Risk, and Automobile Accidents.*

   The table below contains information collected concerning the number of sober drivers on the road at the beginning of a time period and scaled factors representing the number of single-vehicle fatal accidents involving sober drivers. When are the most people on the road? When do the most fatal accidents occur? Develop models for:

   a. traffic as a function of time

   b. accidents as a function of time

   c. accidents as a function of traffic

Time	Traffic	Accidents	Time	Traffic	Accidents
Mid.	1343	76	Noon	5723	119
2 am	770	66	2 pm	5856	152
4 am	957	65	4 pm	7030	153
6 am	3492	103	6 pm	5452	112
8 am	4850	114	8 pm	3420	101
10 am	5194	130	10 pm	2376	90

Looking Beyond

10. Based on your experiences in this teaching unit, describe the changes that have taken place in your conception of mathematics as a usable subject. What have you learned that you did not know before?

11. Based on your experiences in this teaching unit, what changes have taken place in how you might teach secondary school mathematics when you enter your own classroom?

12. What features did you see in the structure of the lessons in this unit that might be related to comments in the NCTM teaching standards?

Posing Mathematically:
A Novelette

SECTION 1
The Problem Generation Gap

THE BLACK/WATERS MATH CLUB

It is winter sometime in the early twenty-first century and Sy Black and Martha Waters are math teachers at Cutting Ej High School in Hyper Post, a large urban city on the East Coast. They are popular with the students and have made joint presentations to the math club many times over the past few years. What the students particularly enjoy is the way the two of them work together and how they also encourage their students to explore new ideas on

*their own. For this week's meeting the students have asked Mr. Black and Ms.
Waters to present some interesting ideas that extend what they have already
been taught about the Pythagorean theorem. The students have heard that the
Pythagorean theorem is a rich topic in mathematics and they want to find out
more about it. Mr. Black and Ms. Waters decide that they would like to introduce the students to some fascinating properties of Primitive Pythagorean
Triples. They ease their way into the topic gently.*

Mr. Black: Remember in the tenth grade we studied the Pythagorean theorem. What are some things you learned?

Sam: We learned that if you have a right triangle, then if you draw a square
on each side, you can add the areas.

Rita: Can't you always add the areas of squares on the sides?

Ms. Waters: Sam, what do you think of Rita's point?

Sam: She's right of course. I was talking fast. What I really meant was . . .

Mr. Black: Rita, what do you think Sam meant?

Rita: I remember that $x^2 + y^2 = z^2$, but nothing about areas.

Ms. Waters: Mr. Black, why don't I get some graph paper next door and see
if we can use it to extend some of what Rita is thinking?

Ms. Waters: If we put a right triangle on a piece of graph paper as I do here,
then what's the area of each of the squares on the two sides of the right
triangle?

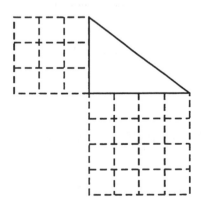

Figure 1

Rita: That's easy. The picture shows they have area of 9 and 16.

Sam: Then obviously . . .

Mr. Black: Wait. Sam, why don't you and Rita cut out a number of different-sized squares from graph paper and show us all visually what conclusion you are reaching?

Sam: Why are we cutting out graph paper?

Mr. Black: Okay, work with Rita and perhaps she will help you see how what we are discussing relates to graph paper.

Rita and Sam cut out square pieces of graph paper and finally they arrive at the sketch in Figure 2.

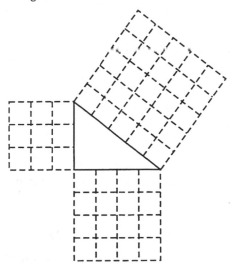

Figure 2

Rita: Hey, that's cool. I never thought of the Pythagorean theorem that way before. So, when the sides of the triangle are 3 and 4, the number of little square units on each side is 9 and 16—or 3^2 and 4^2. And then the number of little squares on the third side is 5^2. So $x^2 + y^2 = z^2$ is not just algebra.

Robert: Wasn't this the theorem you got so excited about in grade ten? You proved it to us in about five different ways. Wasn't President Garfield one of the people who came up with a proof?

Ms. Waters: Yes! You do remember the Pythagorean theorem. We have seen an instance of it in the case of a 3, 4, 5 right triangle. We are about to do some very interesting exploration based upon it that you most likely have not seen before. Let us begin by looking at what I have written on this overlay:

$$x^2 + y^2 = z^2, \text{ What are some answers?}$$

Robert: That's easy. We just saw an answer. It's 3, 4, 5.

Ms. Waters: Good. Are there any other answers?

Sam: There was another we used in the tenth grade a lot. Wasn't it 5, 12, 15?

Mr. Black: Good. Any others?

Ms. Waters: Mr. Black, is Sam's suggestion correct . . .?

Mr. Black: Let's continue, Ms. Waters. We can return to that later on.

Doris: I have another one. How about 6, 8, 10?

Ms. Waters: How did you get that? Did you also remember it from tenth grade?

Doris: No, it's easy. If 3, 4, 5 works, then so does 6, 8, 10 because of similar triangles.

Ms. Waters: Nice, does anything else also have to work if 3, 4, 5 works?

Rita: Sure, 9, 12, 15 also has to work for the same reason.

Ms. Waters: Why?

Rita: Oh, wait. 12, 16, 20 has to work; so does 18, 24, 30.

Ms. Waters: Just to be sure we are not making silly errors, may I ask Doris and Sam to check all these answers on their calculators while we continue getting more of them?

Sam: Yes. They all work.

Robert: I have another one that works: 0, 0, 0. *A little laughter by the others.*

Doris: Wait a minute. The one that Sam said, 5, 12, 15, doesn't work.

Mr. Black: Why not?

Sam: $25 + 144 \neq 225$.

Doris: Actually, I can think of another reason for believing that 5, 12, 15 has got to be wrong.

Ms. Waters: What's that?

Doris: Well, if 9, 12, 15 works, as we found out, then how could 5, 12, 15 work?

Mr. Black: I think I know what you mean, but of course there are a lot of interesting questions lurking behind that observation. You seem to be suggesting that we . . .

Ms. Waters: Mr. Black, why don't we wait for them to come up with your insight on their own?

Mr. Black: I bow to your good judgment. Any other answers?

Sam: I see something. You gave us 3, 4, 5. Doris and Rita then came up with 6, 8, 10; 12, 16, 20; 18, 24, 30 because of 3, 4, 5. We could use their idea and go on forever. But then I'd never get to baseball practice.

Mr. Black: A great observation. You seem to have an answer to a question that we haven't exactly made explicit. Do you think you can make it explicit?

Sam: Yes. How many triples work?

Robert: The answer "an infinite number" follows from what I think is Sam's point. But all of the triples are really just multiples of 3, 4, 5. If you think of 3, 4, 5 as "rock bottom," then I wonder how many "rock bottoms" there are.

Ms. Waters: A fine question. How many do we have so far?

Sam: Let's see. We have: 0, 0, 0 and 3, 4, 5.

Yisroel: Wait, I just got another. We noticed that 5, 12, 15 won't work. But when you add the squares of 5 and 12 you get 169. My calculator tells me the square root of 169 is 13. Then 5, 12, 13 works too!

Ms. Waters: Good. Any others?

Robert: Well, I said something stupid before—that 0, 0, 0 works. I got another silly thing to say: 1, 0, 1 also works.

Mr. Black: Let's not be so fast to claim that anything is silly. I wonder what we can do at this point.

Doris: Well, we then have four "rock bottoms": 0, 0, 0; 1, 0, 1; 3, 4, 5; and 5, 12, 13.

Ms. Waters: Good. We are beginning to collect triples and furthermore, we are beginning to organize them. Do you see how it is that Doris not only listed the results, but organized them as well? Can you come up with any others?

Yisroel: Well, one way is sort of by luck—like when I tried some things with my calculator.

Mr. Black: Good. Are there others?

Robert: Well, we could do what you're always telling us to do. We could look for patterns. We have triples beginning with 0, with 1, with 3, and with 5. I wonder what we can come up with.

Sam: Hold on. I just came up with one that messes up your pattern. How about 1, 1, $\sqrt{2}$? *Lots of laughter.*

Rita: Hmmm. That makes me wonder about what we're really looking for. Look at what Ms. Waters wrote on the overlay when we first began. She wrote:

$$x^2 + y^2 = z^2. \text{ What are some answers?}$$

Ms. Waters: I think you are up to something really interesting here, Rita, but our time is just about up for today, so we'll ask Rita to bring it up at the beginning of our next meeting. In the meantime, we have some things we'd like you to think about.

Mr. Black: A mathematical question that I would be most interested in having you explore is how you might go about trying to figure out what "rock bottom" triples work other than the ones beginning with 0, 1, 3, or 5.

Ms. Waters: I have something else for them to think about.

Mr. Black: Go to it!

Ms. Waters: Well, Sam suggested early on that 5, 12, 15 works and I was about to challenge him on that. But Mr. Black told me not to do so at that point. Do you have any idea what might have been behind Mr. Black's reluctance to have me correct an obvious error?

Mr. Black: I have one just like that for them to think about. Doris observed that if 9, 12, 15 works, then 5, 12, 15 could not also work. When I was about to suggest several interesting questions behind that observation, Ms. Waters told me to wait and not raise them. I wonder why she did that.

Ms. Waters: I'm still intrigued by the observation Rita made. I can't wait to get back to it. Mr. Black, do you think you see what she's getting at?

Mr. Black: No, not really.

Reflective Problem 1

1. *Mr. Black:* What problems do you think I might have posed based upon the "obvious" realization that if 9, 12, 15 works then 5, 12, 15 cannot work?

2. *Ms. Waters:* Based upon Doris's organization of triples, what observations can you make? Based upon these observations, what questions might you ask?

3. *Mr. Black:* At three or four places in the dialogue above, put notes in the margin that would help inform a beginning teacher what it is that one of the teachers or students is doing. For example, possible entries to the right of a comment by Ms. Waters or myself might be: "The teacher is trying to encourage a reluctant student to take herself seriously."

4. *Mr. Black and Ms. Waters:* Take a look back at our dialogue with the students and either make an observation or raise a question of a pedagogical nature that derives from the lesson but which the two of us did not raise by the end.

5. *Mr. Black:* In this particular case, how was the error made by Sam eventually detected? What would you have done if it were not detected at all during the class period? Can you come up with any good reasons for not correcting errors made by students even when they are not detected by the end of class?

6. *Ms. Waters:* Look at the question I put on the overlay at the beginning of the period. What do you think Mr. Black and I were hoping to have the students investigate during this lesson? What do you think Rita had uncovered? How do you think she might have felt about discovering it? mentioning it? [Small Group Activity and Essay]

IN THE TEACHERS' ROOM

"I'm dying for a cup of coffee, Sy. How about you?" asked Martha. They both walked into the teachers' room, exhausted at the end of the day. After sitting there and making small talk with the other teachers for about fifteen minutes, Martha looked at Sy, commented on the usual mismatch between the colors of his shirt and tie, and finally blurted out what she had been thinking for the last hour or so.

"That was probably the best lesson we've done in years."

"Yes, it did go well. I think the best part may have been the way in which we controlled each other," Sy mentioned. "There you were ready to pounce on Sam for coming up with 5, 12, 15 as a Primitive triple," he continued, "and look at the wonderful thing that happened by waiting. Not only was the error found eventually by Doris, but her observation that if 9, 12, 15 works, then 5, 12, 15 cannot also work was clever. More important, that observation leads to many other interesting problems for students to pose. Thanks by the way for saving the day by telling me to stifle it."

"Let's talk a little bit about what happened in that sequence," Martha commented. "I agree that it was clever for Doris to realize that Sam's triple could not be correct without actually calculating it, but why did you get so excited about that observation?"

"I got excited about it for the same reason that I loved the two observations that Robert made: that 0, 0, 0 and 1, 0, 1 are triples, though he thought of them as 'silly' observations," said Sy.

"Well, they are a bit trivial, Sy. Tell me more about what turned you on in the case of Doris's observation. Do you think she has a crush on you?"

They both turned a bit red, but Sy was used to such honesty from Martha. After teaching together for fifteen years, she felt comfortable commenting to him on his mismatched clothing and ever-increasing bald spot in the back of his head; he teased her about her wrinkled crow's-feet between her eyes and her ostentatious jewelry. Seeing Martha's comment as a serious rather than a teasing remark, however, he remarked that he too had observed the signs of a crush, but he attributed it to the fact that she had not yet been discovered by the boys. He dropped the subject at that point and returned to Doris's observation. "Don't you see the kinds of problems they are able to pose once they focused on common elements among different triples?" Sy commented.

"No, not really, Sy. After all we want them eventually to come up with a scheme to generate triples. I think they are very close to seeing, for example, that if 3, 4, 5 and 5, 12, 13 work, then there might be another triple that follows an obvious pattern beginning with the next odd number—7. We wanted them to see how they could always find a 'next' triple if they have a previous one. Within a couple of hours, I am sure we could have gotten them to come up with a formula for generating triples that begin with odd numbers."

"I realize that's where we're headed, but as soon as Doris made her observation that we can't have both 9, 12, 15 and 5, 12, 15 work, it began to raise a wonderful question, which I hoped the students would eventually raise on their own."

"Which is what?" Martha queried, her crow's-feet curled to the limit.

"As a start, Doris's observation raises for me the question of how many terms two different sets of triples can have in common. We already have two triples that have one term in common: 3, 4, 5 and 5, 12, 13. In the case of the first triple, the common term, 5, is the largest element of the triple; in the second case, the common term is the smallest element of the triple."

"I see what you're getting at, Sy. Even Robert's supposedly silly observation leads us to raise that kind of question."

"And while these examples raise interesting problems for us to explore, something even more fascinating is suggested by thinking about 9, 12, 15 together with the incorrect one 5, 12, 15. Let's always list the triples from smallest to largest element. Then, we see right away you can't have both 5, 12, 15 and 9, 12, 15 satisfying the Pythagorean relationship. But do you think it is possible to have two triples with the same largest term but different smaller terms?"

"And you were hoping that the students might pose those kinds of problems?" Martha asked.

"I really was not thinking of what the students might do. I myself was so excited by the mathematics that I wanted to pose those kinds of problems when you wisely stepped in and got me to shut up."

"Sy, would students pose problems of that sort on their own?"

"No, not easily, but with appropriate coaxing they might," he said.

They sat for a while sipping their coffee and staring into space. Sy liked the way Martha had tried to retrieve the Pythagorean theorem for Rita by using a visual example rather than a verbal abstraction at first. Not only did it turn out to be a helpful way to encourage recollection, but some students (Rita for example) actually understood the theorem in a new light. Martha liked the way in which Sy tried to assess what it was that Rita understood about Primitive Pythagorean Triples by asking her to come up with others rather than asking her to state it as an equation with variables. They both had been to a conference recently in which they heard a speaker discuss the many different ways in which understanding of a concept can be assessed and they both agreed they had overstressed formal verbal summary as a measure of success.

While they were both thinking through some of these issues, they noticed the chair of the department, Eloise Farrong, walk in. Slightly younger than Sy and Martha, she was tall and blond with short cropped hair and, unlike Martha, rarely wore any accessories other than a gold locket around her neck. She was a bit jealous of the camaraderie Sy and Martha shared. She didn't like the fact that they were so popular with the students, but as department chair she tried hard to hide her jealousy and to give the illusion of being supportive. Every so often, however, a snide remark slipped out, especially in reference to their popularity.

"What kind of coaxing might you use, Sy?" Martha wondered, almost in a whisper so as not to attract the attention of Eloise.

"You know me, Martha. I think I would begin in a somewhat philosophical mode. I probably would begin by pointing out Robert's two triples and mention that though he considered them to be trivial, one should never dismiss anything as a trivial observation. We can always use something that seems trivial as a start. A slight twist on the trivial can lead us to wonderland."

He was getting excited and talking a bit louder than usual.

"I would then move from the idea of trivial to the power of picking up on something that is supposedly wrong. I would take Doris's observation and would probably observe that she is correct in pointing out that you cannot have both triples satisfying the Pythagorean relationship. But then I would observe that we are asking *too much* of something that has built-in restraints. I wonder what they could ask for that is a little *less greedy*."

"I love your metaphors and images, Sy. I wish we could get the kids to think with such imagery."

He was flattered, but a bit annoyed, because he was sure Eloise had been eavesdropping on their conversation despite the fact that she pretended to be grading papers across the room.

Martha was intrigued and wanted to support Sy, but she did wonder how much the kids would actually be able to latch on to such precious ways of thinking. After all, it was only recently that she had begun to be persuaded that there was value in problem posing itself, no less than using metaphors like *greedy*. Eloise brought over her cup of coffee to the table where her colleagues were seated. She offered them each a chocolate brownie that her sister had baked.

"I hear the kids in the math club are all excited about what you did with them today. What exactly did you do? What were you trying to teach them?

"It's very simple." Martha always felt the need to protect Sy against Eloise. She knew the comment was directed to both of them, but she appreciated that Sy was more vulnerable than she to Eloise's attacks. She also knew how to be more ingratiating than Sy.

"By the way, do thank Ellen for these delicious brownies. Ralph and I must have the two of you over for dinner sometime during the Easter break.

"Actually we are trying to get them to come up with a formula for Primitive Pythagorean Triples. I think they are already intrigued by a pattern: it isn't quite focused yet, but we hope that by starting with 1, 0, 1; 3, 4, 5; 5, 12, 13, they will wonder about whether or not every odd number might have a triple associated with it and will further explore a pattern suggested by the other two elements of the triple."

"Well, Martha, that sounds like a worthwhile goal. And you know that I go along with the NCTM *Curriculum Standards* and am in favor of encouraging students to 'discover' things on their own. But the quotes around the word 'discover' are important.

"You probably realize I was listening to some of the comments you made to each other a few minutes ago. You have to admit I have come a long way in using strategies to encourage the kids to think that they are seeing patterns or even solving problems that look to them as if they are the first people in the world to do so, but aren't you pushing the limit a bit? In this case, you have as your goal to teach them a formula for generating Primitive Pythagorean Triples. It is true that you are dealing with the math club and you feel a lot less pushed to 'cover' stuff in a set time, but don't you feel the need to be a bit more directive?

"If you start to encourage them to pose problems of their own and to listen to all that talk about the value of errors and metaphors such as *greed*, then you'll never end up covering what you need to get through.

"Also, these kids are *la crème de la crème*. It is possible that they will pose problems that neither they nor you know how to solve."

Sy wasn't sure where to begin. He thought he would respond first by finding common ground. "We both do agree that problem *solving* by kids is important and that we should not just be spoon-feeding them the material."

"No doubt about that," commented Eloise, fidgeting a little and beginning to wonder why she did not take Ellen's advice—not to try to change anyone else's mind about their most cherished beliefs regarding their own teaching. "But still, *you* are the one in charge of what gets done in the classroom, what problems students choose, and which answers are correct."

Sy continued, "Wouldn't you agree that students would be better motivated to *solve* problems that they have posed on their own?"

"Maybe," said Eloise, "and you can sometimes give them the illusion that they are posing the problems to solve. You can even sometimes actually let them do it. But you can't make that a steady diet. You would never cover anything in the curriculum."

"As a start, don't you think we should admit that students are always pos-ing problems on their own?" Sy began. "Even if we don't acknowledge it, don't you think they are asking questions like: 'Why did the teacher put an x on this side of the equation and not that side?' Sometimes the problems are about the math we try to teach; sometimes about the purpose of doing it all; sometimes about their daydreams to escape from it all."

"But it's one thing to be aware that they are doing that. It's another thing to acknowledge and honor that kind of activity as part of the curriculum," said Eloise, again realizing that she was not heeding Ellen's warning.

Sy became a bit distracted. Rather than continue the conversation with its confrontational overtones, he wanted to think more about some of the as-sumptions Eloise was making. The most interesting one, he thought, was the assumption that if kids pose problems on their own, then the only rational thing to do is to pursue those problems. He was wondering what else kids could do with problems they posed than try to solve them. He also wanted to talk to her about the psychological advantages of problem posing, especially in light of the fear so many of his students had of mathematics.

Martha was thinking about some of the practical problems she had in get-ting kids to pose problems in the first place. It wasn't a bed of roses, and she always preferred an honest dialogue about the difficulties she experienced in her teaching to a defense of her strategies. She knew that she and Sy were mak-ing headway, but she was the first to admit that there were major difficulties.

She wondered what Eloise really meant by problem solving. Maybe Eloise was really looking for a set of rules to follow to guarantee that they would be able to solve any problem she gave them. She wondered if Eloise realized that there are very important connections between problem posing and problem solving.

Suddenly Eloise looked at her watch and realized that she had to pick up Ellen at her law office. "We have got to talk more about this. I know that the two of you are terrific teachers and that you are not only popular but you get results, even though some kids come to my office almost daily to complain."

Sy and Martha were relieved to see Eloise leave. As they started to pack their books and papers, Sy remembered the comment Martha had made in the hall after math club.

"I still don't see what so intrigued you about Rita's last observation about the overlay. Where do you think she was heading?"

"Well, I can't be sure," Martha said, "but look again at what we wrote on the overlay." She pulled it out of the manila folder it was in.

$$x^2 + y^2 = z^2 \quad \textit{What are some answers?}$$

All of a sudden Sy had the most embarrassed look on his face. It occurred to him that he had been caught in his own game. "She's right! Look what we did. We asked students to *answer* a question as if we had really asked a question. In fact $x^2 + y^2 = z^2$ is not a question at all. We were so blinded by what we were trying to teach about Primitive Pythagorean Triples that we never realized that we assumed a whole lot of unspoken baggage in writing the expression $x^2 + y^2 = z^2$."

"Yes. She sure got us where we're most vulnerable," Martha agreed. "What lessens the bite a bit, however, is that aside from the clever observation of Sam's—that 1, 1, $\sqrt{2}$ works—isn't the implied question pretty clear? We really weren't so far from the mark as Rita might lead us to believe."

Sy was about to point out how much cleverer Rita's observation was than Martha realized when another thought occurred to him that was even more compelling. He had just read about a National Science Foundation grant that would release high school teachers from half their teaching load for a semester in order to write curriculum material for beginning teachers. The project had to be done in collaboration with colleagues at the State College at Hyper Post. Neither Martha nor he had taken any professional leaves in their teaching careers and he thought the timing was perfect to do so.

"Martha, I have a great idea. How about applying for a National Science Foundation grant so that we might write a unit on problem posing for beginning teachers? We could make use of some of the presentations we made at local National Council of Teachers of Mathematics meetings and create new materials as well. What do you think?"

"It sounds terrific, but do you really think we have a chance of getting it? We'd have to spend most of the summer putting the grant proposal together. Ralph and I are planning to go to my son's in Colorado for a couple of weeks, but otherwise I'll be home most of the time. Let's try to do it."

Reflective Problem 2

1. *Ms. Waters:* One way of seeing the significance of Rita's last observation is to realize that $x^2 + y^2 = z^2$ has not only one but a very large number of possible questions one might ask. What are some?

2. *Mr. Black:* A lot of pedagogical issues related to problem posing and problem solving were raised in this section. What are the most interesting ones?

3. *Ms. Farrong:* No set of beliefs exists in isolation. Taking what you see as the position advocated by Ms. Waters, Mr. Black, or myself, think about what some of the other beliefs are that they might hold about teaching that derive from or that lead to the ones they expressed in this section. Write a paper of about two typewritten pages in which you summarize that person's beliefs.

4. *Mr. Black:* Look over the format of the text of this chapter to this point. The style represents an alternative to the standard math text or even the standard text on education. Discuss what are the strengths and weaknesses of dialogue or of a "novel-like" approach.

5. *Ms. Waters:* Take some unit from a standard curriculum that you might be expected to teach and in about three or four pages, introduce the topic using the format either of the dialogue or the "novel-like" narrative. Whichever format you choose, use only two or three characters.

SOME PROBLEM-POSING ACTIVITIES

It is early April, and the crocuses are just beginning to peek through the still-hard soil. Sy and Martha have begun to think about some interesting problem-posing activities that they would like to incorporate in their National Science Foundation proposal. They decide to test out their ideas with some prospective teachers who are taking a course being taught by their favorite professor, Stuart Braun from the State College at Hyper Post. They visit him at the university and he agrees to collaborate with them on the project and to give the problems they have created to his students. Sy and Martha discuss with Professor Braun how they should handle these problems. They agree that it would be best to have them do the problems leisurely at home rather than in class. Professor Braun then gives the prospective teachers in his course the following directions:

Find a quiet place at home and write up your answers to the following. Save your write-up because we will want to refer to what you have said at other times in the course.

Exploration 1

1. Ask and try to answer two questions about the following arithmetic progression: 7, 10, 13, 16, 19, 22, . . .

2. There are nine Supreme Court justices serving on the U.S. Supreme Court. Every year, in an act of cordiality, the Supreme Court session begins with each judge shaking hands with every other judge. Ask a question based upon the above.

> 3. Given that you have an isosceles triangle (a triangle with at least two equal sides), what else do you know or might you investigate?

Reflective Problem 3

Professor Braun: I assume that you have all written your answers to these questions. Get together with two or three other people in the class and pool your answers. Were any of them unexpected among members of the group? If so, how would you characterize the unexpected responses?

Professor Braun has collected the written reactions to the problems and glanced over them after making a photocopy for his colleagues at the local high school. Based upon earlier conversations with Mr. Black and Ms. Waters, he is sure he will be able to incorporate both the problems and the conversations that result from them in his own course on problem solving. He runs into Ms. Waters as she is picking up tickets at the travel agency to go to Colorado and Professor Braun asks her why she selected these particular problems and about reactions Mr. Black and she encountered in the past with them.

"My experience has been that there is generally a very narrow and predictable range of responses to the above questions—especially if people have been exposed to these ideas in some form before," Martha remarks.

"The most common question asked in Problem 1 (see Exploration 1, p. 13) involves a search for a formula to designate a particular term or sum of terms. Were there any sorts of questions asked by your university students that were different?"

Stuart admits that his own students for the most part did the same sort of thing, though there were some more creative responses by people who were supposedly weak in math.

"Seen as a problem in combinatorics, the Supreme Court scenario (see Problem 2 in Exploration 1, page 13) usually results in asking about the total number of handshakes," Martha comments to Stuart. At that point, Stuart recalls that it was one of the supposedly weaker students who wondered how the situation would be affected by the fact that one of the judges was blind. Martha could not wait to tell Sy about this reaction. She then offered the following on the isosceles triangle problem:

"Most people claim that what follows from the fact that we are given an isosceles triangle is that the base angles must therefore be congruent. Occasionally a statement is made about the relation of the base angles to the vertex angle."

She asks Stuart for his opinion on why they all seem to have such a limited and predictable repertoire of responses.

Professor Braun hesitates a bit and admits he is more intrigued by the question than by his ability to answer it. He comments, "Part of what is involved in being educated is developing a common language. Quick and limited associations allow us to short-circuit discourse that would otherwise be unnecessarily verbose (like this sentence). We don't usually elaborate upon what we really mean because our students come to fully understand our intended meanings. In the example you discussed with me, we frequently establish the convention that $x^2 + y^2 = z^2$ signals that we are searching for or dealing with Pythagorean Triples. When we are given an isosceles triangle, we frequently need to make use of the information that the base angles are congruent. These are all good arguments in defense of the students who had produced the original list of Pythagorean Triples even when a question was not asked."

Martha realizes that this is a good argument to explain uncreative responses. She asks the travel agent for a pen and paper and she jots down the following reflective problem with the intent of including it somehow in the material that she and Sy are hoping to develop.

Reflective Problem 4

In order to be convinced that one of the ironic consequences of "being educated" is that our vision may become limited, give Problem 1 in Exploration 1 to a friend of yours who has not majored in math or science. Get a tape recorder and have your friend think out loud in coming up with answers to the questions. Replay the recording. Write a paper in which you summarize the kind of response made by your friend and compare the answers of your classmates and your friend.

TAKING PROBLEM POSING SERIOUSLY: A LOCAL MATH CONFERENCE

It is a weekend in mid-May and Sy and Martha have been invited to organize a session on problem posing at a local National Council of Teachers of Mathematics Conference in Hyper Post. They have selected a panel of five presenters from throughout the United States and Canada. Martha gives the audience of about 200 people the following directions.

Listen to the reasons the speakers give in defense of including problem posing in the school curriculum and decide how to allocate 100 points any way you wish among the five people depending upon how you judge the relative importance of their arguments:

Dr. Pfeffer's Talk

"I think a lot about why it is that so many students fear mathematics. Don't listen further to what I am about to say until you have thought about it a bit yourself. The following 'Peanuts' cartoon (Figure 3) will remind you of the reality of the situation I would like to address.

PEANUTS reprinted by permission of United Features Syndicate, Inc.

Figure 3

"One reason may be the lack of leeway and control students have over the content. Problems are given to students by teachers or by textbooks. In addition, students are told the 'correct' ways of viewing the problems.

"If they are given very little opportunity to define problems in the first place, to choose which ones they will explore, to question why it might be worth investigating those problems, then they may not only feel a lack of ownership and identification with the task, but they may feel emotionally 'hemmed in' as well. They may very well be left with a fear that they will not be able to *see the world correctly*. Problem posing is a different kind of activity. When you look at something in order to pose new problems or ask new questions, you are not so closely hemmed in. There is not the same kind of fear of being wrong, because there are no 'right' questions to ask."

Dr. Saltine

"Fear is an interesting issue, but as a math teacher my main concern is more with making sure that my students *understand* mathematics. What is involved in understanding mathematics? I have a quotation by the famous mathematician Henri Poincaré almost a century ago. Listen to what he says and then think about whether you agree with him and how you might challenge his commentary. Here goes:

> How does it happen that there are people who do not understand mathematics? If mathematics invokes only the rules of logic such as are accepted by all normal minds; if its evidence is based on principles common to all men, and that none could deny without being mad, how does it come about that so many persons are here refractory? That not everyone can invent is nowise mysteri-

ous. That not everyone can retain a demonstration once learned may also pass. But that not everyone can understand mathematical reasoning when explained appears very surprising when we think of it. And yet those who can follow this reasoning only with difficulty are in the majority; that is undeniable, and will not be gainsaid by the experience of secondary school teachers.

"I would like to direct your attention to one small section of Poincaré's quote: 'That not everyone can invent is nowise mysterious. . . . But that not everyone can understand mathematical reasoning when explained appears very surprising when we think of it.'

"That remark has always confused me. It assumes that it is possible to understand mathematical reasoning *without* inventing. That is, it assumes that it is possible to 'merely follow' an argument without inventing new questions and problems on your own in an attempt to follow.

"I am not at all surprised that people cannot understand mathematical reasoning *when explained* because it is necessary not only to *follow* an explanation but to create side paths and to create new problems of your own in order to understand anyone else's explanation."

Mr. Presolv

"I come to you not with a cartoon and not with a quote by a famous mathematician, but I have a problem for you to think about. After you play with it I will tell you why I think problem posing is important. Here's my problem:

Exploration 2

A fly and a train are 150 km apart. The train travels toward the fly at a rate of 30 km/hr. The fly travels toward the train at a rate of 70 km/hr. After hitting the train, it heads back to its starting point. After reaching the starting point, it once more heads back toward the train until they meet. The process continues. What is the total distance the fly travels?

"Some people try to solve the problem by calculating how far the fly has traveled the first time the two objects meet. Then they figure out how much farther the train has traveled when they meet a second time. This leads to the analysis of the sum of an infinite series. It might be interesting to sketch a graph of the distance traveled as a function of the time passed. That is a clever way of approaching the problem, but there is another approach that provides considerable insight into the problem without ever committing pencil to paper. See what happens when you focus attention not on the desired object, the fly, but elsewhere. Though many things are changing throughout the problem, there is an interesting constant—the travel time of the train and the fly. Suppose we then ask a question about the object of less interest: How long is the *train* moving by the time the fly is squashed? Here is a task a grade school student can respond to, and from this bit of information, might figure out how long the *fly* traveled and therefore how far.

"Unlike the train's influence on the fly, I won't beat the problem to death. My point is that it is impossible to solve this problem *without posing some new problem along the way*. I think that every act of problem solving also requires an act of problem posing or question asking."

Ms. Post

"I too would like to select a problem for you to think about. I will provide you with a slight addition, however. A picture:

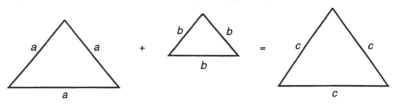

Exploration 3

Given two equilateral triangles with sides of length *a* and *b* respectively, find *c*, the length of the side of a third equilateral triangle whose area is equal to the sum of the other two. (See Figure 4.)

Figure 4

"As in the previous case, think about this problem for a while before I talk about its significance in terms of problem posing.

"It is sometimes the case that we do not fully appreciate what we really have solved unless we follow it by additional problem generation after the problem has supposedly been solved. Exploration 3 is a good example of that point. Using the fact that the area of an equilateral triangle can be expressed as $(s^2 \cdot \sqrt{3})/4$ for s a side of the triangle, we can calculate that the length of the third side, c, of the new equilateral triangle, must be such that:

$$c^2 = a^2 + b^2$$

"Now if we look at the above conclusion, we have supposedly solved the problem. From another point of view, however, we have barely begun. Because of the puzzlingly familiar nature of the conclusion, we are tempted to ask a whole new set of questions in order to understand why something so unexpected, the Pythagorean theorem, is implicated in this result. Actually, 'tempted' is too weak a word to describe our inclination at this point. It is perhaps more accurate to say that we are 'haunted.' So frequently it is not until we ask questions or pose new problems about what it is we think we 'solved' after we have supposedly solved it that we truly understand what we have done."

Mr. Hume

"I also would like to begin with something of a problem. It is, however, a problem in teaching mathematics rather than mathematics per se. Respond to the following before you hear my reaction.

Exploration 4

Given the set of natural numbers, a prime number in that set is defined as a number that has exactly two different divisors. Suppose you were to teach a bright but naive (in the sense that they did not know anything about primes) group of students a unit that began with this definition. What *kinds* of things would you include in the unit following the definition? For example, would you include concepts, propositions, or examples that focused primarily on prime numbers? Are there reasonable alternatives?

"I would like to have you tell me how you responded to this question, but I can tell you from having spoken to other teachers about this question that most of them search for well-known propositions about prime numbers. For example, they single out propositions like the fundamental theorem of arithmetic: that any number can be factored into a product of primes in exactly one way (except for the order of the factors). They might also try to persuade the students that there are an infinite number of primes, or they might lead them to investigate something about twin primes.

"I would like to suggest a different direction. What Dr. Saltine said about the need to invent for the purpose of understanding makes a lot of sense to me. But I would challenge something implicit in her comments. I am not interested exclusively in students' understanding the concept of prime. I want them to understand important things about *themselves* and how they see the world. So, given a definition of prime, I would love to encourage them to pose many problems that they can subsequently reflect upon regardless of whether or not they try to solve them. I would like them to think about the *kinds* of questions they ask. For example, which students are interested in *why* the concept of prime has been defined? Which ones seem to be searching for a visual representation of the idea? Which ones feel the need to find a practical application of the idea? I would then want them to talk about these kinds of issues in order to encourage them to understand that people 'see' the world differently and are motivated by different kinds of questions when they aren't bound by an academic straitjacket."

Reflective Problem 5

1. Martha to the Audience: Pass in your papers in which you were given a total of 100 points to assign among the five points of view expressed at our conference. Those of you who are interested in attending a special session tomorrow, write a brief essay indicating why you made the selection you did. Put it in my box at the conference and I will pass them along to a colleague of mine who will lead a special session tomorrow afternoon based upon your essays.

2. Sy (who is leading the session the following day at the conference): Form groups of three colleagues who have assigned points in the previous problem very differently. Read each other's essays and then discuss what seem to be the important value differences you hold. Are any of you persuaded to reassign points after discussing the different essays you have written?

RECOLLECTING PROBLEMS AND ADDING NEW ONES

By mid-June Sy and Martha have collected additional problems for teachers to think about. Some of the problems have been inspired by events in their own lives and they have injected a personal flair in such cases. Some have been suggested by Eloise, who was moved (but not without mixed feelings) by the success of the conference organized by Sy and Martha last month. They have a notebook in which they keep a record of all of them. Though they are not yet sure how they will make use of these problems in their National Science Foundation grant proposal, they do know that each of them raises some interesting questions about the purpose and role of problem posing and solving. Professor Braun has agreed to give these problems to teachers in a workshop that he is offering on a weekend at the end of June. He hands out a paper that contains both old and new problems of Sy and Martha. Some of the teachers in the workshop were in his course the previous semester, but others are meeting him for the first time.

Old "Friends"

Problem A (from page 3)

$$x^2 + y^2 = z^2$$

What are some answers?

Problem B
(Problem 1, Exploration 1)

Ask and analyze two questions about the following arithmetic progression: 3, 9, 15, 21, 27, 33, 39, 45, . . .

Problem C
(Problem 2, Exploration 1)

There are nine Supreme Court justices serving on the U.S. Supreme Court. Every year, in an act of cordiality, the Supreme Court session begins with each judge shaking hands with every other judge. Ask a question based upon the above information.

Problem D
(Problem 3, Exploration 1)

Given that you have an isosceles triangle (two equal sides), what else do you know or might you investigate?

Problem E
(Exploration 2)

A fly and a train are 150 km apart. The train travels toward the fly at a rate of 30 km/hr. The fly travels toward the train at a rate of 70 km/hr. After hitting the train, it heads back to its starting point. After reaching the starting point, it once more heads back toward the train until they meet. The process continues. What is the total distance the fly travels?

Problem F
(Exploration 3)

Given two equilateral triangles with sides of length *a* and *b* respectively, find *c*, the length of the side of a third equilateral triangle whose area is equal to the sum of the other two. (See Figure 5.)

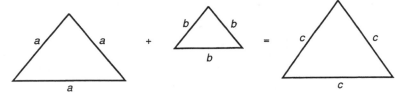

Figure 5

Problem G
(Exploration 4)

Given the set of natural numbers, a prime number in that set is defined as a number that has exactly two different divisors. Suppose you were to teach a bright but naive (in the sense that they did not know anything about primes) group of students a unit that began with this definition. What *kinds* of things would you include in the unit following the definition? For example, would you include concepts, propositions, or examples that focused primarily on prime numbers? Are there reasonable alternatives?

"New Friends"

Problem H

What do you observe when you look at the following data?

$$1 \cdot 3 = 3$$
$$2 \cdot 4 = 8$$
$$3 \cdot 5 = 15$$
$$4 \cdot 6 = 24$$
$$5 \cdot 7 = 35$$

Problem I

Below is a proof that 2=1 based upon some conceptions of multiplication and some ideas from the calculus. Look at the proof. What reaction do you have? What question(s) do you find yourself asking?

Since multiplication is a form of repeated addition, we can express x^2 as $x + x + ... + x$ x number of times. For example, $7^2 = 7 + 7 + 7 + 7 + 7 + 7 + 7$ seven times. Since x^2 is identical to $x + x + ... + x$, we can conclude that their derivatives are equal as well.

Therefore: $2x = 1 + 1 + ... + 1x$ times. But $1 + 1 + ... + 1$ taken x times equals x. Therefore $2x = x$. If we assume that x is not 0, we conclude then that 2 must equa

Problem J

The Fibonacci sequence is one of the most famous sequences in mathematics. Its fame is due in part to the fact that it connects many different fields of inquiry (including geometry, art, architecture, and of course, the reproduction of rabbits). It was investigated originally by the Italian mathematician whose name, surprisingly enough, was Fibonacci (which in Italian means "son of Bonaccus"). The first few terms of the sequence are: 1, 1, 2, 3, 5, 8, 13, 21, 34, 55, 89. There may be a number of different ways of seeing how it comes about, but it is usually defined recursively as follows: The first two terms are 1,1. To generate any other term of the sequence, just add together the two preceding terms. Acting in a playful manner, see if you can come up with a number of interesting properties of the sequence. If things get dull, take a look at any two adjacent terms. What is their product? Now look at the product of right-hand and left-hand neighbors of each of the adjacent terms. Finally, come up with some variation of the Fibonacci sequence and explore some properties of the new sequence.

Problem K

Mr. Black's daughter is about to be married. At the wedding, there will be lots of guests he has not seen in a long time (many of whom he was of course obligated to invite for a variety of reasons). The last time he saw many of the relatives from Florida, he had a 38" waist and his daughter had a 30" waist. Since then, his daughter has been working very hard as a veterinarian and has had no time for exercising; her waist is now up to 36". Mr. Black's culinary experience has consisted mostly of eating at lots of fast-food places. His waist is now just about 44". His relatives (most of whom unfortunately have memories that have not faltered) are fixated on looks, and he of course is wondering what they will be saying about how much each of their weights has changed. Assuming that both his daughter and he have waists that were and remain perfect circles, and assuming that what accounts for the perception that their weights have changed is an estimate of the increase in radius of their waists, which of the two of them would you predict would be hounded more by their relatives? Before doing any calculation, give an intuitive answer to the question. Try to come up with some reasons for your intuition being what it is. Draw a sketch that you think would be helpful to depict "before" and "after" for each of them. Then carry out the calculation. Finally (as their relatives would relish doing), criticize the question however you wish.

Problem L

Black and Waters decide to cash in on their popularity with students by opening up the Personalized Pupil Pizza Parlor on weekends. They combine the selling of pizzas with individualized tutoring of students (not their own). They sell a variety of pizzas with many different crusts and toppings. The following chart is part of their menu for a standard pizza with no toppings (and no tutoring included):

Size of Pizza (Diameter)	Price per Pizza	Price for 1/4 Pizza
8"	$5.20	$1.75
12"	$10.00	$3.50
16"	$18.50	$6.00
20"	$27.75	$8.75

Fred and his friends walk into their parlor, hoping to order a pizza, and they find out at the last moment that they have only a couple of dollars among them. Ms. Waters tells them that she will give them the 20" pizza for whatever money they have, provided they can figure out which is the best buy. Help Fred and friends acquire a free pizza by 1. giving them a few hints that will enable them to solve the problem; 2. writing your actual solution on a napkin for them if they get stuck.

Problem M

Ms. Waters is visiting her son in Colorado. She is traveling along a highway in Fablunjet, New Mexico, that has traffic lights placed at intervals every so often. She finds that she is stopping quite frequently. She decides to record the location of traffic lights on the highway and notices that they appear about every mile and a half. She also looks at her car clock and notices that the light is red for about one minute. She has a CB radio in her car and she calls a driver of an eighteen-wheeler who is by coincidence also stopped at the next light ahead of her. He confirms that the red light is on for the same length of time and simultaneously with hers. He also tells her that when he stopped at a truck stop he noticed that the light was green for one minute as well. She assumes that the pattern of traffic lights is the same for the entire highway. What would be an optimum speed at which she could travel so that she minimizes her stopping?

Reflective Problem 6

Professor Braun: Some of you may have come across some of these problems before. Many of them will be new for all of you, however. If you have worked on them in the past, you need not do so again (unless you have new insights as you come across them a second time). All of you should find a quiet spot to respond in writing to those you have not seen before. Allow about an hour and a half to do so. All of you should keep this list of problems handy, however, for we shall be referring to it again either in this workshop or in some coursework that I may be fortunate enough to have you in for the future.

Section 2
Beginnings: Problems and Situations

GENTLY INTRODUCING AN IMPORTANT DISTINCTION: PROBLEMS AND EXERCISES

Sy and Martha get together in early July to further map out their plans to apply for an NSF (National Science Foundation) grant. They wonder about the format they ought to propose for the purpose of passing along their ideas to teachers. Sy tries to persuade Martha that they ought to write a text, at which point her crow's-feet again assume a prominent position. She claims that they need something with a bit more pizzazz. She suggests that they do something with cartoons, or with video, or using a computer program with Hypercard. Both of them agree that they ought to make use of the problems they have been collecting, especially since they have some interesting feedback from the students who worked on them in Professor Braun's class. They think some more about the matter, and though they cannot yet come up with a definite format, they agree that whatever they do, their pedagogical and mathematical problems ought to be handled in an open-ended and nonpreachy manner. Martha then comes up with a bright idea. She comes to the realization that what teachers need most is not only experience in math problem solving, but also something analogous to it that deals with teaching. Sy picks up on the thought and suggests that pedagogical problem solving is in many ways like math problem solving. He remarks that just as kids should view math problem solving in an open-ended way—one in which neither the answers nor the procedures are always so clear—so teaching should be viewed in a similar way. Martha agrees that whatever the format of their product, they ought to find a way of honoring that analogy. Piggy-backing on the idea, Sy comes up with the suggestion that they have Reflective Problems throughout—problems of the sort they have been recording in their notebooks as well as new ones— and comments that it would be nice if they could encourage teachers to come up with their own heuristics for solving and posing pedagogical problems related to problem solving by kids. Martha begins to feel a bit overwhelmed. She needs to prepare for her trip to Colorado. Sy picks up on her tension and offers to write a rough draft of what he calls "an enticement section" for their NSF proposal. It is his way of trying to convey to the National Science Foundation folks how Martha and he expect to communicate with teachers—light in tone, not too preachy, but not shying away from getting at deep issues. He decides to begin by addressing questions about problem solving for kids in the spirit of the NCTM Standards *written in the early 1990s because he knows that teachers will be grabbed by that topic. He picks up on the popular distinction between problem and exercise, and plans then to move to something less well developed: the relationship of both of these to situations, and eventually to problem posing. He sees it as a real challenge to weave in analogies between mathematical problem solving and pedagogical problem solving. What follows for the rest of this subsection (up to the section entitled "Two Faces of Problem Posing") then is Sy's attempt to engage teachers. He hopes to include it in the NSF proposal.*

You most likely know that problem solving is a theme that began to dominate the field of mathematics education in the early 1980s—though of course the concept had appeared much earlier. It finally became front row center in two documents published by the National Council of Teachers of Mathematics, *An Agenda for Action* (1980) and *Curriculum and Evaluation Standards* of 1989 (see bibliography).

Here are excerpts from each of those documents:

> Problem solving must be the focus of school mathematics for the 1980s. Performance in problem solving will measure the effectiveness of our personal and national possession of mathematical competence . . . . Problem solving involves applying mathematics to the real world, serving theory and practice of current emerging sciences (*An Agenda for Action*, 2).

> Mathematical problem solving, in its broadest sense, is nearly synonymous with doing mathematics. . . . Problem solving is much more than applying specific techniques to the solution of classes of word problems (*Curriculum and Evaluation Standards*, 137).

Reflective Problem 7

About one third of the class should do the following activity. Take a look at an algebra book written sometime between 1950 and 1980. Notice what is meant by *word problems*. Two examples would be "age" and "distance" problems. How many different kinds of word problems can you detect? What seems to be meant by *problem solving* in connection with word problems? That is, what is the student taught to do? The answer is probably most easily seen if you look not at standard textbooks but at review books (like Amsco review books) designed to summarize (for the purpose of test-taking) strategies for solving word problems.

Reflective Problem 8

About one third of the class should do the following activity. You most likely have come across more modern-day notions of problem solving in your class discussions even before taking this course. While we will not be coming up with a definition at this point, it would help for you to understand some of the differences between the older and newer versions of the concept. In order to do so, take a look at a post-1990s algebra text for high school students. Also take a look at pages 137 to 142 of the *Standards* mentioned above. For further clarification, look in your library for any book or article written by or about G. Polya. As a start you might look in the bibliography of this unit or in the indices of the December issues of the journal *The Mathematics Teacher.* Look for words like *heuristics,* or *strategies* for problem solving. Interestingly enough, Polya wrote most of his work before 1960, but his point of view was not much appreciated until much later.

Though there are significant differences between how problem solving was conceived before 1980 and since the 1990s, there is an important commonality. That is, in both cases, problem solving was viewed as something quite different from the doing of exercises. Here is a typical example of how exercises were handled in the "olden days" in much of the curriculum:

> To multiply two fractions, we have shown that we multiply their numerators to get the numerator of the answer; we multiply their denominators in order to get the denominator of the answer. So:

$$(a/b) \cdot (c/d) = (a \cdot c) / (b \cdot d).$$

An example would be:

$$2/5 \cdot 3/7 = (2 \cdot 3)/(5 \cdot 7) = 6/35$$

Do the following exercises:

$$2/8 \cdot 3/5 =$$

$$5/3 \cdot 3/12 =$$

$$7/8 \cdot 9/7 =$$

$$23/5 \bullet 13/27 =$$

Reflective Problem 9

About one third of the class should do the following activity. See if you can locate other exercises of the sort described above in algebra texts that were written before 1950. How would you describe what an exercise is?

Reflective Problem 10

After you have done the three Reflective Problems above, form groups of three classmates, each one having done a different activity from among the above three. Compare your answers to the question of what problem solving seemed to be in two different eras and how problem solving compares with exercises.

PROBLEMS AND EXERCISES *VS.* SITUATIONS

Look at Problem L on page 24. The question that my colleague, Ms. Waters, asked in the notebook we are keeping is: Which pizza is the best buy? That is a good question to ask given the situation, but it is important to appreciate that there is a *situation* here that could be used to generate many problems other than the one Ms. Waters suggested to Fred.

Reflective Problem 11

I overheard the conversation between Ms. Waters and Fred's friends and I devised another scheme to help keep them out of a financial bind. I suggest that we offer one 8" pizza free to the group member who comes up with the most problems to pose based upon the situation. What is the situation? Can you help Fred and his friends out? Half the class work on this task. The other half work in groups of three or four. Then make a list of all the problems you can come up with.

Reflective Problem 12

Take a look at the number and kinds of problems posed in the two grouping arrangements of Reflective Problem 11. Do you notice any significant differences? To what would you attribute the differences?

What is the *situation* that could be used to generate the many different problems you have come up with? It may not be so simple to answer that question. One person might say that it is merely the table of costs as indicated below:

Size of Pizza (Diameter)	Price per Pizza	Price for ¼ Pizza
8"	$5.20	$1.75
12"	$10.00	$3.50
16"	$18.50	$6.00
20"	$27.75	$8.75

Others might say that the table is just a start. There is a lot more in the description of Problem L. For example, read Problem L up to the sentence about Fred and his friends. We have an interesting situation but no problem has been stated so far. If we include that sentence, many problems are implied. What are some? Part of what makes mathematics so interesting to some people and so dull to others is that frequently, the "stories" that generate a problem are considered to be important by some and mere "fluff" by others. The main object for some becomes one of removing "irrelevancies" from a problem so that the details are ignored rather than incorporated into the problem.

Reflective Problem 13

How do you react to the above observation? To what extent do you enjoy stripping a situation of particulars? To what extent do you enjoy imagining how the particulars might be elaborated upon? This is a good question to discuss among your classmates. It would be particularly worthwhile for you to discuss it with friends of yours who have a literary or artistic bent. That discussion might even provide a clue to analyzing why so many people in the past have been turned off by mathematics.

Part of what is involved in maintaining interest for many people in a situation is injecting rather than eliminating "irrelevant details." In "real life" people have many interests other than maximizing the cost of an object. As soon as people realize that some of the following issues are important as well, they are in a better position to come up with some fascinating new questions other than cost in the pizza problem:

- the time it takes to cook different-sized portions
- the relative taste of different-sized portions
- questions of waste of food
- the potential to incorporate the cost of tutoring
- the possibility of using the pizza parlor to motivate interest in math (as in running contests of various sorts)

PROBLEMS AND EXERCISES VS. SITUATIONS: STEPPING BACK

In the previous subsection, we have implied that there is a difference between a problem (or exercise) and a situation. That is a very important distinction. One way of generating new problems is to do what we did in the previous section. We took a problem (Problem L) and "loosened things" a bit so that instead of a problem, we had a situation.

Whether something is a problem or a situation is not always so easy to determine, for frequently we must look beyond the logic of a statement or an event itself to consider other information or values that a person possesses in order to determine whether something is a problem or a situation. Thirty years ago most people (especially men) would have considered the fact that women earned less money than men for comparable work to be a situation rather than a problem.

Reflective Problem 14

1. What are some of these other values that we are more explicitly aware of today that relate to the observation that women earn less money than men for comparable work?

2. Meet together with someone else in your class and come up with several clear-cut examples of problems and several clear-cut examples of situations in mathematics. Try to come up with an example that has some ambiguity.

Without striving for a technical definition, a *problem* (and also an exercise) tends to impel us to *do* something with or to it. A *situation*, on the other hand, is more nearly a neutral thing—something to be observed or perhaps even appreciated, but not impelling us to some sense of further *action or resolution.*

Reflective Problem 15

What do you think of the above attempt to distinguish a problem (or even an exercise) from a situation? Can you refine the difference a bit? Surprisingly enough, there are very few analyses of the concept of "problem" that go very much below the surface. One excellent analysis is provided by Gene P. Agre in his article "The Concept of Problem" (see bibliography).

BEING AWARE OF "EXCESS BAGGAGE": APPLYING THE DISTINCTION BETWEEN PROBLEM AND SITUATION

We all frequently carry along "excess baggage" that plunges us into viewing situations as problems. Problem A, page 21, is a good example of something that is closer to a situation than a problem; yet most people view it as a problem because they have an implicit question that is tagged along with equations in general, namely, "What is the solution?"

Once we find out that we have held on to an implicit question about a situation, we are perhaps in a better position to pose new problems and to ask questions.

If you are given $x^2 + y^2 = z^2$ and you realize that you are not compelled to search for Primitive Pythagorean Triples as "solutions," you are in a position to move beyond the standard responses most people give. For example, $(1,1,1)$ would be a good response to some question other than "What are some solutions?" One such question would be: Can you find a triple that misses the condition of equality by one?

Once you see $(1,1,1)$ as an answer to a potentially new question, you may be inspired to pose other related problems you had never thought about before.

Exploration 5

Can you find other triples of natural numbers that miss the Pythagorean equality by one?

Having appreciated that you have searched for such triples among natural numbers, you might alternatively try to find *rational* numbers (that are not integers) for which the equation is true.

Exploration 6

Investigate what is implied by the above observation.

Noticing that all our new questions—as well as the implicit original one—seem to have an algebraic or arithmetic perspective, you might try to come up with a geometric alternative.

Exploration 7

Come up with a geometric question about Pythagorean Triples. If you are stumped, think about graphs and dimensionality.

Suppose you apply some of this thinking about the concept of "situation" to the arithmetic progression 7, 10, 13, 16, 19, 22, 25, . . . (Problem B, page 21). What question did you ask and analyze? Like the previous example, it may appear on the surface to be superfluous to request that one ask and analyze a question, for the concept of a sequence is usually so closely connected with the search for a generating formula. Once you come to appreciate that we do have something that is more of a situation than a problem, there are a host of new and interesting questions to explore. As a start, we might ask a rather simple question:

How are odd and even numbers distributed in the sequence?

The above question still has a rather trivial ring to it since it is one that is so easily analyzable.

Exploration 8

Realizing that the issue of parity introduces the category of *divisibility*, come up with some less trivial-sounding question.

If you relax your sights a little, you might observe something about the sequence of unit's digits in the original sequence. The first few are: 7, 0, 3, 6, 9, 2. What would you predict the next unit's digit would be?

. . . .

Exploration 9

Ask some new question about the unit's digit of the new sequence.

. . . .

FURTHER OPPORTUNITY TO EXPLORE
THE PROBLEM/SITUATION DUALISM FOR
PROBLEM GENERATION

Take a look once more at Problem M from page 25.

Reflective Problem 16

We have posed one problem about the situation of Ms. Waters. Making use of some of the thinking of this section, how would you describe the situation that has generated the problem? Once you have described the situation, can you generate other problems?

Paradoxes are a wonderful teaching source for many purposes. They can be used as a way of assessing how students perceive and misperceive fundamental mathematical ideas. In trying to locate the source of the paradox in Problem I, for example, many students overlook the rather subtle issue that multiplication is not always repeated addition, but reveal instead an uncomfortable feeling about taking the derivative of both sides.

What is not so obvious about paradoxes is their potential to generate new problems in light of the distinctions we have made between situation and problem. Since paradoxes challenge our most fundamental beliefs, we tend not to be aware of the fact that we assume that the only reasonable question to ask about the "situation" is: What's wrong? How could that be? They provide fertile ground for problem generation once we become explicitly aware that the paradox is not born with a tag that asks only, "What's wrong?" In this case, for example, we could try to muddy things even more than they have been muddied so far.

If x^2 can be expressed as $x + x + ... + x$ taken x times, then we might try to see what conclusion we would arrive at if we search for an analogous way of expressing x^3.

```
• • • • • • • • • • • • • • • • • • • • • • • • • • • • • • • • • • • • •
•                                                                    •
•                      Exploration 10                               •
•                                                                    •
•   Try to formulate an analogous derivation for the expression x³ and see   •
•   what other paradoxes you might come up with.                     •
•                                                                    •
• • • • • • • • • • • • • • • • • • • • • • • • • • • • • • • • • • • • •
```

Try to formulate an analogous derivation for the expression x^3 and see what other paradoxes you might come up with.

Any geometrical shape, like a rectangle, or an isosceles triangle, or a conic section, is in some sense a situation that does not come tagged with a question—though it does have all kinds of associations. In fact, most of the curriculum questions we do pursue are such a small part of the potential marketplace of ideas that it is almost an embarrassment to realize how much we channel the thinking of our students and ourselves as well.

Look at Problem D on page 21—the isosceles triangle question. I gave it to teachers in Professor Braun's class recently and discovered that though there are a large number of relevant questions to ask, the content of the curriculum establishes a quite limited number of associations. Before reading on, try to come up with questions that expand upon the one(s) you think they may have asked when first seeing this situation. Below are some questions that are significantly different from what they asked:

- How many already known shapes can you make by stringing together congruent copies of the given isosceles triangle?
- How many lesser-known shapes can you make in the same way?
- Take an isosceles triangle and place it perpendicular to another plane, tag one of its vertices, and rotate it against the plane. What shape seems to be formed by the tagged vertex?
- What already known figures can you inscribe in a given isosceles triangle? How would you refine the question so that it makes more sense?
- If you know the perimeter of an isosceles triangle, can you find its area? What else might you have to be told?
- What do you think might have been some of the circumstances that got people to investigate the isosceles triangle in the first place?

It is worth stressing that, though I can suggest *strategies* for coming up with some of the above questions, just being *invited* to unchannel your thinking on at least some occasions may provide the necessary inducement to pose new problems and to ask new questions.

Reflective Problem 17

1. Take any problem in your present curriculum. Neutralize it by creating a situation rather than a problem. Now create four new problems/questions based upon the neutralization.

2. Figure 6 summarizes some of what we have discussed in this section

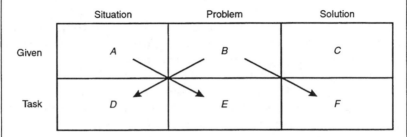

Figure 6

The nonpointed end of each arrow indicates what students might be "given" and the pointed end indicates what their associated "tasks" might be. Most problem-solving activity is summarized by the movement from B to F. That is, students are given a problem and expected to come up with a solution. Meet together with two other students in the class. One of you should draw new arrows; another should determine whether or not the new arrows make sense; a third ought to record comments made by the others in the group.

3. [Sy speaking] Everything in Section 2 up this point is a draft of my NSF proposal intended to show the NSF how I would entice teachers. Realizing that it is only a portion of the proposal, how would you evaluate it? What assumptions does it make about what interests teachers? Did you find it "grabby?" too wordy? serious enough? What rationale was presented for teaching teachers about problem posing? Do you think the enticement was explicit enough? How would you make it more explicit?

SECTION 3
Two Faces of Problem Posing

SOME FURTHER REFLECTIONS
ON THE MEANING OF UNDERSTANDING

Sy and Martha get together in Colorado to continue work on the proposal during part of the time that Martha is visiting her son. They spend mornings talking and writing and afternoons socializing with Martha's husband, Ralph, and their son Arthur. They have just finished rereading their notes from the local National Council of Teachers of Mathematics conference they organized in May. They have decided that their book should draw upon some of the problem-posing themes described in that conference. One theme that stands out strongly for them is the relationship of problem posing to understanding. They begin a conversation with that concern.

Mr. Black: There were many different points of view about problem posing and problem solving in that conference. Don't you agree, though, that the concept of understanding is the big reason that problem posing is worth taking seriously?

Ms. Waters: I've got to think about that. There was a lot that was said. I liked the comments by Pfeffer on fear of mathematics. He was suggesting that problem posing allows for a kind of freedom of exploration. I'm not sure yet how it relates to understanding.

Mr. Black: That's a good point. There were a lot of personal or psychological variables mentioned in the proceedings. Hume, for example, got at variables about the self. He said he was less interested in students' understanding the concept of prime than in their understanding things about themselves.

Ms. Waters: That's right, but he's still concerned with the concept of *understanding*, isn't he? He's more interested in self-understanding than in understanding of the math, but isn't there some similarity?

Mr. Black: I guess so, but how do you get people to understand things either about themselves or the subject they are studying?

Ms. Waters: Well, that's where I think problem posing comes in. I think an essential ingredient of understanding is being able to move beyond whatever knowledge has been learned. I have an article in my purse that I just came across by someone named David Perkins. In it he says,

> Understanding a topic of study is a matter of being able to perform a variety
> of thought-demanding ways with the topic, for instance: to explain, muster
> evidence, find examples, generalize, apply concepts, analogize, represent in
> a new way and so on. [See *Perkins, 1993*.]

He doesn't quite come out and say it, but I think that behind each of these ingredients is an act of problem posing.

Mr. Black: Are you saying that problem posing is necessary in order to *demonstrate* that you have achieved understanding—sort of like problem posing is built into the concept of *understanding*?

Ms. Waters: I think I am saying that, but I am saying more.

Mr. Black: Like?

Ms. Waters: Like, not only is the ability to pose problems necessary in order to *demonstrate* that you understand something, but it is also an important ingredient in the *process of learning* as well.

Mr. Black: You mean you can't sort of just teach kids to know a great deal and once they are filled up with knowledge, expect them to demonstrate a new ability called understanding?

Ms. Waters: Right, it's not just an add-on, like putting frosting on an already baked cake.

Mr. Black: Do you think there is a special kind of problem posing that is needed either as part of the "training" of students to lead them to understand or as part of the definition of understanding itself?

Ms. Waters: I think Dr. Saltine has hit the nail on the head when she points out a devastating assumption of the quote by Poincaré. Remember Poincaré wonders:

> That not everyone can invent is nowise mysterious. . . . But that not every-
> one can understand mathematical reasoning when explained appears very
> surprising when we think of it.

Saltine cleverly suggests that it may not be possible to understand mathematical reasoning without inventing. What that means is that it's necessary to reconstruct whatever you learn in order to make it into an act of understanding rather than merely knowing.

Mr. Black: I wonder if we have hit upon one of the most important insights with regard to that concept that was much bandied about in the 1990s—something I think they called *constructivism* when I was taking math ed courses as an undergraduate. University folks like Brown, Cooney, von Glasersfeld, Cobb, and even our dear Professor Braun used to use it a lot, but I am not so sure I understood what it was all about then—maybe because I didn't see connections with problem posing.

Ms. Waters: It could be. But let us come back to this idea of problem posing as an important ingredient of understanding. What kind of problem posing do you think is necessary in order to acquire an understanding of a concept?

Mr. Black: Well, I think one thing we can do is closely related to what good teachers have done all along. That is, they have presented a concept so that students learn all about the *implications, and uses,* of the concept, and they also learn how the concept relates to others.

Ms. Waters: Yes, but these good teachers usually do the posing of problems *for* their students granted that they pose problems about the implications and uses of the concept. I would guess that the best of them have presented the ideas on their own so that they "cover" what is well known about the concept, but in such a way that the students are made aware of the fact that problems needed to be posed and posed well before any progress could be made in their solution. They do it in a way that gets the students to see that the concept developed historically by "the experts" posing interesting questions rather than having instant answers or superhuman problem-solving skills.

Mr. Black: I would guess that the best of them have also presented ideas with enough use of concrete examples and tables and puzzlement so that students sometimes anticipated what the "experts" came upon on their own. Wasn't this called "discovery learning" years ago?

Ms. Waters: Yes, I think so. But there is that other side of problem posing in relation to understanding. That's the side in which teachers arrange their teaching so that students pose problems on their own even if teachers do not rig the situation by use of patterns of all sorts.

Mr. Black: With the obvious risk, as we have found out, that the teachers themselves will not know how to approach the problems.

Ms. Waters: More than that . . . as we have found out. Students who pose problems will frequently end up exploring something other than what the experts would call the "central" ideas related to the concept. They may end up going off on tangents that do not *make use of the concept* in a direct sense, but rather that modify the concept itself.

Mr. Black: Let's see if any of this makes sense in light of material we have taught before. Over the years we have come upon two concepts of problem posing as ingredients of understanding. The first is problem posing that is more "mainstream" in that a concept is explored and developed in such a way that it "grows" almost as it may have evolved historically. "Unfolding" is a good metaphor to describe this first level of problem posing.

Ms. Waters: Yes, and the second level is what you and I have been calling

"What If Not" in much of our teaching. There the concept does not "unfold" as if it is "accepted." Rather the concept is "challenged."

Mr. Black: Do you think we should choose a real-world application of mathematics to point out the two levels of problem posing—the sort of thing that is advocated in the *Standards*?

Ms. Waters: We could. . . .

Mr. Black: Look. Let's not lose sight of the fact that we are trying to encourage beginning teachers to rethink much of their own experience as learners and then to transform that experience into a set of teaching possibilities. Let's choose a math topic that does not require too much background to get started. I think we should take the concept of prime number and see what we can do with it. Some of what we have taught about primes will be familiar to beginning teachers but will have a zing to it as well. They will begin to appreciate the power of "What If Not" thinking. Why don't I write up a brief unit based upon the concept of "unfolding" as a way of looking at understanding and you write up the "Challenging" or "What If Not" approach?

Ms. Waters: Great. Let's call it quits for today. Then tomorrow morning we can each write up our essays. The next day we can compare and criticize what we have done. Eventually we will figure how we want to reorganize these essays for the NSF proposal. We may even be able to use them directly in the material we eventually produce for teachers—that is, if we're ever successful in getting the grant. Why don't you come with Arthur, Ralph, and me to Yankee Boy Basin by Jeep this afternoon? We get there by a mountain road that should have guardrails on the side since not only is it a one-lane road, but for some of the hairpin turns, only three wheels of the Jeep remain on the highway.

Mr. Black: Fantastic! I think that Yankee Boy Basin will not only be a thrilling experience but also a metaphor for the "What If Not" problem-posing activity. With a W.I.N. strategy, we often feel that we are on a precipice that could reveal a whole new world around the bend, but that might lead to something a bit more precarious as well.

Ms. Waters: You know I am glad you thought of bringing along a tape recorder for our conversations. I'd like to have this one transcribed and would like to jot down notes for a Reflective Problem that can come out of it.

Martha jots down the following Reflective Problems.

Reflective Problem 18

Replay the above dialogue several times. Choosing "C" for "Clear," "U" for "Unclear," and "N" for "Not sure," indicate the state of your understanding for about a dozen portions of the above dialogue. Form groups of three classmates who have chosen significantly different patterns of response. [You will have to decide beforehand how to define "significantly different." That might be a worthwhile class activity in itself.] Meet together and see if you can persuade someone else to modify his/her assessment based upon your own. Then look at those assessments of your own that were not modified in the conversation. What accounts for your disinclination to modify your assessment?

Mr. Black: I smell some of that ol' self-referentiality rising to the surface. I will jot down some notes for another Reflective Problem:

Reflective Problem 19

Ms. Waters's Reflective Problem is asking you to assess your own understanding of the concept of understanding itself. What kind of thing do you feel is lacking when you claim that you do not understand a portion of the above dialogue?

MR. BLACK'S ATTEMPT AT ILLUSTRATING THE FIRST FACE: UNFOLDING

Below Mr. Black illustrates the first face of problem posing—an "unfolding" or "accepting" view of the concept of prime number. Take a look at what has been said in the dialogue above about the linkage of problem posing with that face of understanding. As you read through this effort on his part, what new problems do you find yourself posing? Try to maintain an "unfolding" spirit as you pose them. Though the material in the section written by Ms. Waters will most likely be totally new for you, the following essay by Mr. Black will most likely have a familiar ring. That is not surprising since an "unfolding" view of understanding tends to replicate the key ideas that have evolved historically.

There is an interesting problem I asked some teachers in a workshop of Professor Braun to think about a little while ago. I have come to refer to it affectionately as Problem G (on page 22). I wanted to know what *kinds* of things teachers might include in a unit on prime numbers following the definition of prime as a number with exactly two different divisors. My experience is that the *kinds of things* people tend to pose have to do with unfolding what is known, but perhaps in an interesting way.

My purpose will be twofold in my essay:

- To convey something about how problem posing can be used for the purpose of "unfolding" of material that consists of an already established and well-agreed-upon body of knowledge;
- To prepare you for some of the unconventional content and ways of thinking that Ms. Waters will develop in the following section.

Let me start right off the bat and tell you the kind of unit I would develop. I assume the students have already seen the definition of *prime* and have used it a little bit in middle school to reduce fractions to lowest terms (a topic that has gained popularity again in recent years), but have not thought about some interesting mathematical issues that the topic inspires. I'd like to use the unit to give the students a flavor for the nature of mathematical thinking, and will say something at the end of my essay about my selection of these three topics for that purpose. There are actually three issues I would like the students to explore:

1. Given any number, how can you tell if it is prime or not?
2. How many prime numbers are there?
3. Can you represent every even number as the sum of two prime numbers?

For the first question, I will present a possible dialogue with one student to illustrate how I start the process of problem posing both by students and myself. For the other two questions, I will sketch for you how I introduce the ideas with my students. I won't go very far since I assume you are all familiar with the subject matter—just enough to show something about problem-posing strategies:

Mr. Black: Rita, which of the following numbers are prime: 2, 3, 19, 1111?

Rita: Well, 2, 3, 19 are prime, but I don't know about 1111.

Mr. Black: How would you find out about 1111?

Rita: I would see if it has more than 1 and itself as divisors.

Mr. Black: How would you do that?

Rita: What do you mean?

Mr. Black: I guess it sounds like a silly question, but what would you do to find other divisors?

Rita: Well, I would ask my computer brain Shelly to write me a program.

Mr. Black: What would the program do?

Rita: It would divide 1111 by all the numbers less than itself and see if any of them work.

Mr. Black: Good, now why do you think 1111 was so hard to figure out, while 2, 3, 19 were easy?

Rita: I guess it is because 1111 is such a big number compared to the others.

Mr. Black: So, you would say that the difficulty is with the size of the numbers. The bigger the number, the harder it is to figure out if it is prime or not.

Rita: Uh huh.

Mr. Black: I got a question for you: Is 17356909876545788902 a prime or not?

Rita: That's interesting. It can't be prime because it is even and must have 2 as a divisor.

Mr. Black: Terrific. Now, I want you to think about what we have done so far and then choose your own numbers and do two things. Using some of the ideas about prime numbers that we discussed so far, make some observations of your own and ask your own questions:

Reflective Problem 20

Notice what has been taking place with regard to problem posing. Who has been posing the problems? What has taken place in the last part of this interchange that might encourage a turnabout?

Rita: Here are some of the observations and questions that occur to me:

- Any number that ends in 2 must not be prime (except 2 itself of course).
- Are there any other such easy cases?
- Oh, I just realized that 5 acts like 2. I can tell right away that if a number ends in 5, it must be prime.
- What other endings are easy to determine?
- Wait, any number that ends in 4, 6, or 8 must also be even and therefore cannot be prime.
- The culprit then must be odd numbers.
- Is a number ending in 3, 7, or 9 prime?
- Oh, I guess you can't tell in all cases. For example, 3, 13, 23 are prime, but 33 is not.

- Is there some simple way of telling whether a number ending in 3 is prime?

Mr. Black: Very nice. Notice, you have really used two categories but treated them as if they are one. What did you say about numbers ending in 2?

Rita: They can't be prime because they are even.

Mr. Black: What do you mean by even?

Rita: That they are divisible by 2.

Mr. Black: Then you started to look at the last digits, right?

Rita: Yes.

Mr. Black: Well, instead of looking at the last digit, go back to your observation about divisibility by two.

Rita: I don't get it.

Mr. Black: Well, you found out a great way of seeing whether or not a number is divisible by 2, which happens to be to look at the last digit. Think of divisibility by 2 as a special case of divisibility. Then what questions can you ask?

Rita: Okay. Well, I notice that 33 is the first number ending in 3 that is not a prime. It is divisible by 3 and 11. Some questions are:

- How can I tell if a number ending in 3 is divisible by 3?
- How can I tell if a number ending in 3 is divisible by 11?

Reflective Problem 21

1. I am trying to encourage Rita to inquire about the first of the three questions I want the students to explore. I begin my dialogue with her with a question. I think it is a bit "grabby" (looking at the prime quality of four numbers). Why do you think I selected those four prime numbers?

2. I got Rita to pose some problems of her own eventually. How did I do it? I not only had her ask some questions of her own, but I also asked her to do something more. Take a look at what else I asked her to do and see how that other thing related to her question asking and problem posing.

I began to encourage Rita to think about issues that would prepare her to think more about question 1—Given any number, how can you tell if it's prime or not?—but have done so in a gentle way, making use of specific problems rather than asking very general questions.

My colleague Ms. Waters and I have divided up the task of writing for you in this section. I am focusing on the concept of understanding and problem posing as acts of "unfolding"—of drawing out implications of a concept. What I am trying to do is to accept the concept of prime number as given and see what interesting problems flow from it. I am for the most part choosing material that is well known already by most of my colleagues. I think the students who work through my material will have one important kind of understanding—an understanding of some things that follow from the concept of prime number.

I would like to proceed with the other two questions I have listed above. I turn first to the question 2.

How many prime numbers are there?

Rather than continue a dialogue with a student at this point, I will tell you briefly what I would do to encourage students to explore that issue.

As a start, I think I would ask students to create a list of the first thousand prime numbers. That's a difficult task, especially if they do not have a computer program for generating the list, but I assume that what I did with Rita would be just a first step so that they can make use of at least some efficient procedures for creating a list of primes. Some students will be interested in creating their own computer program.

I would then encourage them to organize their data in a number of different ways so that they would get some insight into the density of prime numbers. Below is an example of a chart that they might create.

Range	Number of Primes
1–100	25
101–200	21
201–300	16
301–400	16
401–500	17
501–600	14
601–700	16
701–800	14
801–900	15
901–1000	14

I would encourage them to seek out other means of representing the information. This would be a nice opportunity to use graphs and perhaps even to seek some sort of functional connection.

The chart (as is the case with most information that has been so organized) is a wonderful invitation for problem posing by the students. Though I have a particular agenda in mind (the focus being question 2 above), I would not discourage problem posing and question asking of a more free-floating nature as well. When students of mine in the past have been presented with charts such as the above, here are the sorts of questions, observations, hypotheses that have emerged:

- The number of primes per hundred numbers tends to decrease though the pattern isn't consistent.
- How many primes would there be per hundred in the next thousand?
- The largest number of primes so far is in the first one hundred numbers.
- I hypothesize that there will never be that many again per hundred.
- Will we ever find that there are no primes per hundred as the table is expanded?
- What will we say about primes if that ever happens?
- The pattern per hundred in terms of odd and even so far is: odd, odd, even, even, odd, even, even, even, even, odd, even.
- Can I predict anything from the above pattern?

Exploration 11

What other questions, observations, hypotheses occur to you?

Reflective Problem 22

Take a look at what my students have done above and distinguish among a. questions, b. hypotheses, c. observations. Look at your work in Exploration 11 above and do the same. Can you say anything about how these three categories relate to each other?

I would use this activity as a point of departure to explore question 2: How many primes are there? I have found that without this kind of playful open-ended exposure, my students tend not to appreciate the significance of that question and have more difficulty understanding efforts at proving that there are an infinite number of primes.

Reflective Problem 23

For an informal proof that there are an infinite number of primes, see the unit in this collection entitled "The Design of Teaching: The Pythagorean Theorem" by Wittmann. For a discussion of the formal proof of Euclid

together with commentary on the slippery nature of the proof and pedagogical possibilities, see *Some "Prime" Comparisons* by Stephen I.
Brown (1978). Discuss the connections you see between the formal and
the informal proof.

Question 3:—Can you represent every even number as the sum of two
prime numbers?—is one that has an interesting history. It is based upon a conjecture made in 1732 by C. Goldbach, a Russian mathematician. It is a conjecture whose statement has neither been proven nor disproven in its present
form, though there have been variations of the conjecture that have been prov-
en. What is amazing, however, is that the conjecture itself is easy to understand, and its converse is so easy to prove that a junior high school student
could do it.

I usually introduce my students to this conjecture by actually examining
its converse. I ask them to consider the following:

If I exclude 2 from the set of prime numbers, explore what happens when
I add any two prime numbers. Here are some examples:

$$3 + 3 = 6$$
$$17 + 5 = 22$$
$$11 + 13 = 24$$

If we choose a few more examples, it most likely will not be hard for you
to come up with a conjecture that in fact is easy to prove.

Now for the converse: Given an even number, can you express it as the
sum of two primes? This is a fun conjecture because of some interesting added "baggage" that accompanies the effort to express any even number as the
sum of two primes. The added baggage usually does not come out unless you
have several people working on the conjecture independently who come together to compare results.

Exploration 12

The converse of the above is known as Goldbach's conjecture. Of
course one even number needs to be excluded as a candidate. Which?
Explore this conjecture (using specific examples) by yourself. As you
come across unexpected or interesting findings, make a list of observations, conjectures, and questions. Then meet with someone else who
has done so. Now create an expanded list of observations, conjectures,
and questions based upon Goldbach's conjecture.

I promised I would let you know why I choose these three questions for the purpose of exploring something about problem posing as "unfolding." There is nothing sacred about them, but each indicates something different about the nature of mathematics. The first question leads to a number of surprises for people who have not thought about it before. So much of my students' previous experience has involved the following of rather simple procedures in order to "get results." Further, the procedures usually get results fairly quickly. Here we have a procedure (dividing by all numbers up to the number in question) that works, but is very tedious and might not achieve an answer in one's lifetime for some very big numbers even though an answer is achievable "in principle."

The students are encouraged to explore shortcuts that might work and they may begin to understand the difference between something that works in principle and something that works in practice. They cannot come up with alternative procedures without engaging in some problem-posing activities.

The second and third questions are wonderful because they are simply stated and yet very difficult to answer. The second one—how many primes are there?—has an answer, but the entire issue can hardly be appreciated unless one has done a fair amount of open-ended exploration. Euclid's demonstration that there are in fact an infinite number of primes is one of the briefest and most elegant proofs the students will ever encounter. On the other hand, as the references in Reflective Problem 24 indicate, it is very slippery. One minute you see it and the next you do not. To the extent that you do get the point, it is an example of a creative proof that seems to be so "obvious" only after it has been produced.

The third question—Goldbach's conjecture—is a delightful example of a problem that generates a great deal of problem posing if students approach it by creating many examples rather than trying first to come up with proofs. The most exciting part of this conjecture, however, is that though some headway has been made (much of it humorous), it has been neither proven nor disproven in over 250 years. For a discussion of the humor, see the NCTM publication by my mentor, Stephen I. Brown, *Some "Prime" Comparisons* (1978).

MS. WATERS'S ATTEMPT AT ILLUSTRATING THE SECOND FACE: CHALLENGING THE GIVEN

Ms. Waters had written a first draft of her unit on Challenging the Given late in the evening after they all spent the afternoon at Yankee Boy Basin. She and Mr. Black call that strategy of problem posing "What If Not." She delights in the fact that "W.I.N." is an acronym for "What If Not" since she thinks of it as a "winning" strategy. Below is her essay.

I have been intrigued by a questionable assumption behind the quotation of a famous mathematician Poincaré that Dr. Saltine referred to in a conference that I organized on problem posing. Actually, a quotation that came much closer to my own point of view is one that I found as I was skimming some old *Scientific Americans*. The quote is by Douglas Hofstadter, author of *Gödel, Escher, Bach: An Eternal Golden Braid* (1980), linking math, music, and art.

> George Bernard Shaw once wrote (in *Back to Methuselah*): "You see things; and you say 'Why?' But I dream things that never were; and I say 'Why not?'" When I first heard this aphorism, it made a lasting impression on me. To "dream things that never were"—this is not just a poetic phrase but a truth about human nature. Even the dullest of us is endowed with this strange ability to create counterfactual worlds and to dream. Why do we have it? What sense does it make? (Hofstadter, 20)

How does this quotation apply to the concept of challenging the given as a way of coming to understand—the central idea of this section?

It is important to see what I am doing in this essay against the backdrop of Mr. Black's essay. He took the key idea of prime number, and accepting that as a definition, decided to pursue its implications. He spoke of posing problems himself in ways that would entice his students, and he also indicated how he would encourage students to do their own problem posing. In this essay, I will be less concerned with discussing strategies for teaching students to problem-pose. I would like to consider *you*, my fellow teachers, to be my students and would like you to join me on a venture. The reason that I am focusing less on people you will teach and more on you yourselves is that both the idea of problem posing by "challenging the given"—by asking "What If Not?"—and the subject matter will be novel. I would like you to use yourselves as learning laboratories.

I have read over Mr. Black's draft and I will eventually be considering the three questions he raised there but in different contexts.

Recall the definition of prime that we have been using:

A natural number is prime if it has exactly two different factors.

As a start, notice that the concept of prime number focuses on numbers with exactly *two* different divisors. Mr. Black used that observation as a starting point and examined all kinds of problems that *unfolded* from the definition. We, on the other hand, will use this observation as something to *challenge*.

As a first problem-posing challenge, look at the following table. It lists all divisors of numbers from 1 to 14. The concept of prime number would draw us to focus only upon numbers in that table that have two divisors.

Number	Divisors
1	{1}
2	{1,2}
3	{1,3}
4	{1,2,4}
5	{1,5}
6	{1,2,3,6}
7	{1,7}
8	{1,2,4,8}
9	{1,3,9}
10	{1,2,5,10}
11	{1,11}
12	{1,2,3,4,6,12}
13	{1,13}
14	{1,2,7,14}

A First Challenge: Two Divisors

As our first challenge, we might ask: What if not *two*? Notice that there are some numbers that have exactly *one* divisor; some have *three* divisors; some have *four*. There are all kinds of questions we might come up with if we hold in abeyance the focus on *two* divisors.

Reflective Problem 24

1. From the earlier table what specific questions occur to you when you look at numbers that are not prime?

2. Look back at the *kinds* of questions you came up with in the earlier reflective problem. In an essay of a couple of pages, describe what they were. This is not an easy question. Notice that we have placed the word *kinds* in italics—something we have done on other occasions in this unit. Some categories that might be relevant are perhaps: degree of generality of the questions, degree of vagueness, different substantive focus (for example, were you searching for a formula in some of the questions? What other *kind* of focus was there?).

Exploration 13

1. The first two numbers that have *three* divisors are 4 and 9. These numbers are the first two squares (beyond 1). A reasonable conjecture would be that all squares greater than 1 have three divisors. Is that true? Investigate.

2. Numbers that have *four* divisors are: 6, 8, 10, and 14. Is there some pattern that would seem to describe all such numbers?

3. The number 12 has six divisors. Are there any other numbers that have six divisors? Is it possible to find some number with more than six divisors?

Now we will select the *three* major questions that Mr. Black discussed in the previous subsection. We will approach things, however, from a *challenging the given* point of view. We return to question 1:

Given any number, how can I tell whether or not it is prime?

Notice that the question doesn't really make sense at this point since we are not focusing at all on prime numbers, but rather on alternatives to primes. In order to make sense out of the question, let us call numbers with exactly three different divisors *slimes*—the numbers you explored in Reflective Problem 24, Question 1. We thus transform question 1 into the following:

Given any number, how can I tell whether or not it is *slime*?

At this point, it would be relatively easy to come up with both a conjecture and a proof indicating why it is that certain square numbers (like 49) are *slime* and others (like 36) are not.

Let us similarly take the concept of *slime* number and return to Mr. Black's question 2:

How many slime numbers are there?

Exploration 14

1. Analyze the above question.

2. If one believes that there are a finite number of primes, how would that affect what one believes about the number of slimes?

Finally, we return to question 3—Goldbach's conjecture for *slimes*.

Exploration 15

Goldbach's conjecture states that any even number greater than 2 can be represented as the sum of two primes. The first few *slimes* are 4, 9, 25. Some even numbers can be represented as the sum of two *slimes*. Thus

$$8 = 4 + 4 ; \quad 34 = 25 + 9$$

Investigate which numbers fail and which succeed. It looks like the conjecture fails in general. Is there any pattern to the failures?

A Second Challenge: Un*natural Domains*

All the work we have done so far with prime numbers assumes we are limited to the set of *natural* numbers. That assumption is sometimes so deeply entrenched that not only do most people not appreciate its significance, but they may be totally unaware of the fact that they have made that assumption.

As our first "unnatural" domain let us look at the set of *rational* numbers—the "fractions." Before trying to impose some of the questions Mr. Black asked on that system, we of course need to be able to determine the primes in that system. Assume then that we have the same definition of prime but change the domain to the set Q of rational numbers. So . . .

Definition: *A number in* Q *is prime if it has exactly two different divisors.*

Let's now select any number in Q, like 7 or 4/15. How many numbers divide these numbers?

Exploration 16

What numbers are prime in Q? How does the answer to the question affect our interest in the concept of pursuing primes in Q? of pursuing Mr. Black's questions in Q?

Having come up with empty hands in Q, let us turn to another domain.

Consider roughly half of the numbers of N, the set of natural numbers. That is, let us look at the set of even numbers, $E = \{2,4,6,8,10, . . .\}$.

Exploration 17

1. What are the first few primes in *E*? Be careful in answering this question. One might immediately dismiss 4, 6, 8 on the grounds that they are even, and therefore cannot be prime. What is wrong with this reasoning? Read on.

2. If Problem 1 seems easily dismissible for the reason suggested in the second sentence of the problem, consider why it is that we do not consider 2 to be a divisor of 5 in the domain of natural numbers. What is problematic is not that 2 does not "go evenly" (which it does not) but rather that one part of the trilogy (the original number, the divisor, or the quotient) did not belong to the domain of inquiry. The same analysis applies now to the number 6 in *E*. Two does not divide 6 because the "quotient," 3, does not even belong to *E*.

So 2 does not divide 6. What does divide 6 in *E*? We have quite a peculiar setup here, for there is no number that divides 6 in that domain. The same is true of the numbers 2 and 10. Look at number 8. It does have two divisors, 2 and 4. In a sense, then, the number 8 might be considered prime if we were to take the literal definition of prime and apply it to this domain. But the original definition carries some baggage with it that is not found in the literal quality of the definition itself. That is, the two divisors of a number are 1 (a quite special number from several points of view) and the number itself. Now the number 8 does not have this connotation of prime.

How can we use this last observation in order to forge ahead in analyzing primes?

One way of rectifying the situation is to appreciate that the number 1 is never a divisor nor a "quotient" because it happens to be missing from *E* altogether! We mentioned above that 1 is a very special number.

Reflective Problem 25

There are several ways in which 1 is special. For one thing it is the first element of the set of natural numbers. What other interesting properties does it have in that set? Think of it in relation to the operations of addition and multiplication.

Let us therefore throw 1 into the set E and see what flows from that revision. Then we have a new set:

$$E^* = \{1,2,4,6,8,10,12,...\}$$

Now 2 is prime since 1 and 2 are its only divisors. Four is not prime since it has three divisors, 1, 2, and 4. Eight is not prime since it has four divisors. But (and here is a first surprise), *6 is prime since its only divisors are 1 and 6.* The next prime is 10 (Why do neither 5 nor 2 divide it?); then 14. Now we have something interesting to explore. We turn to the first of the three major questions explored by Mr. Black in his essay and investigate what happens in E. The question then is,

Given any number in E^*, how can you tell if is prime or not?

The primes so far are: 2, 6, 10, and 14. The first few composite numbers in E^* are 4, 8, and 12. Though it may be arrived at in a variety of ways, one is led quite readily to conjecture that all multiples of 4 (in N) are composites in E^*, while those that miss being a multiple of 4 (by 2) are not. It seems then that a number is composite in E^* if and only if it is divisible by 4. A number is prime in E^* if and only if it is not divisible by 4 (with one minor exception).

• •

Exploration 18

To say the above is to claim that any number of the form $4n$ is composite, while any number of the form $4n-2$ is prime in E^*. Show in as many different ways as you can why numbers of the form $4n-2$ cannot have more than two divisors. If you have trouble getting started, find an equivalent way of expressing $4n-2$. Try to find someone who is skeptical of your demonstration, and between the two of you figure out the loopholes in your argument.

• •

Something quite interesting is beginning to emerge. We began by trying to find some means of determining whether or not a number was prime in E. Hitting upon the concept of divisibility by 4 as one way of looking at the issue, we see not only that we can end up with an easy test for primes in E^*, but also that we are on the verge of going much further. We seem to have arrived at an embarrassingly easy formula to generate all the primes (or all the composites) in E^*. Though we did not discuss the issue earlier with regard to primes in N, not only is there no very simple observational scheme for *determining* primes in N, but the related problem of finding a manageable formula to *generate* primes has also met with failure. In E^*, $4n-2$ will generate all primes in E provided we select N as our domain for n.

We turn to the second question Mr. Black raised in his essay in N, but apply it to E^*.

How many primes are there in E^*?

This question is much easier to analyze in E^* than in N.

· ·

Exploration 19

Show that there are an infinite number of primes in E^*. What information are you using about N in order to answer this question? Can you come up with a way of answering this question that does not involve formulas at all?

Using something like the formula $4n-2$, we can actually generate all the primes in E^*. That formula for primes in E relies upon the domain N of natural numbers in finding replacements for the variable n. Can you produce a generating formula for primes in E^*, making use of elements only from E^*?

· ·

We now turn to the analog of the third question Mr. Black raised in his essay in N and apply it to the domain E^*.

Can you represent every even number in E^* as the sum of a pair of prime numbers?

In N, we have an unsolved problem that has turned heads gray many times over for the past two and a half centuries. Is it true in E^* that every number greater than two can be represented as a sum of primes? Let's see what happens when we try a few examples.

$8 = 2 + 6$ and lo! we have a positive instance.
But $10 = 2 + 8 = 4 + 6$ and in neither case do we have
a pair of primes.

Have we thus disproved the conjecture in E^*?

· ·

Exploration 20

At this point explore how you might revise Goldbach's conjecture in E^*—perhaps modifying the statement to fit what appear to be the positive and negative instances above.

· ·

Before giving up on a search for a form of Goldbach's conjecture in E^*, look back at what we have done. We have shown that for at least one even number, 10, there is no way of representing it as a sum of primes. Let us look once more at that number, however. Is 10 an even number?

In one sense, 10 is even and there is very little to debate. But what does it mean to say that a number is even? If we extrapolate from N, we mean that it is divisible by 2. In N, 10 is even because 2 divides it. What about in E^*, however? Since 5 is not an element of E^*, 2 cannot divide 10. So 10 is not even in E^*.

Though 10 is not even, 4 is even and so are 8, 12, and 16. Find a way to persuade yourself that all multiples of 4 (in the domain N) are even in E^* and that (with one exception [which?]) no other elements of E are even. So, all the composites are even. Now let's explore Goldbach's conjecture in E^*.

$$4 = 2 + 2$$
$$8 = 2 + 6$$
$$12 = 2 + 10$$
$$16 = 2 + 14$$

Take any even number greater than 2 in E^* and show that it can be represented as the sum of two primes.

Exploration 21

1. Notice that the above pattern suggests that any multiple of 4 can be expressed as the sum of 2 and another number that is even but not a multiple of 4. Can you come up with a more formal statement of the proof in which you make use of variables?

2. In every case above, we chose 2 to be the first prime in E^* in order to produce two primes whose sum was an even number in E^*. Can you find some alternative to using 2 as the first prime number in E^*?

Thus a problem of two and a half centuries is subdued if we switch our arena of concern—an "if," of course, that is significant.

Exploration 22

As a bit of further enticement regarding the sense in which we take things for granted until we do W.I.N. kind of thinking, consider the following property of natural numbers: Any number can be expressed as a product of primes in only one way. Take the numbers 20 and 36 in *N*. Express them as a product of primes. Now try the same thing with those numbers in *E**. (Make sure to answer these questions on your own first and then compare your answers with someone else's.) For an analysis of this particular problem, see my mentor's discussion of it in *Student Generations* (by Stephen I. Brown, 1987), pages 38–39. With permission of the publisher, some of my present essay derives from issues he raised on pages 33–40 of that book.

I want to stress something that may not be obvious. I have engaged you as teachers in the activity of thinking of questions and problems in two stages. The first one involves challenging the given. So I have taken the concept of prime number and negated it in two ways: I have asked "What if not *two* divisors?" I have also asked, "What if not the natural numbers?"

There is nothing God-given about knowing what the alternatives might be when we ask "What If Not?" We happened to look at numbers with three or four divisors. We also looked at alternative domains, like the set of fractions or even numbers.

Once we chose these alternative worlds, we then asked a question or posed a problem—something I call the second stage of "What If Not" problem posing. There is again nothing God-given about the new questions we can ask about these alternative worlds. We decided to ask questions that were like the ones we asked in N. Nothing, of course, would prevent us from asking totally different questions. Sometimes the "altered state" itself is so fascinating that it almost forces us to generate questions we never thought of asking earlier.

SOME BLACK/WATERS REFLECTIONS ON THE ABOVE

Martha and Sy have read over each other's units. They get together to discuss what they have done and in particular to try to be clearer about how problem posing as an activity can be encouraged.

Ms. Waters: We have done a lot in our two essays. Do you think it might be a good idea for us to step back a bit and think about what messages we want to convey about problem posing?

Mr. Black: Sounds like a good idea. Let's see. I have used a concept without doing a "what if not" on it. I have accepted the definition of prime and based upon that have come up with an essay in which I have raised questions and posed problems. I have also encouraged the students to do that. You, on the other hand, have "challenged" what is given and have come up with some fascinating modifications of the concept of prime—like defining *slime numbers* and changing the domain within which primes are defined in the first place.

Ms. Waters: True, but how have we encouraged problem-posing activities?

Mr. Black: In the case of Rita, I found it helpful to start out by asking questions of my own. They were sort of grabby questions in that she had the competence to deal with some of them but not all. I was trying to get her to stretch a bit. I gave her some questions I knew she could answer without thinking. I then gave her another (finding the prime of 1111) that I knew she could not answer immediately. I thus led her to believe that the size of the number was what was causing the difficulty. By choosing a large even number, I was able to throw her off base a bit, however, and got her to realize that it was not size alone that caused the difficulty. She now was in a position to appreciate that, though she understood the concept in some sense, it had more interesting innuendoes than she imagined.

Ms. Waters: That was a start, but you did other things that might be easier for beginning teachers to apply. You really explicitly asked her to pose her own problems, though you gave her the domain within which she should operate. You told her to create a list of her own prime numbers and to ask questions about them.

Mr. Black: Yes, and I did a bit more. I asked her to intertwine asking questions, making observations, and coming up with hypotheses. That is a very valuable triumvirate in getting kids to problem-pose.

Ms. Waters: As I look back at your teaching in general, you do something else that's important. You make them aware of the questions *you* as teacher are asking.

Mr. Black: Like what?

Ms. Waters: You ask students to think about whether questions are hard or easy. You ask them to think about whether or not they are the kinds of questions you have asked before in other circumstances.

Mr. Black: So, I guess we are saying that it is important to sensitize kids to the kinds of questions *we* as teachers ask and to the assumptions behind the questions. That's a hard thing for them to think about, but it is really important because it invites the kids to be aware not only of the *substance* but also of the *form* of questions. As I look over the problems in your unit, I notice that there was a wide variety of forms you used for teachers to think about.

Ms. Waters: Like what?

Mr. Black: Well, among the kinds of questions were ones that focused on a search for generality, or a desire to find just one more example, or an investigation of a pattern. You asked wonderful questions for teachers reading your essay like:

How many? [Exploration 14(2)]

Are there any others? [Exploration 13(3)]

Is there a pattern (to the failures)? [Exploration 15]

How does the answer affect your interest in the question? [Exploration 16]

Can you express the idea without using a formula? [Exploration 19(1)]

Ms. Waters: I would have to reread what I did, but even though I know I asked these kinds of questions, I wonder if I made the teachers aware of the fact that I was doing so. And how do we make use of these questions in teaching? Maybe they are specific to our unit!

Mr. Black: Well, some may be, but most of them apply to a large number of mathematical situations. If we are trying to sensitize kids to the questions they ask and the problems they pose, then maybe it makes sense to encourage them to keep a journal of the kinds of questions both they and their teachers are asking.

Ms. Waters: That's a great idea. Some students will find that they tend to ask the same kinds of questions regardless of the situation; others will find that their questions are governed by the situation. I can't imagine that they will not expand both the frequency and variety of question asking and problem posing by keeping a journal.

Mr. Black: It would be worth having them exchange journals in order to find out how the kinds of questions they ask compare with the kinds asked by their classmates.

Ms. Waters: Yes, but there is something else I want to think of. Are there ways of presenting mathematical ideas that encourage or discourage problem posing?

Mr. Black: I think so. Look back at the material we used in our essays. We made use of tables that were derived from some abstraction, but the information was easy to latch on to.

Ms. Waters: You're right!—despite the fact that experts have spent lifetimes trying to analyze parts of those tables.

Mr. Black: So tables have a useful problem-posing quality. What is there about the tables? I guess one thing is that they convey a lot of information with a minimal amount of technical language.

Ms. Waters: That's true. I wonder what else might serve that same *function*— so to speak.

Mr. Black: Punning is the lowest . . . Well, we have not made a lot of use of graphics in the unit we presented. I wonder if we might find some sort of geometric way of introducing primes. But let's not get into that now. I would like to think a little more about your essay—the "What If Not" scheme or "Challenging the Given."

Ms. Waters: I wonder what we really mean by "negating."

Mr. Black: I guess in the case of the unit on primes, for example, it means that we begin by denying that we are interested in looking at numbers that have exactly two different factors.

Ms. Waters: Then the negation would be something like a number that has something other than two factors. But that's sort of an abstraction. We need a way to then focus on numbers with three different factors, five different factors, and so forth. We also need to have a way to get people to consider the domain as an issue.

Mr. Black: It sounds to me then as if we really have a number of different stages involved in the W.I.N. scheme.

Ms. Waters: Let's see. We have a first stage in which we select something. In this case, the something is the definition of prime.

Mr. Black: How do we move beyond what you call the abstraction? I guess we do need the abstraction. We need to ask "What If Not?" That is, we ask what if it is not the case that a number is prime if it has two different factors? So just asking the question is itself a stage—stage 2.

Ms. Waters: Then what? We seem to need to consider alternatives. If a number does not have *two* factors, what might it have? We need to be able to consider alternatives. It might have no factors, two factors, three factors. Seeing the alternatives is another stage—stage 3.

Mr. Black: I guess now we are ready to move to the stage of asking questions or posing problems, as we do in "Unfolding" as well. Call that stage 4.

Ms. Waters: Then what? What we usually do is try to analyze the problem. That's stage 5.

Mr. Black: What does all of this "Winning" have to do with understanding of the basic curriculum ideas we try to teach?

Ms. Waters: Look what happened to our basic understanding of ideas that we thought we understood so well before we started to make some supposedly "irrelevant" modifications of the definition of prime. I have taught this unit several times, and each time the students end up saying things like, "Wow, I thought I knew what primes were all about but it never occurred to me how much I depended upon things about the natural numbers that I just took for granted."

Mr. Black: You mean they find out what happens in domains other than N and are surprised?

Ms. Waters: That's true, but that's only part of what they mean. I think they mean that they end up with a better understanding of what these basic ideas are in the set of natural numbers themselves by seeing how trivial answers in N are deep in E^*, for example.

Mr. Black: Or how unsolved problems in one N are solvable by middle school kids in E^*.

Ms. Waters: Let's go back to Arthur's and see if the pictures of Yankee Boy Basin are developed yet. I want to see how close we came to falling off the edge. Meanwhile, I want to jot down some new reflective activities.

Reflective Problem 26

1. On your own, make up a list of basic ideas in the set of natural numbers that you had previously thought to be rather obvious for which you now have gained a deeper understanding by virtue of this section. Get together in groups of three students. Select one person who has been enlightened in one area and see if you can elaborate on the enlightenment even beyond what has been achieved. Write a group essay of about four pages in length in which you discuss a. the state of enlightenment before meeting; b. the elaborations you have achieved based upon your conversations; c. the potential of using the W.I.N. scheme for enhancing such basic understanding for some other topic that you are presently studying.

2. Write down in a couple of pages what you have learned more generally about problem posing and about understanding based upon the activities of this section. Find someone else in the class who has also written about these experiences. Then discuss what has been a common kind of understanding and what has been unique for you. Based upon what is common, sketch out how you might use the problem-posing ideas of this section to teach a topic in school mathematics that you think might be difficult for students to understand.

Section 4
WINning Big: Integration and Surprise

COLORADO ENDINGS

"My favorite picture is the one you took of the Jeep with two of the right-side wheels three-quarters of the way off the road in that hairpin turn on the way to Yankee Boy Basin," commented Martha as she and Sy took a second look at the pictures before settling down to their writing early Tuesday morning.

"I almost put the camera down when I thought the Jeep was going to totter over the side, but then I realized there was nothing I could do to save the three of you if it was your fate for the laws of nature to take over," teased Sy as they continued to flip through the breathtaking pictures.

"Actually, the shots I like the best are the columbines that blanketed the meadows when we got to the top," mentioned Martha.

"I can't believe that columbines come in so many colors. I thought we'd never locate a white one and when we did, I worried that my cheap 35-millimeter would not capture a close-up of its beauty. No amount of jewelry, even from your favorite Cartier's in New York City, would have made it look more splendorous," Sy said as he checked out the beautiful Indian necklace with its green and red stones that she had bought that morning on their way to work.

There were only two days left before Martha would have to drive home to New Jersey with Ralph and Sy would fly to California in order to attend his daughter's wedding. They were both getting tense about finishing the first draft of their manuscript, but they were trying hard to maintain an air of calm.

"Let's plan to spend the entire day today writing and tomorrow morning as well. Maybe then we can have a blast the last night," Martha said, returning to what was the real world for her.

"What should we do, Martha? There's so much more we could do if we had the time. We could talk more about assessing problem-posing activities. That might make NSF happy. We could write about other problem-posing strategies. We could elaborate upon cycles that include *observing, conjecturing,* and *question asking.* That would make us happy. We could just include a lot of examples from the standard curriculum in which problem posing has potential to enhance understanding. Teachers would eat that up. We could expand the list of problem-posing kinds of questions that we discussed after reading each other's units on *understanding* and *problem posing.* That might even help us define our next project."

"I was thinking more about our conversation yesterday," Martha said. "I think there is one big area that we discussed that we should say more about. What we wrote about primes is interesting stuff and teachers at many grade levels do some things with prime numbers, but remember we were searching for a geometric counterpart of primes and we dropped the subject. We felt that many students might be able to appreciate geometric ideas rather than arithmetic or algebraic ones. There's something appealing about visualizing things. You can actually think of moving pieces of paper in space rather than using arithmetic or algebra."

"I like the idea of thinking about what is involved in posing problems that would transform algebraic ideas to geometric ones, but I think we should extend the idea a bit, Martha. It is true that visual imagery might be appealing to many students, but let's not forget the conversation we had following that fantastic lesson with the math club on Pythagorean Triples. You found my use of metaphor and verbal imagery intriguing. Don't forget that there are people who appreciate such things—a clever turn of phrase, a moving metaphor and so forth."

"What we seem to be getting at is the topic of integration," Martha realized. "As I think about it much of the reform movement of the nineties thought of integration in terms of relating math to the real world and maybe also relating different branches of mathematics, but 'real world' was a much more limited concept than I think we are getting at. The real world does include use of poetic imagery, which is more than reading and writing of journals or essays."

Sy's eyes lit up. "And as I think about it, it includes a lot more than that. Most of the applications of math to the real world have related math to the sciences or the social sciences. I wonder if we could encourage a kind of problem posing that is even more real world. There's a lot of interesting stuff on probability, for example, but I don't know of anything that relates math to ethics. How does math relate to questions on the kind of life we lead?"

"What a zinger, Sy. I know of almost no one who is asking questions of that sort. I wonder if we can include at least a glimpse of how math and morality can be integrated in the section we write on integration."

"But you know there's something else that came up in our conversation the other day that we did not pursue," Sy commented with excitement. "I wonder if we might include it as a problem-posing topic. When we spoke of kids learning so much about the natural numbers by doing a W.I.N. and exploring other domains and other concepts of divisibility, I mentioned that it is because they are surprised by some of the comparisons. I said that surprise is only part of the issue. But as I think about it, surprise is probably one of the least understood but most powerful teaching tools."

"What do you mean?" Martha queried, knowing something big was coming.

"Well . . ." Sy's eyebrows were the ones to do a dance this time. "If you ask most people for characteristics of good teaching, they soon come up with a statement like 'She makes things seem easy to understand.' In most cases, I think they mean that good teachers make things seem natural and expected. I think something very important is left out of that observation, Martha. I think good teachers frequently do the opposite. They make what seems natural and expected into something that is a big surprise—sort of like a magic show. Don't you think that many good teachers lead people to expect one thing and when they find out that the opposite is the case, they are startled and are inspired to explore things further?"

"Can we can do anything with surprise and problem posing, Sy?"

"My guess is that we can choose both surprise and integration as themes to play with from the point of view of problem posing. I think they both lend themselves to a W.I.N. conception of problem posing. Why don't we do what we did last time? You write something up about integration and I'll do something with surprise. Let's give it a try. Keep in mind, however, that a number of the publishers interested in our book have asked us not to go overboard on ideas we are just beginning to develop. Let's postpone questions of ethics and of metaphor and poetry for our sequel. Let's focus primarily on geometry, algebra, and surprise—unless we can sneak some of these other topics into integration and surprise."

"Okay. We have covered a lot of ground here. I wonder how much we will be able to develop into curriculum ideas."

Reflective Problem 27

1. Reread some of the conversation at the beginning of this dialogue. Try to find some way of integrating mathematics with the real world expressed before Sy and Martha get down to business.

2. Continue some part of the above dialogue between Martha and Sy that further explores problem posing from the point of view either of integration or of surprise. Write it either for prospective teachers or for kids. Include one mathematical problem in the dialogue.

MARTHA'S ESSAY ON INTEGRATION: A GEOMETRIC PERSPECTIVE

What would seem on the surface to be more arithmetic and not geometric than the concept that Mr. Black and I wrote about in Section 3—prime numbers? Can we view prime numbers from a geometric point of view? You might wonder what there could be about the definition of prime number that might inspire a geometric perspective. To say that a number has divisors is tantamount to suggesting that we seek numbers that multiply together in some way. Thus 7 is prime since $1 \cdot 7$ is the only way it can be expressed as a product of two factors in the set of natural numbers. But thinking about pairs of numbers being multiplied is akin to thinking about getting areas of rectangular shapes.

Such a realization suggests the following possible intuitive way of trying to understand the concept of prime number:

Scenario:
Figure 7 is a rectangle formed by 12 smaller squares.

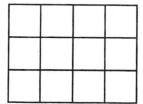

Figure 7

Can you form a different-shaped rectangle from these 12 squares? Notice that you can form not only a 3 · 4 rectangle, but a 2 · 6 and a 1 · 12 rectangle as well. For some shaped rectangles, we do not have so many options. How many different-shaped rectangles can you create, for example, if you start not with 12 but with 11 small squares?

If we think of our task as one of making rectangular arrays out of small congruent squares, then in some cases we can come up with only one rectangular shape (formed by congruent squares in such a way that they abut each other as in standard graph paper), and in others we can come up with many of them.

Exploration 23

Either find a box of commercially produced material like Cuisenaire Rods or cut out a large number of small congruent squares of different sizes from a piece of graph paper. Find the first five rectangles that can be formed in only one way. Call those one-wayers. Find the first four rectangles that are the equivalent of *slime* numbers as we defined them at the end of Section 3.

Reflective Problem 28

1. In more general terms, how would you use a rectangular model for natural numbers to talk about the concept of divisibility?

2. Meet together with two other students in the class. Look back at the work in the sections on "Unfolding" and "Challenging the Given." How much of it can you reinterpret in geometric terms? What new problems have you posed?

As you actually move shapes around on a surface, the chances are increased that you will generate new questions. Such activity is a natural invitation to a "What If Not" way of thinking.

Reflective Problem 29

How do you react to the above comment? At the very least there are people who are more inclined to think pictorially and schematically than propositionally or algebraically. Can you characterize where your preference might lie?

Having gained some appreciation for seeking a geometric counterpart of an apparently nongeometric enterprise, you might look back at Problem H at the end of Section 1. You most likely observed a great deal as you looked at the following data:

$$1 \cdot 3 = 3$$
$$2 \cdot 4 = 8$$
$$3 \cdot 5 = 15$$
$$4 \cdot 6 = 24$$
$$5 \cdot 7 = 35$$

You probably noticed something about how the numbers on the left-hand side increase; you probably noticed something about the increase of numbers on the right-hand side as well.

Reflective Problem 30

Get together with a couple of other students in the course and compare the many different observations and questions and conjectures you may have raised as a result of looking at the data of Problem H.

In addition to my earlier comment about rectangular shapes being associated with products, there is an observation that may almost compel you to wonder if this problem has some kind of geometric counterpart.

That observation is that the numbers on the right-hand side are particularly interesting if you think of them not as what they actually *are* but rather as what they seem to be trying to *become*. Look at the right-hand side from that point of view and what do you observe?

In fact, each of the numbers on the right-hand side is *almost* a perfect square. You might want to think of them as "striving" to become a square.

Reflective Problem 31

"Striving" is a metaphor. Think about your experiences in learning mathematics. Have you made use of such literary devices before? When? Look again at the original list:

1 · 3 *almost* equals 4
2 · 4 *almost* equals 9
3 · 5 *almost* equals 16
4 · 6 *almost* equals 25
5 · 7 *almost* equals 36

Exploration 24

Given what we have said above and also what we said about associating products of numbers with areas, what question do you feel crossing your lips at this very moment?

Reflective Problem 32

1. Using graph paper, cut out an array of rectangular shapes depicted by the products that initiated our metaphor discussion. Thus 1 · 3, 2 · 4, 3 · 5, and so forth. Find someone else in the class who will cut out the associated squares. Work together to persuade yourselves by geometric reasoning alone that no matter what two numbers you start with, if they accord with the above pattern, you will always arrive at an almost square. See if you can justify the conclusion geometrically in a number of different ways. Figure 8 is one picture that might convey what we are seeking here.

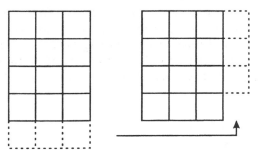

Figure 8

2. Using the "What If Not" strategy, we might very well have been inspired to start with Problem H and come up with the following variation: $1 \cdot 5 = 5$; $2 \cdot 6 = 12$; $3 \cdot 7 = 21$; $4 \cdot 8 = 32$. If you use the same "striving to be squares" metaphor that we used earlier, what do you notice about the right-hand side? Now investigate the above both algebraically and geometrically. Use the W.I.N. strategy to come up with additional variations of the original data, followed by further geometric problem posing and solving.

3. Get a copy of Euclid's *Elements* and look at several of the propositions of Book I dealing with areas of geometric figures. Look specifically at propositions surrounding number 34. Figure out how he has circumvented the use of formulas in dealing with area. Get together with another person and make a class presentation of your findings.

4. Look back at the dialogue over the meaning of the Pythagorean theorem in the first section of this chapter. There we tried to take a look at the Pythagorean theorem from a purely geometric point of view. Select several special cases that would enable you to demonstrate easily that the area on the hypotenuse is equal to the sum of the areas on the other two sides. Remember that "demonstrate easily" means that no algebraic formulas are used to exhibit the equality.

5. Take a look at Proposition 47 in Book I of Euclid's *Elements*. It is the Pythagorean theorem viewed in purely geometric terms. Think through all of the cutting and pasting he is implicitly doing in that proposition. To what extent do you find these geometric approaches more appealing than algebraic ones?

SY'S UNIT ON SURPRISE

I am frequently surprised at how little surprise functions as an ingredient in the teaching and learning of mathematics. After all, wouldn't you think that essentially every new discovery was surprising to the person who first came upon it? What struck both of us is that almost none of our students were able to describe a surprising experience in all of their mathematical learning.

Reflective Problem 33

Get together with one other student who is not in your class but is a mathematics major in college or a high school student who enjoys mathematics. Also locate a tape recorder. Ask the person to think out loud about any surprises he or she came upon in learning mathematics. If nothing is forthcoming, select a few important theorems from number theory—like the one that there are an infinite number of primes, or that Goldbach's conjecture has been around for centuries without proof. Maybe probe the student with something like Euclidean geometry. Are they not surprised to find out that under some circumstances two triangles are congruent if only three parts of each of the triangles are congruent to each other? Don't push too hard. Give the person time to reflect a bit. If the person believes nothing was surprising, try to find out why.

Now see if you can find a professor in the math department of your college or university who is willing to be interviewed—perhaps one who has done research in mathematics. Ask the same question, again taping the conversation. Ask him or her to tell you what role surprise has played in their own research, their teaching and their learning of math. Listen carefully to the interview on tape. Write a brief paper in which you compare the two answers.

We will be looking at surprise from two points of view, both of them having to do with problem posing in general and with "What If Notting" in particular. The first focuses on "finding" surprise and the second on "creating" surprise.

Finding Surprise

The finding of surprise was alluded to by Ms. Post at the local NCTM conference Ms. Waters and I hosted at Hyper Post. She drew our attention to the conceptual link between problem posing and problem solving. Ms. Post pointed out how it is that the surprising conclusion regarding the equilateral triangle example (see Problem F, page 22) almost compels us to ask a new question—a question equivalent to "Why is this happening?" That is, in some cases it turns out that supposedly *solving* a problem is only the first rather than the last step in inquiry. Although we have an answer, the answer may in some ways be puzzling.

What she did not discuss in that section, however, is that such surprise is frequently an invitation for doing a "What If Not" in an attempt to gain a better intuition for something that seems so peculiar.

Look now at an interesting problem about my daughter's forthcoming marriage and relative states of obesity (see Problem K, page 24).

Reflective Problem 34

Get together with someone else in the class and try to discuss what intuitions might have been working that would have led you to conclude whether it was my daughter or myself who would have been more embarrassed by relatives due to the increase in our respective radii.

I will draw a sketch of the two "situations"—my daughter's and my own.

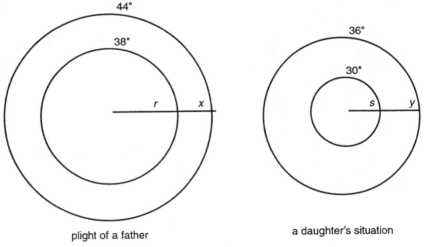

plight of a father   a daughter's situation

Figure 9

Your intuition might very well focus on the difference of the earlier and later circumference for each of the bellies. Since the difference is the same, you might have guessed that the change in radius would be the same. On the other hand, you might have concluded that although the differences are the same (both 6 inches), there is a greater percentage increase in the case of my daughter than myself. If you focused on percentage increase, you might have predicted that the change in radius would be greater for my daughter than for me.

Perhaps there are other aspects of the problem that caught your attention, but let us do the calculation for each of us and see what takes place. In both cases, if we rely upon the fact that the circumference is 2π radii, then we get:
For myself:

$$
\begin{aligned}
44 &= 2\pi (r + x). \\
\text{Then } r + x &= (44/2\pi) \approx 7.006, \\
\text{But } 38 &= 2\pi r. \\
\text{Then } r &= (38/2\pi) \approx 6.051, \\
\text{Thus } x &\approx .955.
\end{aligned}
$$

For my daughter:

$$
\begin{aligned}
36 &= 2\pi (s + y) \\
\text{Then } s + y &= (36/2\pi) \approx 5,732 \\
\text{But } 30 &= 2\pi s \\
\text{Then } s &= (30/2\pi) \approx 4.777 \\
\text{Thus } y &\approx .955
\end{aligned}
$$

Reflective Problem 35

There's a lot to think about and to challenge in this problem. As a start, you might wonder which of the two of us would really be singled out. If we had the same increase in radius, would our relatives (who focus on increase in radius) merely observe that the increase is the same, or would they look at the increase in relation to the original radius? But perhaps it is not the change in radius so much as the increase in area of the ring between the new and old circles that they focus upon. If that is the case, then what can you say about the areas of the two rings? Are they the same, as is the case with the change in radius? If so, would people focus on the actual area or the change in area?

Some of you may have been particularly impressed with the fact that there is a greater percentage increase from the original to the later circumference of my daughter's waist than in my case. Did you use that observation to conclude that there must be a greater increase in the radius for her as well? Such surprise could be used to generate a host of new what-if-not options. Consider the following as a start.

Exploration 25

Was there something a little "fluky" about the fact that the change in radius was the same in the two cases? Select another case where the
change in circumference is the same (6 inches) and see what you get
as the change in radius.

Another what-if-not would inquire into the sense in which circles are relevant. The diagrams below suggest analogous questions to ask about other figures:

Exploration 26

1. Take a look at the diagrams in Figure 10 and make intuitive
   guesses about how the distance between "belts" would compare if
   the circumferences were to increase as they did with the circles
   (that is, a 6-inch increase in circumference).

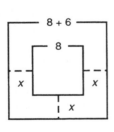

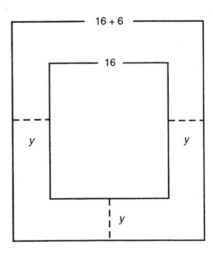

Figure 10

2. Choose some other figure—not a square and not a circle—and
   calculate its circumference. Then place a blown-up version of it
   around the original so that the two are concentric. If the circumference of the larger is 6 (feel free to generalize), then what is the
   distance between the two figures?

Creating Surprise

In the above activities we were motivated to investigate new terrain by virtue of the fact that the finding was surprising—at least for some of you. We have assumed that the surprise was a consequence of the fact that your intuition suggested that the change in radius from smaller to larger concentric circle might be a function of the percentage increase of the circumference and not the differences between the circumferences. Suppose you had an intuition that turned out to be accurate, however. Is there some way in which you might create surprise? Is there some way in which you might find something extraordinary in the expected?

One possibility is to search for a way of exaggerating what you seem to be finding—making an almost absurd case. Consider, for example, the following version of Problem K.

Exploration 27

Suppose we take a belt and put it around the earth (having the same center as the center of the earth). Now increase that belt by 40 feet and place it so that it is concentric (and in the same plane) with the original belt. What do you think might fit between the original belt and the extended one? Try to answer this first by suppressing your findings from above (if that is possible). Do you think a grain of sand might fit? an ant? an aunt? the World Trade Center?

In order to test the reasonableness of an intuition that suggests that it is only the change in circumference that makes a difference, we have created an extreme case. We have made the original belt enormous in length and have made the second almost the same length from the point of view of percentage increase. If we were to place the two belts next to each other, we might have a situation depicted by the following:

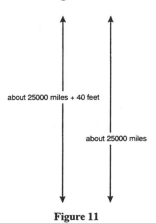

about 25000 miles + 40 feet

about 25000 miles

Figure 11

The percentage increase in length is so insignificant that it is virtually impossible to imagine that anything larger than an ant could fit between the two belts. If we carry out the calculation as we did above, we realize that the difference between the two belts is $\frac{40}{2\pi} \approx$ a little over six feet! The answer to what might fit between the two belts is closer to an aunt than an ant.

The above is a beautiful example of what might happen when we make the familiar strange. In a sense, an original correct intuition for many of you was pushed to the limit. Pushing it to the limit will encourage us to raise many questions. A deep one is the following:

> What draws us to be so much more focused on the ratio (rather than the actual difference in lengths) of the two belts than was the case earlier?

Let us turn to a quite mundane example of how one can make the familiar strange and follow it with some interesting problem posing of the What If Not variety. You perhaps all recall learning something about the conditions under which two triangles are congruent. By definition, they are congruent only if all their parts coincide. So we would expect that we need three sides and three angles to be congruent in order to have congruence of the figures themselves.

Having seen proofs that under certain circumstances the congruence of three corresponding parts is sufficient to establish congruency, we apply these theorems without fully appreciating the sense in which it is a bit of a miracle that we can get away with less than six. How can we push the miracle a bit? Again, devising an extreme case is one possibility.

Exploration 28

The standard theorems of congruence depend upon the fact that we have set up "corresponding parts" between two triangles. Suppose we have established that some pairs are congruent but that they are not necessarily corresponding parts. How many pairs (of angles or segments) can we have congruent and still not have the triangles congruent to each other?

One of the things that makes congruence theorems seem so "natural" and unsurprising is that we have made abundant use of these theorems for triangles. One way of making the familiar seem like a bit more of a miracle than it does would be to explore other figures than triangles in the plane.

. . . .

Exploration 29

Pose a problem about congruence for some plane figures other than triangles.

. . . .

Notice that the above problem is very much in the What If Not spirit, but motivated by the observation that surprise was lacking. In Exploration 28, you had to observe that "threeness" was so taken for granted in all that is done with congruence that we tend not to see it as something that could be "challenged." Then we not only had to find a way of varying the attribute, but also had to search for a question to ask.

I began this section by commenting that one of the most surprising realizations about the concept of surprise is that it is almost totally lacking as a part of the curriculum. We did not always know what we now know, and people who discovered the "truths" that are now so obvious to us must have gone through periods of doubt and surprise as they stumbled upon realizations that were a bit "shaky."

Think, for example, about the theorem that asserts that the medians of a triangle meet in a point. It must surely have occurred to Euclid and his investigators that in *some* triangles the medians meet in a point. But prior to establishing a proof, there had to be considerable doubt about whether or not this held for *all* triangles.

As soon as we put ourselves in a frame of mind such that we try to find the above surprising, we may begin to wonder about the intersection of lines that join vertices not to midpoints but to trisections of sides of a triangle. As soon as we find it to be a bit of a miracle that medians so meet, we can be surprised not only by their meeting, but also by the fact that they do so *inside* the triangle. This raises an activity like the following:

. . . .

Exploration 30

We know that the three medians, the three angle bisectors, and the three altitudes are (respectively of course) coincident for a triangle. Furthermore, the point of coincidence is inside the triangle. Pose analogous problems about lines that represent "What-if-nots" for medians, bisectors, and altitudes. Pose analogous problems for figures other than triangles. Do some investigation. If you have access to the Geometric Supposer Program or one like it, you will find a natural habitat for the posing and investigation of problems of the above sort.

. . . .

Stepping Back

One of the greatest gifts we can give ourselves is to locate the unusual and the extraordinary in the context of what we might previously have seen as humdrum. One of the most valuable sources of motivation is achieved when students are genuinely surprised by something they had anticipated otherwise.

Reflective Problem 36

1. Beginning teachers frequently believe that the most important activity of a good mathematics teacher is to "explain things clearly"—a point that Ms. Waters and I discussed before deciding to choose surprise as a topic to write about. This frequently means that they make things look as if they could not be otherwise. But such a point of view seems to collide with the one described above. How do the two points of view relate?

2. Paradoxes in mathematics are surely a prime (pun?) example of something that generates surprise. There are a number of good books written about paradoxes. You will find some interesting essays in *The World of Mathematics*, a four-volume collection edited by James R. Newman (1956). This collection is actually a classic, and every mathematics teacher should be familiar with it. It has many uses beyond a focus on paradox. There is an excellent collection of text, filmstrips, and tapes in another collection edited by Martin Gardner entitled *The Paradox Box* (1975). The collection has paradoxes about numbers, time, geometry, probability, statistics, and logic. Locate a text on paradoxes in mathematics. Select a paradox that you think would be appropriate to use with high school students. Show how the paradox can be used to:

   • assess conceptions and misconceptions that your students might have.
   • teach them about the difference between a problem and a situation.
   • teach them about problem posing (in an accepting or unfolding mode).
   • teach them about W.I.N. problem posing.
   • teach them about surprise and its value in motivating mathematical ideas.

SECTION 5
A Final Black/Waters Dialogue

Mr. Black and Ms. Waters are about to complete their proposal for NSF. In addition to including a rationale for educating teachers about problem posing, it has some portions of the actual essays they wrote. In some cases they have indicated just the bare bones of the essays because they have not yet figured out the precise format they wish to use in the actual material they produce. They of course have an outline of key topics they hope to address and have also begun to think about strategies they might use to implement their ideas with teachers if they get the grant. Sy is in favor of an extensive workshop over the summer followed by a number of weekend retreats throughout the year. Martha would like to find some way of attracting teachers who are located throughout the United States and Canada, and weekend retreats seem problematic. They are beginning to think about the ways in which they might use electronic communication during the year. They now have a discussion over whether they ought to promise to find some way of summarizing for teachers the chock-full agenda they have generated. Of course it is difficult to make that decision without knowing precisely the manner in which they will express their ideas. Nevertheless, they forge ahead.

Mr. Black: I feel comfortable with what we have put together.

Ms. Waters: I do too, but I wonder if we ought to have some culminating experience that encourages prospective teachers to put together the many different problem-posing strategies and issues we have introduced. After all it is chock-full.

Mr. Black: Should we promise that we will find a way of having them apply what they have already learned to new situations rather than just reflect back on everything they learned? Especially since the concept of application to new situations seems built into the very idea of understanding that we discussed earlier, that might not be a bad idea. Do you have any suggestions?

Ms. Waters: Well, I noticed an interesting "hole" in our collection. There is one problem that we gave to the teachers in Professor Braun's workshop that we never addressed in our essays and that we never mentioned in our NSF proposal.

Mr. Black: Which one is that?

Ms. Waters: Problem J on the Fibonacci sequence. Now Problem J has some nice playfulness to it. In fact, the problem ends with the following suggestion:

Acting in a playful manner, see if you can come up with a number of interesting properties of the sequence. If things get dull, take a look at any two adjacent terms. What is their product? Now look at the product of right- and left-hand neighbors of each of the adjacent terms. Finally, come up with some variation of the Fibonacci sequence and explore some properties of the new sequence.

Mr. Black: Why don't we present the Fibonacci idea in a way that is similar to what we did when we wrote about the two problem-posing approaches for the concept of prime number—my stuff on "unfolding" and yours on W.I.N.?

Ms. Waters: But at that point we were not talking about the relation between Problem and Situation. Also, we were not discussing Integration and Surprise—although I did mention in my discussion regarding my rationale for selecting the three questions I chose that surprise was a motivating factor. By focusing only on "unfolding" and WINning, we'd leave out too much.

Mr. Black: Good point. Should we then write up the Fibonacci problem in a more elaborate way and include Problem versus Situation and Integration and Surprise as well?

Ms. Waters: Well, then we should probably reinvestigate reasons for teaching problem posing in the first place—ideas from the conference that we organized last spring.

Mr. Black: Maybe not. Let that be part of what teachers do on their own in order to make this experience a truly constructive one. Why don't we ask teachers to get together in groups of two or three and have them figure out how each of the categories we have mentioned above either exists already in our discussion of Problem Posing and the Fibonacci sequence or . . .

Ms. Waters: Could be added to the discussion! I like the idea.

Mr. Black: Terrific! Let me get it straight now—what we are asking them to do. We will present the Fibonacci ideas as if we were writing a unit on two modes of problem posing: "Unfolding" and "W.I.N."

Ms. Waters: Then we ask the teachers to see if they can identify where we are making use of the following ideas, even if not mentioned explicitly:

- Moving from situation to problem and vice versa
- Finding and creating surprise
- Integrating branches of mathematics and also rethinking what integration might mean
- Reasons for engaging in problem posing
- Indicate kinds of reflective exercises they would create if they were teaching these ideas to their students

Mr. Black: Yes. Why not label the five items you listed above 1 through 5. We could then ask the teachers to go through our discussion and place numbers appropriately in the margin of each paragraph that illustrates one of the points.

Ms. Waters: With the understanding, of course, that they would have to add comments in order to flesh out their points.

Mr. Black: Okay. Let's indicate in the NSF proposal that we intend to do just that.

Ms. Waters: Okay. Let me list the seven categories that we want the teachers to use in the context of Problem J as a culminating activity:

1. Moving from situation to problem and vice versa
2. Finding and creating surprise
3. Integrating branches of mathematics and also rethinking what integration might mean
4. Reasons for engaging in problem posing
5. Indicate reflective problems they would create if they were teaching these ideas to their students
6. Accepting the given in problem posing
7. What If Not in problem posing

Mr. Black: Don't you think we should actually write out something about Problem J—the Fibonacci sequence—as we did in the case of primes in order to have them get started with 6 and 7?

Ms. Waters: Do you mean that we might start by encouraging them to ask some unfolding questions—the kind of thing we did in our session with the math club in mid-June?

Mr. Black: Yes. I'll get a copy of the overlay we made up to get things going. Here it is:

Take a look back at observations, questions, and hypotheses you can come up with for the following sequence:
1, 1, 2, 3, 5, 8, 13, 21, 34, 55, 89, . . .

Ms. Waters: Yes, and I think we began the process by doing our normal charades that focused primarily upon observations to start. Didn't we have them come up with a list that was something like:

- The sequence generated by the differences between two adjacent terms almost generates another Fibonacci sequence (why almost?).
- There is a pattern of odd, odd, even repeated in the sequence. (Remember, don't worry about perceived triviality.)

- Look at any term and square it. For example, suppose we select the fifth term: 8. Now look at the term preceding and the term following it. What do you notice if you multiply these two terms? Now compare 8^2 with $5 \cdot 13$. Before jumping too quickly to a hasty conclusion, suppose you select 5 as the term to square. Now compare 5^2 with the product of its adjoining terms—$8 \cdot 3$.

- Look at the product of any two "adjacent" terms (for example, 3 and 5). Now look at the product of the "surrounding" terms: 8 and 2. How do the two products compare? Try this for the product of any other two "adjacent" terms and the product of their "surrounding" terms. Compare.

- Take a look at the ratios of adjacent terms (either larger to smaller or vice versa). The first few ratios are:

$$\frac{1}{1} = 1 \qquad \frac{3}{2} = 1.50 \qquad \frac{8}{5} = 1.625 \qquad \frac{21}{13} = 1.619$$

$$\frac{2}{1} = 2 \qquad \frac{5}{3} = 1.60 \qquad \frac{13}{8} = 1.615$$

Exploration 31

Looking at the above observations as a starting point, make other observations, ask questions, and come up with new hypotheses.

Mr. Black: Yes, and then we took a complete backseat. They were off to the races, moving from observations to hypotheses and conjectures—coming up with pages of things to think about.

Ms. Waters: And then they started moving to the W.I.N. stage even without our provocation. They first noticed that we are starting with *two* terms; then that we were *adding* terms; then that the first two terms were 1,1 and could have been something else even if we did not change the operation from addition to something else.

Exploration 32

Choose any of the first five attributes in the numbered list above and perform a W.I.N. on the Fibonacci sequence. As a start just vary the two first terms and then investigate which properties remain the same and which differ from the original sequence.

Mr. Black: We should have videotaped it all. They had no trouble with 6 and 7 on the list, but don't forget that they had been exposed to us for a number of years.

Reflective Problem 37

Look at what you have done in the above two explorations and select some of the categories of 1–5 from the seven listed to analyze.

Ms. Waters: Yes, but if the kids were able to get it after exposure to our teaching, don't you think the teachers for whom we are devising this project will be able to get it through our book and even perhaps through our workshops?

Mr. Black: Wait, what book? We have not yet decided on the format we will use in order to convey our ideas. You just mentioned something about videotaping. Maybe we should create videotapes of our teaching.

Ms. Waters: That might work, but . . . I have an idea! Let us do something really novel as our proposed format to teachers. Some of the essays we have written are already almost in the form of a novel. We want to encourage people to engage their imagination to the fullest—not only as they think about what problem posing and solving are in mathematics, but what they think associated pedagogy might be. We want to minimize a judgmental point of view and wish instead to unleash the creative floodgates. It is true that we have provided some fascinating starting points to think about problem posing, but we want nothing more than for them to come to make this all their own—to personalize it and to develop it further along idiosyncratic grounds.

Mr. Black: So . . . you are suggesting a solution to the format problem that has been nagging us all along . . . that we write a novel! I love the idea. I wonder if we can pull it off. . . I wonder how NSF will react to the idea.

Ms. Waters: We already have collected a number of interesting problems for readers to think about. Do you think we can figure out a way to embed them in the novel so that they do not appear to be inserted artificially?

Mr. Black: I am sure we will be able to figure out a number of interesting schemes. We can devise drafts written by several teachers who are applying for an NSF grant. We can create a conference as part of the novel and speakers can assign problems to participants in the audience. It occurs to me though that the problems we have been collecting are of two quite different sorts. One stream is essentially mathematical, and the other is more pedagogical—though I would not want to make too sharp a distinction.

Ms. Waters: You're right. I'll tell you what. Let's call the problems that are essentially mathematical "Explorations," and let's call the ones that are more pedagogical "Reflection Problems."

Mr. Black: Good, but let's encourage the readers themselves to try to transform the mathematical "Explorations" into "Reflection Problems" and vice versa.

Ms. Waters: Terrific idea. We'll have to figure out a way of building that into the novel. I wonder how. We can always leave that task for the second edition. Or, we might want to offer workshops for teacher educators who use the novel with teachers.

Mr. Black: We are getting a bit ahead of ourselves. Let's see how our application for the writing of a novel is received by NSF and we can always modify what we propose afterwards if the news is good. I wonder what our chances are.

EPILOGUE
Taking Things for Grant-ed

In early December of the year that Sy and Martha submitted their proposal, Hyper Post was not spared the winter of all winters on the East Coast. Snow had begun to fall on November 12 and by the end of November, almost thirteen inches had already been recorded. Sy and Martha were reminiscing in the teachers' room, thinking about the magnificent summer they had spent in Colorado and of the symbolism of the columbines that had covered Yankee Boy Basin.

The semester had been a difficult one. Many of the parents became increasingly concerned that the open-ended and personal perspective that Sy and Martha offered would not get their kids into the best colleges, a point of view that Eloise was not reticent to echo. Though Sy and Martha were convinced that the concern was not well grounded, it is true that their collaboration on the project had encouraged them to be even more experimental over the past couple of semesters.

The bell for the end of the period sounded. As they were heading out to class, they heard an announcement over the loudspeaker from the principal's office. It was that deep, authoritarian tone that was more chilling than the frigid weather that they were to face in an hour. They were mentioned by name. The two of them were to report to the principal's office immediately. What was that tone again? It was the one that accompanied a similar request last spring for the two students suspected by most of the faculty to be heavily involved in drug dealing.

They walked into the principal's office and he handed them each an en-velope. The envelopes had been sent by special delivery from a government agency. The principal wanted them to open them immediately. "If there are charges being made against the two of you, for whatever reason, I need to know immediately. Please open it without further delay," he said. Martha thought she heard a laugh coming from inside the principal's private bath-room, and it seemed to be a familiar voice but she couldn't identify it.

Sy and Martha felt their privacy was still worth something regardless of the obvious intimidation. They left the office. The principal's face was still grim and they returned to the teachers' room. The name and address on each envelope had identical font styles. The three pieces of paper inside each of the envelopes appeared to be the same length and style. They did not quite have the courage to read the letters alone and so they agreed to alternate reading aloud. They decided to read the bottom page first. Sy read out loud.

Dr. Jayne Courtmey, Director
National Science Foundation
Washington, DC

Dear Dr. Courtmey:

Thank you for selecting me to review the NSF proposal of Ms. Waters and Mr. Black. While I certainly found a number of their mathematical problems to be of more than passing interest, and while they express themselves well in writing, I cannot support their project. I fully subscribe to the view that mathematics is a problem-solving activity. As a research mathematician I of course also appreciate the role of problem posing. Both of these activities, however, are a long time in the making. They are not the kind of activity that can be acquired in the absence of a great deal of knowledge and experience with mathematical ideas. What we need if we want to develop good prob-lem solvers and posers is not explicit teaching of heuristics, but rather good teaching of mathematical content at every grade level. We need teachers who can offer good explanations and we need teachers who know what a proof is and who can help students understand when one is necessary.

The use of a novel format is ludicrous because it obfuscates the most fun-damental assumptions about the nature of mathematics. That is, there are very few fields in which it is possible to claim with certainty that something is true or false. Furthermore, there are very few fields in which the truth value can be either established or falsified by deductive proof. Mathematical creativity does not require that students explore issues from a personal point of view, but rather that they understand and create proofs and models that are valid and legitimate.

This proposal is based upon a total misunderstanding of the nature of mathematical thought and I see no way in which I can suggest improve-ments. If the proposal is funded, I personally will do everything I can to see that your division of the National Science Foundation will receive a thor-ough review in the near future.

Martha was shaking. She hoped she could find some clue to identify the critic, but such reviews were anonymous and she knew that if there were any clear identifying characteristics in the original letter they would be eliminated in the photocopy they received. Was there any reason to continue reading? Would the director have included that letter if the decision were positive? Sy persuaded her to read the middle letter out loud:

Dr. Jayne Courtmey, Director
National Science Foundation
Washington, DC

Dear Dr. Courtmey:

What a thorough delight it was to receive the proposal by Waters and Black. They not only have a first-rate understanding of the nature of mathematics as a personal and open-ended enterprise, but they also understand that teaching and learning at every level is an act not only of exploration but of the interplay of doubt and commitment of the deepest sort.

They appreciate that heuristics for doing mathematics are not bought cheaply and so they do not follow those advocates of problem solving who march out an array of general principles that sound good but that have minimal applicability. It is true that with regard to problem posing they speak of two general strategies, but at no point do they convey the idea that these strategies can be applied without careful attention to the details of the situation, and without creating new strategies on their own that fit the situation. I loved the analogies that were made explicitly in the rationale section but which were implied throughout: problem solving and posing in math is to kids as problem posing and solving in pedagogy is to teachers. I have rarely encountered such an interesting array of Reflective Situations and Explorations that buttress this analogy. Their use of "mirror turning," in which they encouraged teachers to use their own learning as a laboratory to imagine what the experience would mean for them as teachers, was masterfully executed throughout.

It serves to remind us that even in the case of math problem solving for kids, there is a need to encourage a point of view that does not consider heuristics as an already developed set of strategies to be imposed by experts, but rather as something that is in a state of flux and that can be refined by the students themselves.

The choice of the novel as a format is a first-rate medium to convey their basic ideas about the nature of creativity and of mind. The most fundamental questions about mathematics itself—having to do with what the field is really all about—are controversial and debatable. I know of no better format to convey this idea than that of a novel.

The proposal is weaker from the point of view of implementing their novel for teacher education. I believe, however, that the authors will work that issue out in greater detail by the time they complete their novel, or they will make a good case for why the issue should not be resolved in an *a priori* manner.

I must say, however, that I would have appreciated seeing some culminating activity worked out in greater detail than they proposed with something like the Fibonacci sequence. I also would have appreciated an entire section devoted to assessment of teaching in the way they advocate. Nevertheless, this is one of the most imaginatively written proposals I have read. It was the first one that did not kill my insomnia. I support it with great enthusiasm.

They both stood dumbfounded. What could they expect from the third letter? In this case, they decided to read it silently together:

Sy Black and Martha Waters
Cutting Ej High School
314159 Main Street West
Hyper Post, New Jersey 012335

Dear Mr. Black and Ms. Waters:

As you can tell from the enclosed two reviews of your proposal, there is something less than universal agreement regarding your proposal. I was tempted to send it out to another couple of referees, but I decided instead to make a decision on my own. I usually try to minimize my own opinion and rely heavily upon that of my referees—hoping for some sort of unanimity, though I rarely get it.

In this case, I cannot help but feel that it is worth taking the risk of supporting your proposal. Your writing is enticing, even though it is sometimes a bit unclear. Put more positively, you seem to have a knack for knowing when ambiguity or vagueness are laudatory attributes—ones that encourage the reader to try to make sense out of a situation on his/her own.

You seem to indicate a healthy balance between viewing mathematics as a collection of statements (to be assessed as true or false) versus an array of open-ended questions. I see the proposal as pedagogically strong, especially in light of the kinds of reflective activities you propose. I like your effort to think about mathematics in relation to poetry, humor, and even ethics, though I realize you chose to deemphasize those points of view in the proposal itself. I would like to encourage you to explore those issues further, however, when you actually put the ideas together in the form of a novel.

You will in fact have the leisure, since as you know, part of the grant proposal will release you half-time from your teaching responsibilities next semester. We also will be supporting you both next summer.

Good luck to you. I look forward to your novel in about a year and a half and also to finding out what it is you find out about teachers as you use the novel in the course you team-teach with Professor Braun next year.

Sincerely,

Dr. Jayne Courtmey
Director, NSF

They returned to the principal's office. As they entered, they heard the noises of party sounds. Banners were flying and balloons were floating. The principal was smiling. He had received a phone call from NSF shortly before the letter was sent to Sy and Martha. Like her emotion, Martha's bladder was full to the brim. She no sooner entered the principal's private bathroom than she smelled a perfume that she had no difficulty identifying. It was the scent of Eloise. She then was able to recall the disembodied laugh she had heard a half hour before. She could not resist creating a name for the perfume: Sent of Eloise; Cent of Eloise; Send Tough Eloise? She came out of the bathroom and saw Eloise give Sy a strong congratulatory embrace. As with her understandings of pedagogical and mathematical matters, she was beginning to acquire a new personal understanding—one that was filled with emotion but did not yet have a name.

BIBLIOGRAPHY

Agre, G. P. (1982). The concept of problem. *Educational Studies* 13 (2): 121–42.

Beiler, A. H. (1964). *Recreations in the Theory of Numbers: The Queen of Mathematics Entertains.* New York: Dover Publications, Inc.

Borasi, R. (1987). What is a circle? *Mathematics Teaching* 118: 39–49.

_____, (1987). *Learning Mathematics Through Inquiry.* Portsmouth, NH: Heinemann.

Brown, S. I. (1966). Multiplication, addition and duality. *Mathematics Teacher* 59(6): 543–50 & 591.

_____, (1971). Rationality, irrationality and surprise. *Mathematics Teaching* 55: 13–19.

_____, (1974). Musing on multiplication. *Mathematics Teaching* 61: 26–30.

_____, (1976). From the golden rectangle and Fibonacci to pedagogy and problem posing. *Mathematics Teacher* 69(3): 180–86.

_____, (1978). *Creative Problem Solving.* Albany, NY: New York State Education Department, Bureau of Mathematics Education.

_____, (1978). *Some "Prime" Comparisons.* Reston, VA: National Council of Teachers of Mathematics.

_____, (1981). Ye shall be known by your generations. *For the Learning of Mathematics* 3:27–36.

_____, (1986). Liberal education and problem solving: Some curriculum fallacies. In *Proceedings of the Philosophy of Education Society,* ed. D. Nyberg, 299–312. Normal, IL: Philosophy of Education Society.

————, (1987). *Student Generations.* Arlington, VA: COMAP (Consortium on Mathematics and its Applications).

————, (1991). Yet one more revolution in school mathematics. *Newsletter of the Graduate School of Education* (University at Buffalo) Spring: 1, 3, 4.

Brown, S. I., Cooney, T. J., & Jones, D. (1990). Mathematics teacher education. In *Handbook of Research on Teacher Education*, ed. R. Houston, 639–56. New York: Macmillan.

Brown, S. I. & Walter, M. I. (1990). *The Art of Problem Posing*, second edition. Hillsdale, NJ: Lawrence Erlbaum and Associates.

————, eds. (1993). *Problem Posing: Reflections and Applications.* Hillsdale, NJ: Lawrence Erlbaum and Associates.

Burton, L. (1986). *Thinking Things Through: Problem Solving in Mathematics.* Oxford: Basil Blackwell.

Butts, T. (1973). *Problem Solving in Mathematics.* Glenview, IL: Scott Foresman and Co.

Cassidy, C. & Hodgson, B. Because a door has to be open or closed. In *Problem Posing: Reflections and Applications*, ed. S. I. Brown & M. I. Walter, 222–28. Hillsdale, NJ: Lawrence Erlbaum and Associates.

Chapin, H. (1978). Flowers are red. In *Living Room Suite.* New York: Warner Brothers Publications.

Connolly, P. & Vilardi, T., eds. (1989). *Writing to Learn Mathematics and Science.* New York: Teachers College Press.

Cooney, T. J., ed. (1990). *Teaching and Learning Mathematics in the 1990's.* Reston, VA: National Council of Teachers of Mathematics.

Countryman, J. (1992). *Writing to Learn Mathematics.* Portsmouth, NH: Heinemann.

Courant, R. & Robbins, H. (1941). *What Is Mathematics?* New York: Oxford University Press.

Davis, P. J. & Hersh, R. (1981). *The Mathematical Experience.* Cambridge, MA: Birkhauser.

Dewey, J. (1910). *How We Think.* Boston: D. C. Heath & Co.

————. (1957). *Reconstruction in Philosophy.* Boston: Beacon Press.

Duckworth, E. (1991). Twenty-four, forty-two, and I love you: Keeping it complex. *Harvard Educational Review* 61(1): 1–24.

Ernest, P. (1991). *The Philosophy of Mathematics Education.* London: The Falmer Press.

Eve, H. (1969). *An Introduction to the History of Mathematics.* New York: Holt, Rinehart & Winston.

Gardner, M. (1969). The multiple fascination of the Fibonacci sequence. *Scientific American* March:116–120.

———. (1975). *The Paradox Box*. San Francisco: W. H. Freeman & Company.

Ghyka, M. (1977). *The Geometry of Art and Life*. New York: Dover Publications.

Heath, T. L., ed. (1956). *The Thirteen Books of Euclid's Elements*. Translated from the text of Heiberg with introduction and commentary by Thomas L. Heath, Volumes I–III. New York: Dover Publications.

Hersh, R. H., Paolitto, D. & Reimer, J. (1979). *Promoting Moral Growth: From Piaget to Kohlberg*. New York: Longman.

Hofstadter, D. (1980). *Gödel, Escher, Bach: An Eternal Golden Braid*. New York: Vintage Books.

———. (1982). Metamagical themas: Variations on a theme as the essence of imagination. *Scientific American* October: 20–29.

Jacobson, B. & Wisner, R. J. (1965). Matrix number theory: An example of non-unique factorization. *American Mathematical Monthly* 72: 399–402.

Kramer, E. E. (1970). *The Nature and Growth of Modern Mathematics*. New York: Hawthorn Books, Inc.

Krulik, S. & Reys, R. E., eds. (1980). *Problem Solving in School Mathematics*. Reston, VA: National Council of Teachers of Mathematics.

Lakatos, I. (1977). *Proofs and Refutations*. Cambridge: Cambridge University Press.

Lehman, H. (1977). On understanding mathematics. *Educational Theory* 27(2): 111–19.

Long, C. T. (1965). *Elementary Introduction to Number Theory*. Boston: D. C. Heath & Co.

Loomis, E. S. (1968). *The Pythagorean Proposition*. Washington, DC: National Council of Teachers of Mathematics.

Martin, J. (1981). Needed: A new paradigm of liberal education. *National Society for the Study of Education*, Eightieth Yearbook, ed. J. F. Soltis, 37–59. Chicago: University of Chicago Press.

Mason, J., Burton, L. & Stacey, K. (1985). *Thinking Mathematically*. Reading, MA: Addison-Wesley.

McGinty, R. L. & Meyerson, L. N. (1980). Problem solving: Look beyond the right answer. *Mathematics Teacher* 73(7): 501–3.

Moïse, E. E. (1963). *Elementary Geometry from an Advanced Standpoint*. Palo Alto, CA: Addison-Wesley.

Movshovits-Hadar, N. (1988). School mathematics theorems: An endless source of surprise. *For the Learning of Mathematics* 8(3): 34–39.

National Council of Teachers of Mathematics. (1980). *An Agenda for Action: Recommendations of the 1980s*. Reston, VA: Author.

———. (1989). *Curriculum and Evaluation Standards for School Mathematics*. Reston, VA: Author.

———. (1991). *Professional Standards for Teaching Mathematics*. Reston, VA: Author.

National Research Council. *Everybody Counts*. (1989). Washington, DC: National Academy Press.

———. (1990). *Reshaping School Mathematics: A Philosophy and Foundation for Curriculum*. Washington, DC: Mathematics Association of America.

Newman, J. R., ed. (1956). *The World of Mathematics*. New York: Simon and Schuster.

Ore, O. (1963). *Graphs and Their Uses*. New York: Random House.

Perkins, D. N. (1986). *Knowledge as Design*. Hillsdale, NJ: Lawrence Erlbaum and Associates.

———. (1993). Teaching for understanding. *American Educator* 17(3): 8, 28–35.

Perry, W. G. (1970). *Forms of Intellectual and Ethical Development in the College Years: A Scheme*. New York: Holt, Rinehart & Winston.

Piaget, J. (1970). *Genetic Epistemology*. New York: Columbia University Press.

Pimm, D. (1987). *Speaking Mathematically: Communication in the Mathematics Classroom*. London: Routledge & Kegan Paul.

Poincaré, H. (1961). Mathematical creation. In *The Creative Process*, ed. B. Ghiselin. New York: Mentor Books.

Polya, G. (1962). *Mathematical Discovery*. New York: John Wiley & Sons.

———. (1954). *Mathematics and Plausible Reasoning*. Princeton, NJ: Princeton University Press.

Popper, K. (1972). *Objective Knowledge*. Oxford: Oxford University Press.

Reshaping School Mathematics: A Philosophy and Framework for Curriculum. (1990). Washington, DC: Mathematics Association of America.

Rucker, R. (1983). *Infinity and the Mind*. Toronto: Bantam Books.

Scheffler, I. (1989). Vice into virtue, or seven deadly sins of education redeemed. *Teachers College Record* 91(2): 177–89.

———. (1991). *In Praise of the Cognitive Emotions*. New York: Routledge, Chapman and Hall.

Schoenfeld, A. (1985). *Mathematical Problem Solving*. Washington, DC: Mathematics Association of America.

Silver, E. A. (1994). On mathematical problem posing. *For the Learning of Mathematics* 14(1): 19–28.

Silver, E. A., ed. (1985). *Teaching and Learning Mathematical Problem Solving: Multiple Research Perspectives*. Hillsdale, NJ: Lawrence Erlbaum and Associates.

Steen, L., ed. (1990). *On the Shoulders of Giants*. Washington, DC: National Academy Press.

Stein, S. (1987). Gresham's law: Algorithm drives out thought. *Humanistic Mathematics Network* 1: 1–12.

Walter, M. (1985). The day all the textbooks disappeared. *Mathematics Teaching* 112: 8–11.